# More Praise for Alice Rivlin
## and *Divided We Fall*

We owe a great debt to Sheri Rivlin and Allan Rivlin for completing this manuscript left unfinished at Alice Rivlin's death. It is a fitting final contribution by a fine thinker and public servant who contributed so much to our democracy. Alice worried that "the American experiment is in danger of failing." This book can help us avert that danger, and points us to a path upward, toward success.

**WILLIAM KRISTOL,** editor at large, *The Bulwark*

———

This posthumously published book by Alice Rivlin is an eloquent *cri de coeur* and an urgent and timely call to renew the basic elements of consensus and common sense that permit democratic government to succeed in a society of sharply divergent viewpoints. No one knows how the current polarized impasse will end, but Rivlin's package of ideas and reforms seems as compelling a solution as any that have been offered. This book is a meaningful contribution in a dark moment.

**JAMIE RASKIN,** U.S. representative (D-Md.) and lead impeachment manager in the second impeachment trial of Donald Trump

———

Alice Rivlin's final book is not only a fascinating insider's memoir but a brilliant analysis of current threats to our democracy. It calls on all of us, both inside and outside of government, to act—including specific advice on what we can do. Buy 10 copies and give them to friends. That is the legacy she wanted and deserves.

**ISABEL SAWHILL,** senior fellow, Brookings

Alice Rivlin foresaw that we would be facing the survival of our constitutional republic. Once again giving of her enormous intellect and her deep compassion for the American people, she spent the last months of her life writing this call to action to end hyperpartisanship. She understood that given the incentives in today's electoral politics, "We the People" must find the faith in each other to demand that our elected officials stop putting party above country and find solutions supported by most Americans.

**CAROLYN J. LUKENSMEYER,** founding executive
director, National Institute for Civil Discourse

———

They broke the mold with Alice M. Rivlin. No single person in recent history engaged in the public arena set a better example of true public service than she. Her final book is a testament to her years of public service which were designed with the one goal of making government work for all of us. The final chapter, addressing the corrosive effects of political polarization in achieving that goal, should be required reading for all elected officials at the federal, state, and local level. Even more so, it should be required reading for all citizens.

**G. WILLIAM HOAGLAND,** senior vice president, Bipartisan Policy
Center, and former chief of staff to Senator Pete Domenici (R-N.M.)

———

Alice Rivlin was one of the true great leaders of a lifetime. Her practical, optimistic, and inspirational voice shines through in this book, and its message is needed more than ever. Every single project, commission, and institution was better for having Alice involved, and the nation would be better if we followed her words of wisdom.

**MAYA MACGUINEAS,** president, Committee for
a Responsible Federal Budget

How fortunate we are to have Alice Rivlin's final, landmark treatise on core threats to American democracy. Infused with insights and perspective from her decades of unparalleled leadership in Washington, *Divided We Fall* calls on us to revive the habit and practice of bipartisanship. Failure, Alice warns, will degrade Americans' economic and social welfare, and imperil our democratic experiment. All of us have something to learn from Alice's brilliant, clarion call for change.

**SARAH BINDER,** professor of political science, George
Washington University, and senior fellow, Brookings

———

Sheri and Allan Rivlin have done a great service in editing and completing Alice Rivlin's last book. Drawing on her decades in public service, Alice reflects on the continued necessity for bipartisanship even in a hyperpartisan era, driving her points home with examples from personal experience and evidence from scholarship. Taking stock of major economic and policy problems, she urges partisans to engage in civil debate, seek common ground, share responsibility for difficult choices, and achieve durable solutions.

**FRANCES E. LEE,** author, *Insecure Majorities:
Congress and the Perpetual Campaign*, and professor of
politics and public affairs, Princeton University

Alice Rivlin was the most devoted public servant I had the honor to know and work with during my public service career in Washington. She was totally committed to challenging both politicians and the public to do whatever was necessary to make our democracy work. This final book by Alice is not just her prescription for fixing our democracy, it is her fervent last prayer that we cannot afford to ignore the dangers . . . it is we the people who must in the final words of her book "defend our constitutional system, seek truth and justice, and see America succeed."

LEON E. PANETTA, chairman, Panetta Institute for Public Policy,
and former secretary of defense, CIA director,
Office of Management and Budget director, and U.S. congressman

---

In these pages are the core symbols of Alice Rivlin's life and legacy: Courage, Integrity, Determination. This diminutive, iconic, powerful presence was revered in Washington, D.C. In my first Senate term, I worked with her in several venues. Added to those above traits, there was a palpable blend of kindness, fairness, and balance. In this book she even describes herself sometimes as maybe naive. No one else would ever confirm that observation!

I'll slip into the western vernacular and just say this: She had a plenty tough job when I first met her, and she was eager and able to speak truth to power. We have a phrase in this part of the country, "If you have a bear of a job, hire a grizzly." She was all that. And she loved the code, "If you have integrity, nothing else matters—and if you don't have integrity, nothing else matters." She was a pure joy to work with and her presence gave birth and nurture to so many remarkable ideas and honest counsel as found in these pages.

ALAN SIMPSON, former senator (R-Wyo.) and co-chair,
National Commission on Fiscal Responsibility and Reform

This book is incredible in many ways. It is a great diagnosis of our current condition, and an even more important and necessary wake-up call and call to action. We are allowed one more opportunity to appreciate Alice's acumen for diagnosing problems, her concern about government dysfunction, her clear understanding of the geographic dimension of economic inequality, as well as her many recommendations for action. I love this book!

**RICHARD FLORIDA,** Rotman School of Management,
University of Toronto, and author, *The New Urban Crisis:*
*How Our Cities Are Increasing Inequality, Deepening Segregation,*
*and Failing the Middle Class—and What We Can Do About It*

---

Alice's last book reinforces her brilliant reputation as a policy bridge builder.

**DONNA E. SHALALA,** former U.S. representative (D-Fla.),
former U.S. secretary for health and human services
and past president of the University of Miami

---

This is a smart book that explains how stupid political fights in Washington are wasting time instead of getting work done and solving problems for the American People. Rivlin gives us concrete action steps to fix our broken politics so we can get our economy moving, invest in American workers, and bring back manufacturing and technology jobs to the cities and towns across the middle of America.

**REPRESENTATIVE TIM RYAN** (D-Ohio)

Alice Rivlin believed that getting the numbers right led to the best public policy. As the first director of the Congressional Budget Office she set a standard of fairness and nonpartisanship that was a service to our country. Under Alice's leadership CBO was an arbiter between conservatives and liberals leading us on a path to good policy and fiscal responsibility. At its best CBO has continued to uphold the bedrock principles Alice put in place.

**JOHN KASICH,** former Ohio governor
and U.S. representative (R-Ohio)

Alice was truly an inspiration. Her passion to bridge the divide within our nation, especially around complicated issues like our economy and healthcare, was only surpassed by her humility. Her ability to clarify was unmatched. Having worked with Alice throughout the years, I am forever indebted to her for her clarity and brilliance. What a legacy she has left!

**MARJORIE MARGOLIES,** Fels Institute of Government,
University of Pennsylvania

In this manifesto, Alice Rivlin warns that the American Experiment is in danger of failing, but with characteristic optimism maps a route to safety and prosperity. Alice is, alas, gone, but her perspective and insight lives on in this call for "a new patriotism" to defend American democracy and finally deal with the nation's big economic problems. Even amid today's bitter partisanship and polarization, she argues that old-style bipartisanship is not only essential if we are to solve today's economic problems, but actually achievable. Alice shines a light through today's darkness, showing the way for citizens to push politicians to get to work on the nation's persistent economic problems.

**DAVID WESSEL,** director, Hutchins Center on
Fiscal and Monetary Policy at Brookings

———————

In her long and storied career, Alice Rivlin embodied the best of public service and public-spiritedness. In this book, the capstone of her life in politics, policy, and scholarship, lovingly completed by her son and daughter-in-law after her death, Alice reflects on the country during her career, examines economics and politics through her own experiences and the best work of scholars in these areas, and offers ideas for improving the process and the country to get through these times of threat to our fundamentals. If you care, as she did, this is a must-read.

**NORMAN ORNSTEIN,** emeritus scholar,
American Enterprise Institute

# DIVIDED WE FALL

# DIVIDED WE FALL

## Why Consensus Matters

ALICE M. RIVLIN

SHERI RIVLIN    ALLAN RIVLIN

BROOKINGS INSTITUTION PRESS

*Washington, D.C.*

*Library of Congress Cataloging-in-Publication data has been applied for.*
ISBN 9780815735250 (hardcover)
ISBN 9780815735267 (ebook)

9 8 7 6 5 4 3 2 1

Typeset in MinionPro

Composition by Westchester Publishing Services

# CONTENTS

# COMPLETING ALICE RIVLIN'S VISION AND MESSAGE FOR A RAPIDLY CHANGING AMERICA

## Sheri Rivlin and Allan Rivlin

In the last year of her life, our mother and mother-in-law, Alice Rivlin, focused as much energy as she was able to muster on completing this book because she strongly believed she had something important to say about the danger that partisan warfare, political standoff, and congressional gridlock pose to the welfare and happiness of the American people. She wanted to warn lawmakers and the public that increasingly hostile political rhetoric and declining congressional achievement threatened future economic prosperity and could lead to a loss of confidence, and potentially a catastrophic breakdown, in America's political institutions. Battling lung cancer with radiation and chemotherapy, she struggled to make progress on completing this manuscript up to within hours of her death. She ran out of time and passed from this earth on May 14, 2019.

Of course, history did not stop on that day—far from it. In the more than three years since Alice's death and before publication of this book, the world has witnessed at least a partial realization of Alice's fears as American democracy came under threat like almost never before. As Alice's two co-authors, we made the decision that as we completed the manuscript, we would not include any facts, events, data, research, or scholarship dated after Alice's passing so some of the statements of fact may seem out of date. Our process is explained in the Acknowledgments section. We have added this preface, as well as an afterword, to frame a context for the book in light of the extraordinary events of 2019–2022, to answer emerging questions, and to offer our best approximation of what Alice would have said in response.

As we picked up the task of completing Alice Rivlin's vision for this book, the Democrats were moving to impeach President Donald Trump the first time for withholding nearly $400 million in congressionally appropriated military aid to Ukraine. The process lasted many months as Trump was investigated, impeached in the House, and tried and acquitted in the Senate. Nearly every vote taken went along strict party lines. Both sides accused the other of treason and unconstitutional disregard for basic facts and the rule of law. Throughout this period, the idea of writing and publishing a book about bipartisan cooperation in Washington seemed preposterous almost to the point of being out of touch with reality.

As the impeachment process was coming to an end, the world was beginning to learn about a novel coronavirus that would be named COVID-19 and would cause a global pandemic, infecting millions of people worldwide, killing a thousand, then two, and eventually more than three thousand Americans a day and more than that worldwide, day after day. The US and global economies came to a screeching halt as governments enacted quarantines and forced business closures.

There was broad bipartisan agreement among policymakers on the need for emergency medical, public health, and economic measures to slow the pandemic, search for a vaccine, and limit the economic damage. Within weeks of the end of the impeachment saga, Congress had passed, and the president had signed, several large spending bills with nearly unanimous bipartisan support. The fastest was an $8.3 billion supplemental appropriation to fund medical research and public health efforts. The largest was the Coronavirus Aid, Relief, and Economic Security (CARES) Act, a $2 trillion spending bill including direct payments to individuals and families, a major expansion of unemployment benefits, and massive grants and loans to businesses closed by the quarantine. Facing a global crisis, Washington was able to pass some of the largest bipartisan spending bills in history. Bipartisanship no longer seemed to be a ridiculous idea, and we no longer feared we were wasting our time completing a book that would be ridiculed as Alice Rivlin's quixotic plea for bipartisan cooperation in a hopelessly hyperpartisan age.

But as spring turned to summer and the fall elections approached, a second wave of the coronavirus turned the number of cases, hospitalizations, and deaths upward again, and bipartisan cooperation gave way to the kind of partisan standoff that had prompted Alice to write this book. Public health measures to stop the spread of the disease became politicized as pundits derided and angry mobs protested business restrictions and the wearing of face masks recommended by doctors and public health experts. As the economic shutdown continued, lawmakers were stuck in a partisan impasse over the size and composition of an additional economic rescue package. Once again, voters and the media were asking, "Why can't you stop the blaming, put the talking points aside, step away from the cameras, go into a room, and get a deal that splits the difference on the areas of dispute for the benefit of 'We the People?'" Months passed as Democrats and Republicans could not work out the details of a COVID relief bill both sides agreed was badly needed. We were frustrated that we had not gotten our work done fast enough to get Alice's words out to her readers in this period where her perspective seemed so relevant to current events.

## RACIAL DIVISIONS ON THE STREETS AND AIRWAVES

In the spring and summer of 2020, thousands of Americans of all ages and races took to the streets to protest under the banner of Black Lives Matter (BLM). The appalling murder of George Floyd by Minneapolis police officers was just one of several deaths of black and brown men, women, and children due to police discrimination, malice, and malpractice that were caught on video, igniting local, national, and even international outrage. Most of the protests were peaceful, but some others turned destructive or violent. Through the mainstream media, millions of Americans engaged in an informal teach-in about the country's history of racial inequality and institutional racism. At the same time, millions of other Americans tuned into right-wing media to hear false assertions that Black Lives Matter represented a threat to white Americans.

Death rates from the coronavirus were also far higher in communities of color than among white Americans. There were many explanations given, but all of them pointed to the persistence of racial inequality. African Americans, Native Americans, and Latino or Hispanic Americans held more risky jobs, earned less money, and had less wealth, less access to health care, poorer diets, and generally poorer health than white Americans. It was an undeniable and painful reminder that racial equality has never been achieved in the United States on many different levels. In chapter 2, Alice suggests some measures to shrink the racial wealth and opportunity divide, but we believe she would go further in this direction if she were writing in 2022 instead of 2019.

## JOE BIDEN WINS THE WHITE HOUSE
## WITH AN APPEAL FOR NATIONAL UNITY

The Democrats surprised many pundits in early 2020 by choosing moderate former Vice President Joe Biden as their nominee rather than several front-running candidates representing the progressive wing of the Democratic Party. Vermont Senator Bernie Sanders, who lists his party affiliation as Democratic Socialist but caucuses with the Senate Democrats, led a large field through the early primary and caucus states with his progressive policies and calls for a "political revolution" earning enough support to place him second for the nomination in both 2016 and 2020. But South Carolina moderate Democrats, following the lead of African American women and Representative James Clyburn (D-SC), changed the direction of the nomination contest, and the rest of the party fell in line behind Biden.

As discussed in chapters 8 and 9, Alice had a deep respect for Joe Biden and an appreciation for the role he played as vice president in leading efforts to reach bipartisan deals with the aggressively partisan Republicans during the Barack Obama administration. There, Biden was on the front lines negotiating every deal in one of the most contentious political environments Washington has ever seen. The negotiations never achieved a "grand bargain" to raise revenue and control projected spending to tackle the long-term debt and deficit threat, but Democrats and Republicans reached many deals to keep the government open and avoid an immediate financial catastrophe.

Biden made ending political division a major theme of his 2020 general election campaign. After selecting one of his principal rivals for the nomination, Senator Kamala Harris (D-CA), to be his running mate, he traveled to the Civil War's deadliest battlefield in Gettysburg, Pennsylvania, to give a speech calling for national unity and a return to bipartisan cooperation. The "Build Back Better" economic agenda at the center of the Biden/Harris campaign, with an emphasis on infrastructure and investments in educa-

tion, job training, and emerging technologies, closely follows Alice's recommendations in chapter 2 of this book.[1] Alice did not come up with the slogan Build Back Better, but if you look under the hood of Biden's plan, the
growth engine is the same. The infrastructure investments Alice champions
in chapter 2 became law through bipartisan action in Biden's first year in
office. We cover the Infrastructure Investment and Jobs Act in the Afterword,
but not chapter 2 because Alice did not live to see this bipartisan achievement.
Alice would have supported any of the Democrats over President Trump, but
she would have been quite pleased that Biden won the Democratic nomination
and then the general election.

## THE PANDEMIC AND POST-PANDEMIC ECONOMY

Despite Alice's reputation as a fiscal hawk persistently warning about long-
term deficits and debt, we are quite certain she would have been comfortable with the massive and mostly bipartisan spending bills of 2020 and
2021 in response to the economic shutdown necessitated by the coronavirus pandemic. She said repeatedly in her writings, and several times in this
book, that she supported high levels of government spending and temporary deficits during an economic crisis. So she undoubtedly would have been
in favor of the large spending bills for medical research, relief to quarantined
workers and shuttered businesses, and general support for an economy on
lockdown. She would have seen this as consistent with her Keynesian perspective rather than an embrace of Modern Monetary Theory (MMT). Although
she never penned a response to the theory that American policymakers have
been too concerned about deficits—a theory that received more attention in
2020—the afterword offers our view of Alice's perspective on MMT and other
dramatic developments that came after the date of her passing.

1. We do not suggest that it is likely, but it is at least possible that someone in the
Biden/Harris campaign was aware of the economic plan presented in chapter 2. Versions of chapter 2 were published on The Hill and on the Brookings website in October
and November of 2019: https://thehill.com/opinion/finance/465185-alice-rivlin-my
-final-thoughts-on-how-to-heal-divisions-in-america, www.brookings.edu/opinions/to
-unite-a-divided-nation-we-must-tackle-both-vertical-and-horizontal-inequality/.

It is a safe bet that she would have nonetheless viewed the recovery and relief spending bills as an opportunity to repeat her warnings about the dangers of long-term deficits. Throughout her career, Alice warned that the United States has developed a bad habit of cutting taxes during economic good times, creating unsustainably large deficits during economic bad times. This belief drove Alice's opposition to the George W. Bush tax cuts in 2001 and 2003 and the Trump tax cut in 2017.

The wealthiest Americans and international investors could have lost fortunes if the global economy collapsed under the weight of the pandemic in 2020, but massive spending by Congress and the Federal Reserve, in coordination with governments and central banks around the world, allowed financial markets to stabilize and soar. This meant investors added to their fortunes despite the death, human suffering, and economic destruction caused by the disease. Even as Alice endorsed the spending bills and extraordinary actions taken by the Fed, she would have also warned corporations and economic elites that they would have to pay meaningfully higher taxes in the future.

For several reasons, Alice would have argued for higher taxes on wealthy Americans and large corporations once the US and global economies were clearly post-pandemic, and she would have expected bipartisan support for this position, as well as support from many high-wealth individuals and corporate interests. First, from Warren Buffet to the Business Roundtable, there was an emerging realization within the corporate sector before COVID-19 that the US economy was out of balance and corporations needed to step up and play a larger role in the communities in which they operate. Wealth and income inequality had reached unacceptable levels, and the pandemic greatly exacerbated the inequality problem.

Second, it is no exaggeration to say the extraordinary actions by governments and central banks saved the capitalist system from a complete collapse and saved the wealthy from losing a substantial share of their fortunes; it is both just and prudent to go to the same people to repay the government so it will be in a position to help them again in the future. Even those who have a habit of questioning the value of government nonetheless turn to it for help in emergencies such as hurricane, fire, pandemic, or economic crisis.

And lastly, both Democrats and Republicans know that the national debt has reached levels that threaten to cause a future economic catastrophe. Even though "Tea Party Republicans" rejected all tax increases in negotiations with the Obama administration, as Alice details in chapters 8 and 9, she would never have imagined that Republicans would fight to protect the wealthy and corporations from tax increases after all Americans, indeed everyone in the world, had just emerged from a pandemic coupled with business closures, millions of lost jobs, and an economic crisis.

Alice would have advocated for a bipartisan tax increase like the tax increases passed after World War II, which she details in chapter 4. But if we know one thing about Alice Rivlin, it is that she would have seen the pandemic as another opportunity to advocate for sensible bipartisan economic policies to maintain the sovereign national debt at sustainable levels while investing in innovation, education, infrastructure, and healthy communities for an economy that produces broadly shared prosperity as detailed in chapter 2. It is clear what America needs to do to set up the economy for success in the coming decades, and the country should not let partisan battles stand in the way of doing it.

## DIVORCING TRUTH, TRUMP CHALLENGES THE 2020 ELECTION OUTCOME

When Alice wrote her concerns that American democracy could be threatened by hyperpartisanship—"The American Experiment is in danger of failing," to quote the first line of the book—she feared she would be viewed as overly alarmist. She could not have imagined how, eighteen months after her death, Trump would seek to invalidate and overturn the 2020 national election and, three months after that, incite an insurrection of loosely allied, anti-democratic, authoritarian, paramilitary groups at the US Capitol.

Months after the events, investigative journalists and a congressional investigative committee now have reporting from multiple sources within the White House and Department of Justice, audio recordings of telephone calls, and contemporaneous notes from participants that detail the steps President Trump took in his efforts to change the vote count in pivotal states, declare the election invalid, and remain in power. It was a deliberate, if inept, attempt at a *coup d'état*. Even months after Trump left the White House, Republican Trump supporters in Congress and in many state legislatures have repeated the "Big Lie" that Biden did not legitimately win the 2020 election, and have made false claims of election fraud as a justification to change voting laws to make voting more difficult for Democratic constituencies and allow state legislatures to overturn election results. It is not an overstatement to view partisan rule changes that create an opportunity to reverse election results as an affront to democracy. As Alice notes in chapter 10 by echoing warnings from her Brookings colleague William Galston, she was very troubled that Trump's actions mimicked turns toward authoritarian nationalistic populism in many other countries in the world. As history has unfolded, Alice's 2019 alarmism now looks prescient.

The British have a simple expression to describe foul play, "That's not cricket." Rather than adjudicating rules or asserting moral disdain, it is simply an observation that some behaviors reveal the absence of a shared agreement on the common purpose. The statement "That's not democracy" best captures our view of how Alice would have responded to Trump's behavior from 2019 to 2021. Alice wrote this book as a call to strengthen US democracy by making government work as well as the American people deserve, and to serve as a warning to all those who care about government, that support for American democracy could be at risk if hyperpartisanship continues to thwart legislative achievement.

Alice evaluates the first two years of the Trump presidency in chapter 10 and points out there were several significant bipartisan achievements among many other frustrating partisan standoffs. Democrats and Republicans had differences on policy that could either be bridged to pass legislation or stall in a standoff, but this is the regular state of the US democratic process. Had she lived to see it, Alice would not have found Trump's behavior in the period from November 3, 2020, to January 6, 2021, to be acceptable in the American constitutional system of democracy. By undermining a national election, rejecting facts and evidence, and inciting violence, Trump crossed lines that made it clear that he was not engaging in democracy.

## BIPARTISANSHIP, BUT NOT AT THE EXPENSE OF DEMOCRACY OR THE TRUTH

A legitimate question is, if Alice Rivlin praised (then vice president) Joe Biden and criticized the tax cuts enacted by Presidents George W. Bush and Donald Trump, and if she was so alarmed by Trump's actions, how can she present this book as bipartisan?

Alice would have viewed this question as important to understanding this book and would have gladly answered, starting with the difference between two closely related but distinct words: *bipartisan* and *nonpartisan*. Alice was a partisan Democrat who served in two Democratic administrations, under Lyndon Johnson and Bill Clinton. She also held many nonpartisan positions, including founding director of the Congressional Budget Office (CBO), president of the American Economic Association, and vice chair of the Federal Reserve Board. Both types of roles, partisan and nonpartisan, informed her thinking for this book.

Bipartisanship is something partisans do. They remain partisans as they work with members of the other party to reach the agreement needed to pass legislation. With this book, Alice is a partisan Democrat calling for more bipartisanship. She is calling on her fellow Democrats (moderates and progressives) and on Republicans and independents to do bipartisanship better and more often, to end longstanding partisan stalemates and achieve progress toward solving America's most pressing problems. So the question of whether this book can be called bipartisan gets answered in the negative. It is not a bipartisan book; it is a call for greater bipartisanship, written by a partisan Democrat. Alice would have hoped there would be calls for more bipartisanship written by partisan Republicans, and some of these voices are rising in the wake of Trump.

But the question illuminates the central tension in this book. Alice was always calling for a reduction in partisan blaming, but she was not asserting that both sides are equally to blame for increasingly dysfunctional partisanship. She could not because they are not. In chapter 10, Alice invokes the political scientists' finding of "asymmetrical polarization," in which over the last five to six decades, Republicans have moved farther to the right on issues than Democrats have moved to the left. To this she adds three of her own informal assertions, based on her observations. The first is that innovations in harsh rhetoric, negative campaign tactics, and hardball negotiation positions have generally, though not exclusively, come from the Republican side, later to be matched by some on the Democratic side.

The second is that there is an asymmetry built into budget negotiations to the degree that Democrats have become the pro-government party and Republicans have become the anti-government party. Democrats need negotiations to succeed to maintain basic governmental functions (passing budgets to keep the government open, avoiding a default on the national debt) while Republicans are more willing to see negotiations fail, causing harm to the public they represent but reinforcing their assertion that government cannot do anything right.

The third assertion is that some Republicans under Trump have made a departure from past Republican definitions of fair play, democracy, and the truth. This point has grown ever sharper following the 2020 election result denials and the Capitol insurrection on January 6, 2021. In Alice's name, we are drawing lines for behavior in the American democracy—lines that she would not have seen necessary to state—the crossing of which should be deemed intolerable. She would expect bipartisan agreement that (1) there is no place for violence in the American political system; (2) even if US politics has historically been driven by racial and ethnic divisions, no modern party should tolerate or take advantage of racism or division for political gain; (3) elections should be free and fair, and open to all eligible voters, and the results of elections must be respected; and (4) political debate should be governed by the truth and based on facts and evidence, not lies repeated as propaganda.

Throughout her career, Alice believed in bipartisanship, but her commitment to bipartisanship was never greater than her commitment to the truth. She believed the truth is nonpartisan, even if partisans sometimes aggressively promote their version of the truth. This was the fundamental rationale guiding the founding direction of the CBO. In the narrow area of economic prediction, and in all things, partisans have their own journalists, commentators, and experts offering different descriptions of the facts, analyses, and predictions. But Alice did not believe anyone can split the difference on the truth. The truth is the truth, even when it is unknown or unknowable, as is often the case with economic projections.

The Congressional Budget Office was designed to offer nonpartisan expertise in economic analysis and projections. The projections would not be perfect, but they would be the best assessments and estimates of unbiased experts. Alice believed that building and supporting institutions designed to produce common frameworks for discussing unknowable future outcomes was the first essential step toward finding common ground in deciding on a path forward—and that is far better than perpetual conflict and policy paralysis.

She believed in bipartisanship informed by the truth, and she was a strong believer in nonpartisan institutions like CBO, the National Institutes of Health (NIH), the Food and Drug Administration (FDA), the Centers for

Disease Control and Prevention (CDC), the National Oceanic and Atmospheric Administration (NOAA), and many others, which are designed to be insulated from political pressures and to bring professional expertise to policy decisions. Even in Alice's lifetime, Donald Trump revealed himself to be the opponent of every one of these truth-seeking nonpartisan institutions.

Perhaps the first tip-off for her would have been the efforts of Trump's then director of the Office of Management and Budget, Mick Mulvaney, to explicitly undermine CBO early in 2017, but it soon became clear that Trump was campaigning to undermine and politicize every corner of the professional civil service, which he derided as the "deep state." For many decades, presidents of both parties have understood the necessity of keeping politics out of policy in such areas as law enforcement, diplomacy, intelligence, health, and safety. There are different laws and norms guiding the relationships between the White House and the various independent departments, agencies, and commissions, but collectively these norms and laws are referred to as the guardrails of democracy.

In most cases, the rules and norms were written following a major abuse of power, catastrophe, or scandal, necessitating a bipartisan investigation, new laws, and enhanced congressional oversight. For instance, most federal government employees are protected from political influence by civil service laws written after the assassination of President James Garfield in 1881. Abuses of power in J. Edgar Hoover's FBI and the Watergate scandal led to bipartisan congressional investigations, reform, and oversight to insulate the Department of Justice and federal law enforcement from political influence. Bipartisan investigations of the September 11, 2001, terrorist attacks revealed the dangers of politicization of military and diplomatic intelligence. Americans are all safer when presidents hear what they need to hear, rather than what they want to hear, about threats to the country.

Before Alice's death, it was clear that Donald Trump did not respect these guardrails of democracy. After her death, it became clear that he was actively working to subvert and dismantle them, with dangerous consequences. From denying intelligence reports of Russian influence in his own election, to politicizing the Department of Justice for not protecting him from investigations and politicizing medical research and the nation's public health response to the coronavirus (causing hundreds of thousands of unnecessary American deaths according to members of his own Coronavirus Task Force);

from his efforts to delegitimize the 2020 election before votes were cast, his denial of the election results, and his efforts to influence state election officials, to the incitement of mob violence at the Capitol insurrection on January 6, Trump's assault on the institutions of democracy reached levels that, at least temporarily, stunned Republicans in the House and Senate leadership.

## JANUARY 6 MUST NOT BE AN EXCUSE TO REJECT BIPARTISANSHIP

If the Capitol insurrection serves as confirmation of Alice's concern about potential threats to democracy, it also comes with an additional challenge to her thesis, to the degree that many Democrats hold the view that it is folly to seek deals with Republicans who enabled Trump's misbehavior by echoing his challenges to the election's legitimacy or voting to acquit him through two impeachments. Alice would respond with her view that partisan warfare contributed to the conditions that allowed Trump to win the White House, and the path forward is not ever-stronger partisanship leading to gridlock. Rather, she would say the path forward is bipartisan agreements leading to legislative wins in the House and Senate, helping average Americans, and increasing confidence that government can solve real problems.

Alice would certainly reject the idea that the threat to democracy has passed. Donald Trump and his allies are clearly still engaged in efforts to ensure his return to the White House by taking greater control of election processes. Further, she says explicitly in chapter 10 that she does not expect the problem of dysfunctional partisanship to diminish simply by removing Trump from the White House. Therefore, Alice would renew her calls for greater bipartisanship to get Washington functioning again. Better laws, even if not perfect laws, and sensible economic policies can deliver prosperity that is more broadly shared, which is a more desirable outcome than populist blame shifting and false promises.

## THE MORE THINGS CHANGE . . .

Alice relates her experiences through two periods in recent political history that share much in common with the start of the Biden presidency: the first two years under Clinton, in chapter 6, and the first two years under Obama, in chapter 8. Both Democratic presidents struggled to pass signature legislation through Congress, even though both came in with Democratic majorities in the Senate and House of Representatives, because lawmakers struggled to craft legislation that was acceptable to the most progressive Democrats in the House and the most moderate/conservative Democratic Senators. Closing this gap is not, strictly speaking, bipartisan negotiation, but the same hard work, respectful listening to the concerns of the other side, and commitment to reaching a deal that are the subject of this book are required to achieve success in negotiations between the wings of the Democratic Party.

In one of many congressional rule changes suggested in chapter 11, Alice makes a strong case for the elimination of the Senate filibuster. She does this for two reasons: (1) the filibuster was not, as some defenders assert, part of the original design of the Founding Fathers to make the Senate the more deliberative body, and (2) as it is currently being used—or more accurately, misused—the filibuster has become an impediment to, rather than an enabler of, bipartisan cooperation. But Alice would reject the assertion that elimination of the filibuster would usher in a period of easy adoption of the broad progressive agenda. The gap between the most progressive Democrats in the House and the most moderate/conservative Democrats in the Senate would remain as a major challenge to surmount in passing legislation. In the first two years of the Clinton and Obama administrations, this gap was a major challenge for their economic agendas even though their bills qualified for budget reconciliation, so they needed only a 51-vote simple majority to pass in the Senate. The tensions between the two wings of the Democratic Party are built into the structure of the American political system.

The wings of the Democratic Party represent vastly different constituencies. Nearly all the House progressive Democrats come from dark-blue cosmopolitan cities or college towns where most voters are seeking to support the most progressive candidate in the Democratic primary, and the primary winner faces only token opposition from the Republicans in the general election. But liberals are far fewer than a majority of voters nationwide (this is also true for conservatives), so to win congressional majorities, Democrats must win a substantial number of House races in congressional districts and Senate races in states where a true progressive would not have a chance. Moderate Democrats win races by campaigning for many core Democratic policies but also promising to "vote my conscience, not my party" when standing against the least popular progressive positions and big spending plans.

Progressives often accuse moderates of lacking a spine, but this is not only insulting—it is inaccurate. Moderate Democrats prove their bravery by winning elections in hostile territory and by standing up to progressives as they promised their constituents they would do. If the history of the Clinton and Obama administrations is any guide, the legislative success of the Biden administration will depend less on whether Democrats eliminate the Senate filibuster, which Alice says they should do, and more on whether progressive Democrats and moderate Democrats can find common purpose. And when Democrats are united, they may find there are more Republicans than they expect who are willing to share credit for popular legislation.

The shared American experiences of the years following Alice's death, 2019–2021, would probably add a few critical items to Alice's long-view national agenda, including greater emphasis on shrinking the wealth and opportunity gaps between the races in the wake of Black Lives Matter and the differential health outcomes from COVID-19, and a call to strengthen US democratic institutions and election infrastructure after Trump revealed there exists a constituency for taking power through anti-democratic means.

Throughout the book, Alice repeatedly returns to similar lists of significant policy areas where she believed bipartisan progress was possible but being thwarted in this hyperpartisan age. It is, if you will, her tally of the policy opportunity-costs of hyperpartisanship. It includes infrastructure investments to achieve broadly shared prosperity (presented in chapter 2 and partially achieved through bipartisan action in the Biden administration), her ongoing concern about the dangers of unsustainable national debt, the threat of climate change, needed new investments in public health, mental health and addiction to opioids and other drugs, and the need to fix a broken immigration system.

To update Alice's agenda for bipartisan progress for the first years of the Biden administration, we would add an item to address racial inequality and an additional item to strengthen American democracy. Alice would call on progressive and moderate Democrats to reach out to independents, as well as to those Republicans who reject political violence and seek to define their party without reliance on white supremacy, or anti-science, anti-evidence, and anti-truth Trumpian propaganda, to build a new consensus in support of America as the greatest democracy in the world.

# Acknowledgments, with an Explanation of Our Process

## Sheri Rivlin and Allan Rivlin

When Alice Rivlin died in May 2019, the manuscript for this book was somewhere between 50 and 75 percent complete. She tasked the two of us with completing this book. We soon realized that Alice had a very grand vision for her final book, combining economic and political analysis and scholarship with her personal memoirs into a warning and a call to action to those both inside and outside of government to come together to save American democracy. Her vision was vast, but she had run out of time, leaving us drafts of many chapters, none of which were ready to be edited and published. Our work on this project has taken more than two years, as history has taken many dramatic turns in the areas that are the subject of this book, as discussed in the preface. In that posthumous works of nonfiction and scholarship are rare, we feel compelled to detail our methods for completing the project and at the same time thank the many people whose dedication made this book possible.

In approaching this project, we feel a kinship with many before us who have had the task of completing an unfinished manuscript, novel, or symphony. As children, we imagined that completing an unfinished symphony meant you had to write an ending—as if Franz Schubert wrote three and a half perfect movements, and someone only needed to write a finale that was as good as the rest. Only if you listened very carefully to the fourth movement could you hear the place where some not-Schubert took over, trying to provide a grand, or at least not disappointing, ending. In the real world, however, the creative process is not so linear.

Alice wrote this book over a period of several years, and only for the last year did she know it would be her final project. At Brookings (and probably in many other academic environments), writing a book starts with an outline listing the chapters and what will go in them. We found about a half a dozen draft outlines for this book, ranging from six to fourteen chapters. We developed an outline with seven chapters, but as we were working through the details, we realized we needed the eleven chapters you see here to complete Alice's vision.

The next step is a request to a research assistant (RA) to collect all the available information about a topic and put it in a memo that forms the basis for the factual content of a chapter. Will Palmisano was Alice's RA during this period, and he is the author of several memos that inform this book. Many Brookings research assistants had a hand in this book from inception through completion. Victoria Johnson and Brieanna Nicker deserve special mention. We also want to express our deepest appreciation to Abigail Durak for her commitment to this project from the time of our first involvement through completion (even as she changed jobs to continue her career). From chapter 3 onward, nearly every page of this book has a footnote, meaning either Abby's or Brieanna's attention has been on that page.

Alice then wrote as much of the book as she could complete. In a series of drafts of each chapter, she made all the points she wanted to make and told all the stories she wanted to tell. She redoubled her efforts with each disappointing diagnosis, but she knew she would run out of time before completing the project. Even if she had completed her draft chapters, she would still have been far from a completed manuscript.

Alice was admitted to Georgetown University Hospital a few weeks before her death, and there she gave us the honor (and the burden, as she well understood) of completing the book. We had several working sessions with Alice in the hospital and then back in her home, where she shared her guidance for completing the book. She had also shared her most pressing thoughts on the necessary changes to chapter 1 with her grandson, Caleb Andrew Jones.

Toward the end of chapter 1, Alice was quite focused on adding a section that we refer to as the *mea culpa*. She felt that Wall Street and Washington

had let down the American people, and truly, the world, by failing to anticipate the financial crisis of 2008–2009. In several labored sessions, Alice dic-
tated versions of this section to Caleb, and to us, which were all merged into
chapter 1. Although she was not asserting any direct causation, she believed
there was some relationship between her own and many other Washington
economic establishment members' close associations with the banking and
investment banking industries, and public doubts and distrust. She thought
that these relationships detracted from the legitimacy, or at least the perceived legitimacy, of the economic policymakers' and regulators' role in
protecting the public interest, especially once people learned that the private and public decisionmakers had so badly underestimated the systemic
risk that caused such devastating economic consequences for millions
around the globe. She believed this contributed to a decline in trust in the
expertise and professionalism of government authorities, and that this
added to the appeal of populist politicians in the US and around the globe.

Alice left us with drafts of many chapters in various stages of completion, and we found many others by snooping in her computer files. We almost missed the most up-to-date version of one of the chapters because she
had saved it with the mistaken file name "Dhapter Two." She had sent many
drafts around to colleagues for comments and received considerable praise
mixed with constructive criticism. Some of the concerns raised fundamental issues with her thesis and key points. While she did not get to do rewrites
based on these comments, we knew she intended for us to treat them seriously and take them into account. And thereby we developed the principle
that guided the completion of the project: Our goal was to complete the book
Alice would have written if she had been allowed enough time to complete
her vision and listen to the wisdom of her friends, colleagues, and us, her
coauthors.

The book has three authors, but it is written in the first person singular
because we were all working to complete Alice's vision, make her points, and
tell her stories. We have made a firm rule to not update the book with events,
scholarship, or research that happened after May 2019. Alice did not live to
see the last two years of Donald Trump in the White House, the two impeachments in the House and acquittals in the Senate, the murder of George
Floyd and the global Black Lives Matter protests, the COVID-19 pandemic
and economic shutdown, the election of bipartisanship champion Joseph R.

Biden, Trump's refusal to accept the result of the 2020 election, or the insurrection at the US Capitol on January 6, 2021. These events happened after Alice's lifetime, so we have left them out of the chapters of her book, but we are confident we know what Alice would have said about these events. The preface and afterword express our own views, informed by our deep involvement in this project and all of Alice's thoughts and writings, as to how Alice's vision would have been altered by the events of 2019, 2020, and 2021.

Alice would not have published any of the chapters in the form in which she left them. Before a book is ready for editing, peer review, and further rounds of revision, there is a process that involves insight, storytelling, scholarship, collaboration, and extensive rewriting. Alice had not completed that process with any of the chapters. This explains why completion of the book took as long as it did. Alice Rivlin had earned expertise and authority in multiple domains, and so, to participate on her level, we had to learn at least a fraction of what she already knew about economics, American history (from the time of the founders), the detailed history of the most recent five decades in Washington, political science, social psychology, and many other disciplines. Each chapter required at least two months attention from us, her coauthors.

Alice was not here to help us, but in addition to all the chapter drafts and the comments on them, including her own, she left us a lot. We had pages of notes and a couple of hours of audiotape of her telling us about her priorities for changes to complete the book. We also had access to nearly every word she had ever published, and we made a copy of her Brookings hard drive and cloud backup containing a terabyte of unpublished writings, drafts of books, articles, speeches, emails, and comments on books and articles written by her colleagues. We found dozens of interviews with Alice, along with magazine articles and oral histories of the Clinton administration and the budget battles of the Reagan and Obama years.

Alice gave us a list of colleagues whose work she planned to rely on, especially for the later chapters. These included Maya MacGuineas for chapters 8 and 9; Frances Lee, James Curry, Sara Binder, and Molly Reynolds for chapter 10; Carolyn Lukensmeyer and G. William Hoagland for chapter 11; and Alice's close friend and Brookings senior fellow Belle Sawhill, who read sections of the book to attest that Alice's voice was coming through authentically. Alice was also counting on the input of Molly Reynolds to review all of the political science scholarship and to be her final reader and advisor. Each of these trusted friends and colleagues came through for her and contributed invaluable assistance, without which the project could not have been completed. If you are not familiar with these names or their work, you will be introduced to them throughout the book.

Molly Reynolds engaged the draft deeply, asking thoughtful questions, making comments and corrections everywhere, and requesting a complete rethinking and restructuring of several of the chapters. We gladly made the changes she suggested, as Alice would have done.

We want to thank several political leaders who graciously shared their time helping us understand how Washington can more effectively help regional economic development to address local realities in small-town America. Huntington, West Virginia, mayor Steve Williams shared his plan to put a former coal town with an opioid addiction problem on an upward path, and he explained the "money chase" for federal, state, and business dollars to clean up the waterfront and rebuild the downtown area of a now-thriving college town. Youngstown, Ohio, mayor Jamael Tito Brown and representative, Tim Ryan, of Ohio's 13th Congressional District, shared their perspectives and plans for industrial revitalization in the American heartland. Representative Jamie Raskin (D-MD) shared his views on politics that speaks to the concerns of all the residents of his district. Like many other congressional districts, Raskin's district runs from dark-blue suburbs of a major city through purple exurbs out to red rural counties (in this case, from the suburbs of Washington, DC, to the Pennsylvania border).

We want to thank several Brookings scholars for the time and attention they have given us in support of this project. Senior Fellows Carol Graham, Martha Ross, E.J. Dionne Jr., William A. Galston, and Elaine Kamarck generously shared their time and perspectives. We want to thank Mark Muro, Alan Berube, and the team from the Metropolitan Policy Program at Brookings (Brookings Metro) for conceptual help with chapter 2 and for generating figure 2-1. We want to acknowledge Lisa D. Cook, who started her career as Alice's assistant (as did Ross and many others) and is now serving on the board of governors of the Federal Reserve.

Beyond our sincere thanks to the research assistants, graphic designers, and peer reviewers, and our copy editor, Carla Huelsenbeck, our deepest gratitude goes to our family, especially Alice's husband, also a noted economist,

Sidney G. Winter. We want to thank Alice's other two children, Cathy Rivlin, a California supervising deputy attorney general and family photo archivist, and Douglas Rivlin, the director of communication for America's Voice, who provided guidance to Alice and us on immigration issues. We want to thank Caleb Jones for his direct contribution to the book in taking good notes on Alice's final thoughts, and another of Alice's four grandchildren, our daughter, Tyler Amanda Rivlin, for her guidance and emotional support during the writing process.

Finally, we want to thank our editor, William Finan. Alice wrote a lot of books and had many excellent editors (including Bill Finan) that she deeply appreciated, but she passed this project to two coauthors who were going through the book writing process for the first time. It is no overstatement to say that Alice's book could not have been completed without the wisdom, talent, patience, and encouragement of our editor. Bill always understood the importance of completing this project even when bipartisanship was least in fashion, and without pressuring or rushing us, he kept us on task through two impeachments, an election, a global pandemic, and an attempted coup.

# INTRODUCTION: THE CHOICE WE FACE

The American Experiment is in danger of failing. The greatest threat to our democracy does not come from any foreign power—it comes from our democracy itself. Hyperpartisan warfare is sabotaging our government's decision-making capacity, eroding the ability of the public to understand the issues, propose solutions, have reasoned discussion, and make informed choices. We are losing the ability to face any challenge, solve any problem, or take advantage of any opportunity.

Balanced solutions to many of America's most pressing problems exist, but they are not getting enacted into law because the federal government's decision-making process no longer functions as it should. Even though presidents and Congress worked across party lines in the past to share both the credit and the blame for making the difficult choices needed to reduce federal budget deficits while extending the life of Social Security and Medicare, the most recent effort to do this died in a partisan standoff. A bipartisan immigration reform agreement that was reached years ago in the Senate would have strengthened our borders, provided a path to citizenship for millions of workers necessary to employers throughout the economy, and reformed our broken immigration system, but it could not get a vote in the House of Representatives. All of the nations of the world have engaged in a process to agree on measures to reduce the carbon emissions that cause global warming, but President Donald Trump removed the United States from the Paris Accords.

Overwhelming majorities of voters support measures to keep firearms out of dangerous hands, and both parties repeatedly call attention to the need to fix dangerous bridges, repair roads, and address other pressing infrastructure needs, but Congress has not yet passed laws to address all these issues. There are many bipartisan ideas to help struggling regions (many still in recession) and people trapped in low-wage jobs lacking economic opportunity, by improving their prospects with worker training, opioid treatment, and economic development as regional divergence continues to worsen along with income and wealth inequality.

Washington has failed to enact substantive legislation in any of these areas as the problems grow worse. Whatever your personal priorities are, it is likely that any hope for real and lasting progress depends on getting Congress back to a place where compromise and progress are possible again. We risk losing the most successful economy the world has ever known—one that in the past has proven it has the capacity to provide broadly shared prosperity to a thriving middle class—but rebuilding this economy will require that we prioritize the people and places that are not prospering today.

In particular, we must acknowledge the reality that the recovery from the Great Recession of 2008–2009 has been uneven, with elements of both income and wealth inequality and, equally important, with regional inequality dramatically worsening and making the lives of too many Americans precarious. Major investments in these left-behind people and places will be critical if America is to live up to its full economic and civic potential and remain a great nation. Democrats and Republicans must work together to craft sensible solutions that can garner broad public support and votes.[1]

We face a major choice. We could prove to ourselves and the world that our version of representative democracy works and that a country as big and diverse as ours can face hard challenges and figure out how to resolve them. Policymakers at the federal level could learn from those state and local governments that have been making progress working across party and ideological lines to solve local problems. We could make a habit of doing what we only tend to do in Washington when there is an attack, a natural disaster, or an economic emergency, and come together as one nation to recover and respond. We could lead the world by working with other countries to solve problems that we cannot solve alone.

Or we could blow it. We could continue to divide into hostile camps—Republicans versus Democrats, conservatives versus progressives, city dwellers versus small town and rural residents. We could assume that the "other" group has corrupt or evil intentions, and that the only path to progress is to vanquish them in the next election.

We could allow partisan warfare to keep us from meeting the serious economic challenges ahead. We could lose the confidence of our allies and the respect of our adversaries. We could become a once-great country with a weak economy and a fractious, dysfunctional government. I am writing this book because I am afraid we are choosing failure over success.

In chapter 10, I review research that shows hyperpartisanship is not even working for the partisans. Neither the far right, nor the far left, nor moderates of either party (nor political independents) are seeing the proposals they champion voted into law. Very little is getting done in Washington, and this does not serve anyone's interests.

## The Case for Bipartisanship

The case for bipartisanship is as simple as this: If you want to have big ideas to make America better, there is nothing wrong with partisanship—we need leaders with bold plans to help people and improve the world—but if you want to see those plans put into action, bipartisanship and constructive partisanship (using the spirit of bipartisanship in intraparty negotiations) are really the only games in town. Partisanship has an important place in our elections, helping to clarify choices for voters, but getting things done for the American people, passing laws, and setting spending levels for government programs is, by design, what happens between elections. In practice, very little of this work has been getting done for the past two decades, but most of the progress that has been made has been when bipartisan agreements were reached.

The American governing system enshrined in the Constitution by the Founding Fathers was designed to force deliberation and compromise.

Presidents cannot make treaties, declare war, enact laws, or spend money to address any problem without obtaining passage through both chambers of Congress. The Constitution and the rules that govern the House and Senate leave us with a cumbersome, decentralized decision-making process designed to frustrate political factions, and it seems to be doing that quite well. It is not hard to find writers representing all political points of view expressing frustration that "their side" never gets what it wants.

But rather than building coalitions with other groups, searching for common ground, and developing compromise solutions, the modern approach seems to be to define the maximal position ever more sharply and to deride anyone who would compromise with the other side, accepting one penny more or less than the maximal position, as a spineless sellout. Very little of substance ever passes into law with this approach, but there is always the expectation that after the other side gets crushed in the next election (and we vote out those on our side that would compromise), then we will get everything we want. If this were true, it would have happened by now.

In chapter 10, I discuss research that finds most bills that become law do so with strong bipartisan support and with support from the leadership of the minority in at least one chamber. Some would argue this is an artifact of the Senate filibuster rule requiring the votes of sixty senators to end debate on an issue. In chapter 11, I add my support to those who argue that the Senate filibuster, as it is being used now, forestalls rather than fosters substantive debate. But the elimination of the filibuster would not bring in an unfettered opportunity to pass legislation without compromise, because the principal exception to the filibuster rule—the reconciliation process defined in the budget law—has proven to be a challenging road that also requires many compromises.

President Bill Clinton found this out in his first two years (as relayed in chapter 6), and President Barack Obama learned the same lesson in his first two years (as described in chapter 8). While both Democratic presidents started their first terms with Democratic majorities in both congressional chambers, they learned they needed to navigate a narrow channel to reach agreement on major legislation that could garner the support of the progressive Democrats in the House and moderate Democratic senators who won election in swing states by promising to be fiscally conservative.

## MY FOCUS IS ON ECONOMIC ISSUES

There are many issues where bipartisan cooperation could lead to important policy breakthroughs, but in this book, I focus primarily on economic issues for two reasons. First, I am an economist, so I know those issues best and I was actively involved in the negotiations between Democratic President Bill Clinton and Republican Speaker of the House Newt Gingrich that successfully led to federal budget surpluses in 1998 through 2001 (as discussed in chapters 6 and 7). I was also directly involved in the negotiations between Democratic President Barack Obama and Republican Speaker of the House John Boehner that failed to reach a "grand bargain." (The gory details are in chapters 8 and 9.)

Second, I believe the case for cooperation on economic issues is at least as strong, and perhaps stronger, than for other policy areas. The economic policies that profoundly affect people's lives and well-being—such as tax policy, health care financing, retirement policy, energy policy—cannot be made by one party alone. They must have broad public acceptance, and that requires buy-in from both political parties. We live in a divided country in which control of the levers of government power shift back and forth frequently, and are likely to continue to do so. If the two parties do not find common ground on major economic policies, we will have either gridlock (where the status quo prevails) or erratic shifts in policy as one party or the other temporarily prevails at the polls. Gridlock and erratic policy both make it harder for businesses and families to plan for the future, and for the economy to move forward toward sustained shared prosperity.

## THE MAIN MESSAGES OF THIS BOOK

This book has three main messages. The first is that Republicans and Democrats must begin working together across partisan and ideological barriers to ensure the shared prosperity that all Americans want. For making effective economic policy, bipartisan problem-solving is really the only path to sustainable success. A brighter economic future for the United States depends on stopping the partisan blaming and on getting Democrats and Republicans talking to each other again, listening to each other, and working to construct policies that most Americans can support.

The second message is that on economic policy, whether regarding how to create growth, control spending, or even find answers to troubling issues around economic inequality and geographic divergence, sensible moderates in both parties, and even committed progressives and strong conservatives, are not as far apart as the political process makes it appear. Bipartisan cooperation has led to very important compromise deals in the past, and it is happening quite often these days at the state and local levels of government. Even in today's Washington, bipartisanship happens more often than many people realize, in part because the media sees cooperation as less newsworthy than conflict and impasse.

Yet, on many of the most critical issues, bipartisan agreement that could achieve economic goals shared by most voters and elected leaders on both sides of the aisle still eludes lawmakers. Working together, they could craft legislation to invest in workers' skills, science, and modern infrastructure; make regulation less burdensome; get Social Security on a firm financial basis for the future; make health care more efficient and affordable; slow the growth of greenhouse gas emissions; enhance the stability of financial markets; and create more opportunity to move into the middle class, especially for the people and places that are experiencing an economic recession even when the economy as a whole is growing. The key to pragmatic problem-solving is members of both parties being able to find areas of agreement and to work together. Party leaders have the power to make this happen or make this almost impossible.

The third message is that the public must save politicians from themselves. Politicians, especially party leaders, are rewarded for winning elections, not for working together to solve problems, and voters decide who wins those elections. If Americans do not demand that politicians stop making speeches decrying the outrages of the other side and start negotiating constructive solutions that most people can support, we will all continue to suffer the dismal consequences.

## WE NEED A CHANGE IN TONE IN WASHINGTON, AND A CHANGE IN THE RULES

I have always been an optimist with a strong faith in the ability of Americans to work together to overcome challenges and obstacles. But right now, I am afraid we are blowing our big chance. Hostility and meanness dominate public discourse. Truth is being replaced by name calling, blame, and innuendo, which people tune out just to survive the reality-show atmosphere of our politics. Our elected leaders are concentrating on shifting blame to the other party in hopes of winning the next election—and there is always a next election—rather than crafting policies that would benefit most Americans. These leaders are failing in the jobs we elected them to do: negotiating and implementing laws that will improve our lives and ensure the broadly shared prosperity and American world leadership we all want.

But this is more than a call for a change in tone in Washington; we also need a change in the rules. The writers of the Constitution gave us a unique system of separation of powers and a cumbersome policymaking process that slows the pace of lawmaking and forces deliberation. For most of our history, this system has nonetheless succeeded in passing important legislation in a timely manner with bipartisan buy-in, but that system seems unable to do so today.

Increasing use of the filibuster[2] in the Senate and the "Hastert Rule"[3] in the House has had the effect of making it all but impossible to pass legislation that has bipartisan support. Without bipartisan support, laws become battlegrounds for reversal when the other party gains power.[4] I have a lot to

---

*I believe the total breakdown of federal budgetary policymaking is a serious threat to our democracy and America's future prosperity.*

—Alice M. Rivlin, testimony before the Subcommittee on Federal Spending Oversight and Emergency Management, Senate Committee on Homeland Security and Government Affairs, February 6, 2018

---

say about congressional rules, budget process reform, election laws, and the norms for political behavior in chapter 11.

## WHY BIPARTISAN BUY-IN MATTERS

When the system for passing legislation into law works as it was designed to, legislators work to forge bills that garner the support of a majority of legislators in the House and the Senate. Even in Congresses of the past dozen years, most bills that actually became laws had substantial support from both parties.[5] This is important for several reasons:

- Political scientists have collected the data that tell the story. Congress has been growing increasingly partisan decade by decade since the 1950s.[6] Major legislation has been more likely to end in gridlock in recent Congresses.[7]

- Bipartisan legislation is unlikely to become targeted by the minority party for reversal in the next election as has been the case for recent landmark legislation such as the Affordable Care Act (aka Obamacare), which passed Congress with only Democratic votes over the objections of Republicans who have attempted to overturn the law over sixty times, and the 2017 Trump tax cut, which passed with only Republican votes. Nearly all of the more than two dozen Democrats who entered the race for president in 2020 made repealing the Trump tax cuts central to funding their plans should they get elected.

- A bipartisan legislative strategy is necessary to do the difficult things leaders must do to govern responsibly. Even though Republicans are associated with tax cuts and Democrats are associated with spending increases, both parties are more comfortable doing those things than their opposites, tax increases and spending cuts. But tax cuts and spending increases add up to large deficits. The only way to reduce deficits is to "all jump together" and share the blame for reducing benefits while raising revenue to take credit for achieving the goal, as Republican President Ronald Reagan and Democratic Speaker of the House Tip O'Neill did in passing the Social Security Amendments of 1983. "The essence of bipartisanship is to give up a little in order to get a lot," President Reagan said in signing the legislation, which reduced cost-of-living increases to Social Security benefits and raised the retirement age for future beneficiaries to extend the solvency of the program. Because revenue increases and benefit cuts are politically unpopular, lawmakers have found that the only antidote to runaway deficit spending is bipartisan cooperation.

As I say spending cuts are unpopular, I can hear the disagreement from partisan Republicans pointing to polling data that says Americans want an end to runaway government spending. And as I say tax increases are unpopular, I can hear the disagreement from partisan Democrats pointing to polling data that says Americans want higher taxes on the wealthy and large corporations. I believe these objections help illuminate the point I am trying to make. Both parties employ pollsters and message strategists to frame issues in ways that garner majority support in polls, but polling does not accurately capture political reality.

Because tax increases are unpopular, Democrats have learned to be very specific about whose taxes they propose to increase. By proposing tax increases only for the wealthy and large corporations, Democrats are telling most taxpayers that they will not have to pay additional taxes. Republicans, by contrast, have learned to be very general in their calls for spending cuts. Because spending cuts are unpopular, it is never in the Republicans' interest to propose specific cuts that could tell voters a program they support is on the chopping block. In the real rough-and-tumble of political debate and elections, neither side gets to frame the issues the way they want, and in a never-ending battle, Democrats charge Republicans with wanting to cut popular programs, and Republicans attack Democrats for their taxing and spending.

## THE NEXT ELECTION WILL NOT DELIVER AN ANSWER

In 2008, Democrats won the White House and control of the Senate and the House of Representatives. In 2016, Republicans won unified control in Washington. But beyond the Affordable Care Act and the Trump tax cuts, neither side achieved much of their partisan agenda. The next midterm elections (in 2010 and 2018) brought a loss of the House, and both sides continued to be frustrated that they did not achieve their major goals. (Democrats did not achieve universal health care coverage, and Republicans did not "repeal and replace" the Affordable Care Act.) Winning the next election is rarely the solution to government dysfunction.

Indeed, the pattern that has played out several times has been bipartisan deals following elections that either brought divided government or left divided government in place. Politicians tend to freeze negotiations when elections are near (which in their view is most of the time), hoping that voters will settle the outstanding issues. When elections leave power divided, party leaders are more willing to make a deal. The "lame-duck" period between election day in November and the seating of the new Congress in January has seen a lot of action for budget standoffs and bipartisan deals. During those times when I was personally involved, as detailed in chapters 5, 6, 7, 8, and 9, my family came to understand that the Christmas holidays would be observed at home in Washington.

It is tempting to blame President Donald Trump for the breakdown of civil political discourse in America and the chaos that has replaced policy-making in the nation's capital. Many Democrats and some Republicans see him as the principal perpetrator of federal government dysfunction. But let us not kid ourselves. The intensification of partisan warfare began long before Trump descended the golden escalator into the political arena in 2015 and will not magically go away when he passes from the scene.

Trump took advantage of the dysfunction in Washington and the public resentment of politics and politicians that it engendered. Like populist leaders in many other countries, he rode that resentment to electoral victory. There were economic, cultural, racial, and other sources of resentment as well. Once in office, Trump has made political discourse uglier and less truthful. He has exacerbated hostility and distrust between the parties, and between America and its allies. But imagining that removing Trump from the scene will usher in an era of civil discourse and constructive bipartisan policymaking is an illusion that will only make it harder to address the real, fundamental problems.

I hope this book will get readers thinking about how we can make our government work better. Politicians are unlikely to fix the system unless we the people help them. The problem is not that politicians are bad people. I have worked closely with many politicians over a long career. I believe that most people elected to public office work hard to serve what they sincerely believe to be the public interest, but they are trapped in a dysfunctional system that they cannot change by themselves. They need us to help them. Pressure for change will have to come from both the inside and the outside.

In this book, I focus on the variety of steps we could take to help our political system function again. Lots of people are thinking about this problem and attacking it from many angles—from changing the rules of Congress or the laws that govern elections, to reaching across economic and cultural divides at the community level and practicing the art of solving problems wherever we happen to be. Many people all over the country are working at the city and county level to build consensus for local projects and regional economic development. I discuss many of these efforts in chapters 2 and 11. My hope is to convince readers to stop complaining about the sad state of our democracy, start thinking creatively and constructively about what each of us can do to fix it, and then start doing it.

I am a moderate Democrat who was proud to serve in two Democratic administrations (Lyndon Johnson and Bill Clinton), but I do not think either party has all the answers on economic policy. The classic John Maynard Keynes versus Milton Friedman debate has gone through a few rounds of updates, and neither party strictly adheres to any economic doctrine; however, on economic matters, the two parties have different values, beliefs, and approaches.

In general, I find that Republicans have too much faith that market forces will produce optimal outcomes without government intervention, and Democrats are too eager to rely on government regulation regardless of the cost. I find Democrats too focused on designing uniform federal solutions to problems that might be more effectively handled at the state or local level. I find Republicans far too eager to believe that cutting taxes can lead to high rates of economic growth that make hard choices unnecessary, and Democrats are too determined to believe that higher income taxes on the very wealthy alone will solve the problem of paying for the government services that most of the public wants.

Bipartisan economic policymaking does not mean Republicans and Democrats must abandon their principles and priorities, homogenize their policy positions, and all become centrists with similar views. Bipartisanship is something that partisans do; it does not mean nonpartisan. We need a diversity of approaches to policy issues. Even members of small groups—families, clubs, neighborhoods, the local PTA, businesses, or college campuses—are bound to have differences about what the group should do. In a big, diverse country like the United States, policy views inevitably differ widely along multiple dimensions. Political parties have proven to be useful tools for organizing policy views and supporting candidates so that they can make their appeals to voters. But parties do not serve us well when their leaders refuse to inter-act with each other to address policy problems. We need our elected lead-ers in both parties to get out of their foxholes and negotiate with each other, look for common ground, and reach consensus on policy solutions that sensible people in both parties—and I believe there are quite a few of us—can support and implement.

It may strike you as crazy, even out of touch, to be pushing bipartisan consensus when Republicans and Democrats are screaming at each other, both in Washington and on the campaign trail, blaming each other nonstop, and barely agreeing on the time of day. Advocates of bipartisan solutions to economic problems are often viewed with intense suspicion by both sides. We are called traitors to the cause—whether the cause is progressivism or conservatism. We are said to be naïve or to lack moral principles. One of my Democratic friends told me bipartisan policy sounded like unilateral disar-mament to him. Many Republicans feel the same way.

Policymaking has come to mean imposing one side's view on the other. The fine art of political compromise, which used to be admired, has fallen into disrepute. But compromise and consensus building are essential to making policy. The partisan rhetoric of political campaigns paints an exag-gerated and oversimplified picture of practical policy differences between the parties. For example, many Republican candidates decry "big government" and say they want to slash government spending, but as noted above, they are not specific about what government activities they want to reduce. They do not advocate cutting Medicare or Social Security or veterans' benefits or the Department of Defense, or not paying interest on the debt, although these items account for most of government spending. They say they want to cut "waste" or "programs that don't work" without specifying what they mean.

Similarly, many Democrats say they favor federal health insurance that covers everyone but fail to provide enough in the way of revenue increases to pay the realistic cost of substituting a universal federal program for the mixed public-private system we have now. Every health care reform effort, from Nixon to Clinton, to Obama, to the Republicans' promise to "repeal and replace" Obama's reform, has been able to claim widespread popular support in polls taken before the real trade-offs emerge as the specifics get hammered out in the legislative process. In the abstract, it is easy to believe that reform will mean more coverage for a lower cost. Support fades when many individuals learn that the specifics of reform will mean that someone (possibly they themselves) will get less of a benefit for a higher cost.

There are almost never two distinct sides to a major policy issue. There are multiple points of view and diverse interests—economic, cultural, and geographic—that must be considered in shaping any policy change. Public policies are necessarily complex (although some are a lot more complex than necessary) and improving them normally involves complicated negotiations in which none of the participants get everything they want. If no one will compromise, nothing will get done. If political leaders do not work together to build the consensus needed to move policy forward, we risk losing the opportunities we have now and becoming a less prosperous, more divided country with diminishing respect around the world.

But don't Republicans and Democrats have their own deeply held values that keep them from finding common ground on economic policy issues— public spending, taxes, how to create good jobs, and health, retirement, energy, and immigration policy? I believe these differences are greatly exaggerated by campaign rhetoric. Most of the difference in values that matter for economic policy are not absolutes or yes/no choices. They are points on a continuum, such as self-reliance versus compassion for people who are struggling. Most people believe in both self-reliance and compassion, but they apply these principles differently in the context of a policy dispute over, say, whether there should be work requirements for receipt of food stamps or for Medicaid. The obstacles to finding common ground on economic policy are not absolutes, but questions of where to end up on a continuum. They are questions of more versus less, on which trade-offs and compromises are both necessary and possible.

To believe that bipartisan negotiation on economic policy can break the gridlock, one must believe that (1) meaningful policies exist that would increase the chances of sustained, broadly shared American prosperity, and

(2) enough members of both parties could find common ground to pass those policies into law. I hope to convince readers that both beliefs are true.

## THE ECONOMIC ESTABLISHMENT'S
## THREE BIG MISTAKES

At this point in the book, but more profoundly at this point in my career and my life, I feel compelled to relate the following thoughts, looking back on the past several years of history, my own role in it, and the role of others in my professional circles. As noted previously, I am a Democrat, but I also have served in many nonpartisan positions, specifically as founding director of the nonpartisan Congressional Budget Office (1975–1983) and as vice chair of the Federal Reserve (1996–1999), and I was president of the American Economic Association in 1986.

I view myself as a part of an informal group of partisan, nonpartisan, and bipartisan economic policy professionals that are sometimes referred to, either approvingly or derisively, as the "economic establishment." This group includes people who work at the Federal Reserve Board (both as governors and many members of the senior staff). It also includes the leadership of the Congressional Budget Office, many nonpartisan career civil servants, and partisan political appointees in the White House and cabinet departments including the Treasury, Commerce, the Office of Management and Budget, and several other departments and agencies.

This group also includes many scholars in colleges, universities, and public policy think tanks like the Brookings Institution, where I am a senior fellow, as well as several other think tanks of differing political perspectives and philosophies. Like me, the people I view as part of this informal economic policy establishment will generally have served in several of these types of organizations over the course of their careers. In addition, many of the people who hold these positions that control economic policy for the nation have also been employed by large corporations, and especially the largest banks and financial institutions.

This bipartisan group has responded to internal crises and external challenges through the decades, including the Great Depression, World War II, and the Organization of the Petroleum Exporting Countries (OPEC) oil price shocks of the 1970s. There have been many debates, differences of policy, differences of opinion, and some policy missteps, but on the whole, the bipartisan economic establishment has gotten a lot more right than wrong and has helped make the nation, and the world, quite prosperous over the years.

But in the recent past, I have reached the conclusion that I personally and this group collectively have made three mistakes that are far better to face than ignore. These mistakes, made over a period of many years, mean the bipartisan economic establishment has suffered a loss of authority that has made it more vulnerable to the challenges from populism on both the right and the left.

The three mistakes were these:

1.  We in the economic establishment did not recognize the full dimensions of the increasing economic inequality, racial inequality, lack of real wage growth, and the anxieties among the poor, the working class, and middle-class workers, exacerbated by technology in the workplace and globalization of economic production—and the need to make substantial investments to help workers transition to jobs in the new economy. There was economic pain and frustration in many households throughout the land, to which Washington seemed totally oblivious. In particular, we missed the geographical dimension of the problem as the largest cities, especially on the coasts, surged ahead riding a wave of digital technology while the rest of America, especially in the deindustrializing Midwest and other agricultural areas, was falling further behind. The North American Free Trade Agreement (NAFTA) is much more important as a symbol than as a cause of this problem, but when NAFTA passed during the Clinton administration, his economic team promised we would do a lot more for the workers who would lose out than, in retrospect, we did or needed to do. We were aware that many people, including many people of color, were trapped in urban poverty, even as we were failing to really solve the problem. We are just beginning to understand how and why the middle of America fell so far behind the big cities on the coasts, and how we can address both forms of inequality (as discussed in chapter 2).

2. The second mistake was not anticipating and avoiding the 2008–2009 financial crisis and economic collapse, the effects of which linger more than a decade later. I did not see the collapse coming, and economic experts disagree on whether the crisis was unavoidable or whether there were signs that were missed. But even if the bipartisan economic establishment was not to blame, the public views the economic establishment as responsible when the economy has a dramatic downturn and millions of families suffer consequences. At the very least, economic policymakers need to do a much better job of monitoring and regulating systemic financial risk, so this kind of crisis does not happen again in the future. In chapter 7, I share my thoughts on how we can do this by building on the Dodd-Frank Wall Street Reform and Consumer Protection Act.

3. The third mistake was a failure to fight the pernicious effects of money on politics and public policy. This problem is far larger than one bad Supreme Court decision in *Citizens United* v. *Federal Election Commission*. A lot of alumni of the Reagan, George H. W. Bush, Clinton, George W. Bush, and Obama administrations, myself included, have become far too comfortable taking lucrative jobs, board of directors' seats, and speaking fees from corporations and financial institutions. I did not think I was doing anything wrong when, after leaving the Clinton administration, I took a seat on the board of the Burroughs Corporation (which then merged with the Sperry Corporation, forming Unisys). There were then, and still are, too few women in corporate leadership. I also did not think I was doing anything wrong when I took speaking fees at a few corporate retreats, but when the issue of Wall Street speaking fees was used in an attempt to discredit Hillary Clinton in the 2016 campaign, I realized quite a lot of us were benefiting from what appeared to be a common practice (for those who have the opportunity).

I do not know whether or to what degree "regulatory capture," which is the tendency of industries to gain influence over the government agencies that are charged with regulating them, contributed to the financial crisis of 2008. But when the practice of taking money for speeches, jobs, and corporate board positions is combined with the large number of people who split time between the Washington economic establishment and the Wall Street banks—plus the failure to both ward off the 2008 crisis and appreciate the hollowing out of whole regions of the country that had been supported by manufacturing and agriculture—the rise of anti-establishment populism on both the left and the right becomes far less surprising.

My point in bringing up these three examples is not to assign fault or blame. That would be a pointless exercise. The actions of the economic establishment did not cause the election of President Trump. But the diminished authority of the economic establishment did contribute to the political environment of distrust of authority in 2016, and we must understand that this continues today. We must take this into account as we try to move forward from here. There is something we can learn by looking at recent history from a variety of perspectives and listening to a wider range of voices.

A lot of people in Washington were surprised by the politics of 2016, when a self-described socialist, Senator Bernie Sanders (DS-VT), could attract large crowds and win primaries against Hillary Clinton, a candidate who was clearly promising to continue the economic policies that had delivered a substantial recovery under President Obama (at least as measured by the national aggregate statistics).

---

*Collectively, those of us who purport to be experts on monetary and fiscal policy and financial markets totally missed the financial catastrophe of 2008 until it was actually happening. And perhaps more surprisingly, we are now totally amazed by the angry populism of the right and the left. Where did Trump and Sanders come from, and why are people cheering them so enthusiastically? They don't really fit in our world view. So, one of the big challenges for the next hundred years at Brookings and elsewhere in the intellectual establishment is to somehow learn to listen more effectively so we won't be so surprised by reality.*

—Alice M. Rivlin, address to
Brookings Institution Board of
Directors, March 2016

---

The surprises, of course, did not stop there. More than a dozen well-credentialed Republican candidates for the GOP nomination were overwhelmed by Donald Trump and his broad assault on the Washington establishment. And then in November 2016, voters in Michigan, Ohio, Wisconsin, Iowa, and Pennsylvania joined voters in enough other states in the South and West to deliver an Electoral College defeat for the Democrats. Donald Trump had run a campaign against the bipartisan establishment in Washington, largely by appealing to white working-class discontent, particularly in the industrial Midwest and other regions that were falling behind economically, and won the White House.

Trump's critics can point to numerous explicit appeals to racism (and sexism) and a larger number of more covert racist comments using words that have meaning in racist communities—sometimes called dog whistle racism because it is pitched so that only racists hear the code words. This is both true and condemnable.

But condemnation of Trump did not prove to be a winning strategy to defeat him. No candidate has ever come close to being condemned by the Washington political and media elites as vehemently, frequently, or consistently, starting with condemnation of his racist remark about "Mexican rapists" in his announcement speech. The consistent media criticism of Trump's statements continued as he added sexist, vulgar, and racist comments with increasing frequency throughout the months of the primary and general election campaigning. Clearly the condemnation was valuable to Trump's strategy, defining him as the candidate the elite opposed and giving him round-the-clock coverage that supported his claim to be the outsider as he ran through a field of Republican insiders and then faced one of the most qualified Democratic insiders ever to seek the office.

Trump's victory revealed a low point in American politics. Even if, as many pundits noted, the 2016 election did not prove that nearly half of American voters were racist (many Trump voters had supported Barack Obama in 2012), it did reveal that for nearly half of American voters, racist statements by a candidate were not, by themselves, a disqualifying factor. The proportions may never be fully sorted out, but Trump supporters were motivated by some combination of racist resentment, economic discontent, and cultural affinity expressed as a desire to vote in opposition to the political elite.

With a bit of time to reflect on this result, we in the economic and political establishment should not have been as surprised as we were. This is not the story of the end of bipartisanship, as bipartisanship has been in decline for many years. The rise of Donald Trump is more properly understood as a symptom rather than a cause of hyperpartisan warfare, which had made Washington completely dysfunctional and unable to address new problems and take on new challenges. Politicians have been running campaigns against Washington since time immemorial, but Trump was doing so at a time when the political establishment of both political parties was particularly vulnerable.

Those of us who want to search for common ground and an agenda of real progress in helping America move forward as one nation need to be cognizant of these mistakes and the attendant loss of authority of the bipartisan policymaking institutions. We will have to be humble and listen to more people, and we must understand that the economic establishment does not speak with as much authority as it once did. We cannot just put forth policies designed to achieve the ends we define as important. Instead, we must listen to the public and make the case that our policies will help achieve the ends that people view as necessary and important.

*"There is nothing wrong with America that cannot be cured by what is right with America."*

—President William Jefferson Clinton

I believe we cannot move forward and meaningfully address the economic discontent of the people and places that have been falling behind until we get government policymaking back on a productive path. Many people in both parties will place their hopes on the next election delivering an overwhelming majority for their side and a complete vanquishment of the other side. Then, they assert, America can follow a path—boldly progressive or truly conservative—without compromise. This fantasy never dies, even though it is never realized. But the far greater likelihood is that with or without Donald Trump in the White House, the American public will remain divided, and politics will remain destructively partisan until we recognize this partisanship as the true cause of our dysfunction and discontent.

This is a contrarian book in both the economic and political dimensions. First, I think it is a mistake to view the American economy as fundamentally weak and struggling with overwhelming, insoluble problems leading to stagnation and decline. It is far more accurate—as well as a more constructive mindset for policymaking—to view the American economy as a machine of proven strength and resilience that is currently well positioned to move to the next level of shared prosperity.

The economy is currently showing enough strength to allow us to take on the full list of problems we face, from automation and extreme inequality to global warming, inadequate public health and mental health infrastructure, a dysfunctional immigration system, and rising national debt. These are extremely serious problems, and some of them could do us in if we fail to recognize how threatening they are and cooperate to confront them. But they are manageable challenges if we buckle down and work together to manage them.

We already know some proven policies that would mitigate these challenges. Throwing ourselves into problem-solving mode would turn up more actions we could take. There is no reason to think that the proven strength and resilience of the American economy and our democracy will suddenly desert us now or that American ingenuity is no longer a national asset. The trouble is that we are not even trying to manage these problems. Our divisiveness and our broken economic policymaking process are holding us back, not the economy itself.

Second, I am a contrarian about our political future. By that I mean I am hopeful our democracy will prove as resilient as our economy, and we can solve our divisions of race, class, and political ideology. My hope is that citizens will become more aware of the costs of division and insist on cooperation. First at the local level and cascading up through state and regional collaboration, groups will come together to solve local problems and move long-stalled negotiations forward. Voters will start rewarding leaders with a positive vision and a record of cooperation and accomplishment more than they reward politicians with a talent for blaming problems on the opposition.

This has happened before in our history when we have faced great challenges, and with this approach, we have achieved greatness. As Americans, we can and must recapture the "can-do" energy and cooperative spirit that brought the opportunity that we have in front of us today and come together to deal with all our most pressing issues.

CHAPTER 2

# THE AMERICAN ECONOMY: HISTORIC OPPORTUNITY OR IMPENDING DISASTER?

Which of the following descriptions of the American economy is true?

**Version one:** The American economy is the strongest, most resilient economy in the world, and even though this economy faces enormous challenges, it is performing better and better. Americans are creating businesses, working harder, and earning their chance to live the American Dream.

**Version two:** The American economy is failing many workers and communities, trapping millions of people between low-wage jobs and poverty. Americans are living beyond their means, with high levels of personal, corporate, and government debt. If Americans fail to manage this and other serious threats to their future well-being, they will face declining prosperity and world influence in coming years.

Most of the discussions on cable TV between representatives of the two major parties sound like this. The spokesperson for the party that occupies the White House tells us the economy is strong and getting better (version one), while the person representing the out party points out the economy's weaknesses (version two).

I will let you in on a little secret: Presidents (and equally true, governors and mayors) have far less influence over the general state of economy than advocates insist or voters believe. Presidents can affect economic conditions at the margins by offering good (or bad) economic policies that will benefit (or hinder) some groups in the short term and can strengthen (or weaken) the economy over the longer term, but economies rise and fall due to many factors, and most of them are outside the control of the executive office. Business cycles (regional, national, and global), external economic shocks (wars, pandemics, market failures, oil price surges), and breakthrough technologies (in computing, medicine, manufacturing) will have a greater effect on American families sitting around the breakfast table tomorrow than the marginal tax rates for the upper brackets or which categories of imports are subject to tariffs. Nonetheless, it is easy to run for reelection when the overall economy is growing and very hard when it is not, so partisans will spend a lot of time quoting statistics to prove that the economy is either wonderful or horrible.

And here is another secret: Most of the time, both version one and version two are true. For decades, the strong, resilient American economy has been growing faster than other advanced economies. Job creation is strong; employment has reached historic levels; average hourly wages are beginning to rise; inflation is not a problem.[1] The national statistics that economists look at most show a rosy picture, sometimes described as a Goldilocks economy—not too hot, not too cold, but just right.

But underneath the national statistical averages is a very different picture. Large numbers of people and large areas of the country are not sharing in the general good news. The rising prosperity has benefited the already fortunate, especially white, highly educated workers living in or near the largest cities. Those without a college degree or advanced technical skills are getting left behind with lower pay, fewer opportunities to earn a middle-class income, high levels of debt, and diminished hope for a brighter future for their children.

The wealth gap between white and non-white American families is as large today as it was in the 1960s and 1970s.[2] If your family was able to buy a home, even a modest one, in a whites-only neighborhood in 1962, it has likely appreciated enough in value to have paid for college educations for generations of your relatives. But only a small proportion of African American, Latino, Asian American, and recent immigrant families at that time could get a job that earned enough income to qualify for a home loan, and those that did were blocked by racist laws and, when these were struck down, racist bank lending practices. Institutional racism has persisted, and rather than shrinking, the racial wealth gap has grown larger in recent years as wealth inequality generally has worsened. America has been called the Land of Opportunity, but it has always heaped more opportunity on those with more family wealth. Of course there are many stories of people of color and recent immigrants who have defied the odds and earned great wealth, but the statistics, not the rarer exceptions, describe the reality most people experience.

The statistics also tell us there are large numbers of white Americans trapped generationally on the wrong side of the wealth/opportunity divide. Today, large numbers of working age, noncollege educated men, both white and non-white, are dropping out of the labor market.[3] There are areas of our inner cities and vast stretches of small-town and rural America where people know the rules of the economy were written to benefit someone else (and they are right about this) and they have few choices other than low-wage jobs with limited chances for advancement. If they are barely getting by day-to-day, they know they are living far short of the American dream, and thus, millions of Americans do not feel like they live in the Land of Opportunity.

The American economy is strong in the national aggregate statistics like the gross domestic product (GDP). If you add up all the goods and services we produce, all that we consume, or all the wealth we create, the numbers are higher than ever. But these statistics are averaging some Americans who are doing extremely well with many others who are just holding on or losing ground. The economy is not just version one above, it is also version two, and this should be completely unacceptable to all of us.

For years, for too many Americans, the economy has been failing to deliver economic security, economic opportunity, and hope that the future will be better. It is not enough to say the economy is doing well because the overall level of production is increasing. It matters how the gains are being distributed—that is, who is and who is not benefiting from the work. The goal for the economy should always be to achieve sustainable prosperity, broadly shared. The current US economy is failing to achieve this goal.

The continuous debate between version one and version two dominates the discussion that most Americans hear about the economy. And the next level of discussion is no more informative as each side paints the other as holding unacceptable views that could never actually come to pass. Supply-side economics makes promises of balanced budgets that never come true, but Republicans are never going to make up the difference by ending Social Security or Medicare as we know it. On the flip side, Democrats hold an expansive view of government, but they are not communists and are not trying to nationalize all the businesses in America.

These never-ending insincere arguments crowd out the conversations we should be having: How can we reach agreement on the policies that actually would grow the economy and create broadly shared prosperity, economic security, and opportunity for more Americans to achieve a better life? How can we make the investments in infrastructure that would make life safer for American families and more productive for American businesses? How can we improve education and job training so workers, young and old, have the skills for the growth occupations of today and tomorrow? How do we develop enough energy to sustain economic growth in a way that will sustain thriving life on a threatened planet? How can we support basic science, research, and development so America leads in the technologies that will shape the future? How do we raise the revenue to pay for the services Americans want and expect so we can reverse the unsustainable levels of borrowing and long-term debt? These are the questions we should be asking, but endless partisan debates are making constructive progress on these questions difficult if not impossible.

## ECONOMIC INEQUALITY: AMERICA'S GREATEST CHALLENGE AND BIGGEST OPPORTUNITY FOR MEANINGFUL IMPROVEMENT

Increasing inequality and the large numbers of people who are stuck in poverty or trapped in low-wage jobs[4] define today's American economic agenda. The good overall economic statistics should not blind us to the critical necessity of the work that must be done to make the US economy work for the people and places that are falling behind. And the good statistics that support version one tell us this is a good time to take on the challenges of version two.

We must seize the opportunity offered by the strong macroeconomy to correct the mistakes of the past and move to a new level of more broadly shared prosperity. The current high GDP growth rate, record stock market levels, and low interest rates reveal the strength of the economy that makes this an excellent time to invest in education, infrastructure, basic science, and public health to help lower costs for business and create a more productive and competitive economy.

## WE KNOW WHAT TO DO TO MAKE THE ECONOMY WORK FOR MORE PEOPLE

The overall strength of the economy is just one of the reasons why now is an excellent time to make investments for economic growth and better-paying jobs. A second reason is we currently have a high level of agreement on what the goals should be for our economy and what policies we need to move the economy forward.

I expect to get both surprise and pushback when I say this out loud to students, academics, political leaders, or interested citizens. We have two political parties employing thousands of people whose job is to make sure every American understands the catastrophe that is just around the corner if the other side gets a chance to enact their disastrous policies. This is the very stuff of politics, but politics is not reality.

In my experience, when it comes to governing, the two political parties are never as far apart as their political campaign rhetoric makes them seem, but right now they are as close together on economic policy as I can remember ever seeing them. Despite the political rhetoric of a presidential campaign unfolding amid a background of impeachment, Democrats and Republicans are describing the economy in similar terms, hoping to get help to the same groups of people, using largely the same approaches.

Now, obviously, version one of the economy sounds like it would be offered by Republicans, the political party that currently lives in the White House, describing the economy in glowing terms. Version two sounds like the Democrats, the party that wants to win the White House in the next election, describing the economy in the most negative light. It was

---

*Both sides are trying to scare people into thinking if you vote for this*
*other guy, it's going to be a terrible time. And Medicare is a good*
*example. Both sides are trying to scare seniors that their Medicare will*
*be destroyed. That's not even remotely possible.*

—Alice Rivlin, "Political Bridge
People," *On Being with Krista*
*Tippett*, October 25, 2012

---

Democrats who echoed version one and Republicans, version two, in the 2016
election, and we can expect the roles to reverse again following the 2020
election if the Democrats prevail. But which party would say this?

The extreme levels of inequality we have now are causing frustration
and resentment, making many Americans feel that they are invisible
to other Americans. The heart and soul of America is not the corporations that trade on Wall Street but the millions of Americans that
own or work for small businesses up and down Main Street. Our goal
must be to make the economy work for more American families by
creating better-paying jobs, especially for the people and places that
have been falling behind in the transition to a globally connected
knowledge economy that has delivered so much in riches to such a
small number of elites. We need to make investments in education
and job skills training, modern manufacturing capacity, and the infrastructure and connectivity that are needed to include more people
and places in the fast-growing jobs of today and tomorrow.

You really could hear this from either party and that is the other reason for
the optimism that we are in a good moment to take action to reduce inequality. What would be different is who each side would say was to blame
for the current problems. Democrats blame big corporations and the wealthy
elites that use undue influence over the government to keep their taxes low
and corporate profits high, harming average workers.[5] Republicans blame
the government for bad policy, overregulation, and high taxes that hamper
business growth, in turn harming average workers.

If we could put aside issues of blame, we would see there is remarkable agreement on the dimensions of the problem: We must do something about record economic inequality. There is also agreement on the goals we are seeking: more broadly shared prosperity that gives everyone an opportunity to get a job that pays enough to support a family and offers economic security and hope for the future.

Still not convinced? Let's try it again: Which party do you think would say the following?

> We should increase taxes on wealthy individuals and profitable corporations to give more help to the poor and middle class.

And which party would say this?

> We should raise taxes in the fast-growing states like California, New York, and Massachusetts to fund infrastructure projects that will help businesses hire more workers in slower-growth states like Michigan, Ohio, Alabama, and Oklahoma.

These are two ways of describing the same set of policies. We are already taxing the wealthy to fund programs designed to help the poor and middle class, but Democrats think we should be doing this to a far greater degree because income and wealth disparities have been growing dramatically worse in recent years. We are already taxing the fast-growing states to fund programs designed to help the slower-growing states, and yet geographic inequality has dramatically increased. With a few exceptions, the states where Democrats hold comfortable majorities pay more in federal taxes than they receive in federal benefits, and the states where Republicans are in the majority tend to receive more in federal benefits than they pay in taxes, but Republicans delight in advocating higher taxes on blue states. For instance, the 2017 Tax Cuts and Jobs Act deliberately increased taxes on wealthy families in the mostly blue high-tax states when it placed a $10,000 cap on state and local tax (SALT) deductions.[6]

Democrats and Republicans have been looking at the same problem— economic inequality—from different perspectives. Economic inequality has many dimensions, including racial inequality and gender inequality, unequal access to housing, education, high-paying jobs, health care services, and nutrition, and unequal treatment in the criminal justice system. All of these dimensions are important and interrelated. Beyond the racial wealth gap discussed above, the statistics tell us that African Americans and Hispanic Americans earn substantially less income, are less likely to have a college degree or an advanced degree, and have less access to health care services, poorer diets, and shorter lifespans than white Americans. Similar differences can be observed when comparing white Americans without a college degree and white Americans with a college degree. So the differences in educational attainment explain part of the difference between the races in income, but certainly not all of it. When we compare African Americans with a college degree to white Americans with a college degree, we find huge differences in wealth and income. The same is true when we look at the gap in earnings and wealth between African Americans without a college degree and white Americans without a college degree. White workers earn more income and have more wealth than non-white workers even when we control for education. And this finding holds up when researchers use sophisticated statistical analytic tools to control for all the potentially complicating factors like age and education levels.[7]

The story for women is similar and also quite complicated, even puzzling. Women are now more likely to have a college degree and more likely to have a graduate degree than men are, yet women still earn less income on average than men do. On average (and controlling statistically for other factors including age, education, and number of hours worked), women earn eighty-five cents per hour for every dollar a man earns per hour.[8]

The researchers who study these data have found at least a partial explanation in the difference between occupations where women and men work. Men are found in greater numbers in higher-paying occupations and women tend to work in lower-paying occupations. Many of the reasons for this are historical, and we have made a lot of progress over the span of my career, but we still have a long way to go. When I was in graduate school in the 1950s, there were no women economists, and women professors were very rare.[9] In any hospital, nearly all the doctors were men, and nearly all the nurses were women. All the business executives were men, and they had female secretaries. Men flew the airplanes, and women served coffee and drinks in the cabin.

We have come a long way since then, but on average, most jobs are either about 75 percent male and 25 percent female, or the reverse, 25 percent male and 75 percent female, and the professions with more men pay better than the professions with more women. It is also true that the higher you look on the corporate ladder of most businesses, the fewer women you see. Women are especially scarce in senior management and on corporate boards of directors.

Women are highly concentrated in the professions that take care of the youngest and oldest among us, and I have long believed that the caregiving professions are far more important than we as a society treat them in terms of respect, attention, and money. One of the best ways to reduce the gender pay gap, better prepare children for school, and improve the general health and quality of life for millions of Americans would be a strategy to train and professionalize caregivers. This would also help reduce the racial pay gap because many minority women work in human service jobs. We need to increase the skill level and the pay for women- and minority-dominated professions that provide early child development, preschool and primary education, special education, eldercare, home health care, and other care of our family members when they most need it.

The government collects a lot of data, and researchers inside and outside of government analyze the data to understand why inequality by such factors as race and gender, geography, and educational attainment has been so durable, and what government can do to help close the gaps, giving all Americans more equal opportunity to contribute to the economy and earn their own measure of success and economic security. But even under rigorous analysis, the complexity of the interrelations between factors remains, and there are few simple answers to the problems of increasing inequality and persistent poverty.

Policymakers, especially Democrats, frequently discuss the problem of economic inequality using aggregate national statistics and the differences

*I think we have to think really hard about how to make human service jobs both more highly rewarded and more highly trained.*

—Alice M. Rivlin, Interview with
*Politico,* June 7, 2016

between the wealthiest Americans and the economic frustrations of everyone else. Republicans have been focusing on the economic frustrations being experienced in rural America and the deindustrializing Midwest and the differences between elites and ordinary Americans. These are really two different perspectives on the same problem of inequality. I find one way of conceptualizing inequality in America particularly useful for understanding how and why Democrats and Republicans look at the problem differently. I like to focus on two dimensions—one that I call vertical inequality (or income and wealth inequality) and the other I call horizontal inequality (or geographic inequality). An economic plan to tackle both dimensions could go a long way toward uniting red state and blue state America and breaking the hyperpartisan gridlock in Washington.

## VERTICAL INEQUALITY AND HORIZONTAL INEQUALITY

For this purpose, I am defining *vertical inequality* as differences in income, wealth, and economic prospects between individuals living in the same community and *horizontal inequality* as differences in income, wealth, and economic growth between different communities. When a homeless person or a moderate-wage worker standing on a street in Seattle, San Francisco, Boston, or New York sees billionaire technology company executives, venture capitalists, or investment bankers getting out of their limousines, going from their corner offices to their penthouse apartments, that is vertical inequality. Horizontal inequality, on the other hand, is when a farmer, a teacher, or a factory worker in a struggling small town in the middle of America[10] sees a banker or a politician on television talking about how great the economy is, but the farmer or worker knows, "It is not so great around here." Both dimensions represent very real problems for the American economy, and we must use public policy to tackle both types of inequality head on.

Republicans and Democrats look at inequality from different perspectives largely because they live in different places and know different people. In a massive shift that demographers[11] and journalists[12] have labeled the Big Sort, Democrats and Republicans now live in different neighborhoods. Most Democrats live in or near large, fast-growing cities, and most Republicans live in small-town, rural, and exurban areas.

If you live in a big city like New York, Los Angeles, Boston, Seattle, or San Francisco, you know where the billionaires live, and you know they live in a different reality than average people. When politicians like Senators Bernie Sanders (I-VT) and Elizabeth Warren (D-MA) first talked about billionaires and fractions of 1 percent of the population having as much wealth as the bottom 90 percent, their views were seen as representing the left wing of the Democratic Party. But they have made their point, and now themes of inequality can be heard from all corners of the party. Most of the Democrats' emphasis is on vertical inequality, which exists in every community but is most visible in the largest cities, where extremes of wealth and poverty exist in close proximity.

The big cities have big problems including poverty, homelessness, alcohol and other drug addictions, gentrification, housing costs that passed "ridiculously unaffordable" for an average family a long time ago. The nation's booming cities are adding new businesses, new residents, and new commuters every day, causing perpetual construction and redevelopment projects, and clogging all forms of transportation. But the poor, and even workers with average incomes, worry about excessive growth not benefiting people like themselves. People of color, low-income families, and even middle-class families are getting pushed out of their neighborhoods through gentrification, and there is a widespread feeling that the system is only really working for those at the very top. In 2018 this reached the point where residents of Long Island City in New York protested and eventually blocked Amazon's plans to build a second headquarters, which would have meant 25,000 new jobs paying six-figure salaries.

Saying "no thank you" to thousands of high-paying jobs seemed almost incomprehensible for many people in the parts of America where good jobs are scarce. In midsized cities, small towns, and suburban and rural counties across America, the economy continues to stagnate, and in many places, it feels like the recession that started in 2008 never ended. This is horizontal or geographic inequality, which for decades has been concentrating most of the nation's economic growth in our largest cities, predominantly on the coasts, and leaving rural and small-town America, predominantly in the heartland,[13] behind.

Typical Republican voters do not live in one of the largest cities and rarely see representatives of the 1 percent, but these voters do know economic activity has been slowing down in their area for decades. They know there was no recovery in their part of the country while President Barack Obama was in office, and this has not changed under President Donald Trump. There is horizontal inequality in every community, with areas of wealth and opportunity separated from areas of poverty and decline (often reflecting *de facto* racial segregation, which is the legacy of formal redlining policies in real estate in decades past and informal redlining policies more recently).[14] But horizontal inequality is most visible in national maps that show the concentration of the nation's economic growth in the largest cities (shown in black and dark gray in figure 2-1), leaving the midsized cities, small towns, and rural counties either stagnant (shown in light gray) or in economic decline (shown in white). Decades of deindustrialization of the American heartland, unreliable prices for agriculture products, and formal or informal racial segregation policies[15] have hollowed out small-town America, leaving declining populations, falling property values, a diminished tax base, and rising rates of "deaths of despair" including alcoholism, opioids, and suicide.

At the county level, there is a remarkable correlation between economic growth and voting behavior, with Democrats concentrated in the fast-growing, high population density cities, and Republicans dominating the slower-growing, lower population density interior states, in the small towns and

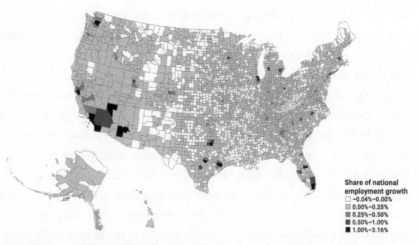

Share of national employment growth
□ –0.04%–0.00%
▨ 0.00%–0.25%
▨ 0.25%–0.50%
◼ 0.50%–1.00%
◼ 1.00%–3.16%

FIGURE 2-1.   Counties Contribution to National Employment Growth, March 2010–March 2019

Source: Analysis of data from the Quarterly Census of Employment and Wages, US Bureau of Labor Statistics, for the Metropolitan Policy Program at Brookings.

rural counties that make up most of the nation's landmass but somewhat less than half of the population. A failure by Democrats to appreciate the economic frustration and pain being felt in states like Pennsylvania, West Virginia, Ohio, Michigan, Missouri, Iowa, and Wisconsin contributed to Trump's Electoral College victory in the 2016 presidential election.

A national strategy to address both vertical and horizontal inequality could appeal to voters in both red states and blue states and unite a divided nation around specific plans to grow better-paying jobs for the people and places that have been falling behind. Among economists associated with both parties, there are many areas of agreement on what should be done to address structural weaknesses and to make needed investments in physical infrastructure and investments in the quality of our workforce to boost the nation's economic capacity. If we did these things with a strategic intent, we could extend economic opportunity to areas of the country and groups of people that have been locked out of the prosperity that other Americans take for granted. We know what to do to make things better, and we need to stop blaming each other and work together to chart a better course.

## TODAY'S AMERICA: ECONOMIC DIVISIONS AND POLITICAL DIVISIONS

In addition to the strong overall economy and the bipartisan agreement that we need to address inequality and spread more of the benefits of the economy to the people and places that have been falling behind, there is a third reason why we must act now: We really have no choice if we want to preserve the democracy we have inherited from previous generations, going back to the founders of our nation.

Our country has flourished for more than two centuries as a capitalist democracy, but the American capitalist system ceases to be politically viable in the American democratic system if the public is no longer confident in the system's ability to deliver opportunity and economic security to the majority of workers. Decades of wage stagnation, corporate downsizing and outsourcing, and increasing inequality of both wealth and power have left too many Americans economically insecure, distrustful of America's economic and political institutions, and disconnected from those who are more affluent and comfortable. Stark differences in current economic security and future prospects between families living in different Americas with vastly different economic realities create anxiety, fear, distrust, and resentment. Persistent and rising inequality diminishes confidence that either political party has the ability to deliver prosperity to average families in the future, and this undercuts faith in our democracy.

Economic frustrations of the past and limited opportunities in the current economy are undercutting confidence about the future. Public opinion polls tell us that Americans are pessimistic about the future, with majorities saying they are not confident that life for their children's generation will be better,[16] and they see America's influence in the world declining, the gap between rich and poor growing wider, and America growing more politically divided.[17] (See figure 2-2.)

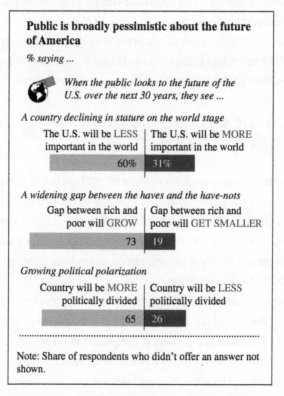

**Public is broadly pessimistic about the future of America**

*% saying ...*

*When the public looks to the future of the U.S. over the next 30 years, they see ...*

*A country declining in stature on the world stage*

| The U.S. will be LESS important in the world | The U.S. will be MORE important in the world |
|---|---|
| 60% | 31% |

*A widening gap between the haves and the have-nots*

| Gap between rich and poor will GROW | Gap between rich and poor will GET SMALLER |
|---|---|
| 73 | 19 |

*Growing political polarization*

| Country will be MORE politically divided | Country will be LESS politically divided |
|---|---|
| 65 | 26 |

Note: Share of respondents who didn't offer an answer not shown.

FIGURE 2-2.   Public Perceptions of the Future of the US

*Source:* Pew Research Center, "Looking to the Future, Public Sees an America in Decline on Many Fronts," survey of US adults conducted December 11–23, 2018.

In my view, and I am not alone in this, we are at a very dangerous time in our history. America is losing one of its greatest assets: our belief that we are one very special country—a belief sometimes known as American exceptionalism. We once had a sense of being one nation having a shared destiny and exceptional qualities that go with being Americans. Even if it was perhaps equal parts myth and reality, and did not as accurately describe the experiences of non-white Americans, our "can-do" spirit helped the United States win two world wars, land on the moon, invent much of the world's economy, and create a working class that was the envy of the world. Now we wonder whether we are a nation coming apart at the seams.

Today, America is divided in ways that recall the great social upheavals of the 1960s or, worse, the Civil War of the 1860s. The rise of red state versus blue state hyperpartisanship has metastasized into increased racism, nationalism, anti-Semitism, xenophobia, Islamophobia, and homophobia that are far too often expressed through violent attacks. I do not know what to do to solve these problems, but I do know we have to try. A truly great nation worthy of a modern exceptionalism would rise to the challenge to heal the wounds of hate and division, giving all Americans opportunities to participate in growing an economy that offers broadly shared prosperity.

We cannot be united states if we have separate economies, with wealthy elites living in penthouses high above struggling streets, or coastal states surging ahead and interior states falling behind. America needs to unite around a plan for economic growth that spreads outside of the cities and includes everyone. A plan that addresses both vertical inequality and horizontal inequality at the same time could unite the country by finding support in big cities in the blue states and the small towns and rural counties of the red states.

## A PLAN TO ADDRESS BOTH HORIZONTAL AND VERTICAL INEQUALITY

Economists call efforts to address vertical inequality "people-based" policies and efforts to address horizontal inequality "place-based" policies. Often these have been seen as alternative approaches competing for the same resources, but clearly this is an area where "either/or" thinking needs to be replaced by a "both/and" understanding.

The distinction between people-based and place-based is somewhat informal and imperfect. People live in places after all, and many of the policies to help them are complicated collaborations between our federal and state or local governments. Generally, people-based refers to laws and programs that people qualify for regardless of where they live (often based on their income as reported to the IRS). This includes the federal tax code, Social Security, and Medicare as well as food assistance in the form of the Supplemental Nutrition Assistance Program (SNAP), housing assistance programs like "Section 8," and child-care assistance. Place-based refers to federal spending and grant programs designed to help a specific town or region. This would include nearly all infrastructure spending and is best exemplified by specific programs like the Tennessee Valley Authority (TVA) project in the 1930s, which was created to extend electric power to families throughout the South.

Of course, the two concepts overlap. Both sides might like to claim education, because federal, state, and, especially, local authorities share jurisdiction and fight over policy.[18] It is also pretty clear that neither people-based nor place-based policies could ever fully succeed without the other. There will never be enough people-based income support and public services to help people survive if they live in a community in stark decline. If businesses, jobs, and people are leaving an area, local hospitals are closing, and schools are consolidating, government programs designed to help needy individuals and families can soften the blow but not reverse the decline. People cannot thrive in a community that is not growing.

At the same time, places working to get their economy and their community moving in a positive direction need people who have enough support to participate in the growth. Hospitals can stay open only if people have health care insurance; schools need students who are well fed and ready to learn. Businesses need customers who can afford to buy food and school supplies. No struggling small town or economic region that is seeking a comeback by making investments to attract new businesses and better jobs would want to see cuts in basic safety-net services that people rely on to get by. Communities cannot thrive if the people who live there are barely surviving.

With the need to address vertical inequality so much more apparent in the blue states and the need to address horizontal inequality so much more apparent in the red states, it is both good public policy and good politics to combine place-based and people-based policies to address both aspects of inequality. We need to tackle both vertical and horizontal inequality, and to do so we need both people-based policies and place-based policies.[19] A new national economic strategy combining both approaches could gain broad support and would bring greater inclusiveness and opportunity to the people and places in America that have been falling behind.

## VERTICAL INEQUALITY

Political progressives have been drawing attention to vertical inequality since the French economists Thomas Piketty and Emmanuel Saez published a paper titled "Income Inequality in the United States 1913–1998"[20] in 2003 with greater attention from the Occupy Wall Street protests in 2011, but recently the position is becoming more mainstream. First the cause spread beyond the left wing of the Democratic Party to include nearly all Democrats, and then many Republicans began echoing the same themes. Then, Speaker of the House John Boehner took up the cause of inequality in 2014, saying, "We do have an issue of income inequality in America. The president's [Obama's] policies are making that problem worse. . . . The top third of America are doing pretty good. The bottom two-thirds are really being squeezed."[21] Later that year, Representative Paul Ryan (R-WI), who was already in the leadership and would become House Speaker the following year, gave a full speech committing himself (and he hoped, his party) to finding new approaches to fighting poverty. In the speech, Ryan offered a plan that would have meant greater flexibility, but no additional funding, for states that devised pilot programs for more personalized delivery of social safety-net services.[22]

More recently, even the nonpartisan Federal Reserve chair, Jerome Powell, has joined the inequality bandwagon, saying in February 2019 that "we have some work to do to make sure that the prosperity that we do achieve is widely spread. . . . Median and lower levels of income have grown, but much more slowly. And growth at the top has been very strong. So we want prosperity to be widely shared, and . . . we need policies to make that happen."[23]

But it is nonetheless the think tanks and political leaders on the left that have developed the most solid lists of proposals designed to shrink the gap between the small number of individuals who have the most and the large

number who have the least. Most serious proposals to mitigate vertical inequality involve increasing the progressivity of the tax code, raising the incomes of the poor by raising the minimum wage and the value of other income
supports, and guaranteeing the provision of basic needs such as food, housing,
transportation, health care, and childcare for the poor and middle class.

A plan to address vertical inequality should include proposals to:

1. **Tax the rich.** The degree to which the political system will support
   tax increases targeting the income or wealth of the richest Americans
   will be hotly debated in the 2020 presidential election. But the tax code
   could be made dramatically more progressive by simply reversing
   the Trump individual tax cuts to raise marginal rates for higher-
   income taxpayers. There has always been room for fruitful bipartisan
   compromise on the general principle of eliminating deductions and
   closing tax loopholes to broaden the tax base if it makes it possible to
   lower middle-income tax rates (as discussed in chapters 8 and 9). We
   need stronger enforcement of tax laws so everyone, especially the
   wealthiest, pay what they owe, and there are many examples of egre-
   gious tax loopholes that need to be eliminated, including the special
   tax treatment for carried interest that benefits hedge fund partners
   and provisions that help specific industries such as oil, gas, and real
   estate development.

2. **Make work pay.** At the other end of the income scale, the Earned Income Tax Credit (EITC) should be expanded and increased. The
   name of the EITC may be unwieldy, but the policy is effective in using
   the tax code to provide badly needed additional income for low-paid
   working families. The EITC has enjoyed broad bipartisan support in
   the past and likely would find bipartisan support now for increasing
   its value and including more people.

3. **Rewrite the rules.** Decades of political dysfunction in Washington
   have given us laws and regulations that are out of date—unable to keep
   up with massive changes in technology and global markets, and
   skewed to the benefit of the most powerful interests in the industries
   being regulated.[24] We need to get Washington working again so we
   can pass up-to-date laws protecting the health, safety, and welfare of
   the public as consumers, workers, borrowers, investors, and families

living near American businesses. To protect us from crisis and catastrophe, we need anti-trust laws to check monopoly power, strengthen labor and worker health and safety laws, environmental laws, and continuous improvement in financial and credit market regulation. And we need to export our values by negotiating trade deals that protect the environment, health, safety, and incomes of workers in the US and in the countries with which we trade.

4. **Help people afford basic needs.** The federal government spends a lot of money to help lower-income individuals and families pay for food, housing, winter heating, and a wide variety of other needs, but proposals to increase the generosity and breadth of these programs tend to receive increased attention during an election cycle. A tax code made dramatically more progressive by increasing top rates and closing loopholes that benefit the wealthy would increase government revenue, funding some of these proposals for new federal spending to help families with college tuition, student loan debt, or health care. Some of the more expansive proposals offered by progressives such as a federal job guarantee, a guaranteed minimum income, and a greatly expanded child tax credit could possibly fit within a sustainable federal budget that brought in more revenue. But the same tax revenues cannot be spent several times over and the 2020 federal deficit is projected to surpass a trillion dollars.[25] Difficult choices must be made across the entire federal budget, including among these worthy initiatives to help working families move from barely surviving to thriving in the modern economy.

The best approaches to helping families at the low end of the income scale are those that help people change their circumstances and advance to a higher level of economic security. Rather than just giving people money, it makes more sense to help adults afford more education and technical skills training so they can get and keep a better paying job, as well as to provide support that helps adults raise healthy families with children who are ready to succeed in school and in life. Transportation assistance is also needed in many areas to help people get to where the jobs are. New policies to raise pay and professional standards for the caregiving professions (discussed above) fit into this part of the plan. Programs that strengthen the ability of childcare, preschool, health care, and home health assistance workers to deliver needed services to children living in poverty and the elderly needing assistance, have the added benefit of increasing pay and career opportunities for many women and people of color, helping to close gender and racial income gaps.

This is a broad outline of the kinds of proposals that should be included in any package designed to reduce vertical inequality. It is based on a clear willingness to use the tax code to address inequality by closing loopholes and raising rates at the very top. It also includes a commitment to continuing the basic social safety-net programs and expand those that help people move to greater success in productive work. Most of these programs function considerably better when they are administered as part of a holistic approach at the local level, so it is appropriate that we set priorities closer to the ground.

## HORIZONTAL INEQUALITY

Republicans have been more consistent in highlighting the pain and resentment in the deindustrializing heartland and rural areas where there has been no economic recovery. Their principal policy, however, including the "Opportunity Zones" in the 2017 tax bill, is not an adequate response to the problem. If Opportunity Zones are well administered by state and local governments, the lower taxes could encourage projects that benefit struggling families in economically challenged communities, but there is at least an equal danger that Opportunity Zones will just be used to lower taxes for developers who are gentrifying those areas.[26] But even if Opportunity Zones perform spectacularly as advertised, they are just a small response to an enormous challenge. There is so much more we could do if both political parties committed at the federal level to join and support ongoing bipartisan efforts at the state and local level to develop strategies and make the investments needed to bring better-paying jobs with security and a future to the midsized cities, small towns, and rural counties across the American heartland.

For decades, place-based policies have not been a priority for many academic economists because they believed such policies were unnecessary.[27] An influential paper by economists Robert Barro and Xavier Sala-i-Martin[28] convinced researchers that the economic performance of US states and regions had a tendency toward convergence and, given time, the poorer states and regions would grow faster than the richer states and regions. The paper was published in 1992, just at the start of the internet age and the "dot-com boom."

Whether the saying is true that "the internet changed everything," it certainly changed this pattern of convergence. The research since the dawn of the internet age makes it clear that the economic fortunes of the states and regions are diverging[29]—that is, the richer areas, mainly the big cities on the coasts, have been getting richer and the poorer areas have been falling behind. Surging cities like San Francisco, Seattle, Boston, and New York are showing clear signs of overcrowding, so it makes no sense to try to move even more people to these hubs of higher-paying jobs. Both the big cities and the rest of America would benefit from public policies that help to move high-paying jobs out of the crowded supercities to the midsized cities, small towns, and rural, suburban, and exurban areas where high-paying jobs are harder to find.

People have worked on placed-based economic development for many years, dating back to efforts to recover from the Great Depression such as the New Deal and the TVA. The John F. Kennedy and Lyndon Johnson administrations brought a focus on the Appalachian region and efforts at urban renewal. From the Peace Corps to AmeriCorps and from the US Agency for International Development (USAID) to international groups like the Organization for Economic Cooperation and Development (OECD), we have developed a network of people with expertise in regional economic development. There have been successes and failures to learn from. Recently there have been several successes to emulate.

I had the honor to be part of a successful turnaround in my hometown of Washington, DC. It still has many problems to solve but is undeniably in better shape than the financially unstable city that, in 1995, was forced by Congress to report to a financial control board (on which I served). A couple of decades later, the city is thriving thanks to a few terrific mayors and several talented chief financial officers. (My friend Anthony Williams was both.)

The DC turnaround is a story that spans decades, yet it is a work in progress. The city still has issues of inequality, poverty, crime, drug addiction, and the development of downtown areas has displaced residents through gentrification, pushing many problems out into surrounding jurisdictions. But there is no doubt the city is in much better shape than it was twenty-five years ago, and this upward trajectory has been matched in cities across the nation. New York, Philadelphia, and Cleveland have overcome their own financial crises. Pittsburgh, Nashville, Atlanta, Houston, and Las Vegas join dozens of other cities in achieving turnaround stories that are correctly described as miracles. The past few decades may not have been the finest hour for our federal government in Washington, but they have been a golden age for city, state, and local government leaders pulling people together and getting things done.

But what about the small towns? Here the news is actually just as hopeful. After the 2016 election, journalists and scholars went out to small-town America looking for hopelessness and frustration. They found that,[30] but they also found heroic examples of small towns and economic regions fighting their way back. New York Times columnist Thomas Friedman went to Lancaster, Pennsylvania,[31] and described a town that had decided to come together to solve its own problems. With little expectation that Washington would get its act together and come riding like the cavalry over the hill, a group of leading citizen volunteers in Lancaster decided the town was going to have to save itself. Business leaders and community leaders representing diverse points of view decided to check their party affiliation at the door and work together to present solutions to local problems and get them enacted by government officials at the city, county, state, and federal levels.

Friedman tells this story of an effective nonpartisan community group in Lancaster called Hourglass (out of a sense that they were running out of time), and in his book Thank You for Being Late, he shares other stories of successful, inclusive, nonpartisan groups coming together to get things done in their communities, including the Itasca Project in Minneapolis, which also brought together government, business, academic, philanthropic, community, and faith leaders to solve regional problems and foster economic progress.[32]

A multitude of reports from researchers,[33] journalists, and, especially, local newspapers (where they still exist) have been published, but few people have visited more small American towns than Deborah and James Fallows.[34] For their book Our Towns, the Fallowses traveled by small plane to more than two dozen small towns across America to spend some time, walk around, talk to people, visit the local newspaper (again, if they still have one), and meet local leaders, asking them what is working (and what is not) to bring a sense of vitality back to economic and civic life. What the Fallowses found gives us a clear understanding of what must happen for a small town or midsized city to mount a successful comeback.

Everyone who has studied more than a handful of examples has a list of eight to ten markers for a successful economic turnaround, and the lists are far more similar than different. Just like Friedman, Jim and Deborah Fallows believe the key to successful local economic turnaround is checking Democrat versus Republican partisanship at the door. The first of ten items on their list is bipartisan cooperation. "People work together on practical local possibilities," they write, "rather than allowing bitter disagreements about national politics to keep them apart." The rest of their list includes having local heroes who inspire others to get involved in the community; revitalizing Main Street; having meaningful public/private partnerships; having local research universities and local colleges that are well integrated into the community; and the existence of a local craft brewery.

What we learn about successful comebacks is that communities need to make smartly targeted investments to move from decline to growth. This includes investments in safe and attractive downtown areas, public parks, libraries, and community colleges. Comeback communities also need investments in schools, teachers, basic education, and advanced technical job training. Communities must make investments in public broadband and Wi-Fi, sustainable energy, roads, and rails. The needed investments will always be more than the local government could afford, so communities will require cooperation and funding from local businesses, foundations, religious groups, civic groups, and state and federal development grants. When communities come together to set priorities for investments in their future survival and growth, the money can be found—some of the time.

And this brings us back to the federal government. The US Congress funds local development through scores of grant programs administered by nearly every government agency. If you talk to small-town mayors, they can tell you about the "money chase" to get funding for downtown lighting and community policing from the Department of Justice; for abandoned factory hazardous waste site cleanup from the Environmental Protection Agency (EPA); for road projects from the Department of Transportation; for job training from the Department of Labor. This does not need to be so difficult.

An office within the Department of Commerce called the US Economic Development Administration (EDA) is already charged with helping regional areas to coordinate federal assistance. The EDA distributes funds to support development projects in all fifty states and in the US territories, and it encourages regions to work collaboratively and strategically by administering competitive development grants that go to the regional teams with the best strategic plans. The budget for this agency is miniscule, at less than $1 billion, and the Trump administration proposed its elimination. Rather than cutting the EDA, I would propose increasing its budget to $5 billion or even $10 billion, as well as giving it a more prominent role within the Department of Commerce, and the whole federal government, in coordinating a new strategy for economic development across America.

A new national economic strategy should not mean greater power in Washington over state and local governments. In fact, it should mean a new relationship of greater balance between the federal government and local leaders in the states and cities. Washington has been criticized for many years, and rightly so, for the failure of our national leaders to reach agreement on coherent economic strategy, but the same cannot be said of many governors and mayors in big cities and small towns across America. Washington can do more to support regional economic planning, spread successful strategies to more areas, and develop a strategic approach to investing for American global competitiveness in the emerging industries of the coming decades.[35]

While the headlines out of Washington have involved budget standoffs and government shutdowns, dozens of cities across the country have done what the Hourglass group did in Lancaster. In most cases the activity has been led by the town's mayor bringing together local leaders, including both Republicans and Democrats, businesses and labor groups, for local economic planning and coordination. The working groups have been putting aside their differences to develop strategies to invest in education, innovation, infrastructure, and community quality of life to attract new businesses, grow local businesses, and create better-paying jobs. Many of these collaborative, regional economic development efforts are starting to gain traction and show measurable success.

Political leaders in Washington would be wise to study the success of governors and mayors in cities like Cleveland, Pittsburgh, Nashville, and Atlanta (although problems and inequality persists in all these examples),

*"Random Innovation" describes a strategy in which individual
communities or schools or health facilities are encouraged to try new
approaches and see how they work. The rationale is simple:
Bureaucracy stifles innovation.*

—Alice M. Rivlin, *Systematic
Thinking for Social Action*, 1970

as well as the many next-level towns that are seeking to follow their path to
success. From Erie, Pennsylvania, to Youngstown, Akron, and Dayton,
Ohio, from Knoxville and Chattanooga, Tennessee, to Dubuque, Iowa, and
Huntington, West Virginia, local leaders are collaborating on the development of regional economic plans and identifying local resources, competitive advantages, and the challenges to be overcome. An economic strategy
sets priorities for long-term investments that are made by combining federal, state, and local funding streams with business investment, foundation
grants, and nonprofit initiatives.

Looking at these local plans, we see investments (both public and private) in four broad areas: education, innovation, infrastructure, and healthy
communities.

1. **Invest in education and job skills training.** Pay teachers more, especially in the districts where per-student spending is dramatically
   below the national average,[36] and modernize and support public
   schools, vocational education, community colleges, job training acad-
   emies, and apprenticeships so that every American has access to the
   skills needed for better jobs in the modern economy.

2. **Invest in innovation.** Identify regional strengths and weaknesses;
   support innovation communities and business start-up incubators;
   build bridges between businesses and researchers at local colleges,
   universities, medical centers, National Laboratories and Technology
   Centers; and make investments to create the conditions for local
   businesses to thrive in future growth areas such as regenerative agriculture, advanced manufacturing, sustainable energy, and knowledge-
   based industries.

3. **Invest in infrastructure.** Repair and modernize roads, bridges, rails, airports, seaports, smart energy grids, broadband data networks, and other critical infrastructure, and invest in public transportation so people can get to work, businesses can get materials and get their finished products to customers, and knowledge businesses can connect to customers all over the world.

4. **Invest in healthy communities.** Rebuild downtown areas and main streets, river walks, and other common areas with better lighting and community policing so people feel safe and business can grow. Invest in areas of persistent poverty, renovating abandoned buildings, turning vacant lots into parks and playgrounds, and revitalizing libraries, community centers, and senior centers. Support local and regional hospitals and wellness centers and bring healthy food to "food deserts" to sustain the healthy, vibrant population needed to attract the kinds of jobs that offer better pay, opportunity, and economic security.

The key to success is commitment to both comprehensiveness and scale. Just as crops need seed, water, sunlight, and fertilizer, and will fail for lack of any one, all four of these investments—education, innovation, infrastructure, and healthy communities—are necessary for success. Job training without economic development is a futile waste of time, as people get trained for jobs that never materialize. Many communities have already experienced this, and it adds to skepticism about the whole exercise. At the same time, development will inevitably become gentrification unless it includes raising the skill level of the local population so they can qualify for better jobs and avoid getting priced out of the region.

Successful economic development stories happen when communities are able to come together and gather the resources to check all the boxes. They are creating an attractive business environment by investing in an educated and well-trained workforce. They are investing in transportation and connectivity infrastructure so businesses can get inputs and move their products to customers. They are investing in innovative businesses, technology business incubators, modern manufacturing hubs, industrial parks, and technology hubs. They are investing in revitalizing their downtown areas, historical districts, main streets, farmers' markets, and river walks, addressing health issues, and working to improve their overall community quality of life. Even though most of the economy's growth over the past decade or more has been captured by a small number of supercities while factories have been closing throughout the heartland, communities including Pittsburgh, Cleveland, Nashville, and Atlanta have blazed this trail to impressive revitalization achievements, and many other midsized cities and small towns have been emulating their success.

## REGIONAL ECONOMIC DEVELOPMENT AS AN ECONOMIC STRATEGY

Throughout my career, I have taken a skeptical view of calls for a Washington-led national industrial policy. Back in the 1980s, when it looked like Japanese corporations were poised to take over the world by succeeding at centralized planning, there were many people advocating the need for an American strategic economic plan, often called an industrial policy, to compete with "Japan Inc." I was unpersuaded that either congressional committees or federal employee work groups could make better investment decisions than the "C-level" executives of our major corporations. The economy is

*Many of those concerned about the lagging American economy have urged the federal government to adopt an explicit industrial policy. Proponents usually envision a huge federal bank with a board allocating funds to industries and areas. Such grandiose notions founder on closer examination, however, in part because of the sheer size and diversity of the economy. Few would trust the federal government to allocate funds wisely or nonpolitically to development projects or programs. . . .*

*Governors and mayors, however, are closer to the scene. They have more ways to generate business, labor, and community support for development and put together an effective program to increase investment and jobs. The best chance of having a successful industrial policy in a country this size is to have a lot of communities, states, and regions competing with each other to improve their own economic prospects.*

—Alice M. Rivlin, *Reviving the American Dream*, 1992

simply too large and complex, and despite Washington's self-confidence in its ability to make decisions and predict the economic future, there is little reason to believe the federal government would be up to the task. Political considerations would inevitably hold more weight than sound economic judgment. I still believe this is true, but new thinking in economics and the regional economic successes have altered my views to some degree.

First, the view that industrial policy must mean top-down decisions, and government planners picking winners and losers in the economic marketplace, may be out of date. Evolutionary economists, including Mariana Mazzucato[37] and my husband, Sidney Winter,[38] have been highlighting the importance of innovation and experimentation in driving economic success. Economic growth follows government investment in the basic building blocks of businesses like infrastructure and public education, and many of America's great business success stories began with government investment in scientific research and direct expenditures for innovative projects, mostly for the military and space exploration.

American businesses lead the world in semiconductors, aviation, pharmaceuticals, and many other technologies that started with government investment. Government investment created the first version of the internet, mapped the human genome, and launched the first global positioning satellites. For decades, America led the world in making these kinds of investments (although more recently China is making investments at a comparable rate), and some American corporations like IBM, Apple, Merck, and Pfizer flourished using technology developed through government investment while others (McDonald Douglas and Chrysler) struggled or flamed out. The government's role should not be about picking winners and losers but instead about creating the conditions that allow some corporations greater opportunities to compete and win in the global marketplace. As Sid Winter writes with three coauthors, "Sometimes, a new industry in the for-profit sector is an almost trivial extension of technical achievements purchased at great expense by the government."[39]

Mariana Mazzucato writes, "This is not about prescribing specific technologies, but providing directions of change with which bottom-up solutions can then experiment."[40] States and localities are now providing the laboratories of economic experimentation, as entities are trying to not only reverse economic decline and turn their economies around for the benefit of local workers, but also nurture economic conditions where local businesses can innovate, grow, thrive, and create better-paying jobs for their workers. Different communities will be able to find their own path forward, emphasizing their relative strength and opportunities. Some will find success building local industries or growing new ones. Some will look to agriculture, manufacturing, distribution, high technology, or travel and tourism. One of the lessons we are learning from these experiments is that success can follow bipartisan cooperation and collaboration at the local level, even as it seems so elusive at the national level.

The federal government is already collaborating with these kinds of activities in many places through the regional offices housing representatives of relevant agencies, but there is far more it could do to support regional economic development if we had a national strategy. Each region could do an analysis of its strengths and weaknesses, identify growth opportunities, and set priorities for the projects and investments necessary for success. To build its productive capacity and attract or grow better-paying jobs, each area would be able to find funds in its local budgets from businesses looking to expand facilities and invest in worker training, from foundations and nonprofits looking to address community needs, and from state and federal grants.

Through thousands of decisions made by regional collaborative groups, America can implement an industrial policy without a Washington power grab. I have long believed that the federal government should look for opportunities to move functions to state and local governments for many reasons,[41] not the least of which is that public opinion polls consistently show that voters trust state and, especially, local government far more than the federal government.[42] Governors, mayors, and county executives, in consultation with businesses, labor groups, environmental groups, community leaders, and other key stakeholders, know what their community needs for economic development, and by placing them in the lead, America can more broadly share the benefits of its prosperity.

## But What Will This Cost?

I have been called a deficit hawk or a deficit scold many times (and I must say I prefer the former to the latter). But there is good reason to worry about the deficit. The US federal budget deficit will surpass $1 trillion in 2020, and it is projected to keep growing to completely unsustainable levels[43] after that as more and more of the baby boom generation stops working and starts drawing Social Security and Medicare. Along with global climate change, the US federal budget deficit, especially in the context of high levels of corporate and household debt, stands as the clearest threat to our future well-being. Neither climate change nor excessive debt is a problem we can afford to ignore, and both should be front and center in every decision the government makes.

All that being said, I believe the investments in more equitable economic growth presented in this chapter must be made and can be made without adding to the national debt if we raise enough revenue to pay for them. We need to make these investments, and we need to pay for them in a way that does not put the burden on the middle class and does not pass the debt on to future generations. The economic plan presented here to address both horizontal and vertical inequality is affordable in budgetary terms for several reasons. First, as noted at the start of this chapter, the US economy is strong (version one), so we can afford to make the needed investments for future growth and a more equal distribution of wealth and income (addressing the needs of version two).

The strong economy creates room for the second reason why these investments are affordable: it includes tax increases on the wealthiest individuals, which can help fund some of the investments. But aren't all tax increases deal breakers for Republicans? Not really. Republicans have agreed to a couple of tax increases at the top of the income scale. This includes the deal that ended the budget standoff detailed in chapter 9, which saw President Obama and Republicans agreeing to continue the tax cuts passed by President George W. Bush for single people earning less than $400,000 per year and couples making less than $450,000 per year, but to raise taxes for filers above those thresholds. More recently, as noted earlier, President Trump and the Republicans increased taxes on high-income earners living in high-tax states like New York, New Jersey, and California by capping SALT deductions in 2017.

The failure of the "Kansas experiment"—the 2012 tax cuts that Governor Sam Brownback enacted[44] and that tax cut enthusiasts promised would deliver jobs and economic growth—and the subsequent rejection of low-tax Republican governors in 2018 in Kansas, Wisconsin, and Michigan may signal a sea change in American politics moving forward. Voters may be attracted to deep tax cuts in the abstract, but they have reversed course when they learn these tax cuts lead to deep cuts in state budgets for roads and schools.

This leads us to the third reason why a bipartisan pro-growth plan to reduce inequality should not be seen as budgetarily unaffordable: The three largest categories of new spending, infrastructure, education and basic scientific research and innovation, are all already assumed to be priorities for bipartisan agreement to increase spending. At the state level, school funding has been increasing in recent years and this is expected to continue, even if federal spending has been relatively flat.[45] At the federal level, Donald Trump is constantly mentioning infrastructure as an area for future bipartisan compromise, even if some congressional Republicans express doubts about his plans.[46]

The need for infrastructure attention is great. The American Society of Civil Engineers issues "report cards" on America's infrastructure, bringing to light concerns about structural deficiencies in bridges (affecting 9.1 percent

*The American economy is the strongest in the world. . . . But with an aging population, slow productivity growth, lagging wages, and increasing inequality, we cannot afford policy gridlock. We need aggressive economic policies to grow the economy faster and create more and better-paying jobs. . . . In recent years we have neglected our public infrastructure, allowed roads, bridges, rail, and water systems to fall into disrepair. We have failed to modernize our airports and air traffic control systems to keep up with the volume of flights or to invest adequately in public health. We have failed to keep the skills of our workforce growing in step with changing technology and to prepare young workers, especially those from low-income families, for the jobs the economy requires. And we have reduced the flow of funding into basic research on which future technological progress depends.*

—Alice M. Rivlin, testimony before the Joint Economic Committee of the US Congress, September 8, 2016 of all bridges according to the 2017 report).[47] Yet, agreement on an infrastructure bill has eluded lawmakers for many years, largely due to Republican opposition to the tax increases needed to pay for it. Business groups that are influential with Republicans, including the Business Roundtable[48] and the National Association of Manufacturers,[49] have been calling for an end to the gridlock and the need for substantial new infrastructure investment.

It is my hope that the conversation about infrastructure can be broadened to include more than just roads, bridges, rails, and ports. Smart energy grids, universal access to broadband for students, and advanced data connectivity that will allow businesses to expand into new areas should also be part of the discussion. I believe support for infrastructure by the public and by elected leaders of both parties will increase if it is understood that priorities for spending will be set not in Washington, but through collaborations at the state and local levels, with businesses and others as part of a strategy to bring better-paying jobs to the people and places that have been falling behind.

There has always been a durable bipartisan agreement to fund basic research in medicine, energy, and the military. Both political parties understand that if America is to succeed in maintaining our global economic leadership, we must increase investments in basic science in areas that could spur business innovation.

And this brings us to the final reason why the proposals mentioned in this chapter should not be seen as unaffordable budget busters: While there is a call for some more government spending, the proposals here are mainly a call for greater collaboration, coordination, and strategic purpose for money that is already being spent. These proposals are best understood as an effort to spur business investment by marshalling local, state, and federal tax dollars for investment in the local conditions necessary to help businesses and workers achieve their goals, bringing economic growth and better-paying jobs to the local community. There would be a role for the federal government in funding some of this activity, including increasing federal budgets for areas such as housing assistance, job training, and environmental cleanup, with greater emphasis on facilitating the coordination of grant programs and other supports that are already in the budget.

One of the government buzzwords with the most bipartisan appeal is "public/private partnerships," which include any time that government partners with business (or foundations, charities, religious groups, or educational institutions). These proposals comprise many examples of public/private partnerships, including basic science to support business innovation and investments in infrastructure to lower distribution costs for the private sector. Many of these proposals combine relatively small (in federal budgetary terms) government grants from multiple departments to support regional priorities defined by governors, mayors, and county executives who are leading teams and leveraging local funds from businesses and nonprofit stakeholders. The Congressional Budget Office has not scored the cost of this approach, but I know enough to know this would not be a major budget buster. Public support, as well as support from political leaders of both parties, is possible to the degree that people understood this is not a huge new spending program, but rather it is a new national strategy to coordinate business investment, combined with federal, state, and local investment, to the task of bringing better-paying jobs and economic growth to the people and places that need it the most.

## A SECOND GILDED AGE?

James Fallows is a leading voice among several who have likened the extremes of economic and regional inequality in the current US economy to the Gilded Age at the end of the nineteenth century. The technology billionaires of today made their fortunes in different industries than the railroad and industrial titans of that era, but they share the same ability to live separate lives from the masses of other Americans. There are also similarities between the politics of the Gilded Age and the current era in that both are seen as dysfunctional and overly responsive to economic elites, with a loss of public trust in the political parties and institutions of government. I take the next two chapters to look carefully at American political and economic history. Chapter 3 covers the founding of the nation to the Gilded Age, and then chapter 4 details how we got out of the Gilded Age with populist and progressive politics and shifting coalitions of government that helped America grow into a position of global leadership and economic prosperity.

# THE HISTORY OF PARTISANSHIP AND DEALMAKING: THE CONSTITUTIONAL CONVENTION TO THE GILDED AGE

Just as Americans endlessly debate two versions of the national economy, switching sides whenever control of the White House changes hands, we also have two versions of American history, but the positions are more durable. In one version, America is the greatest democracy in the world because the Founding Fathers wrote a Declaration of Independence, a Constitution, and a Bill of Rights that delicately balanced federal, state, and individual rights and liberties. In this version of American history, the democratic system has endured because heroes and patriots have defended the flag in battle, preserving our freedom and independence. This is the land of the free because it is the home of the brave.

The other version of American history is a much darker view. It says that from driving the first Americans off their lands to enslaving millions of Africans for generations of cheap labor, to denying the right to vote and other rights to women, to waging adventurous wars around the globe to secure oil and raw materials for our industries, the success America has achieved has come through violence and subjugation.

Once again, both versions are true; America has always been a work in progress. Most people see at least some validity in each version, but the emphasis they place on each depends less on the outcomes of elections than on where people view themselves in the historical and current power structure. Women, Native Americans, descendants of former slaves, and descendants of the many waves of Asian, Latin American, and European immigrants who faced extreme discrimination upon arrival may place greater emphasis on the darker view of American history.

The Founding Fathers wrote documents that have proven to be remarkably durable and resilient in defining the power structure for a new nation, but they were all white male property owners, many of whom owned slaves, and the virtue of the system they created was that it evenly distributed power among white male property owners. It would take decades and centuries for the founders' laws to catch up with their aspiration, stated as self-evident truth, that "all men are created equal." Black men would not get freedom until after the Civil War. Their right to vote (as a matter of law, but not a matter of fact) would not come until 1870. Women would have to wait another fifty years after that to get the vote, in 1920. To this day, true equality for all Americans continues to be an unachieved goal.

This chapter, and the one that follows, are a walk through American history from the drafting of the Constitution to 1980. I spend a lot of time talking about the compromises that led to the agreement to adopt the Constitution and the Bill of Rights, because it was during those negotiations that most of the rules that govern our current political struggles were written. After this I look at political polarization and partisanship through two centuries of United States political history, noting many times where the president and Congress were able to make compromises and reach agreement on landmark legislation even in periods of deep divisions. The exception is, of course, the Civil War, which is certainly a period in history we would not want to repeat.

## THE GENIUS, AND PERPETUAL FRUSTRATION, OF THE US CONSTITUTION

Ever since *Hamilton* opened on Broadway, it has become fashionable to reference the authors of the Constitution, the Bill of Rights, and the *Federalist Papers*. But in a discussion of partisanship, there really is no other option, because the problem the Founding Fathers called factionalism was very much on their minds as one of the greatest threats to the new union they were building. The founders had fought a costly war to overthrow the tyranny of the English king and feared giving too much power to a strong executive who might become another tyrant. At the same time, they were fearful that direct democracy could turn into the type of destructive mob rule that would soon engulf the French revolution.

Steering a course between conflicting dangers, the founders bequeathed us a complicated policy process that separated the executive powers of the president from the powers of the legislature, which they further divided into two separate chambers. The founders saw these separations as a way of balancing the powers of the executive and legislative branches so that each would be able to check the excesses of the other. The founders also created a strong judiciary with the power to declare laws passed by Congress and signed by the president as unconstitutional if they violated the rights of individuals as spelled out in the Constitution and the Bill of Rights.

The Constitution's drafters did not envision political parties as we know them today, but they worried about the threat to government posed by political factions. James Madison defined the term in *Federalist* No. 10:[1] "By a faction, I understand a number of citizens, whether amounting to a majority or a minority of the whole, who are united and actuated by some common impulse of passion, or of interest, adversed to the rights of other citizens, or to the permanent and aggregate interests of the community."

This broad definition would include any group of people united by interests against the rights of anyone else. This definition would apply to our current political parties, the Democrats and Republicans—and subdivisions within the parties, like the Tea Party Republicans and progressive Democrats or even, I remind myself, a group of bipartisan moderates—to the degree that they hold views adverse to the rights of any other individuals or groups. The Constitution drafters did not want anyone taking over, so they wrote the rules to encourage, even force, groups to negotiate and compromise. Everything the Constitution drafters did then to frustrate factions and encourage compromise to pass new laws now frustrates political partisans and encourages compromise to pass new laws in our current government.

In *Federalist* No. 9,[2] Alexander Hamilton responded to fears that the proposed union would fail, just as the Greek and Roman states had failed, due to "domestic faction and insurrection" with his belief that the new political innovations in the representative republic the founders were devising would decentralize power and be stable enough to preserve the United States:

> The regular distribution of power into distinct departments—the introduction of legislative balances and checks—the institution of courts composed of judges, holding their offices during good behavior—the representation of the people in the legislature by deputies of their own election—these are either wholly new discoveries or have made their principal progress towards perfection in modern times. They are means, and powerful means, by which the excellencies of republican government may be retained, and its imperfections lessened or avoided.

The Founding Fathers did not dismiss the concerns of others that the nation would divide, and perhaps come apart, due to the natural human inclination to band together into groups to gain an advantage over the less numerous and less well organized—they wrote the Constitution and the Bill of Rights to protect against these concerns.

The founders took on the daunting task of constructing a decision-making process that would enable thirteen fractious former colonies to work together as a single country to their mutual benefit without falling apart and going their separate ways. The thirteen states had been colonized by different kinds of people and had divergent histories, traditions, and dominant religions. There were huge differences among them in area and population. Some were almost entirely agricultural; others had substantial commerce and emerging manufacturing sectors. Most divisive of all, the southern colonies had large, enslaved populations and heavy dependence on slave labor; the northern colonies had fewer slaves and had influential groups actively opposed to slavery on moral grounds.

As the Constitutional Convention gathered in Philadelphia in 1787, the first attempt to form a national government under the Articles of Confederation was failing because the central government's dependence on the states for voluntary contributions made it virtually powerless. The challenge was to create a decision-making structure for the new country that would enable the central government to function without infringing on the prerogatives of the individual states so much that they would refuse to participate in the common enterprise. The states had huge differences of opinion, and even differences in basic morality on the question of slavery, but in a dangerous world, they found a way to reach agreement that they were stronger together than apart.

## BALANCING POWERS AND RIGHTS WITH CHECKS AND BALANCES—BUT NO FILIBUSTER

The Constitution drafters wanted to do something that may seem impossible: design a government that could actually get things done without anyone being in charge. They were keenly aware of the twin dangers of an overly powerful political majority, lest it become tyrannical, and of requiring a supermajority to pass legislation, lest it empower an obstructive minority—considering but thoroughly rejecting the supermajority as a solution.

Madison and Hamilton believed strongly that a simple majority should decide most issues in the Senate. Both had shared the frustrating experience of the Second Continental Congress, which had laboriously drafted the Articles of Confederation that they were replacing with their new Constitution. They did not want to repeat the mistake of supermajority requirements that slowed progress. The Senate they were designing would be deliberative but also functional and based on majority rule.

Madison argued against a supermajority in *Federalist* No. 58, saying that if there were such a requirement, "the fundamental principle of free government would be reversed. It would be no longer the majority that would rule: the power would be transferred to the minority. Were the defensive privilege limited to particular cases, an interested minority might take advantage of it to screen themselves from equitable sacrifices to the general weal, or, in particular emergencies, to extort unreasonable indulgences."[3]

Hamilton issued a similar warning in *Federalist* No. 22:

> If a pertinacious minority can control the opinion of a majority, respecting the best mode of conducting it, the majority, in order that something may be done, must conform to the views of the minority;

and thus the sense of the smaller number will overrule that of the greater, and give a tone to the national proceedings. Hence, tedious delays; continual negotiation and intrigue; contemptible compromises of the public good. And yet, in such a system, it is even happy when such compromises can take place: for upon some occasions things will not admit of accommodation; and then the measures of government must be injuriously suspended, or fatally defeated. It is often, by the impracticability of obtaining the concurrence of the necessary number of votes, kept in a state of inaction. Its situation must always savor of weakness, sometimes border upon anarchy.[4]

Let that sink in: "tedious delays, continual negotiation," "contemptible compromises of the public good," "the measures of government . . . fatally defeated," "kept in a state of inaction," "weakness" bordering on "anarchy." Sadly, this prediction seems to be reaching fruition in today's Senate.

The Constitution drafters set apart five specific Senate decisions of higher conflict and consequence that they expected to be quite rare and where a two-thirds majority would be required to show the senators had reached a broad agreement. They reserved the higher two-thirds threshold for votes to (1) expel a Senator, (2) ratify a treaty, (3) override a presidential veto, (4) convict a president, justice, or cabinet official on impeachment, and (5) propose constitutional amendments. The first Senate created by the Constitution was majority rule for all other questions.

But if Madison, Hamilton, and the others who designed the government considered and rejected a supermajority requirement to pass legislation in the Senate, how did we end up with filibusters and cloture votes raising the threshold to pass legislation to sixty votes for most bills in the Senate now? The story unfolds over the next 200-plus years, and I pick it back up in the next chapter, starting when Woodrow Wilson needed a change in Senate rules to get authorization to involve America in World War I. But it is wrong to believe the filibuster was something the founders designed to make the Senate the more deliberative congressional body. The filibuster was not part of their plan.

As much as the Constitution writers were concerned about the potential that an obstructionist faction with a minority of the votes could block legislation, they also worried that a faction with a majority of the votes could have unchecked power bordering on the tyranny of an unchecked monarch and impose its will to the harm of a political minority. Madison also raised this issue in *Federalist* No. 10:[5]

> Complaints are everywhere heard from our most considerate and vir-tuous citizens, equally the friends of public and private faith, and of public and personal liberty, that our governments are too unstable, that the public good is disregarded in the conflicts of rival parties, and that measures are too often decided, not according to the rules of justice and the rights of the minor party, but by the superior force of an interested and overbearing majority.

Decades later, in 1859, John Stewart Mill would coin the term "tyranny of the majority"[6] to describe the potential threat to democracy posed by fac-tions or parties formed to further their own interests at the expense of some other group or at the expense of the common good. One of Madison's great fears was that the majority of Americans who did not own land would pass a law allowing them to take land away from the minority who were land-owners. As clearly stated in chapter 2, I count myself among those who be-lieve wealthy Americans should pay higher taxes, but any suggestion that the 99 percent majority should use the tax system to take wealth from the 1 percent minority should be aware of this warning in *Federalist* No. 10:

> The apportionment of taxes on the various descriptions of property is an act which seems to require the most exact impartiality; yet there is, perhaps, no legislative act in which greater opportunity and temp-tation are given to a predominant party to trample on the rules of justice. Every shilling with which they overburden the inferior num-ber, is a shilling saved to their own pockets.

Some might ask, "But isn't this exactly what a democracy is all about: ma-jority rule—and the majority makes rules that benefit the majority?" But James Madison, Alexander Hamilton, and the majority of other delegates to the Continental Congress would say emphatically that this is not what democracy means. In their view, majority rule means leaders elected by a majority should govern for the benefit of all the people, and the founders worried that even leaders elected by a majority could become corrupted by power.

The founders' solution was to define a broad range of rights for individual citizens that cannot be taken away even by laws passed by a majority in the Senate and House and signed by the president. Madison crafted twelve amendments to the Constitution to respond to the concerns of the Anti-Federalists and move toward ratification in the states. Ten of these amendments survived their own ratification process to become the Bill of Rights. Together the Constitution and Bill of Rights define the rights of all citizens and their elected leaders, the president, Congress, judges, and the individual states, giving the judiciary the power to void laws that do not respect those rights. People commonly describe the United States of America as a democracy, but it is more accurately described as a constitutional democratic republic, which is different and a lot more complicated.

## THREE 1787 COMPROMISES THAT ARE STILL CONTROVERSIAL

The framers of the Constitution made many compromises to reach an agreement that would bind the new nation together. Three compromises, in particular, have special relevance to today's circumstances. The first compromise was to reject direct democracy, where policy questions are decided by popular vote, in favor of a republic where representatives are chosen to debate and vote on laws. The second compromise gave a permanent advantage to smaller states over larger states in representation in the Senate. The third compromise addressed the counting of slaves in determining representation in the House of Representatives. All three have been highly controversial throughout our nation's history and continue to fuel political divisions today.

Fearing that bad decisions could be made by a passionate mob, the founders settled on indirect democracy in the form of a republic in which voters, directly or indirectly, selected representatives to formulate and debate policy issues, to balance competing interests and try to find acceptable compromises. The congressional representatives and senators were expected to understand the complexities of issues and the trade-offs implied by proposed laws better than average farmers and merchants could. If voters became dissatisfied with the policies adopted by Congress, their recourse would be to vote their representatives out of office, electing a new set of representatives empowered to try again to find policies that voters support.

For more than a century at the start of the nation, accountability to public opinion was extremely limited. Any claim that the drafters of the Constitution had created government "by the people" would not be accepted as legitimate by modern standards. The House of Representatives, elected every two years, had the strongest claim to holding policymakers accountable, even though only white male property owners could vote in House elections. Senators were selected by state legislatures, and the president, by the Electoral College. As repeated battles were won to expand voting rights for women and minorities, and when the Seventeenth Amendment to the Constitution was ratified in 1913[7] to establish direct election of senators, Americans began describing their government as a representative democracy.

There are many ways of conducting political business that have been part of our traditions for so long, we assume they were written into the Constitution, but in fact they evolved later through a combination of common practices, state election laws, federal laws, and constitutional amendments. Some of the things that go right to the heart of what we assume we mean by "democracy" could be challenged and even be undone through aggressive legal strategies through the courts. The litigation following the disputed 2000 presidential election, culminating in the Supreme Court ruling in *Bush* v. *Gore*, revealed stark differences in popular understanding of our election system and the legal basis for it.

Americans are accustomed to voting for president every four years, but Article II of the Constitution gave the power to select presidential electors to state legislatures. State legislatures may have granted this power to voters, but state laws determine what happens when election results are disputed. Voters might be shocked to learn that a court could decide that voters have less influence and state legislatures have more influence in determining which candidate gets a state's electoral votes than voters had assumed.

## TWO SENATORS PER STATE, SMALL OR LARGE

The second compromise made by the drafters of the Constitution was that each state would get representatives in the House in proportion to their populations but just two senators per state, without regard to their size. In 1787 the largest states, Virginia and Pennsylvania, were roughly ten times more populous than the smallest states, Delaware and Rhode Island, so it is easy to understand why the big states wanted representation proportional to their populations. The small states feared they would be overwhelmed by the big ones, so they wanted each state to have equal representation.[8] In a proposal by the delegation from what was then a mid-sized state, the Connecticut Compromise created the system that endures today—a Senate with two senators from each state and a House of Representatives with members elected from each state in proportion to its population.

The Connecticut Compromise succeeded in delivering agreement on the Constitution to form the United States of America, but it was a hard pill for the larger states to swallow. Even though each voter has the same amount of representation in the House, residents of large states have far less representation in the Senate because a larger number of voters must share just two votes in the Senate. Today the largest state, California, is sixty-eight times larger than the smallest state, Wyoming, and Texas, the second largest, is forty-eight times larger than the second smallest, Vermont.[9] Scholars and political commentators point out how much further out of balance representation in the Senate has grown since the Connecticut Compromise bargain was struck in 1787.

Shifts in the nation's political landscape have conspired to make this feature of the Constitution increasingly intolerable for Democrats. Republicans in small states have far more votes in the Senate in proportion to their populations. These concerns are magnified by the Electoral College mathematics for selecting a president, which gives each state one elector for each congressional representative (proportional) and one for each senator (not proportional), and by the special role of the Senate in ratifying judges and Supreme Court justices. Taken together with other political and demographic trends, this means the Senate, the Supreme Court, and the White House disproportionately give greater representation to those in the electorate who are Republican, conservative, white, and Christian compared with the nation as a whole, today and likely for decades into the future.

As much as Democrats view this as an intolerable departure from democracy defined as equal representation for each person and his or her one vote, I do not think it is likely they will be able to change the two senators per state allocation. The Constitution's authors deliberately made the Constitution very difficult to change. Any amendment that would benefit one party at the expense of the other has little chance of getting over the necessary hurdles. Regardless of the merit of the arguments made for the reform, Republicans have enough power to block this reform and will certainly continue to do so.

One way to address the Republican advantage in the Senate would be for Democrats to win more Senate races in less urban states like Iowa, Nebraska, the Dakotas, and Montana, where Republicans seem to have made it a strategic priority to reverse what was once seen as a Democratic advantage. Democrats held eight of the ten Senate seats representing these five states following the election of 1976 and seven of the ten following the 1992 election. After the 2018 election, Republicans held nine of the ten seats in these states. Perhaps this is an area where Republicans have been doing such a good job of competing within the rules that Democrats now want to change the rules. There are other areas of politics where these roles are reversed.

Of course, another way to redress the Republican advantage in the Senate would be to grant statehood to Washington, DC, or New Columbia as it would then be known, and a strong case can also be made for allowing Puerto Rico to become a state. I have sympathy for California residents because they get 1/700,000 of a vote in the House of Representatives (about the same as residents of every state) and 2/18,000,000 of a vote in the Senate. That's a lot less than the residents of Wyoming who get 1/568,000 of a vote in the House, 2/568,000 of a vote in the Senate. But my sympathy is muted by the fact that as residents of the District of Columbia, my family, neighbors, and I have zero votes in the House and zero votes in the Senate. We pay federal taxes, and many serve in the military, but our license plates have borne the phrase "Taxation Without Representation" for many years.

---

*[Washington,] DC citizens pay our taxes, serve in the armed forces, and if necessary, make the ultimate sacrifice to defend democracy around the world. But here at home we cannot vote for full representation in the Congress of the United States. This is an inconvenient truth about America, which should be changed forthwith.*

—Alice M. Rivlin, testimony before
the Senate Committee on
Homeland Security and
Government Affairs, 2014

---

The DC population of just over 700,000 is larger than that of Vermont or Wyoming, and our economy has a bigger gross domestic product (GDP) than sixteen states, but we are not full voting citizens in this great democracy. It is an historical anachronism and a political injustice that should be rectified, even if it is clear that granting statehood to DC and Puerto Rico would likely add more Democratic votes on the House and Senate floors. Democrats would have to offer Republicans something of great value for them to ever consider lending their support to this worthy cause.

## COUNTING SLAVES AS THREE-FIFTHS OF A PERSON

The third compromise is even more controversial in today's context. It is no overstatement to say the 1787 decision to count slaves as three-fifths of a person (of course, with no voting rights nor any other rights of a free citizen) in defining the population for purposes of allocating representatives is an affront to modern sensibilities.

Even though this book makes the case that compromise is essential to creating public policy in our American system, this does not require me to defend every compromise reached along the way, and I will not defend the compromise that allowed slavery to continue on the American continent. But it is part of our history and must be understood.

This is especially important because, as we see throughout this chapter, America's history of race and racial injustice has been central to the story of partisanship and bipartisanship up to the present day. The "three-fifths compromise" was the first of many historic political compromises that perpetuated slavery, discrimination, and injustice by white Americans over people enslaved in Africa and their American descendants.

Since slaves were considered property and had no civil rights, it seems bizarre that they would be counted at all for purposes of state representation in the national legislature. However, the slave-dependent states of the South, eager to enhance their power in the House of Representatives, insisted on counting slaves along with free persons. States less committed to slavery (or actively opposed to it) wanted to reduce the clout of the pro-slavery states by not counting slaves at all.

One of history's ironies is that after the South lost its fight for slavery in the Civil War, emancipation enhanced the representation of former slave states in the House of Representatives. The newly freed slaves were included in the states' population total, even though voter suppression through violence and intimidation made it impossible for most former slaves to exercise their right to vote. The enhanced political power of the Southern states after the Civil War helped continue segregation and delay voting rights and full citizenship for African Americans for another century. Some political leaders today, like Stacey Abrams of FairFight.org, are continuing to battle against voter suppression, the practice of seeking partisan advantage by deliberately making it difficult for racial minorities to vote.[10] I will discuss the passage of the 1965 Voting Rights Act in the next chapter and the modern-day lingering effects of voter suppression and proposals to protect voting rights in chapter 11.

## EVOLUTION OF THE TWO-PARTY SYSTEM

The Constitution's drafters were concerned about political factions, but by becoming a faction themselves, the drafters unintentionally facilitated the emergence of two parties even before American political life under the Constitution officially began. As the Federalists—a network of political leaders including James Madison and Alexander Hamilton—fought for ratification of the Constitution, they urged that it place the powers to tax, spend, borrow, and make foreign policy in the new federal government. The Anti-Federalists, like Richard Henry Lee of Virginia, Luther Martin of Maryland, Robert Whitehill of Pennsylvania, and Revolutionary War hero Patrick Henry of Virginia, advocated rejecting the Constitution, fearing that a powerful central government would threaten the sovereignty of the states and the rights of individuals. Although the Federalists prevailed, ratification was closely contested in some states, and the Federalists had to promise to add the Bill of Rights to the Constitution to protect the rights of individuals and calm the fears of the Anti-Federalists.

Political parties had varying names and agendas in the late 1700s and up through the Civil War. Hamilton's Federalists were first opposed by Thomas Jefferson's Democratic-Republicans through the War of 1812. Andrew Jackson's Democrats emerged in the 1820s and were opposed by Henry Clay, who would form the Whig Party and then the Republican Party.

Through the decades that the names and leaders of the political parties changed, the main fault lines remained quite stable. The first fault line was economic, pitting the industrial and mercantile cities against the agrarian countryside. This rift was closely associated with geography in that the North was more industrial and the South was more dependent on agriculture. The question of slavery would eventually divide the nation geographically when the South took arms against the North in the Civil War, but before then it took on an association with the major political division in the nation, pitting those who favored a strong federal government against those who wanted stronger autonomy for the states. The political parties were ephemeral and fluid, shifting as issues and personalities rose and fell, but as they formed and re-formed, the tendency to coalesce and divide over these main fault lines persisted.

There is perhaps no better exemplar of the two versions of American history, heroic and dark, which I outlined at the start of this chapter, than our seventh president, Andrew Jackson, who served two terms from 1829 to 1837. Jackson was celebrated as a war hero, having beaten the British at the Battle of New Orleans in 1815. He was a champion of the common man, versus the elites, and a founder of the Democratic Party. The Jefferson-Jackson Day Dinner is the biggest fundraising event of the year for most modern-day state Democratic Parties. But Jackson's other military battles were fought against the first nations to occupy the lands we now call Florida, Georgia, Alabama, Mississippi, Tennessee, and Kentucky. He drove the Seminoles out of Florida and the Cherokee across the Mississippi River into Oklahoma, on a deadly forced march known as the Trail of Tears. As president, he passed the Indian Removal Act and opposed the abolition of slavery.

The Whig Party was formed by Daniel Webster, Henry Clay, and others to oppose Andrew Jackson, and they were successful in electing two presidents, William Henry Harrison in 1840 and Zachary Taylor in 1848, although both died in office. The Whigs collapsed over the issue of whether slavery would be expanded to the western territories, with the Southern Whigs defecting to the Democrats and anti-slavery Whigs forming a new Republican Party.[11]

The debate over whether new states and territories would be free or allow slavery took many forms, including questions of whether the federal government could pass laws opposed by individual states. Clay was nicknamed the Great Compromiser due in part to the role he played in negotiating the Missouri Compromise in 1820. It allowed free Maine and slave-holding

Missouri into the union as new states and set a horizontal line extending west from the southern border of Missouri. New states and territories below the line would allow slavery and above the line would be free.

Thirty-four years later the Kansas-Nebraska Act of 1854 violated the Missouri Compromise by allowing Kansas and Nebraska (both above the line) to decide the slavery issue for themselves by popular vote. Advocates on both sides flooded into the states, and the dispute erupted into violence in "Bloody Kansas" and even in the United States Senate when, in 1856, South Carolina Representative Preston Brooks severely attacked Massachusetts Senator Charles Sumner with a cane.[12] Preston was a pro-slavery Democrat and Sumner was an anti-slavery Republican. The issue that divided them would erupt into the bloodiest war in American history five years later, after anti-slavery Republican Abraham Lincoln was elected President in 1860 without a single Southern state electoral vote. The Southern states realized they would lose future political battles over slavery, so they seceded from the United States.

## RECONSTRUCTION AND THE FORMATION OF THE MODERN TWO-PARTY SYSTEM

After the Civil War, the two main parties we have today, Republican and Democratic, emerged to dominate American politics for at least the next century and a half. However, the two parties were very different from the parties as we know them today. The Republicans, the party of Lincoln and Grant, had won the Civil War and were dominant in the North. Democrats were dominant among white voters in the South and represented those who wanted to ignore the consequences of losing a war fought over slavery and structural white supremacy, to the degree that it was possible to do so.

Most histories date the Reconstruction period as lasting from the end of the Civil War in 1865 to the resolution of the disputed 1876 election in 1877, but Lincoln was drawing up plans for Reconstruction with the signing of the Emancipation Proclamation in 1862 and congressional passage of the Thirteenth Amendment to the Constitution in 1864 (which would be ratified by two-thirds of the non-Confederate states at the end of 1865) freeing all slaves.

The conflicts and violence that led to the Civil War did not end when the Confederate army surrendered at Appomattox, Virginia, in 1865. President

Lincoln was assassinated five days later. Race riots (attacks on freed former slaves by violent white mobs) broke out across the South, with particularly bloody events in Memphis and a massacre in New Orleans in 1866. Slavery may have ended, but Southern plantation owners still wanted cheap labor, so they instituted an exploitative sharecropper system, and vigilante groups like the Ku Klux Klan formed to deny equality, dignity, and economic self-reliance to former slaves.

When Lincoln's vice president, Andrew Johnson, a Democrat who had campaigned with Lincoln on a national unity ticket, became president and moved to allow Southern states to return to the union without any protections for former slaves, he lost the support of the Republicans in Congress. He was the first president impeached in the House, and he won acquittal in the Senate by a single vote.

The 1866 congressional election did not include the defeated states of the Confederacy, and Republicans won supermajorities in both chambers. The Republican-controlled Congress had enough votes to override President Johnson's repeated vetoes of the Reconstruction Acts of 1867, which set the requirements for the "rebel states" to be readmitted into the union and defined the role of the former Union army in keeping the peace in the South. Congress also passed the Fourteenth and Fifteenth Amendments to the Constitution,[13] granting citizenship to all persons "born or naturalized in the United States," including formerly enslaved people; providing all citizens with "equal protection under the laws"; and extending the provisions of the Bill of Rights to the states. This extended voting rights to former (male) slaves. However, by the time former Civil War general and Republican Ulysses S. Grant took office in 1869, violence and brutal treatment against former slaves (and also against Republicans) across the South by the Ku Klux Klan (KKK) and other white supremacy groups was so rampant that the Southern states were in no way functioning democracies.

President Grant took on the agenda of continuing Lincoln's unfinished business, enforcing the Appomattox surrender, and giving former African slaves and their American descendants full rights as citizens, including the right for adult males to vote. He ordered more federal troops to the South to restore civil order in hostile territory.[14] Working with Congress, especially the faction called the Radical Republicans, Grant passed laws against KKK intimidation and conspiracy, and created the first Department of Justice, sending federal marshals to enforce the laws and arrest KKK members.

The federal troops remained in the South for nearly a decade, but Republicans broke faith with former slaves in the South for political expediency, ending Reconstruction in the mid-1870s. As a result of a bargain reached to decide the closely contested 1876 election, Republican President Rutherford B. Hayes agreed to withdraw federal troops from the South. The Democrats subsequently recaptured firm political control of the Southern states, where they reinforced white supremacy and kept African Americans from exercising their voting rights. Southern Democrats passed "Jim Crow laws" through their state legislatures, establishing literacy tests and poll taxes designed to keep former slaves from voting. They also enforced racial segregation mandating separate bathrooms and water fountains, and barring African Americans from shops, restaurants, and hotels.[15]

Now, you may be asking how this could happen in America with our Bill of Rights and after freed slaves had been granted full rights as citizens. The answer is one of the worst decisions in the history of the Supreme Court: The 1896 *Plessy* v. *Ferguson* decision held that segregation laws were constitutional and established the doctrine that "separate but equal" accommodations did not violate the Fourteenth Amendment. This ruling would stand for fifty-four years, until it was reversed by the Supreme Court in the 1954 decision *Brown* v. *Board of Education of Topeka* (Kansas).[16]

The last three decades of the nineteenth century and continuing decades into the next century were a desperate period for former slaves in the fully segregated Jim Crow South. Justice was unattainable when persecuted citizens suspected that the police and judges by day were vigilante group members disguised in white robes by night. African Americans were harassed, threatened, beaten, and murdered, often in ritualized and public lynchings designed to intimidate whole communities. Race riots, in which mobs of whites brought violence, burning, and looting to African American communities, decimated economic opportunities for African Americans to build and maintain businesses, create wealth, invent products, and file patents.[17]

Eventually more than 3 million former slaves and about 3 million of their descendants joined in the Great Northward Migration of African Americans from the Southern states to the cities in the Northeast and Midwest.[18]

## POLITICAL DIVISIONS AND BIPARTISAN
## LEGISLATION IN THE GILDED AGE

There are many ways in which the late 1800s, which Mark Twain termed the Gilded Age, shares important similarities with our own times. In the 1880s, new technologies (the telegraph, railroads, and mass production using coal, steam, and steel) were creating brand-new industries and vast wealth, especially in large cities like New York, Philadelphia, and Chicago. A small number of industrial titans became fabulously wealthy as economic inequality hit record levels. By 1890 the top 1 percent of the public controlled 25 percent of the nation's wealth.[19]

But things were not going as well for most Americans in the big cities and across the land. The Civil War had destroyed the economy of the South, bringing widespread poverty. The South had trailed the North economically, but after the war this geographical inequality reached new levels. The railroads helped distribute goods from factories and farms in the South, Midwest, and West to customers in the big cities, but this meant the railroads had a chokehold on the economy, allowing them to profit at the shippers' expense. New production methods were increasing agricultural yields but driving down the price of crops, and these methods were capital intensive, leaving farmers deep in debt and vulnerable to getting wiped out by a setback that could arrive in the form of storms, droughts, or locusts and other pests. The new factories, mostly in the North, were dirty and dangerous. Labor unions formed to fight for higher pay and safer working conditions, but also to protect white workers from competition from the African Americans fleeing the South in the Great Northward Migration.[20]

In addition to the economic similarities between the Gilded Age and the current period in American history, there are similarities in politics. The vast wealth in the hands of a small number of plantation owners, industrialists, and railroad tycoons, generated by advantageous relationships with the mass of Americans in the factories and on the farms, was used to purchase advantage through control of the political system. The two parties were viciously battling, less over ideology and national policy than over the spoils from serving the interests of the wealthy titans of industry and commerce.

Frances Lee has studied congressional voting patterns of the late 1800s and finds very small ideological differences between the parties that were divided by political personalities and battling over political opportunities for enrichment. Both parties represented business interests (although not necessarily the same ones) that wanted tight monetary policies and high tariffs to protect their goods from foreign competition (but low tariffs on goods they wanted to import). The industrialists wanted protective tariffs to keep out foreign competition for the manufactured goods they produced, but Southern tobacco and cotton producers opposed protective tariffs on goods they wanted to import in exchange for their exports.

In a paper titled "Patronage, Logrolls, and 'Polarization': Congressional Parties of the Gilded Age, 1876–1896,"[21] Lee reviews the work of many political scientists and historians like Arthur Schlesinger Jr.,[22] and concludes, "The Gilded Age illustrates that political parties are fully capable of waging ferocious warfare over spoils and office, even despite a relative lack of sharp party differences over national policy."

The two parties were at nearly equal strength in those years, and control of each chamber changed hands more frequently than any time in our history—except now. The parties were geographically divided, with Republicans dominant in the North and Democrats dominant in the South but also holding strongholds in several Northern cities. Both parties were split with factions from the West that believed they received too little attention from the East. They were also split by religion and race. Protestants and Lutherans of northern European origins tended to be Republicans, while Catholics and many of the more recent southern and eastern European immigrant communities aligned with the Democrats. Where African Americans were allowed to vote, they were strongly aligned with the Republicans, the party of Lincoln and emancipation.

Competing business interests drove the agendas of the two political parties during the Gilded Age. Southern Democrats represented the former plantation owners searching to expand markets for agricultural products and cotton. Republicans championed the big business and banking interests of the rapidly industrializing Northeast, but several big-city Northern Democratic governors and mayors, like the corrupt "machine" politician William "Boss" Tweed, who ruled from New York's Tammany Hall, also championed business interests in their states.

The parties fought over patronage jobs in government and public works projects, and they fought over taxes and tariffs. Both parties agreed that tariffs, as the principal source of government revenue, needed to be high enough to fund government's needs, but fought political battles over which specific goods (wool, cotton, glass, iron) would face tariffs of what level. It was an era of big money in politics, where politicians were understood to be "owned" by business interests and legislation could be passed by making sure it allowed enough politicians to meet the needs of their wealthy constituents.

The policy differences between the parties tended to be far smaller than the animosity between the political leaders. Politics in the Gilded Age was as vitriolic as ever, leading to long legislative stalemates, but the two sides were able to come together and pass legislation. In addition to the "logrolling" ("I will vote to fund your project if you vote to fund mine"), other bills passed by strong bipartisan margins when a large number of business interests wanted the same policy. The Interstate Commerce Act of 1887, which attempted to curtail the monopoly power of the railroads, and the Sherman Anti-Trust Act of 1890, which penalized monopolistic practices in restraint of trade, both passed the Senate and House with few "no" votes. Lest you think these were anti-business laws, remember that they saved a large number of businesses from being hijacked by a very small number of businesses that had discovered choke points in the emerging industrial economy.

The pressures for change that brought about the end of the Gilded Age were building in the farms of the West, Midwest, and South that were organizing cooperatives to fight the monopoly power of the railroads, and in the newly unionizing factories in the North. For decades, the two political parties had become detached from the concerns of anyone other than their wealthy patrons with legislative battles that pitted the interests of one set of titans against the interests of another set of titans and ignored the interests of most voters of lesser means.

Both the Republicans and the Democrats favored a strong currency backed by gold, which was supported by banking and industrial interests but opposed by farmers, who were deep in debt. Calls for looser monetary policy backed by silver as well as gold caused a breakaway "populist" faction to persuade the Democratic Party to nominate William Jennings Bryan, a young congressman from Nebraska (raised in Illinois) in the presidential election of 1896. Bryan's skills as an orator, as well as his constituency among the "common man" farmers and ranchers in the South and West, were a threat to the industrialists and power brokers running Wall Street and Washington, who coalesced behind pro-business Republican William McKinley. McKinley won the election and continued the Gilded Age policies into the end of the century. But when his vice president, Garret Hobart, a New Jersey businessman, died in office in 1899 and the Democrats again chose William Jennings Bryan for their 1900 presidential nominee, McKinley tapped New York Governor Theodore "Teddy" Roosevelt to be his running mate. McKinley beat Bryan again in the rematch but was assassinated six months into his second term, and Roosevelt, an activist reformer, took the presidential oath of office. This was September 1901; the Gilded Age had ended, and the Progressive Era had begun.

CHAPTER 4

# REFORM AND REALIGNMENT: THE PROGRESSIVE ERA TO THE SOUTHERN STRATEGY

On one level, the 1900s play out as a continuous struggle between business interests and progressive reformers. In the Gilded Age, business had co-opted both parties, but at the end of the nineteenth century and start of the twentieth century, business interests were losing their grip in the period that would come to be known as the Progressive Era. The reformers were on the rise, and the corrupt, business-serving, and largely unproductive political establishments in both parties could not continue to defend the traditional East-coast centered order in an American democracy that was modernizing and expanding westward. Populists and progressives called for political reform in both parties at the federal, state, and local levels.

Power that had been tightly controlled in the hands of a few business tycoons devolved to the masses as representative democracy was more fully realized with the 1912 passage and 1913 ratification of the Seventeenth Amendment to the Constitution, giving voters in each state, rather than state legislatures, the power to select US senators through direct elections. Women waged a decades-long campaign for the right to vote that found success in many Western states and was granted nationally by the Nineteenth Amendment to the Constitution in 1920. Farmers were forming cooperatives, factory workers were organizing into unions, and child labor laws were passed, shifting power from the few to the many.

A series of boom-and-bust economic panics in 1893 and 1896, the Spanish-American War in 1898, and then more economic panics in 1907 and 1910 weakened the traditional order in both parties, allowing progressive reformers like William Jennings Bryan and Robert M. La Follette to build large followings. It was in 1901 that Republican Theodore Roosevelt became president following the assassination of William McKinley.

Maverick President Theodore Roosevelt did not fit the McKinley mold for Republicans. He was an activist Republican who had challenged the political order as New York governor, making friends as well as enemies. Many of Roosevelt's "Square Deal" policies would not be called pro-business by current Republican standards. He regulated business practices, passing the Pure Food and Drug Act and other consumer and worker protections.

Roosevelt perceived dangers in concentrated business power and in the massive economic inequality of the day, saying, "There can be no real political democracy unless there is something approaching economic democracy."[1] Supported by a Republican Congress, he used the Interstate Commerce Act and the Sherman Anti-Trust Act—passed in the administrations of Grover Cleveland and Benjamin Harrison but ineffectively implemented by McKinley—to "bust the trusts," breaking up big oil and railroad monopolies. In taking on the railroad and oil monopolies, Roosevelt was challenging and defeating the wealthiest and most powerful men of the era, including J. P. Morgan and John D. Rockefeller.

Roosevelt was also a pioneering conservationist who created national parks and forests to protect public lands from private exploitation. However, an estimated 86 million acres of the land transferred to the national forests had been Native American ancestral land taken by force.[2] Teddy Roosevelt's record on race relations was mixed at best. He famously dined at the White House with Booker T. Washington, but Roosevelt's papers and letters reveal this was a departure from his general belief in the superiority of the white European race.[3]

After serving nearly two terms (one inherited from McKinley and one of his own after winning the 1904 election), Roosevelt backed William Howard Taft for the Republican nomination, and Taft went on to win the 1908 presidential election. Taft is not often thought of as one of the great reformers, for several reasons. He was a one-term president who was more aligned with the conservative, pro-business wing of the Republican Party than Roosevelt, who ran against him in 1912. In fact, Taft ran for the White House against three icons of political reform: William Jennings Bryan in 1908 and, in 1912, both Teddy Roosevelt, who split the Republican vote by forming the Bull Moose Party, and Democrat Woodrow Wilson, who would prevail against the divided opposition.

But I suspect the real reason Taft is not viewed as a reformer is that his best claim to meaningful reform is loved by almost no one. Taft pushed through the Sixteenth Amendment, launching the income tax and corporate tax system that has evolved into our current tax system. It was a substantial reform because the system of tariffs and sales taxes it replaced put most of the burden on the less well-off. The progressive income tax and corporate taxes enacted by Wilson after ratification of Taft's amendment shifted the burden far more equitably up the income scale.

Although Wilson was from the other party, his record of activism in the White House rivals that of Teddy Roosevelt. In addition to instituting the first income tax, Wilson, backed by a Democratic majority in Congress, strengthened anti-trust policy and created the Federal Reserve System, which was a major advance toward stabilizing the currency and the banking system. Even if the banks buckled at the start of the Great Depression, the system was necessary to restarting them again and has stood through many tests in the years since.

Wilson was reticent to involve America in Europe's Great War, and his campaign slogan, "He kept us out of war," was one of the primary arguments made by his supporters for his 1916 reelection, even after German U-boats (submarines) sank dozens of merchant ships, some of them American, and passenger ships, including the RMS *Lusitania*, in 1915. But when Germany reasserted its blockade and U-boat attacks resumed and intensified in 1917, Wilson asserted US rights under international "freedom of the seas" treaties and mobilized the nation to enter the war on the side of the British and the French. However, in the Senate, Wilson was frustrated by an anti-war minority that refused to end debate on his war resolution.

On March 4, 1917, Wilson issued a statement to the public, calling on the Senate to amend its rules to allow senators to cut off debate. Wilson decried the Senate as "the only legislative body in the world which cannot act when its majority is ready for action," adding that a "little group of willful men, representing no opinion but their own, have rendered the great government of the United States helpless and contemptible."[4] He proposed a new rule, later named Senate Rule 22, that gave a two-thirds supermajority a mechanism to invoke "cloture," ending debate on an issue so that it can be brought to a vote. The Senate adopted the rule, and by April, Congress had passed a declaration of war.

With Wilson taking direct action to reign in the filibuster, this is a good time to get back to that story. Up to this point, the history of the filibuster was less about any deliberate actions and more about inaction and accidental outcomes. We now must go back to the early 1800s to pick up the thread.

## THE ACCIDENTAL FILIBUSTER

So far, all I have said about the Senate filibuster is it was not created by the Founding Fathers to make the Senate a more deliberative body. We know this because Alexander Hamilton and James Madison designed the Senate to be majority rule. In fact, the filibuster was not created by anyone for any reason; it arrived totally by accident.

My Brookings Institution colleague Sarah Binder exhaustively researched the filibuster for a book she wrote with Steven Smith, called *Politics or Principle? Filibustering in the United States Senate.*[5] As Binder told the story in very accessible testimony before the Senate Committee on Rules and Administration[6] in 2010, the filibuster is an unintended consequence of a Senate rules reform supported by Vice President Aaron Burr (shortly after his deadly duel with Alexander Hamilton) in 1806. Burr insisted the Senate rule book was too long and complicated. In the simplification, the senators inadvertently eliminated the rule to "call the previous question"—in other words, to get back to the business at hand.

Although it had not yet been used this way in either chamber, the House soon learned to use the previous question rule (which was never eliminated from their rules) to cut off debate. It would be decades before the senators realized, in 1837, that having eliminated their chamber's previous question motion, any minority of senators could block votes just by holding the floor and continuing the debate, and thus the filibuster was born.

Over the next fourscore years, the filibuster was used with increasing frequency and obstructiveness until 1917, when President Woodrow Wilson was frustrated by filibusters blocking his domestic reform agenda and his plan to enter the war in Europe. With the new rule allowing two-thirds of senators to cut off debate by invoking cloture, the Senate supermajority came to power for the first time. In Wilson's view that was better than having the Senate governed by a faction amounting to a handful of senators or even a single senator.

For the next half century, filibusters were reserved for rare times when a minority of senators believed the majority was making a grave mistake, often on the wrong side of history, including the famous filibusters by Southern Democrats against civil rights laws in the 1950s and 1960s. The threshold dropped from two-thirds to three-fifths in 1975, and use of the tactic climbed from rare to commonplace in the last three decades of the last century. But it was not until the start of the second Barack Obama administration, in 2013, that use of the filibuster became so routine that a sixty-vote supermajority was the *de facto* threshold needed to pass legislation through the Senate. In chapter 11, I offer many recommendations to make Congress work better in our highly polarized times, and one of the suggestions is the complete elimination of the filibuster.

## FDR's NEW DEAL BECOMES THE MODEL FOR DEMOCRATS' ECONOMIC POLICY

The self-serving corruption of Northern and Southern elites in the Gilded Age, new voting blocks of women, immigrants, and in the western states, and several economic panics shook the Eastern establishment and brought in reformers. But it was the catastrophe of the Great Depression under pro-business Republican Herbert Hoover that opened the door for Franklin D. Roosevelt (FDR) to do something that had never been done before. His "New Deal" coalition united former slaveholders among the Southern Democrats and former slaves in the North with poor and working-class whites against the Northern Republicans. And then, facing a broken economy and the enormous challenge of World War II, FDR made deals with the Republicans to get more done than any other president.

Economic devastation of the Great Depression propelled Democrats, led by FDR, into unprecedented federal activism. In a flurry of crisis responses,[7] the Democrats created numerous national institutions and infrastructure projects to put the unemployed to work, relieve the suffering of the destitute, rescue the failing banking system, and implement social insurance programs to protect workers against future income losses due to unemployment and retirement.

People look at the Democratic majorities during the FDR and Harry S. Truman administrations and assume, incorrectly, that this is what made the New Deal legislative successes possible. To hold this view is not only false, but also anti-liberal. Remember, any legislation Roosevelt passed with only Democratic votes implicitly meant he was making a deal with Southern Democrats who were still defending segregation. He often did govern this way, more than some of his advisors would have liked—his politically active wife, Eleanor Roosevelt, tried unsuccessfully to press him to support anti-lynching legislation[8]—but he also passed legislation over the objections of Southern Democrats, and of conservative business-oriented Northern Democrats, by forming bipartisan coalitions.

The nation was deeply divided over civil rights, labor rights, and many other issues, and Congress was often chaotic, but FDR and his allies, the progressive Democrats, were able to form shifting coalitions to pass legislation—sometimes including conservative Northern Democrats, sometimes including Southern Democrats, and at other times including progressive and moderate Republicans.

Even while the Roosevelt administration was creating major new roles for the federal government in stimulating the economy and protecting the vulnerable, it was taking criticism from the more conservative Democrats like Al Smith, the Democratic candidate for president in 1928 and former governor of New York. America's business interests, who had stood in opposition to the initiatives of a series of presidents, with the exception of Hoover, were even more focused on opposing Roosevelt's New Deal. Board members from corporations including General Motors, DuPont, and the Sun Oil Company formed the American Liberty League, which Al Smith joined along with a long list of former politicians and federal officeholders.

With conservative business-oriented Northern Democrats opposing some elements of the New Deal and conservative Southern Democrats opposing other elements, bipartisan cooperation with progressive Republicans was necessary to help pass the New Deal reforms into law.[9] Republican Harold Ickes, as secretary of the interior, was instrumental in developing the Pub-

lic Works Administration.[10] Senator George Norris (R-NE) helped create
the Tennessee Valley Authority,[11] and the Social Security Act passed Congress with strong bipartisan support.[12] The American Legion helped drum
up bipartisan support for the GI Bill to educate war veterans.[13]

The scramble for votes to pass the New Deal often caused Roosevelt to be
dependent on the support of Southern Democrats, who were committed to
maintaining white supremacy in the former Confederate states. Southern
Democrats in Congress, who rarely had to face a serious electoral challenge,
attained the seniority that led to committee chairs and Party leadership positions. In return for allegiance to the Democratic Party, they prevented Northern liberals from using the powers of the federal government to interfere with
segregation, discrimination, voter suppression, and even lynching in the South.

Many New Deal programs contained racially discriminatory provisions,
such as federally sanctioned redlining in the underwriting manuals of the
Federal Housing Administration (FHA), which instructed insurance companies against writing policies for African Americans seeking to buy a home
in a white neighborhood.[14] The first version of Social Security covered neither agricultural nor domestic service jobs, which were disproportionately
held by African Americans, so they were left out of the benefit pool until a
1950 reform bill extended coverage to more categories of workers.[15] There
are many other examples,[16] but perhaps the most damaging was the Agricultural Adjustment Administration, which paid white landowners to keep
their land fallow but made no provisions for the African American or white
tenant farmers and sharecroppers who had been working the land and were
now without income at the height of the Great Depression.[17]

Roosevelt was elected president four times, but he died in office just five
months after the 1944 election; Vice President Harry S. Truman inherited
the White House, World War II, the New Deal agenda, and the monster federal budget deficits. He also inherited the 94 percent top marginal personal
income tax rate that FDR had adopted to help pay off all the war debt.

Some people hear about a 94 percent tax rate and assume the economy
must have been terrible because such a high rate would discourage people
from working to earn higher incomes. But we know that the high tax rate
continued for decades, and the post-war period was one of the best, if not
the best, economic environments in history. It is important to understand
that no one paid 94 percent of their income in taxes. The top marginal rate

only applies to income above a certain threshold. In 1944, the 94 percent tax rate applied to income over $200,000, which is about $3 million in today's dollars. But the wealthy paid 81 percent on income up to $200,000 (after deductibles and exclusions, etc.).

There were twenty-six tax brackets then, each with a different tax rate ranging from 23 percent on the first $2,000 of taxable income up to 94 percent for the top bracket, so things were a lot more complicated. Even families earning the median income of $13,500 paid 36 percent on their taxable income, paying more in federal income taxes than we do now. But back then, most people saw paying taxes as their patriotic duty. Most Americans supported the war effort and wanted the armed forces to have whatever they needed to fight the war. Everyone understood that the nation was now deeply in debt, and paying taxes was a small sacrifice compared with the sacrifice of thousands of GIs who had lost limbs or given their lives to win the war.

The high taxes worked to get the nation's budget under control, and after years of huge deficits to fund the war, the federal government ran budget surpluses in 1947, 1948, and 1949. But the economy struggled in the first two years after the war ended, and Truman's popularity plummeted. The spending caused a severe bout of inflation, labor strikes shut down the national railroad, and the economy struggled to find jobs for all the returning GIs. The women who had answered the call of "Rosie the Riveter" to do men's jobs in the factories during wartime were told they were no longer needed.

Democrats lost control of both chambers of Congress in the 1946 midterm elections. By 1948 the Democratic Party was splintering, and in addition to facing the Republican governor of New York, Thomas E. Dewey, Truman was challenged by two former Democrats who formed their own parties; former Vice President Henry Wallace and the Progressive/American Labor Party on the left, and South Carolina Senator Strom Thurmond and the "Dixiecrats" on the right.[18]

Despite famous predictions of his defeat, Truman won the 1948 election and worked to hold the bipartisan New Deal coalition together to support his "Fair Deal," uniting enough Southern Democrats, progressive Northern Democrats, and Republicans to raise the national minimum wage in 1949, provide 800,000 new houses for the poor, and expand Social Security in 1950.[19] But he was challenged by a coalition of conservative Republicans and

Southern Democrats on several issues, especially the anti-union Taft-Hartley Act that Congress passed by overriding Truman's veto. While Truman did not have the votes to pass civil rights legislation, he integrated the military by executive order (although it would take years to overcome resistance within the military).[20]

In the post-war period, America was far more unified on foreign policy than on domestic policy. This changed when the Korean War bogged down after China joined forces with North Korea. The far right turned aggressively anti-Communist, led by Senator Joseph McCarthy (R-WI) with his exaggerated assertions of Communist agents and sympathizers throughout government and the entertainment industry. McCarthy was eventually censured by the Senate for making false accusations.

As the Cold War and the challenges posed by the Soviet Union and China took shape, America's attention turned to foreign policy. So, the 1952 election of retired Army General Dwight D. Eisenhower, who had led the D-Day invasion of Normandy Beach and was credited with victory in World War II, was unsurprising.

## PRESIDENT EISENHOWER CEMENTS THE NEW DEAL WITH INFRASTRUCTURE

At the age of 21, I was eligible to cast my first presidential vote in 1952, and as a Democrat, I voted for Adlai Stevenson then and again in 1956. But Eisenhower was very popular and won every state outside of the Deep South, Kentucky and West Virginia. Even if I did not vote for him, I must agree with polls of historians that rank Eisenhower among the best American presidents, especially when it comes to his economic policy. He maintained the New Deal and the high taxes to pay for it; he added new investments in infrastructure and science; and he worked with a Democratic Congress to achieve balanced budgets.[21]

Eisenhower's landslide victory in 1952 brought with it a Republican majority in the House of Representatives. The Senate switched to the GOP by the narrowest of margins, 48 to 48, with Vice President Richard Nixon there to break the tie in favor of the Republicans. But Democrats won back the House and Senate in 1954, elevating Lyndon Johnson (D-TX) to majority leader in a divided Washington, and even though Eisenhower won reelection in 1956,

Democrats would hold the Senate for the next twenty-six years and the House for forty years. Even with divided government, Eisenhower and the Democrats on Capitol Hill proved capable of passing major legislation.

"Ike" labeled himself a moderate Republican opposing the "old guard Republicans" who favored repealing the New Deal and Fair Deal policies. In addition to standing up to communism around the world and strongly supporting NATO—which he had helped create but many isolationist Republicans opposed—Eisenhower had domestic priorities that included bringing down the federal budget deficit and national debt, and support for infrastructure spending, particularly for the Interstate Highway System. Responding to the Soviet Union's launch of the Sputnik satellite, Eisenhower started the National Aeronautics and Space Administration (NASA) and made a strong push for public school science education.

It is well worth noting that these successful bipartisan efforts to build consensus for sound economic policy geared toward the long term preceded an extended period of economic growth in America and the rise of the great American middle class. Beginning with FDR and Truman's GI Bill, New Deal and Fair Deal economic policies, and support for organized labor, nearly two decades of successful bipartisan leadership were rewarded with an unprecedented and unequaled period of prosperity and global leadership. A similar economic policy enacted today would set the economy on a path to broadly shared prosperity, as I outline in chapter 2.

But lest this version one view of America seem overly nostalgic for the Eisenhower administration, the 1950s were also historic for version two of the American story. It was a far better time to be middle-class and white in America than to be poor and Native American, African American, or an immigrant. The median family income for African American families in 1954 was just slightly more than half that for white families[22] (a ratio that has remained stubbornly stable through the years). White men living in rural areas earned far less than their urban counterparts. A woman's place was said to be in the home, where the man was said to be the ruler of his castle. The female labor participation rate, which had risen dramatically during World War II, dropped back to nearly pre-war levels to just above 30 percent in the early 1950s but then began a long upward climb until the end of the century. The decades-long civil rights and equality movements were struggling against determined and often violent resistance in the 1950s.

Eisenhower was a reluctant champion for racial equality. He had not been an initial supporter of Truman's order to integrate the military, but after the Supreme Court's 1954 decision in *Brown* v. *Board of Education of Topeka*, Eisenhower moved vigorously to enforce public school integration as the new law of the land. To overcome resistance from the school board of Little Rock, Arkansas, he sent in units of the 101st Airborne, took command of the Arkansas National Guard, and addressed the nation, saying, "Our personal opinions as to the accuracy of the decision has no bearing on the matter; the responsibility of the Supreme Court to interpret the Constitution is unquestioned."[23] In saying this, Eisenhower was underscoring the centrality of the Constitution in the argument that Thurgood Marshall, chief counsel for the National Association for the Advancement of Colored People (NAACP), had made and that had won the court's unanimous opinion. Despite Eisenhower's speech and actions, resistance and delay in implementing the *Brown* decision was effective in keeping more than 90 percent of Southern Black students in segregated schools for the 1960 school year.[24]

## Kennedy and Johnson Break with Southern Democrats over Civil Rights

The civil rights movement was taken up in the 1960s by President John F. Kennedy. When Martin Luther King Jr. was arrested in Atlanta, Georgia, shortly before the 1960 election, Kennedy telephoned King's wife, Coretta Scott King, to express support—earning the endorsement of King's father, Martin Luther King Sr., and eventually, 70 percent of African American votes, helping Kennedy win a very close election.[25]

Kennedy remained cautious on the issue for fear of angering Southern Democrats, but eventually the freedom rides, sit-ins, and boycotts of the civil rights movement compelled him to act. His brother and the attorney general, Robert Kennedy, sent 400 federal marshals to the South to protect the freedom riders. President Kennedy addressed the nation in 1963 to define civil rights as a moral crisis and call for new legislation, but he was assassinated before he could pass it.[26]

President Lyndon B. Johnson (LBJ) picked liberal Senator Hubert Humphrey of Minnesota to be his champion to shepherd the Civil Rights Act through a long and arduous legislative process. The official US Senate history of the Civil Rights Act of 1964 quotes Johnson urging Humphrey to court the Senate Republican leader, Everett Dirksen (R-IL), saying, "The bill can't pass unless you get Ev Dirksen. You get in there to see Dirksen. You drink with Dirksen! You talk with Dirksen. You listen to Dirksen."[27]

Johnson and Humphrey needed Dirksen because Southern Democrats, led by Senator Richard Russell of Georgia, were in a full-on rebellion, which took the form of a filibuster lasting sixty days. Dixiecrat Senator Strom Thurmond (D-SC) had set the filibuster record, holding the floor for 24 hours and 18 minutes against the Civil Rights Act of 1957,[28] and he joined a solid block of Southern Democrats for a two-month long filibuster in 1964. But Johnson and Humphrey had already worked with the ranking Republican member of the House Judiciary Committee, William McCulloch (R-OH), to get enough votes to pass the Bill through the House. Then Johnson and Humphrey got Everett Dirksen to corral enough Republican senators to break the filibuster and pass the Civil Rights Act of 1964 with broad bipartisan support.[29]

Johnson chose Humphrey to be his vice-presidential running mate in 1964. Their enthusiastic endorsement of Kennedy's stalled agenda of civil rights continued with passage of the Voting Rights Act of 1965, the Fair Housing Act in 1968, and several other pieces of legislation that clearly established the Democrats as protectors of minority rights and cemented the bond between African Americans and the Democratic Party. Of course, the passage of anti-discrimination laws did not end racism in America—that struggle continues today—but it did put the government, which had actively participated in perpetuating racism, firmly on the side of fighting it, which was progress.[30]

On economic policy, LBJ saw his legacy as the continuation of FDR's New Deal. Johnson laid out his vision for the "War on Poverty" in his 1964 State of the Union address,[31] and he described a "Great Society . . . where no child will go unfed, and no youngster will go unschooled" in a speech to students at Ohio University[32] and in another speech at the University of Michigan[33] in May 1964.

Johnson's efforts to pass Medicare and Medicaid, which many regarded as the last missing pieces of the New Deal, were blocked by Southern Democrats, particularly Wilbur Mills, representative from Arkansas and the chair of the House Ways and Means Committee. But after Johnson won in a landslide election that November, liberal Democrats gained the upper hand in Congress, and Mills turned from an adversary to an ally of Medicare and

Medicaid.[34] He worked the compromises and crafted legislation that could pass with broad support of liberal and conservative Democrats as well as a fair number of Republicans in both chambers.[35]

Medicare and Medicaid often get lumped together, but they are very distinct programs, and each has many subparts that provide different services for different groups of people. Both were originally opposed by many interest groups, including doctors and insurance companies, and by many Republican lawmakers, but the two programs have become so popular that even former opponents now vow to maintain them. They are also so complicated and have become such a large share of the budget that there are many proposals to improve them.[36] There could be substantial opportunities for bipartisan improvement in both programs if we could put aside politics and unite around the goals of delivering better care to the elderly, disabled, and poor and near-poor children and adults more efficiently and at a substantially lower cost. The Affordable Care Act (2010) attempted to do just this and succeeded substantively, but it failed to win Republican participation or support.

## GOLDWATER AND THE BIRTH OF MOVEMENT CONSERVATIVISM

The presidential election of 1964 was a disaster for Republicans but played an important role in moving the party to the right and setting the agenda for the party for decades to come. Republicans passed over moderate New York Governor Nelson Rockefeller to nominate Barry Goldwater, a senator from Arizona and an avowed small-government conservative. It is fair to view Goldwater as the first hyperpartisan Republican, and his book, *The Conscience of a Conservative,*[37] was widely admired by conservative intellectuals. William F. Buckley Jr., an articulate conservative thought leader and the lively host of a popular television talk show, referred to it frequently.

Goldwater wanted Republicans to stop apologizing for their conservative ideology (as in the often-stated moderate slogan, "conservativism with a heart," which implied that other conservatives were heartless), and to make the moral and constitutional case for individual freedom as unhampered as possible by government interference. He valued self-reliance and personal responsibility, and thought it was good for people to make their own decisions, even bad ones, instead of depending on help from government.

He believed the founders had enshrined limited government in the Constitution, spelling out the necessary powers of the central government and entrusting all others to the states and the people. He regarded the New Deal's expanded federal role as unconstitutional and wanted to roll it back, including the popular Social Security program.

Although Goldwater lost badly in 1964, Ronald Reagan would be elected sixteen years later based on what Buckley would later term "a platform indistinguishable from what Barry had been preaching."[38] Today's Tea Party Republicans and House Freedom Caucus, with their small government agendas, emphasis on states' rights, and professed allegiance to traditional Christian values on social issues, owe a lot to Senator Goldwater.

It should be understood that, throughout American history, the term "state's rights" has been closely associated with the rights of states to allow slavery before the Civil War, and the rights of states to allow racial segregation and discrimination thereafter. Goldwater, an active member of the Arizona NAACP,[39] denied that he was a segregationist, but he was one of only six Republican senators to vote against Johnson's Civil Rights Act (joining twenty-one Senate Democrats in opposition). Goldwater stressed that education is not mentioned in the Constitution and was therefore among the powers reserved for states. He believed states should be able to respond to the desires of their citizens without federal interference from Washington, and although he said he personally favored integrated schools, he did not believe Washington had the right to dictate school policy to states that rejected racial integration in the schools.

Goldwater's stand on states' rights in school integration earned him the endorsement of segregationist Senator Strom Thurmond of South Carolina, who switched parties from Democrat to Republican,[40] and the electoral votes of five Deep South states (Mississippi, Alabama, Louisiana, Georgia, and South Carolina), the only states he won besides his home state of Arizona in the Democratic landslide of 1964. It was the first time the "solid South" voted Republican.

The 1964 election was also important for many other reasons. It marked the first real use of negative attack ads, with the Johnson campaign hiring Tony Schwartz and the Madison Avenue advertising agency Doyle Dane Bernbach (DDB) to make a series of ads like the famous "Daisy" countdown commercial,[41] suggesting that Goldwater would be unreliable in a crisis and likely to use nuclear weapons,[42] and in Northern and Western states, ads suggesting he was too sympathetic to the Ku Klux Klan.[43]

The LBJ landslide in 1964 was off all previous charts. Johnson won 486 electoral votes to Goldwater's 52 and captured 61 percent of the popular vote to Goldwater's 38 percent. The Democrats controlled the House by 258 to 176 and the Senate by 68 to 32. Nevertheless, Goldwater had inspired conservatives to embrace limited government, Christian values, personal responsibility, and states' rights, appealing to white former Democrats in the South. "Movement conservativism" became a force to be reckoned with.

Lyndon Johnson presided over a period of rapid economic growth. In the middle of the decade often referred to as the "go-go '60s," the average rate of gross domestic product (GDP) growth was over 5 percent per year from 1963 through 1968.[44] Johnson is credited with some of the greatest legislative achievements of any president. Of course, I may be somewhat biased because I worked in the Johnson administration as the assistant secretary for planning and evaluation, at the US Department of Health, Education, and Welfare (HEW), so I wrote a lot of reports and analyses that went into the

---

*[Health, Education, and Welfare] was . . . my first experience inside the federal government. What I learned most that has been a theme in the rest of my career is how difficult it is to make policy—especially social policy of the HEW sort—from Washington, because the country is so big and so diverse, and the interaction with states and localities is difficult. It was an eye-opener.*

*We were in the middle of the war on poverty and all of the activism of the '60s. . . . We were trying to make it work. . . . So I became much more skeptical of the ability of the federal government to run things centrally, and very interested in what could be done at the state level and things like revenue sharing and other programs. I wrote a book about it in the early '70s, Systematic Thinking for Social Action, where some of those themes come in.*

—Alice M. Rivlin, interview for the
UVA Miller Center Presidential
Oral Histories Project,
December 13, 2002

---

implementation of some of those policies. But Johnson also inherited an unpopular and probably unwinnable war halfway around the world in Vietnam, and amid widespread public protests, he chose to refuse the Democratic nomination to run for a second full term in 1968.

## RICHARD M. NIXON: THE SOUTHERN STRATEGY AND POLICY MODERATION

In many ways, the 1968 Republican presidential nominee, Richard Nixon, represented a different faction of the Republican Party than Goldwater, but Nixon continued to base his campaign around appealing to Southern white voters. His Southern strategy placed less emphasis on directly opposing civil rights, but his messages against government dependency and supporting "law and order" were effective in helping him win the presidency over a beleaguered Democratic Party torn apart by the Vietnam War and facing an independent challenge from segregationist Alabama Governor George Wallace, who won five states in the Deep South.[45] The realignment by political ideology was by now well underway, and over the next two decades, white Southern conservatives would move to the Republican Party, and districts formerly represented by more liberal Republicans in the Northeast would elect more and more Democrats.

As president, Nixon was fairly moderate. Rather than running against the New Deal, Nixon embraced it and even expanded government's reach in many areas. Working with a Democratic Senate and House, Nixon was able to add a major new element to the Social Security system with Supplemental Security Income (SSI) for elderly and disabled citizens, and large increases in Social Security, Medicare, and Medicaid benefits.

Environmentalism in America has bipartisan roots that include President Teddy Roosevelt's efforts to protect public lands, and Rachel Carson's influential book *Silent Spring* at the start of the 1960s. But it was President Nixon who created the National Oceanic and Atmospheric Administration (NOAA) and the Environmental Protection Agency (EPA), giving it broad enforcement power through amendments to the Clean Air Act, a new Safe Drinking Water Act, and the Endangered Species Act. Herb Stein, the chair of Nixon's Council of Economic Advisers, would later write, "Probably more new regulation was imposed on the economy than in any other presidency since the New Deal."[46]

As Nixon took office, the economy that had been so strong under LBJ (although with large budget deficits to fund the "guns and butter" of the Vietnam War and the Great Society) started to deteriorate. The unemployment rate was very low, but inflation was rising, crossing above 6 percent at the end of 1969.[47] Growth slowed, and the economy went into a mild recession in 1970. It would be the first of many economic slowdowns in a decade of frustratingly slow growth after so many years of economic success.

Even though Nixon was moderate on domestic policy, relations with Congress were often tense. Nixon stretched the powers of the presidency in ways both overt and covert, as would be uncovered in the investigations following the Watergate scandal. In one of the overt acts during the summer of 1974, Nixon threatened to withhold congressionally appropriated funds from programs he did not support—a practice known as impoundment. Congress responded by passing the Congressional Budget and Impoundment Control Act of 1974. Facing near-certain impeachment in the House over Watergate, Nixon resigned in August.

The Congressional Budget and Impoundment Control Act of 1974 turned out to be no small element in my life. The act reasserted Congress's control over spending by making it clear that presidents cannot redirect appropriated funds without going to Congress for permission. The act set up a new congressional budget process and a timeline of required actions by certain dates. The first day of the nation's fiscal year changed from July 1 to October 1, when the old budget ran out and a new budget needed to be in place. The president was required to submit a budget proposal in February; Congress had to pass identical concurrent budget resolutions by May 15, which are then used to guide the authorizing and appropriating committees in each chamber. The budget resolutions could include reconciliation instructions, requiring the passage of a reconciliation bill to align the House and Senate spending limits. Reconciliation bills were specifically exempted from being filibustered in the Senate, requiring only a simple majority to pass a budget resolution to help the Senate complete the budgets on time. In other words, the new budget act was defining a new "regular order" for passing budgets. The act also created standing budget committees in both the House and the

Senate, and created the Congressional Budget Office (CBO) to give the committees their own source of unbiased, nonpartisan expertise for economic and budgetary analysis so they would not be dependent on the White House Office of Management and Budget (OMB).

At the time, I was at Brookings writing about the federal budget and the budget process, and some of my ideas made it into the legislation. Senator Ed Muskie (D-ME) was named chair of the Senate Budget Committee, and he ran a search committee that held hearings to find a CBO director. The search committee selected me for the job, but that was not the end of it.

The House Budget Committee, chaired by Representative Al Ullman (D-OR), conducted its own search and selected the deputy controller general, Phillip "Sam" Hughes, to be the CBO director. I knew Hughes, and he would have been great in the job. So now, the House had a candidate and the Senate had a candidate, but there was no process to decide between the two of us. The standoff took months, but then fate lent a hand in the form of a drunk-driving congressman and an exotic dancer named Fanne Foxe.

Remember Wilbur Mills, who was chair of the House Ways and Means Committee, from earlier in this chapter? He was often referred to as the most powerful man in Washington, but the power went to his head, and we can assume so did quite a lot of alcohol. In a well-publicized scandal, he was pulled over by the US Park Police (the police force that patrols the national monuments and national parks in the heart of Washington) beside the Tidal Basin, and Ms. Foxe tried to flee the scene by jumping in the water. The incident cost Mills his committee chair, and Al Ullman was named to replace him on Ways and Means. Representative Brock Adams (D-WA) replaced Ullman as chair of the House Budget Committee, and since he did not care enough to continue the standoff with Muskie, I got the job as the first director of the CBO.

Muskie and Adams did something that is very unusual in Washington: They helped me isolate the CBO from political pressure. I was allowed to ignore calls from political leaders to hire their politically connected constituents, and just hire the most qualified experts in such areas as budget analysis and economic modeling. The CBO's goal was to estimate the budgetary cost of policy proposals five or ten years into the future, knowing it was impossible to get it exactly right. The policies were complex, and the future is unknowable, but after a few rocky missteps, the best estimates of unbiased, nonpartisan expert analysts proved to be valuable in moving the policy debates forward.

It did not help that this was a time when the national economy was frustrating for just about everyone. "Stagflation" was the name given to periods of slow growth (aka economic stagnation) amid high levels of inflation. The word would continue to return throughout the 1970s as first President Nixon and then Presidents Gerald Ford and Jimmy Carter had to deal with oil shocks caused when the emerging Organization of Petroleum Exporting Countries (OPEC) restricted the world's supply of oil, driving up the price and slowing the economy. The inflation rate was over 10 percent when Nixon resigned due to the Watergate scandal in 1974. Ford struggled with stagflation but was able to bring the inflation rate down in time for the 1976 election, which he nonetheless lost to Georgia governor and peanut farmer Jimmy Carter.[48]

Economists working for Ford and those working for Carter were facing an especially difficult challenge because there are no easy answers for an economy experiencing slow growth, high unemployment, and high inflation all at the same time. Keynesian economic theory, and its focus on fiscal policy, was locked in a debate with monetarist theory, most associated with Milton Friedman from the University of Chicago, and its focus on the supply of money as controlled by the Federal Reserve Board. Each theory had an answer for slow growth: loose fiscal policy (more government spending), from John Maynard Keynes, or loose monetary policy (lower interest rates), from Milton Friedman, to give the economy a boost, but both policies would make inflation worse. And each had an answer to high inflation: tight fiscal policy (less government spending) or tight monetary policy (higher interest rates), but both policies would drive up unemployment.

If at any given time you ask people, or the politicians who reflect their preferences, they will tell you looser is better than tighter when talking about monetary or fiscal policy. Unemployment is a severe hardship that compounds other problems in a family, including health, mental health, divorce, and children's education. Unemployment also hits the poor, women, minority, and immigrant communities more severely.

But if we always choose loose fiscal policy, in the form of lower taxes and higher government spending, the deficit will soar and eventually inflation will follow. Similarly, if we always choose loose monetary policy, in the form of larger money supplies and low interest rates, eventually inflation will hit unacceptable levels. These policies are popular in the short run but have long-term consequences that are undesirable and unsustainable. Inflation also harms families and is especially brutal to those with low or limited incomes, who struggle with rising costs for food, housing, and transportation, and to meet other basic needs. Because both unemployment and inflation cause hardship, but politicians generally are more inclined to support looser policies, the Federal Reserve evolved to be insulated from political pressure. And this is what Congress wanted to do for its fiscal policy planning, by insulating the CBO from politics.

Eventually, Federal Reserve Chair Paul Volker made a decision that was very politically unpopular, because it caused a lot of short-term economic pain starting in 1979 and accelerating through 1980, which was an election year. He and the Federal Open Market Committee he chaired tightened the money supply, driving interest rates to extraordinary levels, slowing the economy, and causing the unemployment rate to spike. The unemployment rate hit 10 percent once again and was much higher among specific groups including African Americans and Hispanic Americans. The deficit soared as tax receipts slowed, while spending for unemployment insurance and other supports increased. The pain of this decision would be felt immediately, but benefits would not arrive for several years, in the form of the ability to grow the economy back with a much lower inflation rate. All of this was bad news for President Carter, but he was facing a run of bad luck on many fronts.

Carter faced a second major OPEC embargo, and separately, there was a world food crisis that caused food prices to surge by nearly 10 percent in 1978 and 11 percent in 1979, so the economy was slowing but inflation was surging. Stagflation had returned, and Ronald Reagan, former California governor, actor, and Republican nominee for president, started using the term "misery index," which is the sum of the inflation and unemployment rates. And then in November 1979, almost exactly one year before the 1980 election, fifty-two American diplomats and citizens were taken hostage in Iran. In a self-imposed restriction to acknowledge the hostage crisis, Carter refused to leave the White House to campaign for reelection, choosing a "Rose Garden" campaign strategy, and Reagan easily won the presidency in 1980.

## THE DEMOCRATIC AND REPUBLICAN PARTIES SWAP CONSTITUENCIES ON RACE ISSUES

From the start of the 20th century to the Reagan Revolution in 1980, the political parties take shape as we know them today, with racial politics continuing to be at the center of the drama. Over the span of 100 years, the two parties had switched places geographically and on questions of racial inclusion versus segregation. The political parity between the two parties that held from the Gilded Age into the start of the century yielded to Democratic Party dominance following the Great Depression, only to return near the end of the century. But, as we have seen, the mid-century period of Democratic strength was based on an uncomfortable alliance of liberal Northern and conservative Southern Democrats, which proved unsustainable when the "Solid South" protested, and ultimately abandoned the Democratic Party over the issue of civil rights for African Americans. The nation's population and a measure of political power was moving westward, as California overtook New York to become the largest state at the start of the 1960s. Southern Democratic defenders of white privilege like South Carolina Senator Strom Thurmond eventually realigned with the 1964 presidential candidacy of the presidential candidate from Arizona, Barry Goldwater, and the "Southern strategy" of Californian President Richard Nixon. Another Californian, Ronald Reagan, also a Goldwater ally, would eventually help return the Grand Old Party (GOP) to parity with the Democrats in the 1980s.

CHAPTER 5

# THE BIPARTISAN BUDGET NEGOTIATIONS OF THE REAGAN-BUSH YEARS

During the eight years (1975–1983) that I served as the first director of the Congressional Budget Office, I interacted every day with members of the House and Senate and their staffs. I found Capitol Hill a fascinating and rewarding place for a policy analyst to work. Ideological differences between the parties were less sharply defined than they are now, and partisanship was less intense. Personal relationships among members, while sometimes tense, usually appeared friendly and collegial, especially in the Senate.

The political realignment of the South was well under way during this time, but the advantages of incumbency and committee seniority kept many conservative Southern Democrats in important positions of power in the Senate. Staunch segregationist James Eastland (D-MS) was chair of the Judiciary Committee; John Stennis (D-MS) was chair of Armed Services; and Russell Long (D-LA) was chair of the Finance Committee. Liberal Republicans like Edward Brooke (R-MA), John Chafee (R-RI), Jacob Javits (R-NY), Charles "Mac" Mathias (R-MD), and Mark Hatfield (R-OR) held influential positions. Within many Senate committees, Democrats and Republicans worked out their differences and brought bills to the floor with bipartisan support. The Senate Budget Committee, newly created by the Budget Reform

Act of 1974, started out under the leadership of its first chair, Ed Muskie (D-ME), and ranking member Henry Bellmon (R-OK), who were both proud of their close working relationship. Their solid bipartisan cooperation helped me create a strong tradition of nonpartisan analysis at the fledgling CBO.

In the House, relations between the two parties were more fraught. The Republicans had been the minority for a long time (and were to remain so until 1994). Resentment of their seemingly permanent underdog status sometimes made the House minority testy, but relations between the leadership of the two parties were remarkably cordial by contemporary standards. Congressman Bob Michel (R-IL), who was prominent in the Republican leadership for much of his long career, was liked and respected by Democratic leaders, and he frequently orchestrated bipartisan legislative compromises. In those years the House, like the Senate, had liberal Republicans who sometimes voted with the Democrats and Southern conservatives who remained Democrats but sometimes voted with Republicans. As detailed in chapter 10, the great ideological and geographical sorting of voters and their elected representatives into two camps, conservative Republicans and liberal Democrats, was just beginning to take shape.

## WHEN CAPITOL HILL WAS LESS DOMINATED BY PARTY

Members who served in Congress in the 1970s and 1980s still like to reminisce—and perhaps exaggerate—the cordial relations that existed between the parties in those years. Politicians talk about defending their different views vigorously in committees and on the floor but then socializing together at the gym or the bar. (Alcohol flowed freely on Capitol Hill then, and still does.) In those days, members tended to bring their families to Washington and return to their home state or district less frequently than they do now. The spouses got to know each other, kids played on the same soccer team, and informal interaction across party lines was normal, not exceptional. Hill staff also socialized and formed friendships across party lines more easily than they do now.

As CBO director, I was impressed, and sometimes overwhelmed, by the amount of time members spent discussing and debating policy issues. The legislative process—now nostalgically called "regular order"—was slow and inefficient. Bills moved from subcommittees to full committees to the floor and finally to a conference committee charged with finding a bill acceptable to both chambers. Bills were usually debated and amended at each stage. Before bringing a bill to the floor, the bill's sponsor had to get a rule governing the time and conditions for floor debate, but "open" rules allowing consideration of amendments were normal. Committee and subcommittee chairs exercised more power in those days than they do now that House and Senate leadership has taken a stronger role in steering legislation.

There were too many committees and subcommittees, with fragmented and often overlapping jurisdictions.[1] As a result, there were seemingly endless hearings. On budget-related matters, numerous committees and subcommittees wanted to hear from the CBO director as well as from executive departments and nongovernment witnesses. When Congress was in session, I was often called upon to testify several times a week on different subjects—occasionally twice or even three times in the same day. It was like exam week in college, cramming to get up to speed on energy policy, then moving on to national defense or health. Members' questions often reflected their partisan or ideological points of view, but they were generally polite and focused on the issue at hand. While I was often exhausted by the time-consuming inefficiency of these hearings, I realized that the members and their staffs (not to mention the CBO director) were learning a lot about policy issues from the process and the wide range of stakeholder views that were represented at hearings.

I was also surprised at the profound difference between the pragmatic, consensus-building leaders of the House and Senate that I worked with every day and the shrill partisan rhetoric they indulged in on the campaign trail.[2] The prime example was the change in Senator Bob Dole (R-KS) when he ran for president against Bill Clinton in 1996. By then I had known Dole for many decades as a giant of the Senate—sensible, businesslike, brokering compromises across the aisle, and willing to stand up to the Reagan administration "supply-siders" when they went too far claiming miraculous economic growth would follow from cutting taxes. But in his 1996 campaign, Dole embraced supply-side economics,[3] promising to cut taxes for families and investors in half.[4]

To be fair, I also knew Bob Dole as the senator who for years had consistently been working for compromise solutions to shore up the financing for Social Security and Medicare. But back in 1965, he had voted against the original Medicare bill, and so the Democratic National Committee ran devastating ads in 1996 designed to scare voters into believing Dole wanted to eliminate Medicare.[5] I was dismayed by the strident partisanship (on both sides) in the campaign, but after Clinton won the election, Dole went right back to the pragmatic Bob Dole I had always admired.[6]

To my surprise, the gulf between the House and the Senate was sometimes more evident than the gulf between the parties. The two chambers had different cultures and, often, limited communication with each other. In private conversations, many House members frequently disparaged senators as self-important grandstanders with superficial understanding of technical issues. In turn, senators would say that House members had narrow perspectives and did not get the "big picture." I remember House Budget Committee Chair Bob Giaimo (D-CT) once asking me to call Senate Budget Committee Chair Ed Muskie (D-ME) to explore what he was thinking about a budget issue. I wondered why Giaimo did not call himself, but then I realized I had stumbled on a House/Senate sensitivity about status.

## BUDGET DEFICITS DO MATTER, AND TAX CUTS NEARLY ALWAYS MAKE DEFICITS WORSE

The election of Ronald Reagan in 1980 ushered in a sea change dramatically changing American politics and economic policy debates. I say a lot about the change in political dynamics later in this chapter and then give the political scientists' broader perspective in chapter 10, but at the time I was deeply involved in the political debates. Like every new president, Reagan had campaigned on a political philosophy and set of promises that would be challenged by the realities of real-world policymaking, and as CBO director, I was often in the position of delivering the reality check message. Reagan had promised deep tax cuts, but his economic team embraced a then novel economic doctrine called "supply side economics" that convinced them that the budget deficit would not balloon out of control. Decades later the two political parties are still reckoning with the fact that this prediction proved false. In 2002, President George W. Bush's secretary of the treasury, Paul O'Neill, tried to warn then vice president Richard (Dick) Cheney about the danger that ballooning deficits posed to the economy, but Cheney demurred, saying, "You know, Paul, Reagan proved deficits don't matter."[7] I must say I disagree with Dick Cheney; deficits do matter, and

*Left to their own devices and knowing that they must remain popular*
*with voters to keep their jobs, politicians tend to spend more, tax less,*
*and pass the debt on to future politicians and taxpayers—and they*
*know it. They turn to budget technocrats to help keep themselves*
*honest and responsible. . . . [The Congressional Budget Office] has*
*become increasingly important in recent years for reasons that are*
*common to all advanced countries: the difficulty of making budget*
*decisions that balance the needs of an aging population with*
*opportunities for the young in the face of slower economic growth*
*and rising debts.*

> —Alice Rivlin, Keynote Address at
> the 9th Annual Meeting of OECD
> Parliamentary Budget Officials,
> Edinburgh, Scotland, April 6,
> 2017

that is exactly what the presidencies of Ronald Reagan and his vice president and successor, George H. W. Bush, proved.

Cheney was speaking from the perspective of politics, and I am speaking as an economist, and that may be the real source of the discrepancy. In my view, deficits do not matter as much as they should to voters, and the politicians who represent them, because the harm deficits cause is, most of the time, some years off in the predictable future. The most concerning danger of our current deficit and national debt is that we have made far too little accommodation for the aging of our population as the baby boomers pass through their retirement years.

The budget outlook for the United States over the next couple of decades is truly scary. If we do not change our current tax laws and federal spending policies, deficits will continue to grow, and we will have to borrow more and more each year. Obligations to our country's creditors will pile up faster than even optimists think our economy can grow. Interest owed on those obligations will displace essential government services the country relies on. Recent projections of the likely implications of current policy show national debt rising from about 78 percent of our gross domestic product (GDP), which is already extremely high, to about 106 percent in ten years.[8] The federal debt was this high during World War II, peaking at 119 percent of GDP in 1946, but the economy was growing and taxes were dramatically higher in the war years, and they stayed high until most of the war debt was paid down.[9] The difference now is that current policy has debt sustaining high levels as far into the future as the models project.

I have been sounding warnings about the danger posed by long-term deficits since the Reagan administration, when I was the director of the Congressional Budget Office (CBO). Before telling the history of the budget battles of the 1980s, allow me to lay out some basic facts, and define some important terms, about the national debt and deficits and why they should matter to all of us.

The federal budget sets targets for national revenues and spending, but the actual amounts are not known until the year is over. National revenues come from taxes, tariffs, fees, and other sources. The Internal Revenue Service (IRS) can make quite accurate estimates, but it does not know how much revenue is going to come in until it arrives (with tax forms where individuals and businesses must show the amount they owe).

The amount of spending is also an estimate. It is unknown because many programs are defined by law to be available to everyone (individuals or businesses) who fit certain criteria. Spending goes up automatically in a recession because more people qualify for benefits when they lose a job and drop below the income levels specified for each program. The programs that shrink and grow due to economic conditions are known as automatic stabilizers because they provide what is called countercyclical spending. Deficits always get bigger in a recession, but this is a good thing because it helps smooth out the business cycles by pumping more money into the economy when it needs it most.

When the government spends more than it takes in, it must borrow the difference by selling Treasury bills (T-bills), Treasury notes, and Treasury bonds.[10] There would be nothing wrong with the government running a deficit, even a large deficit, in a bad year if the government would then pay down the debt by running a budget surplus in the next good year. The problem now is that we are racking up huge deficits in good years and bad years, and worse, we have not been making plans to deal with the ticking timebomb of an aging population. The huge baby boom generation is now entering retirement, or close to it, and when the boomers retire, they stop paying taxes and start using Social Security and Medicare. We have known for a long time that this will make deficits a lot worse, and it is starting now.

The thing is, deficits do not matter until they do, and then the economy is in for some real trouble. As we have learned in recent decades, when there are sustained high deficits, there eventually will be a piper to be paid. The pain may arrive in the form of high interest rates or high inflation, or both at the same time because the two are related. As I write this, interest rates and inflation are both at very low levels, so some people on both the right and the left are saying our current deficits are not such a great concern. I do not disagree with this assessment of the deficits the government is running this year and next, and I have argued that the obsession of central bankers about future inflation may be an outdated concern, a "dragon" of the last century that we have already learned to vanquish. Since the global financial crisis of 2008–2009, the Federal Reserve and central bankers around the world have been more concerned about the danger of deflation than inflation, and they have been using low or very low interest rates (even negative interest rates, in some countries) to boost economic activity.

But this is not a permanent condition, and eventually interest rates and inflation will return to more normal levels. (Or if they do not return to normal, the economy will develop other problems, even if economists do not know exactly what would happen if the economy stayed abnormal for a sustained period.) It is the long-term deficits, projected over the decades when the

---

*Suppose that the major advanced economies actually face a new "normal," in which inflation is low on the list of threats. In this new world the top-of-the-list threats to prosperity in large, advanced economies are financial instability, slow growth with tendencies to deflation, and the concentration of income, wealth, and political power in the hands of a small number of people.*

—Alice M. Rivlin, "Thoughts About Monetary and Fiscal Policy in a Post-inflation World," remarks to the Economic Policy Conference, National Association for Business Economics, March 10, 2015

---

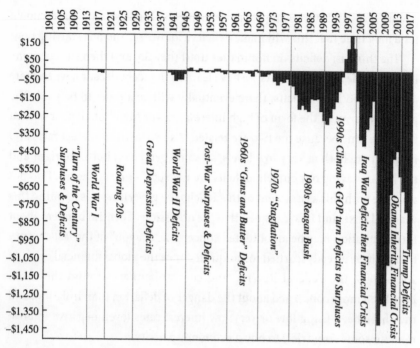

FIGURE 5-1.   US Federal Budget Surplus or Deficit (current dollars, in billions)
*Source:* White House, Office of Management and Budget Historical Tables.

baby boomers will be retiring, that are unacceptably likely to cause us problems. We will probably first notice the problem in the bond market. If people
begin to worry that the government is running up larger debts than the economy can grow out of, they will be unwilling to buy bonds at the Treasury auction and the price will fall, which means interest rates on the bonds will spike.

## SURPLUSES, DEFICITS, AND JOHN MAYNARD KEYNES

Historical tables from the Office of Management and Budget (OMB)[11]
show that America ran a net surplus from the time Alexander Hamilton set
up the first national bank through the middle of the 1800s, then ran surpluses and deficits netting out to less than $1 billion through 1900.[12] Sim-
ilarly, for the first sixteen years of the next century, the plus and minus
years netted out to a cumulative surplus of $66 billion. Then World War I
(1917–1919) was financed by $23 billion worth of debt, but when the war

was over, the government went back to small surpluses in each year for a decade—which all together added up to $3.4 billion in surpluses from 1920 to 1930. That is when the Great Depression hit, and the way we think about budget deficits changed.

The British economist John Maynard Keynes is famous for teaching the world not to obsess about balancing the budget. Keynesian economic theory tells us deficit spending can be the best medicine to stimulate a stalling economy with slack capacity and high levels of unemployment. The deficits run up during the Great Depression were very large compared with anything that had gone before, but they were seen as successful in helping the needy and in rebuilding consumer demand to get the national economy moving again. Those deficits were then far exceeded by the deficits created to pay and equip the troops in the field, air, and seas during World War II. Even as a percentage of the then rapidly growing national output (GDP), World War II produced a massive amount of government debt.

Figure 5-2, showing deficits and surpluses as a percentage of total output (GDP), is a better way of looking at deficits than figure 5-1, which shows deficits in dollars (not adjusted for inflation). When deficits are shown as a percentage of GDP, you can see that the World War II deficits were massive, and policymakers were very brave to run them. But these deficits were less of a concern because they were understood to be temporary, and after the war ended, the government ran a surplus in four out of the next five years

---

*In the period post-World War II, the US had run up a large debt in relation to the size of its economy. But we weren't in any kind of economic trouble because of the debt. We were growing rapidly, and we reduced the debt as a percent of the economy very rapidly. Not because we reduced the debt so much, but because we grew the economy. So, debt per se, until quite recently [starting in the 1980s], has not been a big economic concern.*

—Alice M. Rivlin, interview by
Martin Meeker with Patrick
Sharma, August 23, 2010, UC
Berkeley

---

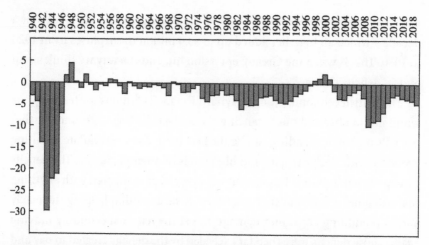

FIGURE 5-2.    US Federal Budget Surplus or Deficit (as percentage of GDP)
*Source:* White House. Office of Management and Budget Historical Tables.

and seven out of the next fourteen years through 1960 (although this was aided to a large degree by the agreement to move the Social Security Trust Fund and the US Postal Service "off budget" starting in 1937).

For the next thirty-seven years, from 1961 to 1997, the federal budget would only achieve balance one time: the last budget under President Lyndon Johnson for fiscal year 1969. For most of this period, politicians—especially Republicans when they were out of the White House and not in the majority in Congress—would complain that the deficits and the growing national debt were too high. But conservatives in the mold of Barry Goldwater and Ronald Reagan disliked taxes more than they disliked deficits, so they needed a new theory, and they received one in "supply-side economics."

## SUPPLY-SIDE ECONOMICS

The supply-side economic theory contains some insightful improvements to economic thought. However, the element that is most useful to its adherents but most destructive to nonbelievers is the promise that tax cuts could stimulate enough growth in the economy to offset the lost revenue. In other words, tax cuts would be self-financing, generating more new revenue through economic growth than the revenue lost from the tax cut. This is a great story, and one that influenced many people in the Reagan, G. H. W.

Bush, and G. W. Bush administrations, and now in the Donald Trump administration as well. If only it were true. Tax cuts have sometimes been followed by modest economic growth and sometimes by more rapid economic growth, but the tax cuts under Reagan, both Bushes, and the 2017 Trump tax plan have never come close to generating enough growth to offset the lost revenue, and deficits have continued to soar.

At the beginning of the Trump administration, Republicans—the party that had made such an issue of deficit spending when Barack Obama was president—chose to make the deficit outlook far worse. They enacted a huge tax cut, promising repeatedly that the tax cut would pay for itself,[13] but an analysis by the Tax Policy Center finds decisively that it did not.[14] We have developed a bad habit of cutting taxes in economic good times and then blaming countercyclical spending for the deficits that predictably arrive when the economy stumbles. We end up with a deficit that never decreases and tax rates that are too low, especially for Americans with the highest wealth and income. Each time we make this economic policy mistake, we hear the same false promise that the growth that follows the tax cuts will replace the lost revenue.

It is important to pay attention to the supply side as well as the demand side of the economic equation. The heart of Keynesian economics is the countercyclical government spending to maintain demand during an economic downturn. Our habit of cutting taxes whenever there is an upturn in the economy is what has been creating problems. Rather than tax cuts to assist the supply side of the economy, I support policies that increase needed investments, both public and private, in the conditions that lead to future productivity gains and broadly shared prosperity (as described in chapter 2). Government spending boosts demand, but investments in infrastructure, research and development, a well-educated and well-trained workforce, and public health lead to a more prosperous economy well into the future. This, in my opinion, is a better way to address the supply side of the economic equation.

## TWELVE YEARS OF DIVIDED GOVERNMENT AND TWO BIG BUDGET DEALS

From 1981 to 1992, Republicans held the White House while Democrats were in control of the House of Representatives and the Senate switched hands three times. Ronald Reagan served two terms and was followed by his vice president, George H. W. Bush. Throughout the Reagan years, there were many commentaries that Washington had become more contentious, coarser, and nastier than ever before, and political campaigns were becoming increasingly driven by negative attack ads. The political parties were divided from each other along partisan lines, and also internally divided, on big questions about the role and size of government, and appropriate levels of taxation and spending priorities. Nonetheless, the two sides were able to reach bipartisan agreement to move the public's agenda forward, most notoriously in two celebrated deals that strengthened the long-term fiscal stability of Social Security and reduced the nation's deficits and debt.

In his 1980 campaign for the presidency, Reagan railed against the federal government, saying in his campaign speeches and his first inaugural address, "Government is not the solution to our problem, government is the problem."[15] Reagan promised to cut income tax rates, boost military spending, and reduce domestic spending. Unfortunately, in a stagnant economy these policies fueled by the administration's wishful thinking about self-financing tax cuts and the growth effects of deregulation combined to create an unexpectedly expansionary fiscal policy that threatened to push the nation's finances deeper into the red.

The task of realizing Reagan's campaign promises fell to his new budget director, David Stockman, who put the new administration's budget proposal together with amazing speed. As CBO director, I had worked with Stockman when he was a congressional staffer and later a Republican representative from Michigan. I knew he was smart, conservative, and a workaholic dedicated to shrinking the domestic programs of the federal government.

To pass a budget, the Reagan administration needed to work with a long-held Democratic House and a newly Republican Senate. They employed a different strategy for each chamber to gain effective control of both. The parties were not as polarized or sorted as they are in the present, and the Democratic majority in the House disguised a potential center-right coalition of Republicans and Southern Democrats (known as the Boll Weevils, named after a beetle that infested southern cotton crops in the early twentieth century and was highly resistant to eradication).

The Reagan administration focused its negotiations to pass the budget through the House on the Boll Weevils and won their votes, joining House Republicans in overpowering the Speaker of the House, Thomas P. (Tip)

O'Neill, and Budget Committee Chair James Jones (D-OK). Boll Weevil Democrat Phil Gramm (D-TX) who would later change his party affiliation to Republican, paired with Delbert Latta (R-OK) to write a technically bipartisan alternative budget proposal to the one written by Jones and the Budget Committee. Their second version, given the name "Gramm Latta II," had enough support from Republicans and Boll Weevils to pass the House and become the basis for the final legislation.

The Republicans did not have enough votes to end a Senate filibuster,[16] so Stockman worked with Senate Budget Committee Chair Pete Domenici (R-NM) to use the reconciliation process outlined in the Congressional Budget and Impoundment Control Act of 1974 in a way it had not been used before. At the time, I had great respect for Domenici, and we would much later become close professional colleagues and co-chairs of the bipartisan Debt Reduction Task Force discussed in chapters 8 and 9. Stockman and Domenici's novel plan was to pass the entire Gramm-Latta II budget as one large Omnibus Budget Reconciliation Act.

Senate Democratic majority leader, Jim Wright (D-TX), and the rest of the Democrats had no opportunity to filibuster the Reagan Budget or any of the appropriations bills because once the Omnibus Budget Reconciliation Act passed the Senate and an identical bill passed the House and was signed by President Reagan, it became the law of the land. The Republicans had found a loophole in the 1974 Congressional Budget Act that allowed the majority to pass legislation using the reconciliation process sidestepping any possibility of a filibuster by the minority. Stockman used the same strategy to pass Reagan's tax cuts as the Economic Recovery Tax Act of 1981.

The rush to pass the budget bill was so great that no one proofread it, notes on sources of estimates were left in, and a CBO staffer was surprised to find her phone number printed in it by mistake. Democratic leadership in the House and Senate was caught by surprise and felt betrayed by the conservative Democrats. Jim Wright called out his protégé and fellow Texan, Phil Gramm saying, "Caesar had his Brutus, and I have my Phil Gramm."[17]

By the time the Reagan budget was approved by Congress, the tax cuts and spending increases had grown, but the spending cuts were left vague and noncommittal. Income tax rates would be cut across the board, with the top rate falling from 70 percent to 50 percent. The increase in military spending

*Probably the high point of my name recognition on streets and in airports was at the beginning of the Reagan administration. I was at that time director of the Congressional Budget Office and testified a great deal on the Reagan budget. We warned that the Reagan budget would create high deficits. We were right. But actually, we didn't know the half of it. The deficits were much worse than anything predicted by CBO.*

—Alice Rivlin, interview by David Levy for *The Region*, Federal Reserve Bank of Minneapolis, June 1, 1997

was much larger than even Budget Director Stockman had anticipated. Meanwhile, the budget assumed substantial cuts in domestic spending, but left them unspecified—a gambit that came to be known as the magic asterisk. Ultimately, Congress cut little from domestic programs while enacting the tax cuts and military spending increases. The administration's wishful thinking about Congress's willingness to cut popular domestic programs was one reason why the deficit grew suddenly in the early 1980s. Congress, it turned out, was not willing to make deep cuts in popular programs, and the Republicans had neither the ability nor the desire to force them to. Republicans had not even been willing to state what programs they wanted to cut nor how deeply. Those were the details hiding behind the magic asterisk.

Another example of the Reagan administration's wishful thinking producing budget deficits was visible in the administration's growth projections about the economic benefits of tax cuts, spending cuts, and deregulation, dubbed the "rosy scenario" by Democrats. Reagan was strongly influenced by the supply-side economist Arthur Laffer, who argued the growth effects would be so great that total revenue would not fall. The claim sounded too good to be true because it was.

No one in the Reagan economic team ever publicly espoused the extreme supply-side claims that tax cuts would pay for themselves, but the unrealistic projections for economic growth (and thus, lower deficits) illustrated

TABLE 5-1.    Administration and CBO Budget Projections, Fiscal Years 1981–1984 (in billions of dollars)

|  | 1981 | 1982 | 1983 | 1984 |
|---|---|---|---|---|
| *Outlays* | | | | |
| Administration | 655 | 695 | 732 | 770 |
| CBO Alternative | 662 | 721 | 766 | 818 |
| *Revenues* | | | | |
| Administration | 600 | 650 | 709 | 771 |
| CBO Alternative | 599 | 654 | 707 | 769 |
| *Surplus or Deficit(–)* | | | | |
| Administrative | –55 | –45 | –23 | 1 |
| CBO Alternative | –63 | –67 | –59 | –49 |
| *Actual deficits* | –79 | –128 | –208 | –185 |

*Source:* Alice M. Rivlin, CBO Director, in testimony before the Senate Budget Committee, March 31, 1981. *Actual deficits* added to chart taken from congressional testimony.

the supply-siders' influence. Likewise, the Reagan administration believed that cutting the "waste" in government programs, especially for "welfare," would greatly improve low-income Americans' incentives to work, further growing the American economy (and government revenues) via supply-side improvements.

Over at CBO, where I was in the middle of my second term as director, we were considerably less optimistic about the economy. Based on what we believed were more realistic economic assumptions, CBO projected higher deficits than predicted by the Reagan OMB. My testimony on behalf of CBO[18] received enormous press attention and cemented my reputation, not only as a deficit hawk, but also as an analyst willing to "speak truth to power." In fact, CBO and I got more credit for accurate forecasting than we deserved. Our estimate of the deficit was larger than the administration's estimates but not nearly large enough. For example, the administration had projected that deficits would decline and that by 1984 there would be a surplus of $1 billion. At CBO, we estimated the 1984 budget would have a deficit of $49 billion. But the actual 1984 deficit was $185 billion. The economy, which had been recovering from the recession of 1980, plunged into a deeper "double-dip" recession in 1982, due in large part to efforts by the Federal Reserve chair, Paul Volker, to stop inflation by dramatically raising interest rates. When the economy recovered, the "Reagan deficits" declined but did not disappear, and they dominated economic policy debates for more than a decade. The stock market crash of 1987 was widely, albeit somewhat dubiously, attributed to huge deficits, and the level of taxes and deficits were central issues in the presidential elections of 1988 and 1992.

This pattern—of Republicans proposing and often passing large tax cuts, large military spending increases, and large but unspecified cuts in nondefense domestic programs while expecting strong economic growth, leading to large and increasing budget deficits—would repeat itself several more times. The tax cuts happen, the military increases happen, but the growth does not happen, and the cuts in domestic programs are not made—and so, the red ink piles up. Republicans blame Democrats when the domestic spending cuts are not made, but this is not entirely fair.

The Republicans are not brave enough to specify which spending programs should be cut, and the Democrats know that the public does not support cutting specific programs. Government spending in general may be unpopular at times, but the public opposes specific cuts to programs like Social Security and Medicare, education, food safety inspections, national parks, veterans' benefits, and on and on until there is nothing in the entire domestic budget that the public will approve of cutting. If it were easy to specify unpopular government programs to cut, Republicans would do so, and David Stockman would not have needed his "magic asterisk."

Within a year of passing the budget for fiscal year 1982, policymakers and economists of both parties, myself included, were concerned that the United States was "living beyond its means" by accumulating public and private debts that future generations of Americans would have to deal with. Even the White House and both parties in Congress were realizing the tax cuts had gone too far. Bipartisan tax bills like the 1982 Tax Equity and Fiscal Responsibility Act and the 1984 Deficit Reduction Act reversed a substantial part of the revenue loss from Reagan's earlier cuts. Ronald Reagan is not generally thought of as a tax raiser, but he signed bills that raised income taxes, payroll taxes, gas taxes, a telephone excise tax, and taxes on distilled spirits and cigarettes, and eliminated business deductions in nearly every year of his presidency after the first one.

## RONALD REAGAN AND TIP O'NEILL
## "SAVE SOCIAL SECURITY"

The most celebrated of all the big bipartisan agreements was the 1983 deal reached between Ronald Reagan and Tip O'Neill to strengthen the long-term financing for Social Security. Reagan had campaigned against the New Deal and suggested Social Security should become a voluntary program. After beating Jimmy Carter to win the 1980 election, Reagan put those ideas into a 1981 proposal that was quickly shot down in Congress by lawmakers on both sides of the aisle. But actuaries and budget analysts like me were warning that the system for paying for Social Security was unsustainable.

Reagan created the National Commission for Social Security Reform, headed by Alan Greenspan (before he became chair of the Federal Reserve) and with members appointed by the president, Tip O'Neill, and Howard Baker (R-TN), the Senate majority leader. The commission floundered in the months leading up to the 1982 election, in part because Democrats were using Social Security as an issue to gain seats in the House, but after the election, Senators Daniel Patrick Moynihan (D-NY) and Bob Dole (R-KS) revived the stalled talks, engaging a "gang of five" senators to negotiate with the White House chief of staff, James Baker.

The breakthrough came when Democrats in the gang of five, who had been proposing increases in revenue to close the fiscal gap, started to privately float some reductions in outlays, which the Republicans were seeking. Together, they reached an agreement in principle that the gap would be filled by equal amounts of revenue increases and benefit reductions, and they evaluated dozens of proposals, seeking the least politically painful combination of changes to achieve the needed closure of the funding gap. Both sides knew that neither side could have done this alone, because the other side would beat them up in the next election for hiking the payroll tax or cutting grandma's Social Security benefits. They reached an agreement to all jump off the cliff together, with a package of Social Security changes under which Reagan and the Republicans and Tip O'Neill and the Democrats would share both the credit for "saving" the Social Security system and the blame for the unpopular benefit cuts and tax increases necessary to do it.

The final deal moved all federal government employees and members of Congress and their staffs into the Social Security system, delayed the scheduled cost-of-living adjustment (COLA) for six months, and indexed benefit increases to the lower of the change in wages or consumer prices. The deal raised the employer and employee shares of the payroll tax rate in stages spread out over fifteen years, from a little over 6 percent to 7.65 percent. It also raised the retirement age for full benefits by one month per year. (That meant a retiree in 2007 would have to wait until age 67 to get full benefits— two years longer than a retiree in 1983, when the deal was signed, who could retire at age 65.) The plan worked: the life of the Social Security Trust Fund was extended, and most people agreed that there was more credit than blame to share around.

## THE BYRD RULE REDEFINES THE BUDGET RECONCILIATION PROCESS

As we can see over and over, what happens in Congress is determined by (1) the Constitution, (2) the laws Congress passes, (3) the rules the majority party sets for the Senate and House, and (4) norms of behavior guiding how senators and congressional representatives choose to use their authorities under the Constitution, laws, and rules. The first two change only rarely; it is the other two that change from Congress to Congress. In 1985, the new norms in the Senate stretched the rules too far, so an influential Senator wrote and was able to pass a new Senate rule limiting the use of budget reconciliation.

In the fifth year with Reagan in the White House and Republicans holding a narrow majority in the Senate, the Republicans had raised to an art form the practice of sidestepping potential Democratic Senate filibusters by passing legislation through budget reconciliation. Even many Republican Senators were growing uncomfortable that a process intended to make it easier to pass budgets was being used to pass provisions that had little or nothing to do with taxing or spending. Senator Robert Byrd (D-WV) objected, citing 122 provisions in the reconciliation bill then under debate that he called "extraneous" to the budget and an "abuse of the budget process."[19] He persuaded the entire Senate to adopt his new rule by a voice vote without any objections.

The Byrd Rule (passed in 1985 and amended in 1990) added six conditions that must be met to qualify a bill for reconciliation. Among the conditions, a reconciliation bill must change outlays or revenue, it cannot touch Social Security, and it cannot add to the deficit longer than ten years into the future. However, even with these limitations, the congressional budget process has been upended by the unintended consequences of adding a reconciliation process to the 1974 Congressional Budget Act. The law was intended to aid Congress in the passage of 12 appropriations bills to fund the parts of the government under the jurisdiction of different committees, but over time, reconciliation bills have come to bear more of the weight of the legislative process because they could pass without any role for senators in the minority party.

## THE UNREWARDED COURAGE OF PRESIDENT GEORGE H. W. BUSH

The approach that led to the Social Security Amendments of 1983—a bipartisan commission followed by high-level negotiations and a legislative fast track—would serve as a model for Washington to address many difficult issues. These included reducing the number of military bases following the end of the Cold War; reorganizing the national security and intelligence agencies after September 11, 2001; and especially, efforts to reduce the deficit and national debt while paying for the government services and benefits the public expects and needs. Sometimes this led to success, and sometimes not so much.

There were several efforts to impose greater discipline on congressional budgeting in the late 1980s. In 1985, Congress legislated a complex set of budget rules, known as the Gramm-Rudman-Hollings Act (GRH), which had bipartisan support. (By this point, Phil Gramm was a conservative Republican from Texas; Warren Rudman was a moderate Republican from New Hampshire; and Fritz Hollings was a conservative Democrat from South Carolina.) The act required Congress to set a deficit target in the budget resolution. Exceeding the deficit target would trigger a proportional spending cut in many programs, a procedure given the ugly name of "sequestration" because it was intended to be an unpleasant "sword of Damocles" hanging over congressional budget policymakers to compel responsible behavior. However, sequestration proved ineffective in practice. When Congress made small cuts, the formula used to determine their magnitude was successfully challenged in court. The rules were rewritten to get around the challenge, but the real problem was that Congress was unwilling to invoke sequestration to punish itself for unexpected deficits that could not be attributed to congressional action—a deficit, after all, is the sum of many tax and spending decisions, plus changes in the economy. In practice, one very small sequester took place, but others were not enforced. After several years, budget policymakers realized that GRH embodied a worthy idea but did not provide a workable set of rules to achieve budget discipline. The idea of sequestration was not invoked again until the ill-fated Budget Control Act of 2011 and the "super committee" it set up, which failed to reach agreement on sufficient cuts to avoid the threatened sequester. In this episode, discussed in chapter 9, the sequester proved similarly unpleasant and ineffective.

George H. W. Bush, who served as president from 1989 to 1992, deserves more credit than he usually gets for the late 1990s surpluses. By working constructively with a Democratic Congress, not only did he reduce the deficit during his own term in office, but he also helped establish the "pay-as-you-go" (PAYGO) budget rules and discretionary spending caps that were instrumental in producing budget surpluses long after the elder President Bush departed from the White House.

By 1990, both the Bush administration and the Democrat-led Congress were concerned about the continuing deficits, but President Bush was strongly opposed to any solution that involved raising taxes. Republicans were growing increasingly adamant in their opposition to taxes, largely driven by the emergence of a movement founded and led by Grover Norquist. Called Americans for Tax Reform (ATR), this movement was designed to pressure Republican candidates into signing a pledge not to vote to raise taxes in any form. Norquist, an outspoken opponent of government, espoused the "starve the beast" idea that lower tax revenues would force policymakers to reduce spending. He is known for colorful anti-government statements such as his quip, "I'm not in favor of abolishing the government. I just want to shrink it down to the size where we can drown it in the bathtub." He joined supply-siders in fighting against high income tax and corporate tax rates, which he believed punished work effort and investment. His pledge combined both ideas by committing the signer to never vote for higher rates and to oppose all reductions of tax deductions and credits (also known as tax loopholes).[20] President

Bush had aligned himself with the spirit of the ATR pledge by making his own in accepting the Republican nomination at the 1988 Republican National Convention, using a popular expression to promise, "Read my lips: No new taxes." Although he had good reason to worry about deficits, he rightly perceived the high political cost of breaking this promise.

A year and a half after that speech, early in 1990, the size and trajectory of the deficit was alarming leaders in both parties, so Bush tasked his OMB director, Richard Darman, with engaging congressional leadership to orchestrate a bipartisan budget summit at Andrews Air Force Base. Several days of vigorous negotiation produced a deficit reduction agreement that included both tax increases and spending cuts, and that projected declining deficits over five years. To achieve agreement with the Democrats, President Bush reluctantly broke his promise by agreeing to an increase in the top bracket income tax rate, from 28 percent to 31 percent, and walked away from the capital gains tax cut he had advocated. He made a courageous decision that revealed how deeply he felt that big deficits posed economic risks and how well he understood that he would have to compromise with Democrats to reduce those risks.

Unfortunately for George H. W. Bush, the Gulf War and subsequent 1990–1991 recession sent deficits back up again, so he never got credit for his political courage and came to regret that he had broken his pledge on taxes. He faced a primary challenge from Republican commentator Pat Buchanan, who hammered the "read my lips, no new taxes" pledge,[21] and in the general election, Bill Clinton ran ads repeating the quote[22] to make the charge that Bush was unreliable and a tax raiser. At the same time, independent candidate H. Ross Perot made the growing deficits the centerpiece of the 30-minute and longer "infomercials" that defined his campaign.[23]

Bush's bipartisan budget summit and his decision to break his "no new taxes" promise may have cost him reelection, and they did not show any immediate success in lowering the deficit in the short term, but the effort made a crucial contribution to the eventual surpluses achieved during the presidency of Bill Clinton. The Budget Enforcement Act (BEA) of 1990 spelled out budget rules that worked much better than Gramm-Rudman-Hollings and helped achieve the surpluses by the end of the 1990s. The BEA imposed caps on discretionary spending, which Congress appropriates annually to fund a wide variety of federal activities, from the armed forces to national parks, federal prisons, and scientific research. Separate caps for domestic, military, and international programs specified annual dollar limits on discretionary spending. The BEA also specified PAYGO rules to keep Congress from adding to deficits by cutting taxes or adding to entitlement programs without offsetting the deficit impact with a tax increase or entitlement cut.

The enactment of those rules and their enforcement by both parties until they expired in 2002 proved essential to creating the budget surplus in the Clinton administration, as discussed in chapter 6. The spending caps and PAYGO requirements did not reduce aggregate discretionary spending, but they restrained increases at a time when strong growth in the economy was causing substantial increases in revenues. The Budget Enforcement Act required both parties to specify offsets for any new spending increase or revenue reduction that would otherwise add to the deficit. So even if the PAYGO rules and budget caps did not actually reduce deficits, they kept politicians from making the deficit bigger by cutting taxes, adding to entitlements, or adding to discretionary spending above an agreed-upon limit. Although George H. W. Bush lost the 1992 election to Bill Clinton, Bush's legacy helped

TABLE 5-2.  Federal Budget Outlays, 1991–2001

| Year | Discretionary Outlays | Mandatory Outlays* | Total Outlays | Total Receipts | Surplus or Deficit (−) |
|------|------|------|------|------|------|
| 1991 | 533.3 | 790.9 | 1,324.2 | 1,055.0 | −269.2 |
| 1992 | 533.8 | 847.7 | 1,381.5 | 1,091.2 | −290.3 |
| 1993 | 539.8 | 869.6 | 1,409.4 | 1,154.3 | −255.1 |
| 1994 | 541.3 | 920.4 | 1,461.8 | 1,258.6 | −203.2 |
| 1995 | 544.8 | 971.0 | 1,515.7 | 1,351.8 | −164.0 |
| 1996 | 532.7 | 1,027.8 | 1,560.5 | 1,453.1 | −107.4 |
| 1997 | 547.0 | 1,054.1 | 1,601.1 | 1,579.2 | −21.9 |
| 1998 | 552.0 | 1,100.5 | 1,652.5 | 1,721.7 | 69.3 |
| 1999 | 572.1 | 1,129.7 | 1,701.8 | 1,827.5 | 125.6 |
| 2000 | 614.6 | 1,174.3 | 1,789.0 | 2,025.2 | 236.2 |
| 2001 | 649.0 | 1,213.8 | 1,862.8 | 1,991.1 | 128.2 |

Source: White House, Office of Management and Budget Historical Tables, whitehouse.gov/omb /historical-tables/.

*In addition to Social Security, Medicare, and other "entitlement" programs, the Mandatory Outlays column includes net interest on the national debt.

the nation achieve a balanced budget—something that seemed unachievable throughout the dozen years Bush was in the White House as vice president and then president.

## TAKING A BROADER VIEW OF THE REAGAN-BUSH YEARS

In chapter 10, I bring in the voices and research of a lot of political scientists to try to gain insights into the causes of the polarization and hyperpartisanship we are currently experiencing. From that vantage point, the twelve years of the Reagan and Bush administrations stand out as the crossroads of so many of the major trends in American politics that it is difficult to extricate the contributions of each of the factors. Although there is even greater complexity when we get to chapter 10, allow me to draw attention to three major trends at the end of this chapter: 1) major party parity, 2) the Southern realignment, and 3) issue and ideological sorting.

1. **The arrival of major party parity:** Chapter 10 looks at the thesis of Francis Lee's 2016 book, *Insecure Majorities: Congress and the Perpetual Campaign*,[24] where she argues that the 1980 election was a major turning point in bringing the two parties to near parity. Democrats were the majority in both the Senate and the House from 1954 until 1980, and Lee posits that this changed the relationships between members. This would explain my experience of relatively cordial relations that I describe at the start of this chapter. Republicans were accustomed to being in the role of the minority and did not expect that to change with the next election, so they made accommodations to the majority party to gain influence over policy. This changed dramatically when Reagan won the White House, sweeping in a Republican Senate majority, and then the Republicans worked with the Boll Weevil conservative Southern Democrats to gain an effective majority in the House as well. Republicans would not gain actual control of the House until the 1994 election, but as that possibility drew closer, they became more confrontational and combative.

2. **The culmination of the Southern realignment:** When many of the Boll Weevils eventually switched their party affiliation from Democrat to Republican, often to seek higher office, they were joining

countless other politicians, mostly from Southern and rural states. Many Republicans in urban and suburban areas in New England and the Midwest switched in the other direction or were replaced by Democrats. A larger number of seats changed party hands through elections than party switching. Still, a very long list of Southern Democrats, including Strom Thurmond (SC) in 1964, Phil Gramm (TX) in 1983, and Richard Shelby (AL) in 1994, switched to the GOP as the flow gained added momentum in those periods. The list also includes New Yorker Donald Trump and Hoosier Mike Pence (IN). While there may be many reasons to align with the Republican Party—after all, many people support smaller government, lower taxes, and other Republican priorities—Democrats and many political scientists see racial politics as a prime driver of much of this realignment. Nixon's Southern strategy replaces George Wallace's overt appeals for the votes of racists, with subtler references to race in calls for law and order and against affirmative action. Examples of this include the Willie Horton ad,[25] made by a political action committee (PAC) supporting George H. W. Bush in the 1988 election (and Bush mentioned Horton many times in debates), and the "Hands" commercial for Jesse Helms[26] in his 1990 North Carolina Senate campaign, where he falsely charged his opponent, African American Democrat Harvey Gantt, with supporting racial hiring quotas. We examine these trends in greater depth in chapter 10.

3. **Issue and ideological sorting:** Chapter 10 also tries to bring coherence to many different aspects of the political sorting of voters and of political leaders into two political parties that are more distinct in 1992 than they were in 1980. At the start of the Reagan administration, there were many liberal Republicans and conservative Democrats. It was easy to name dozens of pro-choice Republicans and pro-life Democrats holding public office. There were many Republicans strongly associated with gun control and environmental issues, and many Democrats supporting gun owners' rights or representing coal country in West Virginia, Kentucky, and Pennsylvania.

By the end of the George H. W. Bush administration in 1992 and certainly by the end of the Clinton administration in 2000, nearly all elected Democrats were pro-choice, pro-environment, and anti-gun, and nearly all elected Republicans would take the other side of these issues. There may be many reasons for this, but at least part of the explanation was the evolution over the Reagan-Bush years of issue group strategies and tactics. Groups like Grover Norquist's Americans for Tax Reform put relatively little attention on trying to persuade Democrats to support lower taxes, instead working to define Republicans as supporting the maximalist position by signing the "no tax pledge." Other groups that were new or rising in prominence evolved strategies to define Republicanism as a commitment to conservative positions on a wide range of issues and to define Democrats by their adoption of purely liberal positions.

With President George H. W. Bush boxed in by interest groups opposing compromise on taxes, the Democratic challenger, Bill Clinton, defined his appeal around compromise by cofounding the Democratic Leadership Council, a group dedicated to developing moderate policy options. Democrats had lost three presidential elections in a row, and Clinton wanted to appeal to some of the voters who had left the party, who were collectively called Reagan Democrats. Even though Clinton won the election, the trend toward issue purity and polarization in both parties continued and accelerated.

Alice Rivlin shortly after being named the first director
of the Congressional Budget Office in 1975.

Author meeting for *Setting National Priorities: The 1974 Budget.*
From left to right: Edward R. Fried, Alice, Charles L. Schultze, and Nancy Teeters.

*Setting National Priorities* press conference, May 1983.
Alice, Charles Schultze, and George Perry.

Presidential candidate Bill Clinton reading *Reviving the American Dream*.

Alice briefing President Bill Clinton, Vice President Al Gore, and senior staff, 1993.

Director of the Office of Management and Budget Alice Rivlin walks with President Clinton's chief of staff, Leon Panetta, to a budget meeting on Capitol Hill. Clinton adviser George Stephanopolus trails.

RICHARD ELLIS / GETTY

Alice meeting with President Clinton in the Cabinet room at the White House.

RIVLIN FAMILY

Alice and Senator Pete Domenici in discussion at an
event at the Bipartisan Policy Center.

Speaker of the House Paul Ryan and Alice, 2010.

Secretary of State Hillary Clinton and Alice greeting
each other at a Brookings event in 2010.

Alice on one of her beloved trekking expeditions: Front Row: Sidney Winter, Alice, Donna Shalala, Second Row: Sarah Kovner, Betsy Levin, Jennifer Howse, Lin Butler.

A relaxed Alice on vacation in Vermont in 2004.

CHAPTER 6

# PRESIDENT CLINTON TAKES ON THE DEFICIT

President George H. W. Bush had to defend a struggling economy during his 1992 campaign for reelection against Bill Clinton. At the start of 1992, growth was slow and the deficit and, especially, future deficit projections were a leading national concern. Just eight years later, at the end of Bill Clinton's second term in office, the economy was roaring and the budget was more than balanced. As a nation, we were able to make important investments to make the economy more productive and put together four years of budget surpluses in a row.

This chapter and the next offer a personal telling of the story of the Clinton years, but from the perspective of bipartisan cooperation there is one central insight: Divided government may actually be helpful in achieving good policy. In the first two years, Democrats held the White House and both chambers of Congress but struggled while passing legislation that balanced necessary spending to strengthen the economy with the need for meaningful deficit reduction, in the face of Republican opposition and divisions among Democrats. The Republicans then swept into power, winning control of the Senate and the House in the 1994 election and bringing a level of partisan warfare not previously seen, but the peace treaty that followed two contentious government shutdowns gave rise to budget cooperation that allowed both sides to claim credit for the strong economy at the end of the 1990s.

## BILL CLINTON FORMS HIS ECONOMIC TEAM

Early in his first term, Ronald Reagan talked a lot about "new federalism," which was his plan to devolve more government responsibilities to the state governments. His critics correctly charged that this was largely just a plan to reduce federal spending by placing more burdens on the states. I actually believed there was something to the idea, but only if it was combined with a commitment to ensure there was enough revenue raised to fund the programs that the public relies upon and supports. I wrote my ideas for sorting out those responsibilities that are best handled by the federal government from those that are best addressed at the state level, in a book called *Reviving the American Dream*, which was published in May 1992. I stressed the importance of getting deficits under control and advocated for devolving major chunks of federal programs (such as housing and community development, elementary and secondary education, and most transportation) to the states, while enacting a national value-added tax (VAT) shared with the states in proportion to population.[1] I believed this plan would enable states and their localities to adapt public services to the needs of their citizens better than the federal government could; make it easier for voters to hold public officials accountable for services delivered; and reduce borrowing by

---

*I wrote a book called* Reviving the American Dream, *which is heavily focused on dividing the responsibilities between the federal government and the states in what then seemed to me a more sensible way. Bill Clinton was a governor, and he loved [my ideas]. He read that book, and as you know, when he reads something, he really reads it. So our first conversation—not our very first conversation, but our first conversation when he was interviewing me for the OMB job— related a lot to that subject. He kept coming back to it as [staffing for] the presidency progressed.*

—Alice M. Rivlin, interview for the
UVA Miller Center Presidential
Oral Histories Project,
December 13, 2002

---

giving both states and the federal government a dependable new source of revenue.

Bill Clinton was then the governor of Arkansas and a candidate for president, and he thought this was a terrific idea. Still thinking like a governor, he responded positively to my ideas for giving states more resources and autonomy. I knew that Clinton read *Reviving the American Dream* during his presidential campaign, because the *Washington Post* ran a picture of him reading it. I was an enthusiastic supporter of Bill Clinton in the 1992 election but not an active participant in his campaign, unless you count responding to a few late-evening phone calls from Gene Sperling, the economic strategist of the Clinton campaign. I had met Bill only once, when my friend Peter Edelman asked me to talk with him in 1987. We had spent an hour or so chatting about the economy. I was impressed with the charm and intelligence of the young governor of Arkansas, who asked insightful questions, listened intently, and had practical ideas about economic policy.

In November 1992, I was excited to find myself on the short list for director of the Office of Management and Budget (OMB) in the new administration. Not long after the election, I flew to Little Rock, Arkansas, for an interview with the president-elect at the governor's mansion. I was very nervous and eager to make a good impression. I was also unsure how high a priority the new president would give to deficit reduction—never an easy sell for a politician—and resolved to ask him. I did not have to. Clinton started the conversation by stressing how important it was to get the deficit down. If he failed to reduce borrowing, he thought it would be impossible to accomplish the other parts of his agenda. He made clear that he knew my reputation as a deficit hawk and considered it a plus. I was flattered that he wanted to talk about my book and amazed that he had evidently read it so carefully. On the way home, I thought of all the things I should have said.

Clinton did not initially pick me for the top job at OMB. He chose Leon Panetta, an able, eight-term member of Congress from California, who was then chair of the House Budget Committee. I was very disappointed but not surprised. Leon was a great choice. I had known and admired him for a long time, and worked with him on Capitol Hill when I was running the Congressional Budget Office (CBO). I knew he was smart, likeable, and totally dedicated to the public interest. A couple of days later, the president-elect asked me to be deputy director of OMB, making me a member of the "economic team," and I accepted.

With the election behind him, Clinton made it clear that his highest priorities were the economy and health care. He announced the economic team right away, with considerable fanfare, and told us he wanted us to produce a budget proposal that would reflect his priorities and bring deficits down. We were to get to work immediately, not wait for the inauguration or Senate confirmation. The Senate cooperated and held hearings on the economic team's nominations before the January 20 inauguration ceremonies so that we could be confirmed on day one of the new administration. The health team, including the new secretary of Health and Human Services (HHS), my talented friend Donna Shalala, was on a similarly fast track.

The economic team had impressive credentials. Besides Panetta and myself, the initial team included Clinton's nominee for secretary of the treasury, Lloyd Bentsen, and the deputy secretary, Roger Altman; Robert Rubin, soon to head the newly created National Economic Council (NEC); Laura D'Andrea Tyson, to be named chair of the Council of Economic Advisors (CEA); Alan Blinder, prospective CEA member; Robert Reich, designated the secretary of Labor; and Gene Sperling, who became one of Rubin's deputies. Like Panetta, Bentsen was coming from a powerful job on Capitol Hill. He had been the 1988 vice presidential nominee, had served as senator from Texas for more than twenty years, and was currently chair of the Senate Finance Committee. Reich was a Harvard professor and had known Bill Clinton since they were Rhodes scholars together at Oxford. Rubin and Altman came from successful Wall Street careers—Rubin at Goldman Sachs, where he had been cochair. Tyson and Blinder were well-known academic economists, whom I had known and respected for a long time.

To emphasize their commitment to improving the economy, Clinton and his vice president-elect, Al Gore, held a televised "economic summit" in Little Rock in December. More than 300 corporate, labor, community, and academic leaders interacted for two days with the president- and vice president-elect and the new economic team. Clinton and Gore led the conversations and showed off both their eagerness to improve the economy and their knowledge of the issues. Critics thought the summit was too talky and technical, but it was policy-wonk heaven—earnest conversations, on and off camera, about possible policies combined with new-administration optimism.

## DEMOCRATS GO IT ALONE: THE FIRST TWO CLINTON YEARS

It was not obvious on election night that the first big initiative of the newly elected Democratic president would be deficit reduction. Indeed, many of his supporters and campaign staff who helped him get elected were dismayed, and some were deeply disappointed, when he put deficit reduction first. On the campaign trail, Clinton's economic message had mostly blamed Bush for a weak economy, which was struggling out of a recession as the presidential campaign got into full swing in 1992. "It's the economy, stupid!" said the sign that chief strategist James Carville posted above his desk to answer the question, "What is the message of the campaign?" Most of the time, this meant turning attention to the shortcomings of the Bush economy, with its slow growth rate, high unemployment rate, and high interest rates.[2]

The Clinton campaign laid out its economic strategy in *Putting People First*, coauthored by Clinton and Gore but largely written by Gene Sperling. It advocated growing the middle class by rewarding work (with the earned income tax credit) and cutting middle-class taxes, and making the wealthy pay their fair share of taxes, curbing health costs, and moving to universal health coverage. There was a lot of emphasis on making investments for future growth, with major infrastructure modernization, new technology research and development (R&D), improvements to education, and worker training initiatives. Clinton saw himself as the champion of "people who work hard and play by the rules."

Bill Clinton was a leader of the moderate wing of the Democratic Party, who called themselves the New Democrats. They worked to bring working-class "Reagan Democrats" back into the party after Democrats Walter Mondale and Michael Dukakis lost the presidential elections in 1984 and 1988, respectively. The New Democrats thought the party had veered too far to the left to capture the votes of middle America. There was some emphasis on fiscal responsibility, as well as economic growth, and welfare reform ("ending welfare as we know it"), cracking down on crime ("putting 100,000 more cops on the street"), protecting the environment, and reducing government waste and bureaucracy.

There was a nod to deficit reduction in *Putting People First*, and on the campaign trail, Clinton promised that he would cut the deficit in half in four years. However, the issue was not front and center in his campaign. More-over, as is usually the case, campaign documents included some assumptions and numbers that would prove to be overly optimistic. The best example was the suggestion that enough savings could be squeezed out of health spending to allow expansion of coverage to the uninsured without additional cost. As the health care reform plans were being developed and analyzed by OMB, it soon became clear that this assertion was not realistic.

Why, many of Clinton's supporters were asking, would he prioritize deficit reduction? Understanding the answer to this question requires recapturing the political atmosphere of the early 1990s, when public concern about government debt and deficits was stronger than it is now. The Budget Enforcement Act of 1990 (BEA) was evidence of bipartisan commitment to responsible budgeting during the presidency of Clinton's predecessor, George H. W. Bush, and interest rates were much higher, which made servicing the debt much harder than it is now.

It was independent candidate H. Ross Perot, not Clinton or Bush, who focused on deficits and debt in the presidential campaign. Perot was a Texas billionaire who founded a data technology company (Electronic Data Systems, or EDS) in 1962 but had no prior experience in public office before running for president in 1992. His self-funded campaign used infomercials illustrated with colorful charts to talk about the dangers of deficit spending, the burden of growing debt, and jobs he predicted would be lost to Mexico due to the North American Free Trade Agreement (NAFTA) that Bush had negotiated and Clinton pledged to continue. "That giant sucking sound," Perot warned, was the jobs and dollars that would be sucked down to Mexico. He received almost 19 percent of the popular vote (more than a quarter of the votes in seven predominantly rural states) and, having proven his ability to communicate with voters about the importance of the federal budget deficit, NAFTA, and several other issues, he compelled Bush and Clinton to respond to those issues, lest his share of the vote expand. Although Clinton won a decisive victory over Bush (370 to 168 electoral votes and 44.9 million votes to Bush's 39.1 million), Perot's share of the three-way vote was enough to keep Clinton from winning a majority of the total popular vote.

The outgoing Bush administration's budget proposal showed larger deficits than it had previously reported. The deficit for fiscal year 1992, which had ended in September, was $290 billion or 4.5 percent of gross domestic product (GDP). Earlier Bush numbers, already deemed unrealistic during the campaign, had shown the deficit declining in the upcoming year, but that prospect was replaced by projections of substantially rising deficits if policies did not change. The new numbers gave the incoming administration an excuse for decrying the fiscal situation it had inherited and saying, in effect, "The deficit problem is even worse that we thought. We have to reduce it quickly." As a deficit hawk, I believed then, and now, it was an act of presidential leadership and political courage that made the late 1990s budget surpluses possible, but as the political folks feared, it also contributed to the Democrats' loss of congressional control in the 1994 midterm elections.

## SIX MONTHS OF WRANGLING FOR AN ECONOMIC BILL

Clinton made clear to his economic team that he wanted a budget proposal that reduced deficits, but there were differences within the group on how aggressive the goal should be and how fast we should try to achieve it. The economy was recovering from the recession of 1991, which had meant slow growth and sluggish job creation. In hindsight, we know the economy was picking up speed and generating more jobs by the end of 1992, but the economic team did not yet have evidence of that new strength as we began formulating the new administration's budget plan.

The economic team met with Clinton around his dining room table in the Arkansas governor's mansion in early January 1993. It was our first chance to talk through with the president-elect what the main outlines of his budget proposal should be. Gore participated actively (he and Clinton were operating very much as a team), and Hillary Clinton also joined the group. It was a long, talky meeting, with a lot of charts and graphs. We all understood that the goal was deficit reduction; the question was, how much and how soon. The deficit hawks argued for an aggressive deficit reduction target and a quick start, the "doves" for a slower start and a less ambitious goal. Tyson, Blinder, and Reich (the doves) were concerned that immediate spending cuts or tax increases would derail the fragile recovery, so they urged a more cautious plan. Panetta and I favored more aggressive deficit reduction and were supported by Gore, Bentsen, and Altman, who argued that an ambitious deficit reduction plan would impress the bond market and bring interest rates down quickly. Lower interest rates would not only encourage private investment, but also cut the cost of paying interest on the debt itself.

The budget talks continued for the next two and a half months, with meetings in Little Rock, Washington, Camp David, and eventually settling into the Roosevelt Room of the White House. In addition to Bill Clinton, Gore, and the economic team, the meetings often involved the communications and political teams, and the political consultants from the 1992 campaign, who continued to stress the need to direct our policy decisions and communications to helping middle-class American families.

I use the terms "hawks" and "doves" because we used them at the time. Bob Woodward, skilled veteran reporter at the *Washington Post*, plays up the conflicts as he details these discussions in his first book about the Clinton administration, *The Agenda: Inside the Clinton White House*.[3] Laura Tyson did an extended interview about her reflections on this period with WGBH for the PBS television show *Commanding Heights*, where she disputed Woodward's account, saying, "We weren't internally split. . . . If you actually look at the numbers involved here, it is impossible to make that case. We were basically disagreeing about $20 billion over five years."[4]

My personal recollection of the period is far closer to Tyson's view than Woodward's, especially within the economic team, where experienced and knowledgeable professionals discussed policy option details at a very high level in service of a president, vice president, and first lady who were intellectually curious and eager to hear from advisors with diverse points of view. Even when you expand the circle to include the top political and communications advisors and the political consultants (the full cast of characters in *The Agenda*: George Stephanopoulos, Sperling, Carville, Paul Begala, Mandy Grunwald, and Stan Greenberg, among others), there still was a common purpose and general agreement on the policies the administration should support. The disagreements were less over policy than over priorities and sequencing—not what the administration should try to accomplish, but when it should push for each goal.

There were more than two sides in this debate, and all sides had valid and valuable points of view. (Perhaps I understand this better now than I understood it at the time.) The doves cared about what was best for the American people. They, and especially the political consultants, believed in the message of the Clinton/Gore campaign—that the middle class had been working harder, playing by the rules that society expected of them, but not getting ahead because the costs they had to pay were going up faster than their paychecks. The doves believed in the promises Clinton made to help middle-class families, including a tax cut, public investments in education and job training, and, especially, increasing access to affordable health care.

But we deficit hawks also cared about what was best for the American people. We also wanted to keep the campaign promises. We supported the goals of health care reform and the investment agenda—infrastructure, job training, and R&D that would lead to better jobs in the future. We were perhaps more aware that the campaign promises had never added up budgetarily—you cannot cut taxes and increase spending on the middle class, and then extend health care coverage to millions of families without going into the red. And then when the Bush administration confessed to the level of deficits they had run up and projected into future years, we now had legitimate fears for the whole economy.

But we hawks also believed that the middle class would benefit a great deal from lower interest rates, which would make it much more affordable to buy a home, a car, or anything on a credit card, and this in turn would stimulate the economy. We believed a strong signal that the new administration planned deficit reduction would lead private investors, foreign investors, and the Federal Reserve to lower interest rates.

Lower rates can also stimulate private investment that spurs future productivity by building new production plants or investing in R&D for future technological breakthroughs. We did not know this would happen, but we hoped it would—and in hindsight, it looks like a lot of it did happen. The rise of the internet is a terrific example of a public/private partnership:[5] Government R&D at the Pentagon's Defense Advanced Research Projects Agency (DARPA) created the internet, university researchers adapted it for civilian use, and private investment made it remarkably valuable to all of our lives. And the dot-com boom was fueled by the low interest rates of the 1990s. We did know low interest rates were better than the alternative of rising interest rates, higher deficits, and a slower-growing economy, which would really hurt the middle class. The American people had just lived through high interest rates in the 1980s and did not like them.[6]

Clinton's budgeters worried that high deficits, interest rates, and inflation could form a feedback loop that could spin out of control. Most, although not all, economists believe high deficits, also called loose fiscal policy, can cause interest rates and inflation to increase. High interest rates add to the deficit because they raise the cost of borrowing. If deficits and interest rates kept reinforcing each other, the cost of servicing the debt would crowd out other needed spending. We could soon reach a point at which it would be necessary to raise taxes or cut spending just to pay interest on the growing debt. Some less developed countries had experienced just such a self-perpetuating cycle of exploding debt; we could not let that happen to the United States.

Throughout this period, President Clinton was torn between two impulses and was searching for a synthesis. He wanted to keep his campaign promises and especially his agenda of investing in the middle class, but he was also committed to deficit reduction. Clinton saw merit in both sets of arguments he was hearing, and early in the discussions, he offered a

---

*Bentsen and Altman were convinced that deficit reduction would be good for the markets and would bring the interest rates down, and that the interest rate stimulus would offset any negative fiscal effect, but Blinder and Tyson were not so convinced of that. What we decided on was, "Okay, we do this deficit reduction package, which reduces the deficit over four years, but we also want to do some investment in some of the things that the President had talked about in the campaign." By then I think we realized we couldn't have a major infrastructure package. It was just too expensive. But we had some infrastructure—there were some roads and bridges in there. But mostly it was human resource investment. Investment became a term for anything good we wanted to do. These were plausible things in workforce development, education, health services, and so we put together this deficit reduction package on the one hand and this short-run stimulus, which was bringing forward into the summer of '93 some of the things that we would have been spending in the next fiscal year. That was the answer to the question, "How do you know you won't tank the economy with this deficit reduction?"*

—Alice M. Rivlin, interview for the
UVA Miller Center Presidential
Oral Histories Project, December
13, 2002

---

compromise that he hoped would appeal to both hawks and doves. We would announce an aggressive target and propose a large deficit reduction package for fiscal year 1994, which would begin on October 1, 1993. Simultaneously, we would ask Congress for a small but immediate "stimulus package" that would increase domestic spending in the current fiscal year (1993). The hope was that the stimulus money would create additional jobs and give the recovery enough momentum to offset any negative impact of the coming deficit reduction. We continued to work on both packages, although there were further robust discussions about how large each should be.

## FINDING REAL MONEY A FEW BILLION DOLLARS AT A TIME

"Cutting the deficit will reduce interest rates" was a prominent theme of Clinton economic policy. Although the national debt was far smaller in relation to the size of the economy than it is today, interest rates at the time were so much higher that servicing the debt was a bigger burden than it is now. Debt held by the public at the end of fiscal year 1992 was 47 percent of GDP compared with 77 percent at the end of fiscal year 2018.[7] But net interest paid by the government in fiscal year 1992 was 14.4 percent of total outlays and 3.1 of GDP, compared with only 7.9 percent of outlays and 1.6 percent of GDP in fiscal year 2018.[8]

At one point, I remember Clinton was irritated at the idea that impressing bond investors with the seriousness of our commitment to deficit reduction was key to getting interest rates down. Bentsen pointed out that it was already working. He had stressed the Clinton administration's commitment to deficit reduction in an appearance on *Meet the Press* on the Sunday after the inauguration, and that was followed by a decline in the thirty-year Treasury bond rate the next day.[9]

This heavy focus on interest rates in the bond market prompted the much-quoted James Carville quip, "I used to think if there was reincarnation, I wanted to come back as the President, or the Pope, or a .400 baseball hitter. But now I want to come back as the bond market. You can intimidate everybody."[10] In fact, the bond market responded even before the Clinton deficit reduction plan was ready for prime time. Interest rates, which had been rising during the campaign period, began dropping immediately after

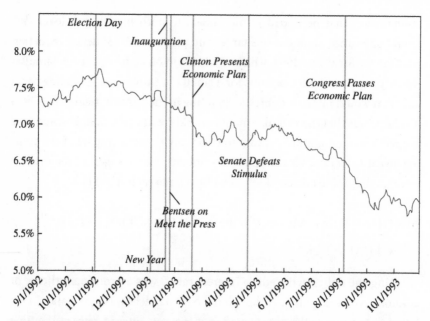

FIGURE 6-1.    Thirty-Year Treasury Interest Rates, 1992–1993
*Source:* US Department of the Treasury, "Daily Treasury Yield Curve Rates" for 1992 and 1993,
treasury.gov/resource-center/data-chart-center/interest-rates/Pages/TextView.aspx?data
=yieldYear&year=1993.

the election and kept falling as the deficit reduction proposals were sent to Congress and eventually became law.

Deficit reduction plans always aim for an impressive total to show serious intent ("Look how big this is!"). Clinton's proposal for almost $500 billion in deficit reduction over five years met this test. A reasonable person might wonder why a $500 billion package was needed to cut a $290 billion deficit in half. The answer is that $500 billion is a five-year total of the amount of deficit reduction and half of the roughly $1 trillion in deficits projected over the next five years. This is a useful way to think about deficit reduction but not always clear to people unfamiliar with the conventions of budget arithmetic.

The hard work, of course, was figuring out exactly which spending to cut, which taxes to raise, and how to get the package through Congress. Both President Clinton and Vice President Gore were personally engaged at every stage of developing this detailed policy. The budget decision process unfolded in a marathon series of meetings—more than fifty hours in all—which were held in the Roosevelt Room and in which both Clinton and Gore were active participants.

The meetings were scheduled for the late afternoon when the president had finished his day's schedule and before his evening schedule began. Staying on schedule was not a Clinton strong point. The meetings often started late and stretched past a normal dinner hour. Late afternoon is my low-energy time of day, so I was tired and hungry by the time the serious work started. I was not alone. When plates of cookies and fruit appeared, cabinet officers grabbed for them like hungry toddlers.

In the Roosevelt Room meetings, we went through much of the huge federal budget line by line, trying to identify potential savings and revenue sources. We talked about hundreds of specific federal activities in excruciating detail—fighter planes and Navy ships, prisons, national parks, vocational education, student loans, and all the rest. There were some comic moments. At one point, in a discussion of whether boat owners should pay for Coast Guard rescues at sea, Clinton convulsed the group by pretending to be a drowning yachtsman desperately waving his credit card to attract the Coast Guard.

Clinton was impressively knowledgeable about the federal programs—food stamps, school lunch, Medicaid, crop subsidies—that affected poor, rural states like Arkansas. Gore was in his element when we turned to the environment and scientific research. Both men relished the wonky policy talk and were reluctant to cut it off. Clinton was terrible at imposing discipline on the discussions and often let them wander on too long. In the early meetings in Little Rock, Hillary Clinton sometimes reminded her husband to move to the next topic. After the inauguration, she dropped out of the budget meetings to focus on health care reform, and Bob Rubin assumed the role of disciplinarian, not always successfully.

Bill Clinton did not initially know much about the congressional budget process or rules like discretionary spending caps or pay-as-you-go (PAYGO).[11] At one point he asked, rather incredulously, whether we had to pay attention to the spending caps. Someone explained that the caps were in current law; we could propose changing them, but we could not ignore them. This was the moment I foreshadowed in chapter 5, where George H. W. Bush exercised real leadership in calling a bipartisan economic summit that led to passage of the Budget Enforcement Act. The effects of these actions would continue to force fiscal discipline on government spending into the Clinton administration. The BEA was the law, and we had to fit our plans into its discretionary spending caps and PAYGO requirements.

We discussed policy changes from two angles: Is it a good idea? And could we get the votes in Congress? With every spending program in the federal budget, there are people who benefit from it or, sometimes, depend on it for a livelihood. We knew that the deficit reduction package would be accepted as fair if it spread the pain broadly by making many small federal program cuts that affect all sectors of the economy rather than a few big ones. Hence, we frequently weighed whether the budget savings from reducing or eliminating a small program were worth arousing the ire of a vocal group of beneficiaries. To show that we were not exempting agriculture from the shared pain, we decided to cut subsidies for producers of honey, wool, and mohair. The cuts were sustained by votes in the Democratic-controlled Senate and House and signed by President Clinton,[12] but they did not last long. The programs crept back into the appropriations in future years when budget-cutting zeal had dissipated.

Political considerations came to the fore clearly when the agenda turned to the revenue side of the budget. Gore and others (including me) thought that a fossil fuels tax would serve the double purpose of cutting carbon emissions ($CO_2$) and reducing the deficit. Treasury Secretary Bentsen agreed to a broad-based energy tax, which was remarkable for a former Texas senator. Unfortunately, someone described it as a "BTU tax," after the British Thermal Unit used to measure heat from fuel consumption. The foreign-sounding term was a messaging liability, but the message would have been unpopular in any case. A storm of protest from energy producers and consumers forced us to retreat to a gas tax increase of a mere 4.3 cents a gallon. Even that small a gas tax increase proved extremely controversial, especially in rural America, where people must routinely drive long distances. The increase did pass, but no federal gas tax has been enacted since.

The revenue side of the Clinton deficit reduction package relied heavily on income tax rate increases on high-income taxpayers. The top bracket rate was 31 percent after George H. W. Bush's courageous broken promise. The Clinton plan added two more brackets for even higher incomes—36 percent for incomes over $115,000 and 39.6 percent for incomes over $250,000. It also took the cap off the 2.3 percent payroll tax for Medicare, which was an additional marginal tax rate increase for affluent taxpayers. Combined with a corporate rate increase, increasing the portion of Social Security subject to income tax, raising the rates of the Alternative Minimum Tax, and a more generous Earned Income Tax Credit (EITC), the Clinton package made the tax code substantially more progressive.[13]

At the outset, I hoped we could put together a budget that at least some Republicans could support. Most Republicans had at least rhetorically opposed deficit spending, and Clinton called himself a centrist Democrat with views that were not radically different from centrist Republicans. I hoped he could put together a centrist coalition in favor of fiscal responsibility. Bentsen and Panetta had both worked successfully across the aisle, and I had good relations with many members in both parties when I directed the CBO. But the plan's reliance on income tax rate increases for the affluent doomed hopes for bipartisan support.

Republicans were not about to vote for any plan that so boldly contradicted Grover Norquist's "no tax pledge," and the lesson widely drawn from George H. W. Bush's recent defeat was that it was political suicide for Republicans to espouse any tax increases. Republicans were talking a good game on reducing deficits and had featured a balanced budget amendment (a requirement that government spending not exceed government receipts in any fiscal year)[14] in their "Contract with America," the list of ten policies nearly all Republican candidates had promised to address should they win the House majority.

On the other hand, even though the tax hurdle was too high to garner even a single Republican vote for the deficit reduction package, when the economy began to grow rapidly in the second half of the 1990s (in defiance of the supply-side economists' predictions) and the stock market roared ahead, taxes on the income and capital gains of the affluent added substantially to the revenue increases that produced the surpluses. From a deficit reduction point of view, we had chosen the right mix of taxes to increase.

As I noted earlier, the White House that I knew, including the Old Executive Office Building (OEOB) where OMB and many other executive staffers worked, was characterized by high-level policy discussions, but I do not want to suggest that there never was heard a discouraging word in months of negotiations over the administration's priorities. I was most aware of this in the middle of February 1993, when we finished putting together the deficit reduction package that was to accompany President Clinton's speech to a joint session of Congress on February 18. Since OMB had the job of making sure the numbers were defensible and writing the slim document that described the plan, I oversaw the write-up and drew the task of briefing the White House staff before the document's release.

I walked into a roomful of angry faces. The atmosphere was hostile, and I got an earful of criticism, although by this time it was too late for more than minor editorial changes. I understood why they were upset. They had worked their tails off to get Clinton elected. Some of them had had a big hand in influencing the campaign message and strategy. At campaign stops across America, others had made sure the mikes worked; arranged transportation, food, and lodging; dealt with security, the press, and local politicians; and sometimes, schmoozed with the candidate. Clinton had depended on them to make it to the White House, but suddenly they were left out. A group of older folks had taken over and, they feared, was leading their candidate, now president of the United States, toward disaster.[15]

On February 18, not quite a month after his inauguration, the president made an upbeat speech to a joint session of Congress, announcing his budget proposal including the stimulus plan. According to our estimates, $255 billion of the $500 billion deficit reduction package would come from spending cuts and the rest from tax increases. A friend who saw me on television in the House gallery as the president spoke said, "You looked exhausted." We all were. Federal Reserve Chairman Alan Greenspan was also in the gallery, in the place of honor between Hillary Clinton and the vice president's wife, Tipper Gore. His presence symbolized his implicit agreement not to let the Fed sabotage our efforts by raising interest rates.

## THE STIMULUS PACKAGE GOES DOWN TO DEFEAT

When the stimulus package was released, it drew far more opposition than we anticipated, with Republicans seizing on tiny programs to ridicule the package as a slush fund. At the time, I thought we had made a mistake by allowing members of Congress to add funding for local projects, in a process the press and the opposition described as hanging ornaments on the Christmas tree. One of the ornaments was "Midnight Basketball," a project to keep at-risk youth out of trouble through organized evening sports.

Midnight Basketball was the ultimate example of a successful local initiative. It was started by G. Van Standifer, who was the town manager of Glenarden, Maryland, a high-crime suburb of Washington, DC, in Democratic

Representative Steny Hoyer's district. The program was created to give at-risk youth an alternative to unsupervised life on the streets during the height of the crack cocaine epidemic.[16] Midnight Basketball had spread to New York, Philadelphia, Chicago, and many other urban areas, with strong backing from law enforcement and George H. W. Bush's Points of Light Foundation. The program was not a silly idea, but it was made to sound so in the hands of Rush Limbaugh on the radio and Newt Gingrich in Congress.

We did not fully realize it at the time, but the stimulus package had run into a newly developing form of partisan warfare that we dissect in chapter 10. After a few weeks of rhetorical attacks on the stimulus package, with many references to "pork" and Midnight Basketball, the stimulus package went down to defeat in a Senate filibuster.[17] The Republicans had launched an effective attack, but there had also been no small amount of behind-the-scenes resistance from moderate Democrats like David Boren (D-OK) and Bob Kerrey (D-NE), whose focus was on the deficit. They challenged the rationale for stimulus as the economy continued to strengthen and interest rates were dropping.

The demise of the stimulus package did not mean the deficit hawks had won out over the doves. We all continued to fight for Clinton's investment initiatives, many of which were moved to the deficit reduction plan (which included the EITC, empowerment zones, student loan reform, and childhood immunizations) or were picked up by Congress as the budget process moved forward. Midnight Basketball was revived in the 1994 Crime Bill, which Clinton signed into law, and which again drew fire from the opposition, especially in ads run by the National Rifle Association (NRA) that clearly wanted the conversation to be about pork, not about guns. By the end of Clinton's two terms, his administration had racked up an impressive record of accomplishments on worker training, community development, technology research, and other investments in the future growth of the economy.[18]

## Now We Had to Pass the Economic Plan through Congress

Throughout the spring of 1993, we were moving forward with the stimulus plan and the deficit reduction package at the same time. When the stimulus failed, all the effort went toward moving the deficit reduction package through the budget process. We certainly could not allow a second effort to fail, so now our job was to persuade Congress to translate the deficit reduction proposal into a budget resolution and, subsequently, into appropriations and tax laws. Without any Republican support, we could not afford to lose many Democrats. The president had to make deals and twist arms to get the last few votes. When the package finally came to a vote in August, it passed by one vote in the House and by one vote in the Senate using reconciliation (as many of Reagan's budgets had), with Vice President Gore breaking the tie.

Even though Democrats were eager to support the first Democrat in the White House since Jimmy Carter's loss to Ronald Reagan twelve years earlier, many congressional Democrats found our deficit reduction package hard to swallow. They rightly perceived political risks in voting for tax increases and for cuts in spending in programs that were important to their constituents.

Some conservative Democrats worried that our proposal did not do enough to reduce the growth rate of "entitlement" spending. They realized that the increase in Social Security and Medicare spending would accelerate as the boomers retired and would exacerbate the debt problem. These Democrats believed that a serious attempt to deal with long-term deficits and debt would have to include programmatic policy changes, or what politicians call entitlement reform, and that postponing action would make the problem harder. They were right, of course, and Clinton fully understood the argument. But on this point, the economic team agreed with the political advisors. Taking on the big entitlements in a major way right out of the box was way too politically risky. We would have to leave major entitlement reform for later.

Bob Kerrey (D-NE) was the last holdout vote in the Senate. Before he agreed to vote for the Clinton deficit reduction package, Kerrey extracted a promise that the president would appoint a commission on entitlements. The Bipartisan Commission on Entitlement and Tax Reform, cochaired by Senator Kerrey and Senator John Danforth (R-MO), was thereby created by executive order in November 1993. The commission would issue an excellent interim report describing the impact of projected entitlement growth on the budget and the economy, but the group never reached consensus on policy recommendations.

In the House, Marjorie Margolies-Mezvinsky, a first-term Democratic representative from suburban Philadelphia, was also concerned the Clinton package did not tackle the projected growth rate of entitlement spending. She got the president to promise to give a speech on entitlements in her district. Some months later, I worked with a White House writer on the speech and accompanied the president when he delivered it at my alma mater, Bryn Mawr College, which was on the border of Marjorie's district. Having won the support of Kerrey and Margolies-Mezvinsky, the budget passed both the House and Senate, and the Omnibus Budget Reconciliation Act of 1993 was signed into law by the president in August of that year.

The representative, known as MMM, had won a district that was previously represented by a Republican for twenty-four years. Politically speaking, she was right to be worried about voting for the Clinton package, with its tax increases and no changes to entitlement policy. She was taunted by Republican colleagues as she cast her vote, and MMM later lost her seat in the midterm election of 1994. Margolies-Mezvinsky was one of many Democrats to lose that year.[19]

Some Democrats, especially those new to the House (many of whom had come in by winning long-held Republican held seats on the coattails of the moderate Democratic president), continued to push for more aggressive spending cuts. A bipartisan bill sponsored by Representatives Tim Penny (D-MN) and John Kasich (R-OH), which would have added $90 billion of additional spending cuts to the package, had considerable Democratic support. Clinton and the House leadership opposed it, winning by the narrow margin of 219–213, but the president had to promise to make additional spending cuts before the end of the year.

A year later, when the books were closed on fiscal year 1994, the president was able to crow about a two-year deficit reduction from $290 billion in fiscal year 1992, the last Bush year, to $203 in fiscal year 1994. The president had shown political courage and won the initial battle for fiscal responsibility. But the Clinton budget plan contributed to the Democrats' loss of control of Congress only two years into the new administration.[20] Republicans, of course, denied that Clinton had much to do with the deficit falling. Senator Pete Domenici (R-NM) wrote an op-ed that said most of the credit went to the discretionary spending caps inherited from the G. H. W. Bush era, the improving economy, and lower interest rates, and only a small amount to the Clinton tax rate increases and user fees. I replied that our team's budget helped the economy and lowered interest rates.

Senator Domenici was right, of course, that continuing to enforce the Budget Enforcement Act caps was a key contributor to lower deficits, and

*[What] made it easier for the Clinton administration to work on the budget deficit . . . was that we inherited from President Bush (senior) the budget rules which had been put together in 1990. . . . Basically two: One was caps on discretionary spending, the spending that Congress votes every year.*

*And the other was an even more helpful rule, which was called the PAYGO rule: pay-as-you-go. That said, essentially, that you couldn't do a tax cut or a benefit increase under an entitlement program like Medicare or Social Security unless you had an equal and opposite proposal so it would not affect the deficit over the next five or ten years.*

—Alice Rivlin, "Debt and the Clinton Years," interview with WBGH for the PBS program *Frontline: Ten Trillion and Counting,* 2009

the Clinton team was increasingly aware of how severe the caps were as we put together our second budget for fiscal year 1995. Freezing discretionary spending without allowing for inflation was hard enough, but we had to find cuts below that level to allow for at least some of the increases in job training, early childhood development, environmental programs, and other investments that Clinton was determined to make. Clinton cabinet members (Shalala at HHS, Richard Riley at Education, Reich at Labor, and others) were unhappy with OMB for not allowing room for more investments. The budget proposal we sent to the Hill for 1995 had cuts that many Democrats opposed, such as eliminating federal subsidies for mass transit operations. By the end of fiscal year 1995, the budget deficit would be down to $164 billion, within easy striking distance of Clinton's original goal, but by then we had plunged into the new world of divided government.[21]

## THE RIVLIN MEMO INCIDENT

A controversy in October 1994 illustrates the stresses of budget politics as the midterm elections approached. Sometime in the late summer, Bob Rubin and I decided it would be a good idea to prepare the president to think about

*Bob [Rubin] thought, rightly, that when we got past the election, the president should take a longer view. It was all very well to shut up about the entitlement programs and Medicare and so forth before the election because the political guys were saying, "You can't do more Medicare cuts, you can't do anything long run. You can't touch Social Security. You'll kill yourselves in the election." And we agreed with that. But then Bob said, "After the dust settles on this election [which we didn't expect to lose], we've got to get the president focused on the longer run, so why don't we give him some idea of how the longer-run budget picture looks and what's going to have to be done. Balancing the budget can't just be done on the discretionary side. It's got to involve entitlement programs, and we've got to give him the big picture." So I volunteered to pull together a memo, which was not a surprising thing for a budget director to do.*

—Alice M. Rivlin, interview for the
UVA Miller Center Presidential
Oral Histories Project, December
13, 2002

a post-election budget strategy that would move beyond the 1993 deficit reduction package. Current projections showed that if policies did not change, moderate deficits were likely to persist until about 2011, when the first of the baby boom generation would become eligible for Social Security and Medicare. After that, the rapidly growing number of seniors drawing benefits would cause spending to rise faster than revenues, with the result that deficits would explode. There was bipartisan concern about the sustainability of Social Security and Medicare. The Kerrey-Danforth bipartisan commission (Senator Bob Kerrey's reward for voting for the 1993 deficit reduction package) was preparing policy options,[22] but the Clinton administration needed a longer-term budget strategy.

With the 1994 election coming up soon, we were determined to avoid a leak that would allow Republicans to claim we were plotting entitlement cuts or more tax increases. We decided not to develop options of our own for long-term deficit reduction; instead, we would write a briefing memo to the president, showing the magnitude of projected deficit increases and illustrating possible strategies by using proposals already suggested by others on both left and right.[23] The briefing memo was Bob's idea, but I thought it was a good one and gave OMB staff the assignment of collecting and analyzing options to be discussed at a National Economic Council meeting ahead of presenting them to the president. I drafted a cover memo to the president for discussion at the NEC meeting.

In the cover memo, I pointed out that the administration was committed to increasing productivity and living standards by investing in technology, infrastructure, and workforce skills. We were also still committed to a middle-class tax cut and universal health care (we hoped to revive the Clinton health reform bill, which had just failed in the Senate). I emphasized the growth of projected federal spending associated with the boomers' eligibility for Medicare and Social Security, and the need to figure out our investment priorities in the face of the boomers' retirement pressures without incurring rapid increases in deficits and debt. Then I listed possible entitlement cuts and tax increases that were all labeled as drawn from outside sources with no OMB recommendations.[24] Pretty routine budget stuff—or so I thought.

After a good discussion in the meeting, we collected the draft memo copies to guard against leaks. However, Treasury Secretary Bentsen was at a finance ministers' meeting in Europe, and his deputy broke the rules by retaining his copy and faxing it (on a secure fax) to the secretary. Bentsen read it, scribbled some comments, and handed it to an aid. Somehow a copy, complete with the secretary's scribbles, ended up in the hands of Republican strategist Bill Kristol.

Suddenly Newt Gingrich, who was then the second-highest ranking Republican in the House, and numerous other Republicans were attacking "the Rivlin memo" as evidence that the Clinton administration was preparing drastic cuts in Social Security and Medicare. Kristol said the memo was evidence of the administration's "craven hypocrisy." The House Republicans, under the leadership of Gingrich, were far more aggressively partisan than their earlier counterparts and highly focused on recapturing control of the House in the 1994 midterm elections after decades in the minority. They were determined to make the Clinton administration and congressional Democrats look corrupt and ineffective, and the Rivlin memo was just one aspect of an assault on many fronts. Still, it handed ammunition to the opposition, and it had to be refuted. Along with Rubin, Panetta, and other administration heavies, I denied any presidential plans to adopt any of the memo's options; indeed, the president had not even seen the memo. But the Republican attacks were shrill and relentless. Within the White House, I took a lot of grief from the political team, who still regarded the 1993 budget package as a mistake and held me particularly responsible.

It was a tough time in my life. I did not think I had done anything wrong, but my memo had caused the ruckus, and people all over the country were blaming me for doing something stupid and damaging to the president. With the perspective of seeing the pattern repeat itself over and over (remember Travelgate, Filegate, Tablegate, and perhaps a dozen other "gates" in the administrations that followed Clinton's?), I have come to understand that Republicans, and then both parties, were employing armies of political operatives in networked party communications structures ready to weaponize anything that has the potential to denigrate the other side. Now anyone in modern public life can suddenly find themselves part of a partisan attack story, where the actual facts are of no importance whatsoever. If you do not believe me, just ask Hillary Clinton, Sandra Fluke, Joseph Wilson and Valerie Plame, or Peter Strzok and Lisa Page.

But the larger point of this incident is one we would see play out over and over again throughout the Clinton administration and then the George W. Bush, Barack Obama, and Donald Trump years: Deficit reduction is hard, and either side can quickly pick up rocks and start throwing. In the elections of 1994 and 1996, both parties wanted to claim to be in favor of lowering the deficit. The balanced budget amendment was in the Contract with America and Democrats were also convinced there was a political benefit to publicly supporting deficit reduction. Even the deficit hawks in the Clinton administration were as surprised as pollster Stan Greenberg himself when his polls started showing public support for deficit reduction. But if deficit reduction is popular in the abstract, specific plans that would actually lower the deficit are unpopular and easy to demonize. Even as both parties embraced a lower deficit, both sides were quick to charge the other with wanting to raise taxes or cut popular programs like Social Security and Medicare. This is why bipartisanship is often required to actually make meaningful deficit reduction progress—the story that is told in chapter 7.

## CHAPTER 7

# WHEN BIPARTISAN NEGOTIATION ACHIEVED A BUDGET SURPLUS

The Republican victory in 1994 was a tidal wave. The GOP won control of the House of Representatives for the first time since 1955, earning Newt Gingrich (R-GA) the Speaker's gavel with a substantial majority. Bob Dole (R-KS) became the majority leader as Republicans won control of the Senate for the first time since 1987. Dole, who would later be nominated to oppose Bill Clinton in the 1996 election, was already taking positions to appeal to the ascendant combative wing of the Republican Party that Gingrich was inspiring. In addition to facing opposition control of both chambers, the Clinton White House was also dealing with a Congress that was more polarized and partisan than ever before.

The White House was in shock after the midterm elections. We had expected to lose seats, as the president's party usually does in midterm elections, but we could not believe we had lost control of both chambers—and lost so big. Republicans picked up eight seats in the Senate and fifty-four seats in the House of Representatives. Even Tom Foley (D-WA), the Speaker of the House, went down in defeat, along with many high-profile Democratic congressional representatives, senators, and governors across the nation.

Speaker Gingrich was riding high and was eager to move his "Contract with America" quickly through Congress. The Republicans had been the minority party in the House for forty years and were not used to being in charge. But Gingrich had plotted this takeover for a long time and saw his chance to lead a partisan crusade for Republican policies.[1] Only the veto pen of a Democratic president appeared to stand in his way.

Gingrich moved quickly to push elements of the Republican Contract with America through the House, including a bill to start the process of amending the constitution to require a balanced budget. Republican congressional leaders challenged Clinton to send up a budget proposal that would achieve balance in five years by making far deeper cuts in domestic spending than he was then contemplating.

Under the rules from the Budget Impoundment and Control Act of 1974, President Clinton was required to send Congress his proposal for fiscal year 1996 in the first week of February 1995. The previous June, the president had made Leon Panetta his chief of staff and asked me to take over as the OMB director, so I was now in charge at OMB. The deficit hawks on the economic team, including me, wanted to send up a budget that enhanced the president's priorities while continuing progress on deficit reduction. But the disastrous midterm elections loss had dampened Clinton's enthusiasm for deficit reduction and strengthened his commitment to investment in education and the environment. He wanted a slower path to balance that would leave more room for these domestic priorities. The fiscal year 1996 budget proposal we sent to the Hill included a variety of spending cuts to cover the cost of a modest middle-class tax cut but no further deficit reduction.

Republicans attacked the Clinton budget as weak on the deficit, although they had yet to produce a budget proposal of their own. Some conservative Democrats also piled on. My colleagues and I found ourselves defending the administration's budget and priorities at extremely hostile hearings. The partisan rancor only got worse as the year wore on.

The new congressional leadership agreed on a budget resolution that accelerated deficit reduction and aimed for balance by 2002 but had trouble agreeing on detailed appropriations bills that reflected their goals. In this situation, the possibility of vetoing legislation is the president's most potent constitutional power. With help from OMB, Clinton developed the veto threat into an art form, using it at every stage of the legislative process to try to preserve the administration's priorities as spending bills moved through Congress. For example, if an appropriations bill cutting programs we valued was moving toward a vote in a subcommittee, OMB would coordinate with the relevant department and send the committee a Statement of Administration Policy (SAP) saying one or more cabinet officers would recommend that the president veto the bill unless certain changes were made. Adding more cabinet officers or the OMB director strengthened the threat. We were careful not to say, "The president will veto," unless we were sure he would.

As it turned out, this was an effective strategy to communicate the president's priorities in a negotiation that would never actually allow him to veto anything. We were already well into the era when budget regular order was quite rare. "Regular order" can be a somewhat imprecise term meaning the way things are supposed to be or the way things worked in some prior period, but in this case, we had the Congressional Budget and Impoundment Control Act of 1974 that spells out quite clearly how the budget process is supposed to unfold each year—and yet, those rules were rarely followed. The twelve appropriations bills hardly ever passed Congress on time, having been replaced by omnibus spending bills, which put all appropriations into one large bill when the two parties are able to negotiate them, and by continuing resolutions (CRs) when they fail to reach agreement. Continuing resolutions keep the old budget in place for a matter of weeks or months to give Congress time to pass new spending bills with different priorities.

This is what happened in 1995 for the fiscal year 1996 budget we were negotiating. By mid-November, the Republicans had little to show for all their budget bravado. As the fiscal year ended, Republicans were forced to fund most of the government departments using a CR. This all-too-common practice, playfully known as "kicking the can down the road," is just one of the costly[2] symptoms of dysfunction that has come to characterize Congress in recent years.

## THREATENING A DEFAULT: REPUBLICANS TIE SPENDING CUTS TO THE DEBT CEILING

There was even greater concern that government borrowing was coming close to the debt ceiling. The debt ceiling is a statutory limit on the total amount of debt the Treasury can incur. In normal years, raising the debt ceiling is a routine task that falls on the majority party in Congress. The opposition may do a bit of speechifying against out-of-control spending, but the majority always has the votes to pass the simple legislation to raise the debt ceiling to accommodate the level of borrowing the Treasury needs to fund the budgets Congress has passed.

In that Congress "holds the purse strings"—that is, Congress passes the taxing and spending bills—it is Congress that runs up the debt. It does not make sense for Congress to limit the debt by triggering a default when Congress has the power to limit the debt by spending less or raising more revenue. But this was not a normal year, and Speaker Gingrich and the congressional leadership made an unusual threat to tie raising the debt ceiling to their spending cuts. To get what they wanted on taxing and spending priorities, the congressional Republicans were threatening to have the US government default on its debt obligations to bondholders—a group that includes many retirement funds, pension plans, banks and insurance companies, corporations, and individuals, both in the United States and around the world. The consequences of a default are impossible to fully calculate, but they would not be good, and would certainly be far worse for the American economy and the American people than a temporary government shutdown.

One of my proposals detailed in chapter 11 is that we defuse this bomb threat to the American and global economy by eliminating the debt ceiling altogether. We have a process to decide how much the government will borrow. We need to improve this process and we need to borrow less, but we do not need a process to decide if we will pay our debt for the money we have already borrowed. There is no argument to be made for the United States to become a deadbeat, losing its status as a great nation and leader of the free world economic order, facing higher interest rates, a collapsing economy at home and abroad, and many other negative consequences. No American political party should be tempted to gain leverage over the other by threatening harm to Americans, so we should remove this temptation to do so.

The Republicans wrapped their proposals into one big omnibus bill that cut deeply into Clinton's priorities but raised the debt ceiling. Speaker Gingrich hoped that the threat of closing the government (undesirable) or defaulting on the debt (unthinkable!) would get the president to capitulate out of fear of being blamed for the consequences. But the Speaker miscalculated. Bob Rubin, who was now treasury secretary, found ways to postpone the date when the government would be missing a debt payment by shifting around budgetary accounts. This stretched out the amount of time we had before the debt ceiling was breached. We now had at least a few more months, and Rubin made it clear he could find more time if he needed to. Hitting the debt ceiling was by far the greater danger; everyone knew there were high costs and incalculable risks if the federal government defaulted on its debts, but with this threat postponed, Clinton took the risk of closing the government rather than sign on to a spending bill with which he profoundly disagreed.

The president's firmness paid off. Speaker Gingrich, overconfident after the Republicans' big victory at the polls, thought Clinton would not dare risk closing the government the Democrats so dearly loved. He thought Clinton could not reject the public mandate that swept the Republicans into power. He also thought that if Clinton dared to allow the government to close down, the public would blame the president for not acceding to the Republican demands. It turned out Gingrich was wrong in all these beliefs.

Gingrich's biggest miscalculation was to underestimate how much the public depended on routine government services. He was quoted as claiming, "We can close the government, and no one will notice." But people did notice. Some had to cancel trips because they could not get their passport renewed; some could not close on a new house purchase without a Federal Housing Administration (FHA) loan approval; others could not start college without a student loan approval; still others had to tell their extended family that a planned gathering was off because a national park was closed. Public annoyance mounted as the standoff continued, and Republicans felt the brunt of the blame.

There were two federal government shutdowns over the fiscal year 1996 budget: the first one only lasted five days, including a weekend in mid-November 1995; the second lasted three weeks over Christmas and New Year's, and ended in a compromise that opened the government on January 6, 1996. It was a cold, snowy Christmas in Washington. Congressional leaders, who wanted to be home with their families for the holidays, spent many hours in meetings at the White House, negotiating the terms of an agreement that would open the government. We all envied the president because he lived in the White House so he had zero commute, while the rest of us struggled to get there through city streets rendered impassable by heavy snowfall.

One of the less pleasant duties of the OMB director is shutting down the government in a budget crisis. We were able to reassure seniors that their Social Security checks would still arrive because neither the Social Security Administration nor the US Post Office are dependent on annual appropriations for their funding, but we had to put a stop to almost everything else the government does, and we did not know for how long. The relevant legislation specifies that "essential services" continue. No one wants military operations curtailed, leaving the nation vulnerable to attack, and the Federal Bureau of Prisons must maintain security and provide food for inmates. I put my able deputy for management, John Koskinen, in charge of making and implementing the hundreds of close decisions as to what was or was not essential. (OMB staff made up a song about John, "Mr. Shutdown.")

One high-profile dilemma was whether to light the national Christmas tree. The huge evergreen was already decorated and waiting for the president to throw the switch. My decision that lighting it was not essential caused a storm of protest and offers of help. The power company said they would donate the electricity; private security companies offered to stand in for the park police. We backed down and went ahead with the traditional tree lighting. We also decided that the technicians who tended to laboratory animals were essential, but the scientists who did the experiments were not. Scientific

---

*I think they [the Republicans] were carried away by their own rhetoric, especially [House Speaker Newt] Gingrich: Government is bad, big government is what we're against. That never has very much content as far as I'm ever able to see. It's always "big government" in the abstract that is the enemy, but these particular programs are fine. But they [Republicans] forgot that. They bought into this rhetoric—because they'd just won, they'd been going around the country talking this way for six months, and they won big. Then they thought, "Here we are doing it [shutting down the big government]." But nobody liked it.*

—Alice M. Rivlin, interview for the
UVA Miller Center Presidential
Oral Histories Project,
December 13, 2002

---

discovery seemed postponable, but we wanted to avoid dead monkeys, rats, and rabbits.

Eventually, the Republicans realized they were losing the public relations battle. Constituents were impatient to get the government functioning normally again. President Clinton made a few concessions, first among them that he would submit a budget that achieved balance within seven years (as certified by CBO rather than OMB—another small concession to build trust with Congress), and the Republicans agreed to open the government.[3] I strongly supported the decision to specify CBO rather than OMB, because I trusted CBO even if the Republicans distrusted the professionalism of our OMB staff. Gingrich and other Republicans realized that their hopes of blaming Clinton for the shutdowns had backfired, and so they did not use the tactic again.

The agreements that ended the government shutdown at the beginning of 1996 set the stage for budget agreements for fiscal years 1997 and 1998 that put the nation on a path to budget surpluses in 1998–2001. The year 1996, however, was a presidential election year, and the path to agreement would remain long and tortuous. After the shutdown ended, President Clinton gave his State of the Union address to Congress, and the headline was his acknowledgement that "the era of big government is over." Both the State of the Union and the GOP response, which was delivered by Senator Dole, included calls for the other side to cooperate in reaching a balanced budget. Soon after, the Clinton White House submitted a budget that the Republicans labeled "dead on arrival," and both sides retreated into partisan rhetoric positioning themselves for the November elections.

The White House actually submitted two budgets for the 1997 fiscal year to Congress in the early months of 1996. The first was about 20 pages long, rather than the usual 600- to 700-page monstrosities we usually sent, but it was important. In addition to meeting the deadline of the first week in February as set in the budget process law, the slim budget document committed Clinton to the agreements he had made with Republicans to get the government open four weeks earlier. And CBO had reviewed our numbers and certified that they added up to a balanced budget by 2002. A full-sized budget document of many hundreds of pages was submitted about a month later. This budget followed the outline of the earlier submission and was also certified by CBO as achieving balance by 2002.

To make the projections show balance in fiscal year 2002, we resorted to some fairly creative budgeting. The best example was the proposal to auction off portions of the radio spectrum to private sector purchasers. Those numbers on your AM/FM radio offer a visual representation of two portions of the radio spectrum; AM modulates at frequencies between 535 kilohertz and 1.7 megahertz, and FM modulates at frequencies between 88 megahertz and 108 megahertz. The FCC has always managed the radio spectrum by leasing specific frequencies (e.g., 88.5 MHz) to radio stations. However, more modern technologies than simple AM/FM radio have valuable uses for other parts of the spectrum—for example, in maritime navigation, air traffic control, mobile telephones, and satellite communications—and the FCC was leasing those parts of the spectrum as well. The new proposal was to sell rather than lease new parts of the spectrum to private industry at auction. This was a defensible policy, and the telephone and satellite communications companies that bought parts of the radio spectrum have made good use of them (or sold them to someone else who would). But to a budgeter, asset sales, unlike spending reductions or tax increases, create one-time savings rather than continuous reductions in the deficit. (The radio spectrum sales ended up netting less than $24 billion[4] over five years, which is little more than pocket change to federal budgeters.) Using asset sales to get to a balanced budget shows how desperate we were to get the projected deficit to zero.

At the end of March, the Republicans finally faced up to the debt ceiling and raised it to $5.5 trillion. At the same time, they passed the "presidential line-item veto," making good on a promise in the Contract with America. This and two other contract items[5] allowed the Republican majority whip, Representative Tom DeLay of Texas, to boast that contrary to conventional wisdom at the time, "the Contract with America is alive and well."[6]

A line-item veto gives the executive branch the power to eliminate specific spending proposals passed by the legislative branch without rejecting the entire spending bill. Most governors have this authority, but the US president did not. Ronald Reagan had pushed for the line-item veto, so it was popular among Republicans even before it was included in the Contract with America. Clinton had a line-item veto power as governor of Arkansas and he requested it in one of his State of the Union addresses, so he was happy to sign the Line Item Veto Act on April 9, 1996.[7] This amounted to a huge transfer of power from Congress to the president, and eventually, in 1998, the Supreme Court would rule that the presidential line-item veto was unconstitutional because it undermines congressional authority. The Constitution gives Congress the power of the purse, and only a constitutional amendment could transfer this authority to the president. By then, however, President Clinton had used the line-item power to veto specific spending proposals eighty-two times.[8]

The whole time—through the 1994 elections, through the government shutdowns, through the budget proposals and counterproposals on both sides of the 1996 elections—the Republicans continued to talk about their balanced budget amendment[9] gimmick, which Clinton vowed to never accept.[10] An amendment to the Constitution requiring Congress to pass a balanced budget is a bad idea for many reasons. It is a simple answer to a very complicated question, because the federal government should run a small deficit in some years, run large deficits in some years, and strive for a zero deficit or a surplus in other years. As discussed in chapter 4, quite large deficits were appropriate when the nation was gripped by the Great Depression, and they grew larger immediately after that when the nation was fighting World War II.

To be fair, the balanced budget amendment spelled out a process where, in special circumstances like a war or an economic crisis, a three-fifths supermajority of both chambers of Congress could vote to allow deficits, but a process to reach such a high vote threshold could dangerously slow the government's response to an avoidable economic downturn, and the system of "automatic stabilizers" we have now works much better and faster. Under current arrangements, tax revenues automatically shrink when economic activity slows, and expenditures automatically grow. For example, when people lose a job, their income drops and they will pay less in taxes; if they start drawing unemployment benefits, government spending increases. If this happens to a lot of workers at the same time, the deficit automatically grows at precisely the best time to stimulate a slowing economy. This is Keynesian Economics 101, and it is one of the most important reasons why the US has gone eighty years without another Great Depression.

There is no good reason to pass a constitutional amendment to break this mechanism that provides automatic stabilization to the economy. Clinton led most other Democrats in opposing this bad idea, saying it would put the United States in a "straitjacket." Of course, the proposal had almost no chance of becoming the Twenty-eighth Amendment to the Constitution and failed to reach the two-thirds threshold in both chambers, on several attempts. If the proposal had succeeded, it would still have needed ratification in legislatures of three-fourths of the states. As discussed in chapter 3, the writers of the Constitution made it almost impossible to change it without a broad bipartisan (or nonpartisan) agreement, as there was in 1971 when the voting age was lowered to 18, matching the draft age as the Vietnam War raged on. In the past fifty years, there has only been one other amendment added, with the 1992 ratification of an amendment proposed in 1789 to ensure that any congressional pay raise that Congress approves does not go into effect until after the next election, so that citizens have a chance to vote out representatives who voted for the raise.[11]

## A No-Change Election Seems to Change Everything

At the end of April 1996, I went to the Federal Reserve to serve as vice chair, so I was not part of the Clinton administration heading into the November election. The 1996 campaign rhetoric included a lot of charges and countercharges related to budgetary matters. Republicans continued to charge Clinton with being a "tax and spend liberal" and campaign on their call for a Balanced Budget Amendment. Democrats attacked Bob Dole and Newt Gingrich for wanting to slash Medicare.[12] There were many proposals and counterproposals but little action before the election, which ended up changing very little. President Clinton won reelection decisively, but Republicans gained two Senate seats and lost three House seats, retaining control of both chambers.

The fact that the election caused little change in the balance of power in Washington may have caused quite a large change in the political dynamics of the budget negotiations. An upcoming election is often used as an argument against making compromises to reach bipartisan agreement because both sides believe they are about to win. Why compromise, the thinking goes, when the public is on our side and will toss out the other side in November? But voters did not punish either party in November 1996, and nearly everyone was back in the same seats when the president addressed the new Congress in January.

Just after the election, both sides expressed a new willingness to work together. Clinton promised to "forge a coalition of the center,"[13] while Gingrich said the new Congress would focus on implementation rather than confrontation.[14] Of course, this happens after most elections, but this time it felt different, and it was different as both sides followed through on the cooperative rhetoric.

I believe what had changed was the Republican strategy. Republicans had tried confrontation and taken it as far as it could go, but they had little to show for it. They had to retreat on the government shutdowns and then again on the debt ceiling. They expected to gain in the elections, but Clinton was still in the White House. It was time to try a different approach.

The Republicans would make one more attempt in January 1997 to pass the balanced budget amendment, but it fell one vote short in the Senate in March. In the midst of this legislative process, Clinton sent a budget to Congress in February,[15] and in a shocking twist, the Republicans pronounced it "alive on arrival."[16] Indeed, they did not even produce their own budget for fiscal year 1998 but instead chose to take President Clinton's budget as a starting point for negotiations.[17]

The two sides were far apart on taxes, Medicare spending, and a long list of other issues, but they were negotiating in good faith. Working groups including the White House team led by Erskine Bowles, who was then the president's chief of staff, and Democrats and Republicans from both chambers on Capitol Hill were working through the compromises, and just before the October 31 deadline, they reached agreement in time to pass all twelve appropriations bills. The fiscal year 1998 budget process would go down as one of the smoothest in history, with no continuing resolutions. Like an actor who becomes an "overnight sensation" after a twenty-year career, the fiscal year 1998 budget agreement was easy to achieve—if you do not focus on the two government shutdowns, more than a dozen CRs, and two hard-fought national elections in prior years that set up the negotiations for success.

It was not that the two parties were closer together on budget policy that made the negotiations successful; they were as far apart as ever. What made the negotiations work was that both Republicans and Democrats wanted the negotiations to succeed. On most issues, it came down to numbers, and the two sides were able find a number that both could live with. As those of us who would like to see more legislative cooperation consider options to make bipartisan negotiations more frequent and more likely to end in success, we should remember that agreement is possible even when it seems the parties are far apart. At least when it comes to budget and economic issue disputes, compromises are always possible if both sides are willing to make a deal. Gingrich and the Republicans had exhausted themselves and the nation by testing the limits of the confrontational hardball tactics of standoffs and shutdowns with nothing gained. When confrontation failed, they tried cooperation and found they were able to accomplish most of their goals.

The final agreements for fiscal year 1998 were put into two bills: the Balanced Budget Act of 1997 for the spending side, and the negotiated tax changes were passed in the Taxpayer Relief Act of 1997. The two bills included a mixture of things both sides wanted, with some Republican priorities and some of Clinton's priorities. Both sides were happy with the tax credit of $500 per child for families with incomes under $110,000, which Clinton and the Republicans had each promoted. The bills contained Clinton's plan for $1,500 tax credits to offset the cost of college tuition, and nearly $40 billion in higher education tax credits. Republicans got their capital gains tax reductions and a big victory in reducing inheritance taxes.

Some years earlier, Republican message gurus had stopped talking about "estate taxes," preferring the term "death taxes" to stand for the same long-held goal of eliminating inheritance taxes altogether. Even if the renaming was effective in ginning up opposition to the taxes in public opinion polls,[18] I always thought it was silly. Everyone dies eventually, but not everyone pays this tax. At the time, there was an exemption for the first $600,000, which meant most families paid no tax when a family member died. The tax applied to families in the top 1 percent who were inheriting what people commonly call estates.

There was some merit to the Republican argument: Because most of the money that made up someone's estate at the time of his or her passing had been taxed when it was earned (as income, rent, capital gains, or other investment income), to tax the money as it passed to the next generation was double taxation. There was even more merit to the concern that inheritance taxes fell particularly heavily on family farms and family businesses that would not have enough cash to keep going and pay the tax as ownership passed from one generation to the next.

Democrats also had a legitimate point of view. With high and rising rates of economic inequality, Democrats believed there was justice in progressive taxation. The wealthy benefit the most from the ordered society that government provides, and the roads and educated workforce that government funds allow businesses to succeed and to generate wealth. Most Americans do not inherit estates, and those that do typically have many advantages in the forms of things like private education and superior health care that put them far ahead of Americans raised in poverty or even in the middle class. In funding (for example) education and police protection for all of society by taxing a portion of the vast wealth that a small number of families accumulate, the nation does not achieve equality of opportunity, but it does come a step closer to equality of opportunity.

Even though both parties were using different language to describe the topic and had different principled points of view on what constituted just taxation, the solution reached in the Taxpayer Relief Act of 1997 was obvious and easy because both sides wanted an agreement. Democrats wanted to maintain or increase the "estate tax" and Republicans wanted to eliminate the "death tax," so both Democrats and Republicans agreed to reduce inheritance taxes, whatever they decided to call them, while changing the details of the law to make it clear it was not death that was being taxed, it was large estates. The solution was just mathematics raising the levels above which the tax would kick in so people inheriting large estates would still pay the tax but those inheriting smaller amounts, small businesses, or family farms would not have to pay. Both sides agreed to raise the exemption from $600,000 to $1 million in stages over ten years, and to exempt an additional $700,000 for family businesses and family farms. The new rules returned the exemptions to approximately where they had been set the last time they were modified (1981), adjusted for inflation, and made it clearer to taxpayers that the taxes were only going to be paid by the very wealthy.

The same approach worked in many areas. The rate of growth in Medicare was trimmed by $115 billion and Medicaid by $13 billion over a five-year period, adding years to the programs' long-term solvency. Republicans had proposed deeper cuts, the difference was split, and a deal was achieved. Critics argued that the negotiators had agreed to some budgetary gymnastics to reach these savings,[19] and they were right. The cuts put unrealistic

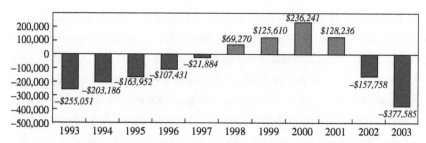

FIGURE 7-1.   Deficits and Surpluses, FY 1993–FY 2003 (in millions of dollars)
*Source:* White House Historical Tables, "Table 1.3—Summary of Receipts, Outlays, and Surpluses or Deficits (–) in Current Dollars, Constant (FY 2012) Dollars, and as a Percentage of GDP: 1940–2021," whitehouse.gov/omb/budget/historical-tables/.

pressure on hospitals and doctors to reduce costs, and when many doctors started dropping out of the programs, Congress had to add more money back every year through a series of "doc fix" bills. This continued as an annual ritual for seventeen years, through the George W. Bush presidency into the Barack Obama administration and even through the passage of the Affordable Care Act in 2010.[20] Eventually this adjustment was made permanent through a bipartisan agreement reached in 2015.[21]

Democrats would not accept Republican efforts to index capital gains against inflation because the Treasury calculated that it would explode the deficit as the decades rolled on. One of the largest gains on the Democratic wish list was about $24 billion of expanded health care programs for low-income children. This was about $8 billion more than House Republicans wanted to spend. The State Children's Health Insurance Program (SCHIP) was far from a full realization of the administration's health care reform aspirations, but it was far more than a consolation prize. By extending health care coverage to millions of children in families with too much income to qualify for Medicaid and too little to afford private health insurance, SCHIP patched a critical need in the American system.

## WHO GETS THE CREDIT FOR THE BALANCED BUDGET?

In the end, the agreement was far more successful than the negotiators expected. Through several years of back and forth with a goal of achieving balance by fiscal year 2002, the economy was improving, and the deficit was declining. As negotiators were battling over the fiscal year 1998 budget and which projections of the deficit to use in February and March of 1997, the OMB projections[22] and CBO projections[23] were billions of dollars apart for fiscal year 2002, but both predicted a deficit of $120 billion for the budget year that would end on September 30, 1998. By the time that date rolled around and the ink had dried on the calculations, it turned out the budget was already in balance![24] Economic growth had accelerated, the stock market was soaring, federal revenues were exceeding expectations, and it was clear that the battle for a balanced budget had already been won. The actual fiscal year 1998 budget surplus was $69 billion. The two sides had achieved their goal four years ahead of schedule.

Both political parties claimed credit for the late 1990s surpluses, and the discussion continues to this day. President Clinton and veterans of his administration, including me, love to point to the surpluses as evidence of Democrats' fiscal responsibility, and Republicans are no less proprietary. The Senate Budget Committee chair, Pete Domenici (R-NM), and Ohio Governor John Kasich, who was chair of the House Budget Committee in the 1990s, both claimed and deserved credit. (Kasich made his role in achieving the surplus a central theme in his Republican presidential campaign in 2016.) Who is right? All of us. The surpluses resulted from ten years of difficult and often unpleasant negotiations within and between the two parties, involving two presidents (a Republican and a Democrat) and leaders of six Congresses.

Cynics who allege that elected officials are inherently fiscally irresponsible now claim that the surpluses of the late 1990s were just a lucky accident, not a bipartisan achievement. The cynics are right that a combination of favorable circumstances made deficit reduction much easier in the late 1990s than it is now. First, the economy was growing rapidly in the second half of the 1990s. The sluggish productivity growth of the 1970s and 1980s began accelerating in 1996; unemployment dropped, average wages and incomes grew, and the stock market was soaring due to the dot-com boom, also called the dot-com bubble (discussed below). As a result, federal revenues rose to record highs—20 percent of gross domestic product (GDP) in fiscal year 2000.[25] Second, the end of the Cold War in 1989 enabled reductions in military spending that lasted nearly to the end of the 1990s, when the Clinton administration realized the disinvestment had gone too far. Third, the baby boom generation was still at least two decades away from eligibility for Social Security and Medicare. Budget watchers were already warning that federal entitlement spending would rise rapidly when the boomers retired, and soaring health care costs were already troubling. The demographic pressure on federal spending that we are feeling now, however, still seemed far in the future.

Although the policy options were expanded by economic, geopolitical, and demographic fortune, it was still necessary for policymakers to seize, not squander, the opportunity they were provided. If leaders in both parties had not worked hard to devise and enforce budget rules to keep spending in line with revenues, the natural inclination of politicians to raise spending and cut taxes—a proclivity that is highly visible in contemporary Washington—would have kept the debt growing. Achieving surpluses took discipline and political courage, not just luck.

In retrospect, we know some of the strength in the economy was an illusion. From June 1996 to September 2000, the inflation-adjusted GDP (or real GDP) was growing at a rapid annual rate of 4 percent or more in every quarter,[26] but we would later look back on this period as representing, at least in part, an unsustainable boom. Large numbers of Americans, and consumers all over the world, were becoming more comfortable buying things over the internet, and new business models designed to take advantage of new opportunities were emerging every day. A huge amount of investment went into the Nasdaq stock exchange and other ways to fund these new companies. Some of the companies, like Cisco, Qualcomm, and Amazon, were to become or remain some of the largest corporations in the world, but many others, like Pets.com, Webvan.com, and eToys.com, were spectacular failures. The Nasdaq Composite stock market index was just over 1,000 at the end of 1995, then rose to a peak on March 10, 2000, at 5,048.62,[27] only to lose more than three-quarters of that value, falling back to just over 1,000 by October 2002. This round trip from low to high and back down to low would be known as the dot-com bubble.

Stock markets do not give a good picture of the real economy that the average person is facing every day, but they do provide a few insights into some problems beneath the surface of the economy. This was a period of increase in both vertical and horizontal inequality.[28] In the 1990s, real family income was growing at the top of the income scale (and also at the very bottom) but declining in the middle, especially for lower-middle income families.[29] As discussed in chapter 2, research points to the dot-com boom as the beginning of divergence between the fast-growing cities, mostly on the coasts, and the slower or negative growth areas outside of the big cities and across the middle of America.[30] These patterns have continued to this day.

## DEALING WITH THE UNEXPECTED SURPLUS

Having fought together and worked together across party lines to get to a balanced budget, Congress and the White House lost the same focus once the balanced budget was achieved. Now the new, difficult political question was what to do with the unexpected surplus. Democrats and Republicans had both embraced the goal of achieving budget balance, and this shared goal had motivated them to abide by the rules (like limits on discretionary spending and pay-as-you-go, or PAYGO, budgeting) they had imposed on themselves in the Budget Enforcement Act (BEA) of 1990. But once the goal was achieved, they had no shared objective with respect to the unexpected surplus.[31]

Republicans remained committed, at least in their public pronouncements, to restraining federal spending and using the prospect of big income tax cuts as a key to winning the 2000 presidential election. Democrats remained committed to increasing public investments and a middle-class tax cut. Both sides talked about allowing some of the surplus to remain in the budget to help pay down the national debt, but Vice President Al Gore put particular emphasis on this as he geared up for his run for the presidency.

The White House continued to push elements of Clinton's investment initiatives and scored a major bipartisan success in 1998 with passage of the Workforce Investment Act (WIA). The ambitious jobs training bill was passed in the Senate by a vote of 91 to 7 and in the House, 343 to 60.[32] It was an impressive bipartisan achievement in a divided government, but it did not continue when Republican George W. Bush won the White House.[33] The WIA was later restarted and renamed the Workforce Innovation and Opportunity Act under President Barack Obama.[34]

Neither side wanted to bear the onus of repealing the BEA budget rules, so they stayed in place until they expired in 2002. However, the spending caps eroded by mutual consent. The BEA allowed spending above the caps in emergencies. During the deficit period, the emergency designation was reserved for hurricanes, earthquakes, and other "acts of God," although modest amounts of other spending was often jammed into an emergency bill. But when surpluses appeared in the budget, all kinds of popular spending programs suddenly became "emergencies." Between 1998 and the 2000 elections, billions of dollars above the caps were added for "emergency" military purposes, agriculture programs, Strategic Petroleum Reserve replenishment, law enforcement, education, and other activities. Nevertheless, despite erosion around the edges, the discipline imposed by the BEA held reasonably well during the period of divided government. Each side was able to keep the other from using the surplus for its preferred purposes.

Near the end of his second term, President Clinton proposed using the surpluses, then projected to be more than $200 billion and rising, to pre-fund Social Security benefits ("Save Social Security First"), but that prudent proposal never gained traction. The History Channel's resident historian, Steven Gillon, wrote a book detailing a secret meeting between Clinton and Gingrich where each agreed to make major concessions to achieve a bipartisan agreement to overhaul Social Security and Medicare, but the accord was derailed by the Monica Lewinski scandal.[35] The deal that never became public would have included some form of partial privatization of accounts (a Republican priority) and adjustments in the retirement age for younger future retirees, in exchange for firm long-term financial footing using a substantial portion of the projected future surpluses.

In his 2000 campaign for the presidency, George W. Bush promised immediate tax cuts that would return the surpluses to taxpayers. "It is your money," he told voters. Vice President Gore campaigned calling for greater spending on health care, education, and the environment, but close to the election he was most associated with Social Security and his proposal to put the surplus funds in a "lockbox" to pay benefits for future generations of retirees. Both campaigns were adding new spending initiatives and additional tax cut proposals as the election drew nearer, believing projections of hundreds of billions of dollars in budget surpluses growing well into the first decade of the new millennium.[36]

As detailed in many other accounts, the 2000 election was a mess. The election night vote count ended in a deadlock followed by highly publicized recounts of the votes in several Florida counties that were halted, resumed, and again halted by the courts. The election was ultimately decided by a 5 to 4 decision of the Supreme Court and a controversial concession from

Al Gore. The country was as divided by partisanship as ever, and many Democrats believe to this day that the election was illegitimate, but Gore acquiesced to the Supreme Court and conceded the election to avoid a constitutional crisis.

At the end of two terms, the Clinton administration left with an economic record that was far more positive than negative, even though there was no small amount of unfinished business. The unemployment rate, which was 7.3 percent when Clinton took office, was 4.2 percent overall as his term was winding down in October 2000. Unemployment among African Americans was still too high, at 8.2 percent, when Clinton was leaving office, but it had declined dramatically from 13.1 percent eight years earlier, and Hispanic Americans also registered a decline from 10.2 percent in January 1993 to 5.8 percent in October 2000.[37] With eighteen quarters in a row of real GDP growth over 4 percent,[38] the overall measures of economic health were all strong, even if income inequality was growing beneath the aggregate statistics and the deindustrialization of the middle of America was well underway. The budget was in surplus, and both OMB[39] and CBO[40] were projecting surpluses to continue on an increasing slope through 2009. The stock market was soaring at the end of Clinton's term, with the Standard and Poor's (S&P) 500 index triple the level it held eight years earlier,[41] although we know some of this gain reflected what Federal Reserve Chair Alan Greenspan warned was "irrational exuberance"[42] and the dot-com bubble.

But most important for real people was Clinton's record of making investments in the economy of the future. There were investments in workers, with many new education initiatives including college tax credits and increased student financial aid that allowed a record number of Americans to go to college and get a degree, and the Workforce Investment Act to increase worker access to job training programs at the local level. From the vantage point of time[43] and many critical analyses,[44] we now know the WIA was a good effort that failed to achieve its goals. Its rules were overly complex, too few workers qualified for the most effective training programs, and often the training was not well matched to the needs of local businesses. The worker retraining was ultimately inadequate to allow workers in the declining sectors of the economy, like manufacturing and agriculture, to find work in the emerging sectors of the economy, like information technology and professional services. This worker retraining deficit contributed to the economic inequality and geographic inequality that have become key factors in our political divisions today, as discussed in chapter 2.

The Clinton administration had a strong record for encouraging government-sponsored, university-sponsored, and private sector-sponsored basic scientific research and discovery, as well as research and development of new products, services, and markets. Medical research made great leaps, and the National Institutes of Health mapped the human genome. The Clinton administration was not able to achieve the goal of universal access to affordable health care, but it did expand coverage to millions of children under SCHIP.

But the biggest area of accomplishment and, at the same time, the biggest unfinished work of the Clinton administration was the four balanced budgets in a row. In several ways, they demonstrated that what seemed impossible was not only possible but also achieved. For years, it seemed like Clinton and the Democrats would never find common ground with Gingrich, Dole, and the Republicans, but they did. For many years, it seemed like a balanced budget was an impossible dream and yet the bipartisan agreement delivered four balanced budgets in a row. However, the long-term issues affecting the fiscal solvency of Medicare and Social Security still proved to be a bridge too far.

The date by which the Medicare Trust Fund would become technically exhausted[45] was extended by a couple of years by shifting some money from Social Security and then extended by decades to 2026 by limiting the amount Medicare pays out to hospitals and doctors. But those cuts were not really enacted. The Medicare Trust Fund is solvent, but future Congresses made up the difference from general revenue. The truth is, this entitlement reform is very hard to do. We know we will need to find more money to provide the same level of support for a population that is aging. The oldest members of the baby boom population bulge are now reaching retirement and are expected to live longer in retirement than their parents receiving medical care that keeps growing more expensive.

Political calculations make it clear that a problem becomes exponentially more difficult to solve if the two parties cannot work together to solve it. If one side tries to do it "their way," the other side will have a powerful attack campaign against the benefit cuts or tax increases. Bipartisan agreement may be the only path to solving the problem of long-term financing of the big entitlement programs: Social Security, Medicare, and Medicaid. Most of the time, the only thing the two sides can agree on is to postpone the question and push it onto future Congresses and presidents. America now has a new impossible dream of finding a fiscally sustainable way to provide the health care and retirement benefits promised by our entitlement programs to an aging population, but at least the Democrats and Republicans in the 1990s proved that the impossible can be achieved.

## THE GEORGE W. BUSH YEARS

George W. Bush took office in 2001, following the closest election in American history, and just as the Clinton administration had struggled in the early months, the latter Bush White House struggled to gain control of the Washington policy process. The Republicans retained the majority in the House by a narrow 221 to 212 seat margin. The Senate was even closer, with 50 Democratic senators and 50 Republicans. When the Senate convened in January, the Democrats were in the majority with Vice President Al Gore able to cast the tie-breaking votes for the majority. When Dick Cheney was sworn in as vice president on January 20, 2001, Republicans became the majority, but in June the Democrats regained control of the Senate when Jim Jeffords of Vermont changed his political affiliation from Republican to Independent and caucused with the Democrats.

While the Republicans controlled the House and Senate, George W. Bush was able to pass the tax cut that had been central to his campaign. As had been the case at the start of the Reagan administration (discussed in chapter 5), Republicans did not have enough votes to end a Senate filibuster,[46] so they used the budget reconciliation process to pass the Economic Growth and Tax Relief Reconciliation Act (EGTRRA) of 2001.

To pass through reconciliation, each element of the tax and spending bill had to comply with the provisions of the Byrd Rule (discussed in chapter 5), and one of those provisions is that the bill cannot add to the deficit longer than ten years into the future.[47] For this reason, many of the tax cuts in EGTRRA were set to expire in 2011, a fact that figures prominently in chapter 9. But if reconciliation was originally designed as part of a new process to reduce deficits, in practice it has often been used by presidents with more than 50 but fewer than 60 votes in the Senate to pass party-line bills that have added to deficits. In the case of George W. Bush's tax cut in 2001, this was the second blow to the surplus he inherited.

The first blow had already happened, even if we did not know it yet. It takes a while before economists know that the national economy has changed direction, but by the end of 2000 the economy was slowing and would continue to be sluggish for many months due to the dot-com bubble bursting in March 2000. As the 2001 tax cut was working its way through the legislative process, the rationale for passage changed from returning the surplus to taxpayers, as George W. Bush had promised on the campaign trail, to stimulating an economy that was beginning to slow down. Then everything changed on September 11, 2001, when the nation was attacked by terrorists about eight months into Bush's first term.

The economy came to a sudden stop after 9/11. The insurance industry losses were immense. Financial markets were disrupted as Wall Street was the target of two of the four attacks. Airline travel dropped to near zero for several months, and hotel bookings declined not only in New York but also nationally and even globally. September 11 deepened the post-dot-com recession, at least temporarily, as businesses pulled back their investments in the face of higher risks (or at least perceived risk).[48] Consumers were starting to go shopping again by November and December, but the United States was preparing to enter into two wars, first in Afghanistan and then in Iraq. The surpluses quickly melted away.

Fiscal year 2001 ended just three weeks after September 11 with a smaller surplus than the year before, but it was still over $120 billion. This was the last budget year of the Clinton administration and the last year the budget would see anything close to a surplus. The fiscal year 2002 budget was $157 billion in the red, and the deficits in fiscal years 2003 and 2004 were record setters (at least in nominal terms) at $377 billion and $412 billion, respectively.[49] In January 2001, CBO had projected that the federal budget would run cumulative surpluses of $5.6 trillion over the next decade if the economy continued to show strength and policies did not change. These assumptions were wildly unlikely because, even without a recession, Congress would probably have used the surpluses either to cut taxes or increase spending or some of each. By the end of 2011, CBO's retrospective evaluation of the previous decade showed cumulative deficits of $6.1 trillion, a negative swing of $11.7 trillion from the projection of 2001.[50] Of course, in January 2001, CBO had not anticipated the September 11 attacks, the wars in Afghanistan and Iraq, or the global financial crisis later in the decade.

Republicans did fairly well in the 2002 midterm elections, holding control of both the House and the Senate.[51] This was largely because the shock of September 11 continued to make Americans feel both patriotic and fearful. As noted in chapter 5, Vice President Dick Cheney told Treasury Secretary Paul O'Neill in 2003 that "Reagan proved deficits don't matter,"[52] and the George W. Bush administration sought, and passed through reconciliation, a second tax cut. Bush also proposed a new prescription drug benefit in Medicare. As there were already three parts of the Medicare systems of coverages (Part A for hospitalizations, Part B for outpatient medical care, and Part C for additional coverage through "Medicare Advantage"), the drug benefit would become known as Medicare Part D. After some difficult negotiations over the details, which included a "doughnut hole" of drug costs paid by the Medicare member, Part D passed with bipartisan support;[53] however, Congress waived the Congressional Budget Act restrictions so there was no PAYGO rule in effect, and thus there were no new taxes or other revenues added to "pay for" the new entitlement benefit.

Congress passed other bipartisan laws. The No Child Left Behind Act required standardized testing to meet performance benchmarks in exchange for federal funding. The McCain-Feingold Act set limits on the amount of soft money given to a political party or spent on advertising and required disclosure of the identity of the funders.

Comprehensive immigration reform, a top priority of the president, was blocked from passage in the Senate. The Senate compromise bill called the Comprehensive Immigration Reform Act of 2007 fell 14 votes short of the 60 needed in a major disappointment. The bill tied border security and workplace enforcement to legalizing 12 million undocumented immigrants. Many Republicans wrongly labeled this "amnesty."

President Bush took the United States out of the Kyoto protocol, an international treaty that set clear targets to reduce greenhouse gases. I was disappointed by his decision and by the hyperpartisan atmosphere in Congress around the issue of global warming, having served in an administration that took climate change seriously.

There was concern about deficits on Capitol Hill, and when Republican Representative Frank Wolf of Virginia first proposed setting up an independent commission to present options to reduce the deficit in 2006, he was applying the approach that had been successfully used several times, starting in 1988, to close military bases following the end of the Cold War. Voting to close a military base in a home state or district can be political suicide for senators and representatives. Loss of the base's jobs, sales, and contracts can devastate the local economy. But military requirements change, and Congress needed a way to close obsolete military bases that did not require forcing members to vote against local interests. In the Base Realignment and Closure (BRAC) process, Congress empowered a group of independent military experts under the leadership of two respected former members of Congress, a Democrat and a Republican, to create a list of bases to be closed. The BRAC process provided that unless Congress acted to disapprove the entire list by a specified date, the secretary of defense was required to close all listed bases. The process was a success. Taxpayers saved billions, and no member of Congress had to cast an onerous vote to close a local base.[54]

Since voting to raise taxes or cut entitlements was also seen as political suicide, it was superficially appealing to apply the BRAC idea to crafting a bipartisan "grand bargain" to reduce the debt.[55] Representative Wolf proposed a sixteen-member bipartisan commission on debt reduction (with two executive branch and fourteen congressional members).[56] The recommendations would be considered under a fast-track authority, which required an up or down vote on the whole package (no amendments) by a certain date. The process differed from BRAC, but the ideas were similar: Republicans and Democrats would join hands and jump in the pool together so that neither could blame unpopular votes on the other in the next election. In 2007, Wolf was joined by Representative Jim Cooper (D-TN), and when Senators Kent Conrad (D-ND) and Judd Gregg (R-NH) took up the cause, the effort was bipartisan and bicameral.[57] The two senators and two house members had recruited an impressive number of cosponsors from both parties but not yet enough to get the legislation passed into law, and no action seemed likely. This would change when deficits soared in the Great Recession.[58]

The national debt began climbing again, under the combined impact of a recession, two tax cuts,[59] increased spending related to terrorism and wars in the Middle East, and the addition of Medicare Part D.[60] The surpluses so many of us had fought so hard to achieve during the Clinton years faded into history—and things were about to get a lot worse.

## THE FINANCIAL CRISIS OF 2008, 2009, . . .

A few years ago, in a classroom discussion of the financial crisis of 2008, one of my students asked, "Professor, did you predict the crisis?" My first thought was, "Who, me?" but I recognized it was an entirely legitimate question. For several decades, I had been a member in good standing of the group of economists and economic policy practitioners who dominated economic policymaking in Washington. Collectively, we had failed to keep the economy out of trouble. As I say in chapter 1, our collective failures contributed to the current situation in which so many people feel disconnected from their government and outraged at the inability of the policymaking process to solve major problems.

Public opinion surveys have been telling us for decades that Americans have been losing confidence in most of the institutions of society, including the military, organized religion, and the business sector, but the data showing a long decline in public trust in government are undeniable.[61] I believe that some portion of this decline is inevitable as society has grown more complex and that some portion has been manufactured for political gain, but I wrote this book because I believe a substantial portion of the decline in trust in government is justified. It has occurred over the same period that increasing political polarization has made government less effective at solving our most pressing problems. (Beyond my own observations, I look at the data to back up that statement in chapter 10.) In chapter 2, I connect this decline to the long-term failure of government of either party to meaningfully address the inequality, both economic and geographic, that has developed as a consequence of the mechanization and globalization of mass production, depressing wages for low- and middle-income workers, and hollowing out the middle of the American industrial belt. But in addition, I fear the failure of government to anticipate and prevent the 2008–2009 financial collapse, and the global economic downturn it caused, will join the Vietnam War and Watergate as historic incidents from which a broad decline in trust in government is understandable and justified.

There have been many efforts by Democrats to blame George W. Bush and the Republicans for the economic crisis. After all, Republicans villainize regulation, and clearly a lack of financial market regulation contributed to the depth and breadth of the economic catastrophe that started in the mortgage lending industry and spread through the US and global economy. My view is, this was a bipartisan economic policy failure that took root in the Clinton administration but really started much earlier than that. The philosophy that minimal supervision and regulation of financial markets was best for the economy was strongly ingrained in Washington policymaking circles ever since Alan Greenspan advised President Gerald Ford and was then named by Ronald Reagan to be chair of the Federal Reserve, holding the post through five administrations. It seemed to work very well until it didn't, and a financial crisis made a lot of people wish they had seen the problem in time to do something to prevent it. I have enormous respect for Chairman Greenspan, and I served as his vice chair of the Federal Reserve Board from 1996 to 1999, and for this and other reasons, I include myself in the list of the many who failed to see what was happening until it was too late.

The Clinton administration was very close to the Wall Street investment banks and the large commercial banks. Robert Rubin had spent more than two decades at Goldman Sachs before becoming NEC director and later treasury secretary, and he then left to take a leading position at Citigroup. Deputy Treasury Secretary Roger Altman came from Lehman Brothers and the Blackstone Group. There were lots of others with close Wall Street ties in positions that had oversight responsibility for financial markets. And the pattern was continued into George W. Bush's two terms, with the most prominent example being Goldman Sachs's Henry Paulson serving as treasury secretary.

The Clinton and Bush administrations certainly share blame for deregulation of the financial markets. Rubin was the driving force behind the Clinton administration's repeal of the Glass-Steagall Act,[62] the law written after the 1929 Wall Street crash to separate banking from investment banking. Even if Glass-Steagall alone would not have prevented the 2008–2009 economic collapse, many economists believe the law's repeal did allow banks to take greater risks and to merge with investment banks and insurance companies, creating the "too big to fail" institutions that required massive taxpayer bailouts and making the crisis far worse than it would have been.[63] But the Bush administration had seven years to change policy toward regulation of the rapidly evolving financial markets, had the administration been so inclined. But its anti-regulation bias kept the issue from rising to the level of action until 2008, which was too late to be in place to avoid the crisis.[64]

Since the financial crisis of 2008–2009, there has been a lot of analysis of what went wrong and who is to blame. My own view is that we all missed it, and that all of the people who assume responsibility for understanding and managing the economy and the financial markets share responsibility for a collective failure. I think Robert Rubin expressed this best when he testified before the congressionally established Financial Crisis Inquiry Commission: "Almost all of us involved in the financial system, including financial firms, regulators, ratings agencies, analysts and commentators, missed the powerful combination of forces at work and the serious possibility of a massive crisis. We all bear responsibility for not recognizing this, and I deeply regret that."[65]

People are correctly suspicious of collective responsibility because they worry that it also means no one is responsible. I share this concern, and that is why I called for the creation of a new government organization to be

---

*Markets cannot be counted on to police themselves. . . . When the financial system fails on the scale we have experienced recently, the losers are not just the wealthy investors and executives of financial firms who took excessive risks. They are average people here and around the world whose jobs, livelihoods, and life savings are destroyed and whose futures are ruined by the effect of financial collapse on the world economy. We owe it to them to ferret out the flaws in the financial system and the failures of regulatory response that allowed this unnecessary crisis to happen and to mend the system so to reduce the chances that financial meltdowns imperil the world's economic wellbeing.*

—Alice Rivlin, "Establishing a Framework for Systemic Risk Regulation," testimony before the US Senate Committee on Banking, Housing and Urban Affairs, July 23, 2009

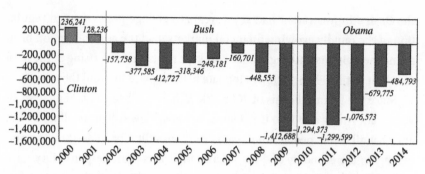

FIGURE 7-2.    Deficits and Surpluses, FY 2000–FY 2014 (in millions of dollars)
*Source:* White House Historical Tables, "Table 1.3—Summary of Receipts, Outlays, and Surpluses or
Deficits (–) in Current Dollars, Constant (FY 2012) Dollars, and as a Percentage of GDP: 1940–2021,"
whitehouse.gov/omb/budget/historical-tables/.

charged with the responsibility of monitoring the financial markets and raising a red flag when any segment of the market looks like it is entering risky
territory. This would make someone specific responsible for monitoring systemic risk. I was not alone in making this suggestion, and some people recommended that it be a part of Treasury while some suggested the Federal
Reserve and others called for an independent agency, office, or commission.
My suggestion was the Fed, but Congress housed the Financial Stability
Oversight Council (FSOC) at Treasury as one of several important changes
in the Dodd-Frank Wall Street Reform and Consumer Protection Act.[66] This
means if a similar financial crisis happens again, we can hold the treasury
secretary accountable because she or he has this responsibility now.

The economic collapse that started in 2008 was forceful and deep. Throughout the second half of the presidential election year, the stock market was
collapsing, banks and businesses were going bankrupt, the economy was in
free fall, and workers were losing jobs at the rate of hundreds of thousands
per month. Home values were diving, and many homeowners owed more
on their mortgage than their house was worth. Voters were ready for change,
and for the first time in the nation's 232-year history, they elected someone
other than a white male as president.

Emergencies facilitate bipartisan cooperation, and even during a heated
presidential election, both the Democratic nominee, Senator Barack Obama
of Illinois, and the Republican nominee, Senator John McCain of Arizona,
joined President George W. Bush, Democratic House Speaker Nancy Pelosi,

and Democratic Senate Majority Leader Harry Reid in supporting the largest bank bailout and one of the largest spending bills in the history of the United States. The Emergency Economic Stabilization Act of 2008, which created the Troubled Asset Relief Program (TARP), meant the taxpayers were buying the bad debt that banks had on their balance sheets so the banks could remain solvent. The massive spending for TARP and other emergency measures to save the economy was necessary to keep it from seizing up altogether and sending the global economy into another Great Depression[67] rather than the sustained global recession we all experienced; however, spending drove the federal budget deficit to more than $1 trillion in fiscal year 2009, President George W. Bush's last budget year.

In winning the 2008 presidential election, Barack Obama inherited what investors call "a falling knife" (which commonly comes with the warning to not try to catch it). Financial markets were plummeting, the workforce was losing thousands of jobs each day, and the deficit was exploding. But the bipartisan assistance that Democrats had offered a Republican president facing a crisis was not reciprocated. Even before taking office, Obama and the Democrats knew that they were inheriting a collapsing economy and that Republicans were not going to give them any help to build it back up.

## CHAPTER 8

# OBAMA AND THE DEMOCRATS STRUGGLE TO MAKE UNIFIED GOVERNMENT WORK

The economy that Barack Obama inherited from George W. Bush was in much worse shape than the economy Bill Clinton inherited from Bush's father, George H. W. Bush, but beyond this major difference, the parallels between the two Democratic administrations are broad and deep. Both Clinton and Obama took over when the public (as measured in opinion polls) was deeply concerned about the current state of the economy but also very worried about the level of the federal budget deficit, and national debt. Both presidents struggled to hold together the liberal and moderate factions dividing the Democratic Party. Both populated their economic offices from the same talent pool, and many key players served Clinton and Obama. Both administrations began with a major economic summit. Both struggled but were able to push their economic bill through despite near total congressional Republican opposition. Both suffered a major loss at the ballot box in the first midterm elections and faced energetic opposition from the victorious GOP congressional leadership threatening government shutdowns and possible default on the federal debt. Both were able to win reelection two years later. Although Obama was able to do what Clinton could not in passing the Affordable Care Act (ACA), a major reform of the American health care system, neither president managed to reach a deal to fully address the long-term fiscal stability of Social Security and Medicare.[1]

## PRESIDENT OBAMA TAKES CONTROL AMID AN ECONOMIC DISASTER

In December 2008 and January 2009, even before the president-elect took the oath of office, Obama was facing difficult negotiations with surprisingly oppositional Republicans and also facing resistance from members of his own Democratic Party as he worked to craft his first economic rescue package. Incomes were continuing to plummet from the global financial crisis that followed the collapse of the Lehman Brothers investment bank in 2008. Unemployment was soaring, housing prices were plunging, and foreclosures were skyrocketing. Millions of Americans were losing their jobs, their businesses, their homes, and their life savings. Many of those who still had jobs were trapped in unsellable houses that were worth less than their mortgages. Everyone was feeling the pain, but as always, the most vulnerable were hurt the most. African American, Hispanic, Native American, and recent immigrant families, as well as many lower-income white families, had little wealth to cushion the blow of lost jobs as businesses closed.[2] Recent college graduates in the millennial generation were also hit hard because they had taken on large student loans but were unable to find jobs that paid enough to support the debt. For many people and many businesses, the effects of the financial crisis were to linger for a decade or longer.[3]

As in any recession, tax revenues had dropped dramatically at the end of the George W. Bush administration; government spending for recession-related programs (such as food assistance and unemployment insurance payments) had risen just as dramatically, so the budget deficit was growing. This automatic stabilization[4] worked to help cushion the effects of the economic downturn. Automatic stabilization provides an economic boost just when it is needed most. It makes no sense to criticize short-term deficits that occur automatically when the nation's economy slows down, because deficits are good policy when they boost demand and stop a downward business cycle. Without passing any new laws, the budget deficit will get larger in an economic downturn because tax revenues fall and spending increases for unemployment benefits, nutrition assistance, and other economic sup-

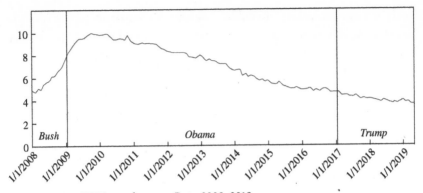

FIGURE 8-1.    US Unemployment Rate, 2008–2019
*Source:* Bureau of Labor Statistics, Household Survey Monthly Reports.

ports as more people need them.[5] But unless the government has been running a surplus and building resources for a "rainy day," the reduced revenue and increased spending will add to the short-term budget deficit. With the deep recession in the Bush era reaching emergency proportions, policymakers were correctly putting concerns about medium- and long-term deficits (brought about by the retirement of the baby boomers) on the back burner, to be addressed once the emergency was over and the economy began to recover.

The economic crisis continued into 2009, but the spirit of bipartisanship that had delivered strong Democratic support for the emergency economic measures proposed by the Republican president late in his final year in office did not continue. The 2008 election was celebrated on the Democratic side as a historic win for the first African American president, but on the Republican side it was viewed ominously. Republicans responded in two distinct ways to the November defeat that saw Democrats gain eight Senate seats and twenty-one House seats to strengthen their control in both chambers. Reince Priebus, the chair of the Republican National Committee, issued a lengthy report calling on the Republican Party to moderate its message to appeal to a younger and more racially diverse electorate.[6] The report suggested a break with the current Republican anti-government rhetoric softening the Party's messages against government assistance to people in need, saying, "To people who are flat on their back, unemployed or disabled and in need of help, they do not care if the help comes from the private sector or the government—they just want help."

Mitch McConnell, the Republican leader in the Senate, took a very different approach, signaling in December that he would be an active opposition leader by voicing skepticism toward president-elect Obama's economic recovery package. Although Obama inherited the Great Recession from his predecessor, Republicans quickly blamed the new president for the "trillion-dollar deficits" that ensued and refused to join in further legislation to mitigate the impact of the recession.

The Obama economic package was the result of a long series of negotiations starting within the White House and then working all sides of Capitol Hill. Obama's economic advisors were divided over the size of the package. The chair of his Council of Economic Advisors, Christina Romer, had studied the Great Depression, and she calculated that the government needed to spend $1.8 trillion to fill the gap caused by the financial system's collapse. Obama's chief economic advisor, Larry Summers, refused to present such a large number to the president, because Summers did not think it was politically viable.[7] The first proposal publicly released by Romer and Jared Bernstein, economic advisor to Vice President Joe Biden, had a price tag of $775 billion. Romer was right about the economics, but (regrettably) Summers was also right about the politics.

---

*I believe the Great Recession would have been longer and deeper without the stimulus package of 2009. If the stimulus had been larger and lasted longer, recovery would have been more robust and the Fed might not have found it necessary to do so much quantitative easing. Indeed, it is pretty crazy economics for a country trying to climb out of a deep recession to put the burden of accelerating a recovery on the monetary authorities—a job they have never been great at—in the face of sharply declining federal deficits that made the task of stimulating recovery with monetary tools a lot more challenging. But that is what we did.*

—Alice M. Rivlin, "Thoughts about Monetary and Fiscal Policy in a Post-Inflation World," Economic Policy Conference, 2015

---

In retrospect, we know Christina Romer was right about the economics because the economy recovered so painfully slowly after the $838 billion package was negotiated and passed. The government was spending about $1 trillion less than she calculated was needed to grow the economy as fast as it had the potential to grow. After leaving the Obama administration, Christina and her husband, David Romer, wrote about the concept of "fiscal space" that captures my own views quite well.[8] Basically, they argue that nations spend less than they should in a severe economic downturn because they run deficits that are too large during normal economic times. Either the US had too little fiscal space or policymakers believed they had too little, because the tax cuts early in the millennium under President George W. Bush meant the government was running larger-than-necessary deficits before the financial system collapsed at the end of the decade. I am known as a deficit hawk because, throughout my career, I have drawn attention to the long-term (well, not so long-term now) budgetary crisis we will face as the baby boom generation reaches retirement, but I actually believe there was too much emphasis on the shorter-term deficit and debt in the first few years of the Obama administration while the economy was still weak.

Larry Summers was, as I said, right about the politics. The deficits caused by the financial meltdown were large in dollar terms, and the public took notice. Republicans were drawing attention to the deficits and debt, as were many moderate Democrats. The Democrats had enough votes in the House to pass legislation and just enough Democratic Senators to avoid a filibuster. Reconciliation could have been used for taxing and spending bills, making a partisan path even easier. But Obama had campaigned for president on themes of national unity and healing the "red state" versus "blue state" national divisions, so he made a firm decision to seek Republican support for his first major economic initiative.

The size of the economic package was a key element of the negotiations, and moderate Republican and Democratic senators, in the name of concern about excessive spending and deficits, set clear limits on the total price tag. They insisted it needed to be closer to $800 million than $1 trillion—and this drove negotiations toward the $838 billion that eventually passed.[9] The moderate Democratic and Republican senators also insisted on a substantial shift in emphasis from stimulus spending to stimulus tax cuts, and roughly one-third of the final package took the form of tax cuts. Nearly every line in the large spending and tax cut bill was hotly debated between the Democrats in the House, and between the moderate Democrats and Republicans needed to win passage in the Senate.

In the end, the Obama stimulus bill passed the House without any Republican votes[10] and received just three votes from Senate Republican moderates, leaving it 1 vote short of the 60-vote threshold needed to break a Republican filibuster.[11] Senator Sherrod Brown (D-OH) had to return immediately from memorial services for his mother to cast the deciding vote.[12] That the Republicans were playing such hardball in negotiations with the new president, winning concessions and then, in return, providing so few votes on final passage, was a clear sign that bipartisan cooperation was going to be very difficult in Obama's tenure as president.

The economy shed 800,000 jobs in January 2009, as the economic decline was growing in speed and depth. The economic stabilizers and extraordinary measures passed at the end of the Bush administration were no match for the accelerating global financial meltdown. Far more action would be needed, but Democrats who had provided most of the votes for George Bush's rescue package for the economy and the big banks were now on their own to deal with the economic shambles. Republicans largely stayed on the sidelines, complaining about the lack of jobs, large deficits, and the "bank bailout" even though a Republican president had passed the Troubled Asset Relief Program (TARP) with a substantial number of Republican votes in the House and Senate. By the time of the midterm elections, Joshua Green, writing in the *Atlantic*, would dub the TARP Wall Street bailout "the forbidden bipartisan success" because Republicans were so actively denouncing it on the campaign trail.[13]

Obama's American Recovery and Reinvestment Act (ARRA, also known as the Recovery Act) did an awful lot of good. It helped turn around an economy in steep decline and put it on a path to steady growth. It provided help to the states in the form of higher Medicaid payments and more support for education. It provided tax cuts for low-income workers, support for those most harmed by the financial crisis (such as increases in food stamps, housing and childcare assistance, and farm loans), and public investments designed to create jobs and increase future productivity (such as road and bridge repairs, and job training programs).[14]

Many economists thought the Obama stimulus package was too small, given the magnitude of the economic catastrophe.[15] Paul Krugman, the

*New York Times* columnist with a Nobel Prize in Economics, was particularly vocal on this point, echoing arguments similar to those Romer had marshaled inside the White House.[16] My own view is that the Recovery Act should have been bigger, but more importantly, there should have been more than one bill. Two or three bills, each smaller than the Recovery Act but adding up to a larger total, would have allowed the administration more time to design and implement a more efficient and effective package of measures.

Believing they had only one chance to pass an economic plan led Obama and the Democrats to shove everything they could think of into the Recovery Act, and this meant there were some bad ideas mixed in with the good ideas. It also meant the longer-term investments were lumped in with the short-term stimulus, making the Recovery Act complicated to design and to explain. Both stimulus and investments can be good policy, but when the distinction is blurred, the case for each of them is weakened.

Economic stimulus is at the heart of the John Maynard Keynes prescription for an economy that has a shortfall in consumer demand. Immediate economic stimulus puts more money into the hands of consumers as fast as possible. There are several ways to do this, including simply sending checks to families and individuals, extending or enhancing unemployment benefits, hiring a lot of people, or cutting taxes (perhaps by cutting payroll taxes or giving a tax rebate). Lots of policies can be stimulative if they get more money to consumers so they can spend it to keep the demand side of the economy going.[17]

There is also a stimulus effect in making investments in the economy that will increase future economic output. These investments yield a double benefit. First, there is the short-term stimulus that puts more money into the hands of construction workers, teachers, job skills trainers, and others who are hired to do whatever work the investments are funding. The second benefit is the longer-term effect on economic productivity of the investment in infrastructure, like improved roads or schools, or in a better educated, better trained workforce. When government investments, including investments in public health, basic scientific research, and development of new technologies, are thought out and well planned, they can have a longer-term benefit on the economy that surpasses the initial stimulative effect.

Putting everything into a single economic bill shifted all the emphasis of communications to immediate stimulus effects. Longer-term investments were being lumped in with stimulus tied to the shorter-term business cycle. In public statements about the ARRA, the projects that were more in the spirit of longer-term investments were tagged with the phrase "shovel-ready" to highlight their immediate effects, but this suggested the selection criteria for projects was speed rather than merit. In the years following passage of the Recovery Act, the Obama White House stopped using the word "stimulus" altogether after political advisors absorbed the results of public opinion polls telling them voters believed the stimulus money had been wasted and they had soured on the term.[18]

> If I'd been designing [the stimulus package], and obviously I wasn't, I would have taken a slightly slower tack on the long-run investment. We need to think carefully about how we're going to do this, and we need over time to pay for them. . . . I would have put it in two packages - one for the immediate stimulus and one for longer-run investment. But I understand why the president wanted to put it all in one because it then looks as though he is really serious about getting on top of this economic catastrophe. And that's what he should be doing.
>
> Alice Rivlin, February 1, 2009

Interviewed by Jacki Lyden, *All Things Considered*, National Public Radio

## MULTITASKING: OBAMA'S FIRST 100 DAYS STARTED BEFORE DAY ONE

The law requires presidents to submit a budget in February, and this is usually the first economic action of a new president, but the Recovery Act had been proposed and passed before President Obama submitted his first budget proposal on February 26, 2009, just weeks after his inauguration. The budget process was further complicated by the fact that Congress had failed to get its fiscal year 2009 work done in 2008, so the government was running on a continuing resolution that was set to expire in March 2009. The Democrats were now in control of the White House, the House, and the Senate, and although the president did not get everything he wanted,[19] the Democrats were able to pass a continuing resolution to fund the government through the end of fiscal year 2009,[20] including funding for the Recovery Act. They then passed the fiscal year 2010 budget[21] in April, which was months ahead of schedule for the fiscal year that would start on October 1, 2009.

The Obama administration had a lot of balls in the air. In addition to passing the Recovery Act and two budgets, it had to administer the TARP bank bailout and the automobile industry bailout it had inherited from the Bush administration. Neither had strong support from a public that was asking, "Where's MY bailout?" A partial answer to this question came in the form of the Car Allowance Rebate System (CARS, aka "Cash for Clunkers"), introduced and passed in June of 2009, which paid people to trade in their aging vehicles for more fuel-efficient models. And because the origins of the financial crisis came from the housing industry, Obama also introduced the Home Affordable Refinance Program (HARP) to help homeowners who were "underwater," meaning they owed more on their mortgages than the homes were worth in the depressed housing market. This allowed some homeowners to refinance and stay in their houses.[22]

The complexity of all these initiatives was overwhelming. President Obama tried to outline all his plans in his first address to Congress[23] and in a "five pillars" speech designed to put all the various initiatives into a framework.[24] But even with all of this going on, Obama kept one eye on the long-term deficit, and that was the focus of the Fiscal Responsibility Summit he convened in late February 2009.[25]

As noted in chapter 7, bipartisan efforts to focus attention on the long-term deficit and mounting debt were being organized on both sides of Capitol Hill. Representatives Frank Wolf (R-VA) and Jim Cooper (D-TN) and Senators Kent Conrad (D-ND) and Judd Gregg (R-NH) had introduced draft legislation in both chambers to create a bipartisan commission for proposing new solutions, but neither effort had amassed enough votes to pass before the recession made the problem far worse. Now the White House was joining the cause.

On February 23, 2009, in the first weeks of their term, President Obama, Vice President Biden, and their economic team invited Democratic and Republican lawmakers and experts to the Fiscal Responsibility Summit to explore how the parties could work together to reduce long-term federal deficits.[26] For those lawmakers who were worried about the near-term deficit increases resulting from recession-related stimulus measures, the summit was meant to offer reassurance that longer-term policies could be put in place to rein in the debt explosion associated with the retirement of the baby boom population.

The Recovery Act and other Obama initiatives, when combined with interventions inherited from the previous administration and aggressive Federal Reserve action to ease credit, certainly helped stop the economic free fall and put the economy on an upward path.[27] The recession officially ended in June 2009,[28] but this was merely a statistical declaration. The American public was still suffering from the deep and long-lasting effects of the economic collapse, with an unemployment rate above 9 percent. But in addition to the devastating impacts the financial crisis and the Great Recession had on households and businesses, the downturn also blew a Grand Canyon-size hole in the federal budget. Rapidly rising deficits, associated both with the recession itself and with measures to mitigate its impact, added massively to the national debt. In 2007 the deficit was 1.1 percent of gross domestic product (GDP), which was a very manageable number, but just two years later, at the start of 2009, the deficit had jumped to 9.8 percent of GDP.[29] Although economists expected the deficit to fall as the economy recovered—and it did—the higher burden of public debt, which had climbed from 35.6 percent of GDP in 2007 to 53.3 percent of GDP by the end of 2009, combined with the demographic time bomb of the aging boomers, was seen as a worrisome sign.[30]

It was in this environment that the White House was also developing its health care reform proposals, so President Obama asked his team to find a way to extend health care to more Americans, but to also do so in a way that adhered to the spirit of the "pay-as-you-go" (PAYGO) rules Congress was no longer living under. When Obama presented his plan for the Affordable Care Act to Congress in September, he did so saying, "I will not sign a plan that adds one dime to our deficits—either now or in the future. Period. And to prove that I'm serious, there will be a provision in this plan that requires us to come forward with more spending cuts if the savings we promised don't materialize."[31]

Obama and the Democrats spent the rest of 2009 working within the multiple constraints of an economy that needed a lot of stimulus, investment, and other interventions to get it moving forward; the need to extend access to affordable health care to millions of uninsured Americans; and a government deficit and debt level that was expanding due to the immediate crisis and also projected to become unsustainable over the longer term due to changing demographics.

The Republicans were positioning themselves as opposing nearly every aspect of the Democrats' agenda. Even though the economic collapse started in the final year of the George W. Bush administration, Republicans were criticizing the Obama economy with the question, "Mr. President, where are the jobs?"[32] Republicans also criticized the deficit and national debt, but at the same time they made it clear they would oppose any tax increase, and especially any tax added to pay for health care reform. President Obama was criticized for not reaching out enough to the Republican leadership, either on the substance of his economic and health care reform bills or socially with invitations to the White House or to play golf, and the consistent message coming from the House Republicans was far from conciliatory.[33] This was symbolically reflected in a break from decorum when Representative Joe Wilson (R-SC) interrupted Obama's address to Congress on the release of his health care reform plan, shouting "You lie!" at the president. (Wilson apologized the next day for the outburst.)[34]

## HEALTH CARE REFORM

From the time Nancy Pelosi (D-CA) presented the Democrats' first draft of the legislation that would become the Patient Protection and Affordable Care Act[35] through eventual passage on March 23, 2010, health care reform dominated the Washington agenda, even though most of the action was happening behind closed doors, in intense negotiations between the president and lawmakers, and especially their staffs.

President Obama had hoped to reform health care through bipartisan cooperation, and he made several efforts to reach out to Republicans for support. From the start, he disappointed the Democrats on the left by rejecting the "single-payer" approach to reform, where government would provide health care to all Americans. Instead, he embraced plans that maintained private health insurance and expanded access to the millions of uninsured Americans through a combination of public and private insurance. The Medicaid program was already providing healthcare for the lowest-income families, but Obama raised the level of income that would qualify for Medicaid to allow more working poor families to qualify. Since Medicaid is administered at the state level, he added money for states to help them with the added burden.

The real challenge was for families and individuals that made more money than the Medicaid threshold but did not have health insurance. Some could not afford the insurance, either because they did not have enough money for a basic plan or because someone in the family had a preexisting condition, which meant coverage was priced out of reach. Other families or individuals did not have health insurance because they did not want to pay for it or they hoped they would remain in good health and would not need it.

The Obama plan changed the rules for insurance companies, forcing them to cover people with preexisting conditions at the same rate as other consumers. But this created a temptation for consumers to wait until they got sick to start paying for insurance, so the plan also changed the rules for consumers, mandating that they either get insurance or pay a tax penalty. The plan offered substantial subsidies for individuals and families to help them purchase private health insurance on managed markets called exchanges, all designed to help lower-middle income and middle-income people find insurance plans they could afford.

The overall approach had been proposed by the conservative think tank the Heritage Foundation and implemented in Massachusetts by Republican Governor Mitt Romney. By relying on the private sector rather than proposing a government solution, Obama was following the playbook that had foundered for President Clinton, but Obama wanted to distinguish his effort by inviting the health care industries into the process (further disappointing the Democratic left flank). In March 2009, the White House assembled representatives from health insurance and pharmaceutical companies, medical device manufacturers, hospitals, doctors, and other stakeholders. Bringing the health care industries into the room worked to keep most of them on board, but the efforts to present a moderate reform plan still were not successful in attracting Republican support.

Republican leaders made it clear they believed they could damage Obama's credibility by blocking health care reform, just as they had done with President Clinton, and that this would help them win the next election. For this reason, the leadership actively discouraged compromise by moderate Republicans in the Senate and did not provide a single Republican vote in the House.

Democrats were back in the same position they had been in when negotiating the economic package: Obama wanted to find the common ground that could earn him a handful of Republican and moderate Democratic votes needed to break a Senate filibuster while maintaining the support of the most progressive Democrats in the House as well as the more moderate House Democrats. After many months of negotiations, even Obama had to admit that there would not be any Senate Republican votes to pass healthcare reform, so every Senate Democrat was needed for passage.

The Democrats, however, were split on several provisions of the bill. Progressives thought there should be a "public option"—a government-run health plan that would compete with private plans to keep costs down. Moderates feared a public option would upset the balance of competition between private companies in the health insurance exchanges, and if the government-sponsored public option had advantages, or even if it simply proved popular, it could ultimately lead to a government monopoly. The public option was eventually dropped from the health care bill when five moderate Democrats voted it down in the Senate Finance Committee,[36] and Senator Joseph Lieberman, a political independent from Connecticut who had been on the Democratic ticket as Al Gore's running mate in 2000, came out against it, giving its opponents a filibuster-sustaining block in the Senate.

My own view is that the battle for and against the public option was more symbolic than substantive. A public option, that could mean allowing people to buy Medicare coverage at younger ages, would be good public policy, but I did not see the need to make this a priority in passing the ACA in 2010. Beyond the expansion of Medicaid to cover more of the uninsured, the heavy legislative lift in the Affordable Care Act was the need to set up the exchanges in each of the fifty states and US territories. You could not have a public option without creating the exchanges where families and individuals choose their coverage, but there is no reason you cannot set up the exchanges and then add a public option at a later point. I expect this is what Democrats will do the next time they are able to make health care policy. My advice to Democrats at the time was that they should put all their energy into passing a bill to expand Medicaid and create health care exchanges that work as advertised and provide access to health care for uninsured Americans.

After dropping the public option, Democrats appeared close to victory, but Senator Ted Kennedy (D-MA) passed away from a brain tumor in August, and in a political surprise, he was replaced in a special election by a Republican. New Senator Scott Brown (R-MA) and his opposition to the Affordable Care Act cost the Democrats their Senate supermajority. After publicly meeting with the Republicans, President Obama and the Democrats determined that a compromise was not possible. Instead, they passed the ACA using some particularly fancy legislative footwork.

The House and Senate had by this point both passed health care reform bills, but they were not identical as required for legislation to become law. They were based on the same approach, but the House bill was more generous and carried a price tag of over $1 trillion compared with the Senate bill, which was closer to $800 billion (even though both versions raised enough revenue to offset their costs). The House refused to just accept the Senate bill, although by many accounts, both President Obama[37] and House Speaker Nancy Pelosi were personally committed to getting the problem solved and passing the bill. The plan they devised had the Senate and House working out the compromises to get the bills aligned. Then the House would pass the Senate bill (even though it was unacceptable to the House), and both the House and Senate would pass a legislative "sidecar" bill that made the changes

---

*Health care policy is far too important to be driven by a single party's ideology. Programs that affect people's lives so intimately must flow from a broad bipartisan consensus. The public's health insurance coverage should not bounce around unpredictably with each party transition in an election.*

—Alice M. Rivlin, "Curing Health
Care: The Next President Should
Complete, Not Abandon, Obama's
Reform," May 4, 2012

---

to bring the Senate bill in line with the House/Senate compromise.[38] The sidecar was designed to qualify as a reconciliation bill under the budget process, so it only needed a simple 51-vote majority to pass rather then the 60-vote threshold normally needed to break a filibuster.[39]

The Republicans howled their opposition to both the substance of the bill and the process the Democrats had used to pass it without any Republican votes. There would be court challenges, and some of them were successful in invalidating important provisions of the law. But President Obama had succeeded in expanding health insurance coverage to the uninsured, even if he had not been able to achieve his original goal of doing it in a bipartisan manner. Obama signed the Patient Protection and Affordable Care Act into law on March 23, 2010.[40]

Officially the Democrats were celebrating a huge legislative accomplishment, but many prominent voices on the left, both in Congress and on the editorial pages, were calling it a partial victory because it relied on the private insurance industry, not single-payer, government-run health care, and because the public option had been dropped from the bill. President Obama was personally disappointed by this reaction, and in an extended response to a question from Jonathan Weisman, a reporter for the *Wall Street Journal*, at a press conference late in 2010, Obama explained his frustration with the elements of the Democratic Party that opposed compromise to achieve progressive change.

"So I pass a signature piece of legislation where we finally get health care for all Americans, something that Democrats had been fighting for for a hundred years, but because there was a provision in there that they didn't get that would have affected maybe a couple of million people, even though we got health insurance for 30 million people and the potential for lower premiums for 100 million people, that somehow that was a sign of weakness and compromise."

Opinionated voices on the left and the right have outsized influence in the American political media landscape, and this contributed to the tepid reaction to the passage of the Affordable Care Act. Cable news is filled with debates between one liberal and one conservative, and often this meant there was no one arguing that the ACA was an unqualified success. It was no surprise that "Obamacare" was pilloried as an unmitigated disaster on Fox News and the editorial pages of the *Wall Street Journal*. The disappointment for the Obama administration was that the ACA was debated as only a partial success on MSNBC and the editorial pages of the *New York Times*. The public was divided but generally more negative than positive toward the ACA in the early years, after passage in 2010 but before implementation in 2013.[41] Implementation came with its own challenges, especially when the website Healthcare.gov was overwhelmed when it debuted and had to be debugged and relaunched.[42] But eventually the ACA proved to be both popular with the public and effective public policy in dramatically bringing down the number of uninsured Americans.

## THE ORIGINS OF THE SIMPSON-BOWLES COMMISSION

Throughout 2009 and into 2010, Senators Conrad and Gregg continued to sign on supporters for their proposal to form a commission that would address the long-term fiscal problem presented by the retiring baby boom generation, and they finally appeared to have the bipartisan support needed to pass their bill in the Senate.[43] But at the crucial moment, prominent Republican cosponsors, including Majority Leader Mitch McConnell, faded away as they realized the process would likely require them to swallow a tax increase as well as spending cuts.[44] In January 2010, the Conrad-Gregg proposal received 53 votes in the Senate—strong support, but short of the 60 votes needed to avoid a filibuster.[45] In the House, the Wolf-Cooper companion bill never made it out of committee.

President Obama liked the debt commission idea, which had already been proposed by his Council of Economic Advisors. The Obama economic team realized that, while the recession-caused deficits would recede as the economy improved, the problem of paying for the promises made to the avalanche of seniors would remain. A strong chapter in the annual Economic Report of the President in early 2010 outlined the dimensions of the longer-term fiscal challenge, emphasizing both the rapidly rising population of seniors and the historical growth of per capita health care costs at 2.3 percent faster than the growth in per capita GDP.[46] The combination of more beneficiaries and rising health care costs would drive a wedge between federal spending and revenues, causing debt to rise faster than the economy could grow. Stabilizing the debt could only reasonably be accomplished by some combination of slower growth in spending (especially for health care) and additional revenues, policies that would require bipartisan consensus. The president thought a bipartisan commission would be a good way to arrive at a plan to reduce the projected growth of debt.

When Conrad-Gregg failed to win Senate approval, Obama announced he would create a similar commission by executive order.[47] The National Commission on Fiscal Responsibility and Reform would be cochaired by former senator Alan Simpson (R-WY) and former Clinton chief of staff Erskine Bowles. It would have twelve congressional members (six Republicans and six Democrats) and six public members, including the chairs. The commission would be charged with reducing the deficit (excluding interest on the debt) to zero by 2015 and stabilizing the debt-to-GDP ratio at an "acceptable level" by the time the economy recovered. The appointment of the commission established President Obama's intention to deal seriously with the debt problem without requiring any action before the November election.

Anti-tax Republicans called the Simpson-Bowles Commission a trap to get Republicans to support tax increases. Grover Norquist, the sharp-tongued anti-tax activist and head of Americans for Tax Reform, denounced Alan Simpson as a "useful idiot" being used by President Obama to endorse tax increases.[48] Some Democrats accused the commission of providing political cover for slashing Social Security and Medicare. Conrad and Gregg were initially opposed to creating a commission by executive order rather than by legislation, since it would be more difficult to bring the recommendations to a vote.[49] (They were right about that.) However, the White House worked successfully to get congressional leadership in both parties to cooperate and appoint strong budget-savvy members to the commission, including the chairs and ranking members of the House and Senate Budget Committees.[50] Speaker Nancy Pelosi (D-CA) and Senate Majority Leader Harry Reid (D-NV) promised to bring the recommendations to the floor for a vote if the recommendations were supported by fourteen of the eighteen members.

Since I had long advocated strong bipartisan action to reduce the growth of debt, I was delighted with President Obama's embrace of the budget commission initiative. I thought it showed that he understood the economic threat of the long-term debt explosion and was prepared to use the power of the presidency to broker a bipartisan solution. I had worked with Erskine

Bowles in the Clinton administration, and I admired his leadership ability and commitment to fiscal responsibility. I had known Alan Simpson since he was elected to the Senate in 1978, when I was running the Congressional Budget Office (CBO), and knew that behind his wisecracking cowboy humor was a strong intellect and solid commitment to finding workable solutions to hard problems. Besides, I was already involved in a parallel bipartisan effort to craft a "grand bargain."

## THE DOMENICI-RIVLIN TASK FORCE

When the Simpson-Bowles Commission was established, I was coleading the Debt Reduction Task Force at the Bipartisan Policy Center (BPC). In the fall of 2009, I had received a call from Pete Domenici (R-NM), who had just retired after thirty-six years in the Senate. Pete had joined the BPC, a think tank founded by former Senate leaders from both parties and dedicated to working across partisan barriers to solve big public problems. I had enormous respect for Pete and shared his deep concern about the threat that the growing debt posed to future American prosperity. When he asked me to join him in co-chairing a Debt Reduction Task Force that would craft a grand bargain to rein in the projected explosion in the national debt, I did not hesitate to accept.

I first met Pete Domenici in 1975, when I was starting CBO. I quickly discovered that the freshman senator from New Mexico was one of the smartest, hardest-working members of the Senate Budget Committee. By the early Reagan years, Domenici was chair of the Budget Committee, where Fritz Hollings of South Carolina, later known for coauthoring Gramm-Rudman-Hollings, was the ranking Democrat. Both were fiscal conservatives dedicated to enforcing the complex rules of the congressional budget process to try to restrain the ever-growing national debt. In keeping with the bipartisan tradition of the Senate Budget Committee, established by its first chair, Ed Muskie (D-ME), and ranking member Henry Bellmon (R-OK), Domenici and Hollings worked closely together. As CBO director, I had good relations with both. I was especially grateful to Domenici for defending the independence of CBO in the face of early attacks from the Reagan administration. In the 1990s, Domenici and I were on opposite sides of negotiations between the Clinton administration and the Republican-led Congress, but we always remained friends and, in the end, each believed the other deserved a fair share of the credit for the budget surpluses that were achieved. I jumped at the chance to work with him again.

When it came to the composition of the membership, the distinctions between the think tank-based Domenici-Rivlin Task Force and the more official Simpson-Bowles Commission may seem quite subtle from an outsider's perspective, but from my point of view they were quite different. Many of the BPC Debt Reduction Task Force members were like me in that we had never been elected to anything, but we had a lot of experience and expertise in evaluating budgetary options. By contrast, most of the members of the Simpson-Bowles Commission were current senators or members of Congress, and therefore had to be conscious of political and party pressures.

For Domenici-Rivlin, we assembled a diverse and highly qualified group of budget experts and former officeholders from both parties, plus a talented staff, and got to work.[51] The group included former governors and mayors, federal officials, and business, labor, and nonprofit leaders. Many task force members had participated in intense budget negotiations at the federal, state, and local levels of government, either as principles or key staff members, including many I had worked with in federal budget negotiations or my work for the District of Columbia and other cities that had managed their way beyond budget crises. Although most task force members had strong party affiliations as Republicans or Democrats, they agreed to work together to craft a debt reduction plan that reflected a consensus view of all the members, even though individuals might not agree with pieces of it in isolation. We all agreed that "everything was on the table," meaning we would not rule out any type of revenue or spending change in advance.

Task force members were motivated by a mutual understanding of the grim projections of deficit and debt increases that would occur over the next three decades if policies did not change. The ratio of debt to GDP, then approaching 60 percent, would surpass 100 percent by the middle of the next decade. This could cause interest rates to rise and then interest payments would soar. The danger would come if payments for major entitlements plus interest would exceed total projected revenue, leaving no funding for all the other functions of government, including defense. The budget trajectory was becoming unsustainable.

The real goal of the Domenici-Rivlin Task Force was as much to show the value of bipartisan problem-solving as it was to show that it was possible to maintain the economic recovery the nation needed, while at the same time raising enough new revenue and cutting the rate of increase in future spending to close the fiscal gap, and doing it without placing additional burdens on the people who would least be able to bear the load.

There were concerns from conservatives and progressives. Progressives worried that we were going to cut needed benefits for the poor or force seniors into poverty. Conservatives worried that we were going to recommend anti-growth tax hikes. But both of these fears were misplaced. There are sensible ways to slow the growth of benefits for those who can afford it while maintaining benefit levels for those who depend on government programs for the bulk of their income. There also are ways to increase revenues that do not choke off economic growth. There were realistic compromise solutions to change the details of policies to deal with both the impending insolvency of the major trust fund programs and the need for more revenues to fund the government the public expects.

The task force agreed on the goal of stabilizing the government debt-to-GDP ratio to about where it currently was, with the total public debt equal to 60 percent of the nation's total yearly output, and then putting this ratio on a downward path. There are three ways to achieve this goal (and we were fairly certain that we would have to do each of them):

1. Increase economic growth
2. Reduce the growth rate of federal spending
3. Increase federal revenue

Increasing the GDP (economic growth) is the best way to improve the debt-to-GDP ratio but the hardest to achieve. More growth means a larger GDP, and it means less debt as government spending decreases and revenue increases.[52] But we were in a slow recovery from an economic crisis, so while everyone wanted more growth, the options to accelerate growth were limited. We evaluated several choices for short-term economic investment or stimulus, including the payroll tax holiday that made it into the Domenici-Rivlin plan.

Although faster economic growth could increase revenues, no feasible rate of growth under current tax laws would produce enough revenue to offset the projected cost of providing Social Security and health care to the growing number of people eligible for benefits. Some combination of

*Budget policy is a disaster because it is the province of our deeply broken legislative system. The ability to compromise and solve problems across party lines is essential to making a budget and this ability has failed us just when we need it most. In a persistently slow growth economy where monetary policy is likely to be relatively ineffective, pro-growth fiscal policy could actually help.*

—Alice M. Rivlin, "Priorities for
Economic Policy," April 21, 2015

restraining benefits and raising revenues would be necessary to control the rising debt. However, for fear of being demonized by the other side and suffering losses at the polls, neither party on its own could propose enough new revenue through higher taxes or enough cuts in spending through lower benefit levels to close the funding gap. Hence, the only hope for reducing the looming debt growth was a bipartisan grand bargain, in which the parties would take joint responsibility for some combination of politically unpopular spending cuts and equally unpopular revenue increases. If both parties owned the bargain, neither could demonize the other. The challenge was to craft a package of spending and tax changes that could gain enough bipartisan support to pass. We hoped our recommendations would help facilitate the process.

Before even discussing revenue increases, we decided to focus on ways of reducing the future growth in federal spending. No one wanted to suggest tax increases without first being sure we had combed through the budget to eliminate wasteful or low-priority spending wherever possible. There are two broad categories of government spending that are given the names "discretionary" and "entitlements." I do not like either of these names because they capture neither the true nature nor the importance of either category. Both are important.

Discretionary spending is the name we give to every line in the budget that the president proposes, and that Congress authorizes through the appropriations process. This includes the funding for the military, education, housing assistance, transportation, justice, management of national parks and lands, public health, and dozens of other smaller categories of spending.

But all of this is less than one-third of what the government spends, and it has not been rising as a share of the national economy (GDP). Although it was not projected to contribute to the future rise in debt, we proposed a freeze on discretionary spending as a clear signal that it was not going to be the part of the budget that was either problematic or spared from fiscal discipline.

The entitlements (also called mandatory spending) make up the other two-thirds of government spending. These include Social Security, Medicare, Medicaid, most veterans' benefits, and a long list of much smaller programs like food assistance (Supplemental Nutrition Assistance Program, or SNAP), civilian retirement benefits, and anything that people are entitled to if they fit the criteria defined in the law establishing the program. The budget's mammoth programs, Social Security, Medicare, and Medicaid, accounted for nearly all the projected spending increases, so we mainly looked for ways of gradually phasing in entitlement changes that would restrain the growth rate of spending on these programs, with particular emphasis on higher-income households, while maintaining or even increasing benefits for the neediest beneficiaries.

We proposed a plan that would have placed Social Security on a sustainable fiscal track with a balanced set of incremental benefit reductions and revenue increases. These included lower benefits for the highest earners, a phased-in delay in the retirement age for future retirees, and calculating the cost-of-living adjustment more accurately. This was one of the easier parts of our challenge.

The plan included a controversial structural reform of Medicare, known as premium support,[54] which we believed could deliver better care to seniors while helping control the growth of health costs. With premium support, instead of providing health care services directly, as Medicare does, the government would give people money to buy health insurance on a private insurance marketplace like those created by the Affordable Care Act. The government would regulate the basic health care services the plan must deliver and provide data to consumers about comparative patient health outcomes. Many Medicare beneficiaries already have experience getting their health services delivered this way through Medicare Advantage plans, which were first proposed as "Medicare+Choice" by President Clinton and then expanded by President George W. Bush in the Medicare Prescription Drug Improvement and Modernization Act of 2003.[55]

The hope and expectation were that Medicare beneficiaries, armed with good information about the cost and health outcomes of the plans, could choose the best and most cost-effective plans, and that competition for customers would reduce waste and poorly delivered services. We believed that the insurance companies would have strong incentives to coordinate their patients' care, emphasize prevention, and avoid duplicative testing and the excessive charges that plague the traditional Medicare fee-for-service system.

At this time, premium support was championed by many Republicans and opposed by many Democrats. This to me was an apparent inconsistency because the broad outline of the proposal was to do for Medicare what the Democrats had done in the Affordable Care Act, which was still drawing intense Republican criticism. The ACA featured consumer choice among competing private health plans combined with government subsidies to make the insurance affordable for families and individuals who would otherwise find it difficult to afford. Republicans were not shy in attacking the ACA, holding countless House votes to repeal it. But at the same time, they were proposing converting Medicare to a premium support model, which would combine consumer choice among competing private plans with government subsidies to defray the cost of Medicare coverage. While rejecting the ACA, even though it was based on ideas developed in Republican-leaning think tanks, Republicans proposed those same ideas for Medicare beneficiaries, expecting that a subsidized choice among competing health plans would deliver higher quality care more efficiently and at a lower cost. Democrats were no less self-contradictory in defending the ACA while attacking premium support as a voucher program that would "end Medicare as we know it."[56] To be fair, however, there were many versions of premium support (as discussed in chapter 9), and this criticism is valid for premium support proposals that are mandatory rather than the optional version of premium support we included in the task force report.

A voluntary plan needs to attract enough participation to make a budgetary difference, so the Domenici-Rivlin Task Force version of premium support deliberately set the level of the subsidy fairly high (compared with other proposals for premium support) and set the rate of increase higher

*American health care is expensive compared to that in other developed nations and its quality is uneven. Part of the reason is that so much health care is compensated on a fee-for-service basis, which encourages providers to deliver more services but does not reward quality, efficiency, or positive health outcomes.*

*There are two possible approaches to improving the performance of health providers along these lines. One is to change incentives in traditional Medicare by regulation. The other is to foster competition among health plans on a regulated exchange or marketplace. In the original Domenici-Rivlin plan, we recommended doing both— improving traditional Medicare by regulation, but also introducing the option of competition among integrated health plans in a premium support model. Subsequent analysis has suggested that it may be possible to introduce the competitive element more smoothly by ensuring that Medicare Advantage plans compete in a more transparent marketplace with effective incentives to improve health outcomes and lower costs.*

—Alice M. Rivlin, "Growing the Economy and Stabilizing the Debt," testimony before the US Congress Joint Economic Committee, March 14, 2013

as well, at the rate of GDP growth plus 1 percent. This meant our proposal was more generous and most seniors would be able to meet their medical needs without going deeply into their own pockets, but it also meant the long-term budgetary savings from Medicare were smaller than those in other proposals. We also proposed allowing Medicare to negotiate pharmaceutical prices as an additional cost-saving measure.

By the time we had exhausted the list of spending cuts and other savings in both discretionary and entitlement spending that could gain bipartisan consensus, even the more conservative Republican members on our task force realized we would not be able to reach our debt stabilization goal without revenue increases, so we turned to tax reform. We agreed on a thorough revamping of the income tax that would raise more revenue while reducing tax rates. This seeming miracle is nonetheless achievable by using an approach that had been around for many years and had strong bipartisan support among tax experts. The basic idea is to broaden the income tax base by limiting deductions, exclusions, and special provisions (popularly known as "loopholes") that narrow the tax base. There is actually a large amount of income that is sheltered from the income tax, especially among the wealthiest of taxpayers who own large homes, or more than one home, have lots of tax-preferred investments, and can hire tax advisors that know how to take advantage of the tax code.

The task force agreed on a specific tax proposal, authored by our two tax experts, Len Burman and Joe Minarik, which remains a strong model for future tax reform. It capped the exclusion of employer-paid health benefits, then lowered the cap gradually to phase out the exclusion over ten years. It also converted the home mortgage deduction on new mortgages to a tax credit, which would benefit low- and moderate-income taxpayers more but provide much less generous benefits to high-income homeowners with big mortgages on expensive homes. By closing these loopholes, more revenue could be gained even as tax rates were lowered in percentage terms.

We also discussed taking some of the burden off the income tax by adding an additional tax source, either a gradually phased-in carbon tax, which would discourage use of fossil fuels, or a national sales tax to shift some of the burden of taxation from income to consumption. We opted for the latter in the first version of our report, with a proposal for a 6.5 percent national sales tax.[57] Recognizing that recovery from the recession was still incomplete, we proposed a one-year payroll tax holiday as a temporary stimulus to increase consumer spending and increase employment.[58] This was similar to the approach we had taken early in the Clinton administration, when we proposed a short-term stimulus package at the same time we were making proposals to address the long-term debt.

## DOING DOUBLE DUTY

While we were setting up our task force at BPC in 2009, Pete and I talked with Senators Conrad and Gregg about their hopes to create a bipartisan budget commission by legislation. They thought having a bipartisan group working the debt reduction problem outside the government would be helpful even if their legislation passed, and they encouraged us to move ahead.

When the Conrad-Gregg legislation failed, President Obama announced the Simpson-Bowles Commission, and Larry Summers called from the White House to ask me to join it. I hesitated, citing my commitment to Pete and BPC, but ended up serving on both. Having a common member improved communication between the two groups and was a fascinating, if somewhat frazzling, experience for me.

The two groups were dedicated to the same objective—crafting policies that would gradually put the national debt onto a sustainable path without derailing the current economic recovery, and that members of both parties could support. Both had approximately equal numbers of Republicans and Democrats and had cochairs from different parties. However, due to the different environments in which they existed, the two groups operated in quite different ways.

Unlike the collegial think tank milieu of the Bipartisan Policy Center, Alan Simpson and Erskine Bowles were working in an intensely partisan atmosphere. Appointed by an embattled Democratic president facing the 2010 midterm elections in November, they had the daunting task of guiding a group with eighteen appointees, twelve of whom were sitting members of the House or Senate, toward a bipartisan agreement. The congressional members were taking big risks. If they even discussed draft proposals for tax increases or entitlement cuts, there was always the chance that a leaked proposal would be pinned on them and used to demonize them, either by candidates of their own party in a primary contest or by the other party in the general election. ("He will raise your taxes!" or "She will cut your Medicare!")

To guard against such leaks, the commission never discussed proposed solutions as a group. Except for a few ceremonial open meetings, we met behind closed doors, which infuriated the press. Only a small number of highly trusted staff were allowed in the meeting room. Outside experts presented projections of the budgetary outlook and analysis of alternative policies (their own, not the commission's). Members of the commission discussed the proposals, raised questions, or offered comments. The discussions were thoughtful and civil. In fact, I was surprised that members who were vociferously attacking opponents and their policies on the campaign trail could gather on Wednesdays on Capitol Hill and engage in such constructive dialogue. Republicans who had adamantly refused to talk about tax solutions began to realize that the benefits most citizens wanted for seniors could not be financed at current tax rates. These Republicans began to discuss how to increase the government's revenue, especially if it could be done without raising income tax rates. Democrats who had been equally adamant in rejecting all entitlement reductions began to realize that the rising overall cost of current and future benefits was not sustainable without changes either in the benefits or taxes, and that some benefits go to households that could afford to pay for them. These Democrats began to discuss ways of focusing the benefits more on the people who needed them the most.

Because of the possibility of leaks that could cause political harm to commission members, Simpson and Bowles never risked open debate on a complete plan in a full commission meeting. Instead, they listened to the discussions of specific programs (e.g., Medicare or the corporate income tax), talked with individual commission members and their staffs, and privately produced a draft plan (a "chairman's mark," in Hill parlance). Then the two shared their proposals and negotiated with individual members in an attempt to modify the plan enough to win their support.

In the end, Simpson and Bowles had a majority of the commission on board but lost too many of the congressional members from both parties to achieve the demanding fourteen out of eighteen (78 percent) needed for approval.[59] But this is getting ahead of the story—and the story was about to change dramatically. Both Domenici-Rivlin and Simpson-Bowles had been meeting and deliberating for many months, but they were to make their final reports public after the upcoming election. Elections are news-making events, and as with Bill Clinton before him, Barack Obama's Democratic Party would lose his first midterm elections surprisingly badly. The "Tea Party" was coming to Washington, and there would be some very tense negotiations to keep the government open and avoid a default on the national debt.

CHAPTER 9

# WHEN SEVERAL ATTEMPTS TO REACH A "GRAND BARGAIN" FAILED

The two deficit reduction committees I served on, Domenici-Rivlin and Simpson-Bowles, publicly released their plans just after an election that brought big changes. Like President Bill Clinton's first midterm elections in 1994, the 2010 midterm elections delivered a surprisingly large disappointment for President Barack Obama. In what he called a "shellacking," Republicans scored a dramatic victory, gaining six Senate seats and sixty-three House seats to recapture control of the lower chamber they had lost in 2006.[1]

The new House majority included two new movements within the Republican Party. One was the "Young Guns," so labeled in a 2007 *Weekly Standard* magazine cover story. The group had formed to pick up the pieces after Republicans lost the House in 2006 and gained more influence after Obama's big win in 2008 swept a larger majority of Democrats into office, in what many pundits called a generational power shift.[2] By 2011 the Young Guns were rising into positions of power.[3] Eric Cantor (R-VA) became the House majority leader, the second-highest position behind incoming Speaker of the House John Boehner (R-OH). Kevin McCarthy (R-CA) became the House majority whip, and Paul Ryan (R-WI) became the chair of the House

Budget Committee. In 2010, the Young Guns had recruited ninety congressional challengers running as anti-tax, anti-spending Washington outsiders, and sixty-two of them had won their races, giving the trio (Cantor, McCarthy, and Ryan) a loyal following within the new House majority.

The members of the other group, calling themselves the "Tea Party," sometimes dressed in colonial costumes and three-cornered hats to commemorate the 1773 Boston Tea Party. "Tea," they explained, stood for "Taxed Enough Already," and they proclaimed their opposition to tax increases and government deficits. At that time, I was deeply involved in explaining to decisionmakers and the public that these two positions were contradictory unless you planned to make drastic Social Security and Medicare cuts. I doubt the Tea Party would have been popular if it declared this intention.

The Tea Party started spontaneously after an on-screen rant by Rick Santelli, a CNBC reporter on the trading floor of the Chicago Mercantile Exchange. In February 2009, just before the market bottomed out at the start of the Obama administration, Santelli railed against government bailouts for underwater mortgage holders, which he called subsidizing "the losers' mortgages."[4] His tirade sparked people to form a movement. At the beginning, the Tea Party lacked coherence and leadership as several organizations competed to raise money using the name and a loose set of values. Over time, the Tea Party took shape as a movement based less on policy preference (other than aversion to taxes) and more on an attitude of anti-Washington grievances among middle-aged, nonurban, white small business owners and retirees,[5] the group we would later recognize as the Trump base.

The movement's appeal to Republican primary voters became undeniable when Tea Party candidates defeated Republican congressional incumbents and won several key Senate and gubernatorial nominations. The general election was more of a mixed result for the Tea Party, with its candidates winning forty-three congressional seats (of the 242 in the new Republican majority). This included some overlap between candidates recruited by the Young Guns who chose to also identify with the ideologically similar Tea Party. Tea Party candidates also won five Senate seats but lost three high-profile Senate races, allowing the Democrats to retain a narrow Senate majority, although importantly, Democrats were far short of the 60-vote margin required to end a filibuster.

The 2010 election was about far more than the rise of the Young Guns and the Tea Party. Even if it was an unfair judgment, voters were sending a message to the new president and Democrats in Congress that they were not happy about the state of the union. Many voters were upset about the bad economy (even if Obama was turning around a terrible mess he inherited); they had negative views of the bank bailout, the auto bailout, and the stimulus plan (some of which were also inherited, and all of which were necessary policies); and they had negative views of the Affordable Care Act (ACA), even if majorities liked the individual elements of the new law and would eventually come to appreciate the whole of "Obamacare." Fairly or not, the one-sided election outcome convinced the incoming Speaker, John Boehner, and the rest of the resurgent Republicans that they had a mandate to take the country in a new direction, which they interpreted as a call to "repeal and replace" Obamacare, cut taxes, and balance the federal budget.[6]

## OBAMA GETS A BIPARTISAN STIMULUS DEAL (JUST DON'T CALL IT A "STIMULUS")

Like many of us in the Clinton White House after the Democrats' electoral catastrophe in 1994, many in the Obama White House were stunned after the "shellacking" in 2010, but according to multiple reports, the president saw an opportunity within the first 24 hours.[7] The big tax cuts passed under George W. Bush in 2001 were set to expire at the end of the year—even if Congress did nothing at all. Obama made the judgment that Republicans, fresh off their big victory, were not going to give him what he wanted, which would have been to allow the tax cuts for the top two brackets to expire but keep the lower taxes in place for middle-class earners. If he fought for that, he would get nothing; there would be a budget standoff and the tax cuts would expire for everyone, which would hurt the middle-class and be another negative shock to the still-shaky economic recovery. Obama decided that a better outcome could be achieved in a deal with Republicans in the "lame-duck" session of Congress, after the election and before the new Congress commenced in 2011.

After convincing his skeptical staff, Obama tasked Vice President Joe Biden with the job of leading the negotiations between the White House and Boehner and Senate Minority Leader Mitch McConnell (R-KY). The offer was to give Republicans what they wanted, an extension of the tax cut for all income brackets for two years, in exchange for an extension of unemployment benefits and whatever else the Democrats could get. By the end of the lame-duck session, just before Christmas, the Obama administration had gotten quite a lot, in what commentators called one of the most productive lame-duck sessions in congressional history.[8]

In addition to the two-year extensions of the Bush tax cuts for all earners and a thirteen-month extension of unemployment benefits, Obama, Biden, McConnell, and Boehner agreed to a temporary reduction of the payroll tax,[9] a new $1,000 per child tax credit, and a college tuition tax credit.[10] The compromise bill also included an expansion of the Earned Income Tax Credit (EITC), a unwieldly name for a great program that helps low-income workers and generally garners strong bipartisan support.[11] These elements taken together added up to a strong boost of economic stimulus, with a price tag larger than the 2009 Obama stimulus bill Republicans had blasted throughout the campaign.[12] Still, neither party to the negotiations wanted to use the word "stimulus." Republicans did not want to embrace it after criticizing it, and Obama also steered away from the word, in tacit agreement that the Republican political attack had been effective.

Immediately after getting agreement on the tax package, many other deals were struck, including passage of a law ending "Don't Ask, Don't Tell" and allowing gays to serve openly in the military; an overhaul of the nation's food safety laws; a health care bill for 9/11 first responders; and ratification of the "New START" arms control treaty with Russia. The Democratic leadership was involved in the negotiations and supported the progress, but neither the Speaker of the House Nancy Pelosi (D-CA) nor the Senate Minority Leader Harry Reid (D-NV) was present at the signing of the tax compromise bill, and left-wing Democrats were vocal in their opposition. Many Democrats saw the Bush tax cut extension as a continuation of tax breaks for the rich. They were also disappointed that the deal did not include progress on immigration reform by passing the DREAM (Development, Relief, and Education for Alien Minors) Act.[13] Democratic Representative Lloyd Doggett, from the liberal oasis of Austin, Texas, said of the tax deal during the negotiations, "We were told yesterday by the vice president this was a take-it-or-leave-it deal. We're saying, 'leave it.'"[14]

Pleased with the bipartisan progress he was able to achieve so soon after the midterm setback, President Obama was somewhat perturbed at the criticism he was receiving from the left-wing of his own party. During a press conference, he brought up the criticism he had received on the Affordable Care Act, from supporters of the public option back in 2009, suggesting they were setting too high of a standard for legislative success:

> If that's the standard by which we are measuring success or core principles, then let's face it, we will never get anything done. People will have the satisfaction of having a purist position and no victories for the American people. . . . That can't be the measure of how we think about our public service. That can't be the measure of what it means to be a Democrat. This is a big, diverse country. Not everybody agrees with us . . . and people have a lot of complicated positions, it means that in order to get stuff done, we're going to compromise.[15]

Of course, I was delighted by this. I cannot make a better case for bipartisanship than President Obama did at that press conference. But I will point out that this was a bipartisan deal to make the deficit larger, with lower taxes and higher spending. The important elements of this deal were all temporary, and I was not opposed to the short-term economic stimulus that they would provide. The Domenici-Rivlin plan had included economic stimulus in the short term for the struggling economy. But my point is, it is always a lot easier to reach bipartisan agreement to increase the deficit than to reduce it either by increasing revenue or reducing spending, or both, which is what we were trying to do in both deficit reduction committees.

## Two Plans Driven by Common Arithmetic

It is important to understand that not all deficit reduction is created equal. There are smart ways to reduce the deficit and less smart ways, and the difference is in more than just the mix between spending cuts and revenue increases. Important distinctions must be made between short-term and long-term spending cuts, and between reductions for discretionary spending and entitlement spending. In some senses, it is easier to cut discretionary spending, as implied by the name, and that is what budgeters had been doing for decades. Discretionary spending as a percentage of gross domestic product (GDP) was already quite low by historical standards at the start of these negotiations,[16] and when discretionary spending is too low, there is too little money available to fund military defense, as well as highways, public health, scientific research, development of new technologies, and other investments needed for future economic growth.

The heart of the problem facing both deficit reduction committees was not on the discretionary side of the ledger, it was on the nondiscretionary side. We knew we had to do something about entitlements, specifically long-term Medicare spending due to larger numbers of beneficiaries and rising costs for medical care, so our approach to closing the gap was to balance spending reductions and revenue increases and focus the spending reductions on cutting the rate of increase in long-term health care spending. Sadly, after a long and arduous road, we ended up with exactly the opposite: a "sequester," or the imposition of automatic, across-the-board spending reductions, which brought us deep cuts in both short-term military and non-military discretionary spending and almost no balance in terms of new revenue. The long-term issue was not meaningfully addressed.

The environment in which the two deficit reduction commissions released their reports was both far more partisan and far more bipartisan than any of us had expected or even realized at the time. The huge Republican election victory and rise of the Tea Party faction meant government would be even more divided and harshly partisan than it was leading into the election. But at the same time, President Obama was secretly negotiating sweeping bipartisan agreements with the congressional leadership in the "lame duck" deal. This period has served as something of a life lesson for me—that even when partisanship is at unprecedentedly vitriolic levels, bipartisan agreement is always within reach if leaders on both sides want to make progress.

The National Commission on Fiscal Responsibility and Reform (Simpson-Bowles Commission) released its budget plan on November 10, 2010, eight days after the election. One week later (November 17), the Domenici-Rivlin Debt Reduction Task Force released its budget plan. The main outlines of the two plans were similar: capping discretionary spending, restraining the growth of entitlements, and raising future revenues with lower income tax rates by broadening the tax base. This similarity had little to do with my ser-

*We face two huge challenges simultaneously. We must recover from the deep recession that has thrown millions out of work, slashed home values, and closed businesses across the country. We also must take immediate steps to reduce the unsustainable debt that will be driven by the aging of the population, the rapid growth of health care costs, exploding interest costs, and the failure of policymakers to limit and prioritize spending and to pay for new programs. Some observers have argued that policymakers need to choose between economic stimulus and deficit reduction. The task force, however, firmly believes it is important to take action on both fronts at once—accelerating the recovery and phasing in deficit reduction.*

—Senator Pete V. Domenici and Dr. Alice M. Rivlin, "Restoring America's Future: The Domenici-Rivlin Debt Reduction Task Force Report," November 2010

vice on both committees. I did not have nearly as much influence on the Simpson-Bowles report because I was not a cochair, and because the two chairs tightly controlled deliberations for fear of leaks that could do damage. But when I read the report, I was not surprised by the similarities.

The commonalities were driven by the arithmetic of the problem. Rapidly rising health care costs and the demographic tsunami of the boomers' retirement were forcing spending for Medicare, Medicaid, and Social Security higher in coming decades.[17] It was not realistic to expect enough cuts in military spending and other government services to offset the rising spending for seniors. Additional revenues were needed to keep debt from growing faster than the economy. Like Domenici-Rivlin, the Simpson-Bowles plan relied on the tax reform strategy of broadening the tax base and lowering tax rates, but the Simpson-Bowles plan went one step further in how the options were presented.

The Simpson-Bowles plan dramatized the income tax reform opportunity by presenting several options to show how far income tax rates could be lowered if deductions, credits, exclusions, and other "loopholes" were eliminated or severely restricted.[18] Their most drastic option, the "Zero Plan," raised substantially more revenue than the current system, with three tax rate brackets of only 9, 15, and 24 percent. Because it severely restricted tax benefits such as the home mortgage deduction and the exclusion of employer-paid health benefits, which are of greater advantage to upper income people, the plan would have been far more progressive than the current system while arguably enhancing economic growth with lower marginal rates and greater simplicity. The analysis then offered legislators estimates of how much they would have to raise rates if they wanted to restore beloved tax advantages that were aggressively curtailed in the drastic Zero Plan.

The plan was a remarkable presentation of policy options. The tax rates in the Zero Plan were eye-poppingly low and designed to give any politician, Republican or Democrat, a real reason to brag in the next election, and yet the plan raised an additional $80 billion each year that was applied to deficit reduction. The plan also put nearly every tax deduction in the tax code on the table for potential elimination, calling on the special interests that had worked to get the deductions into the tax code to justify their existence. Some especially popular tax deductions, like the deduction for charitable giving and the home mortgage interest deduction (for primary residences), were spared elimination below certain dollar thresholds, but not so for mortgage interest on second homes or for the scores of deductions that are less popular and are known mostly by corporations, tax lawyers, and accountants. Many of those specialized tax breaks would not have survived if Simpson-Bowles had been introduced into Congress and used as the basis for actual legislation.

Both Simpson-Bowles and Domenici-Rivlin used a variation of the broaden-the-base, lower-the-rates tax strategy, believing that the political win-win on taxes would act like the spoonful of sugar to help the medicine of budget cutting go down with lawmakers. The combination of greater tax revenue, responsible cuts in benefits for wealthier retirees, and efficiencies to slow the rate of increase in the provision of medical care would put the federal budget on a sustainable path over the long term. This dose of economic medicine could be expected to deliver many benefits to average workers and consumers. Solving a long-term threat to economic stability would reduce economic uncertainty, lower interest rates, increase business investment, and allow greater government investment where necessary to further economic productivity. All of this would lead to greater economic growth and long-term economic stability.

In the end, neither plan was voted into law, so neither could be called an unqualified success. On the other hand, elements of the plans have been used as the basis for subsequent policymaking, and both plans were successful in proving the long-term budget challenge that America still faces can be solved without drastic cuts in benefits to retirees, the poor, or the middle class by using policies that reflect the values and perspectives of policymakers representing the center-left and center-right in American politics.

## MANY PLANS TO REACH FISCAL SUSTAINABILITY

A short time after the release of these two plans, Democratic Representative Jan Schakowsky of Illinois, who was a member of the Simpson-Bowles Commission, released her own deficit reduction plan.[19] It proved that America's long-term budget challenge could be met from a progressive set of values. President Obama would produce his budget proposal in February of 2011, and soon this would be joined by a conservative plan from the House Budget Committee chair Paul Ryan (R-WI), one of the Young Guns, who was also a member of the Simpson-Bowles Commission. (He would run for vice president in 2012 and eventually become the Speaker of the House in 2015.) By April, America would have two bipartisan committee plans, Schakowsky's progressive plan, Ryan's conservative plan, and President Obama's plan.

Representative Jan Schakowsky's progressive budget restored many of the Simpson-Bowles discretionary budget cuts that she believed would hurt the middle class, and included increased spending for job training, education, and infrastructure that she believed would help spur economic growth. The Schakowsky budget nonetheless achieved the deficit reduction target through much deeper military spending cuts and raised more revenue through taxes on the wealthy, largely by closing loopholes as done in the Simpson-Bowles Zero Plan. The Schakowsky plan also let the Bush tax cuts for the top two brackets expire (the same policy President Obama was just then postponing for two years to get his "lame duck" deals with Republicans).

For some people, such a large number of budget proposals (and there would soon be dozens of other plans offered by various other groups and members of Congress) would be a version of federal budget hell, but as a budget geek, I was in heaven. Every week brought a fresh crop of articles and

*This rising debt burden is a particularly hard problem for our political system to handle because it is <u>not</u> a crisis. Nothing terrible will happen if we take no action this year or next. Investors here and around the world will continue to lend us all the money we need at low interest rates, with touching confidence that they are buying the safest securities money can buy. Rather, the prospect of a rising debt burden is a serious problem that demands sensible management beginning now and continuing for the foreseeable future.*

—Alice M. Rivlin, testimony before the Joint Economic Committee of the US Congress, September 8, 2016

analyses of the relative merits of the plans.[20] All of the plans were serious and substantive attempts to deal with the long-term budget challenge, and all would have brought the nation's projected future deficits down to, or at least much closer to, the goal of 60 percent of GDP. Further, the competing plans were made of elements that had been proposed, discussed, and, in many cases, costed out by the Domenici-Rivlin and Simpson-Bowles teams, and of course the Congressional Budget Office (CBO) was doing its own analyses of the various options. In the negotiations that would follow, all the negotiators could be working from common sets of budgetary impact estimates of the many alternative proposals. As always, I was optimistic that with all these efforts to address the long-term challenge, a grand bargain would be attainable.

## DRAMA AND CHAOS IN 2011

At the start of 2011, many members of Congress from both parties recognized the ultimate danger of debt growing faster than the economy, but it was clear the 2010 election had changed the political landscape and bipartisan cooperation was going to be more difficult than we on the deficit reduction committees had hoped. Republicans had moved to the right and were more adamantly opposed to tax increases than ever. Democrats had moved to the left and were increasingly dug in against reductions in entitlement benefits.

There were several senators in both parties that realized serious efforts to rein in the debt would have to include some additional revenues as well as major efforts to slow the growth of Medicare, Medicaid, and Social Security. A stalwart bipartisan group of six senators (four of whom had been members of Simpson-Bowles) kept meeting off and on for months in hopes of reviving the grand bargain. Mark Warner (D-VA) and Saxby Chambliss (R-GA) had formed an unlikely friendship, and frequently met at Warner's home in northern Virginia. They were joined by Kent Conrad (D-ND), Dick Durbin (D-IL), Mike Crapo (R-ID), and Tom Coburn (R-OK) to form a "gang of six" that periodically announced they were making progress but had a hard time closing a deal.

Early in the new year, tragedy struck. On Saturday, January 8, 2011, outside a supermarket in Tucson, Arizona, Democratic Representative Gabrielle Giffords was addressing supporters when a lone gunman shot her in the head and hit seventeen others, killing six. Because the shooter appeared to have political motives, there were immediate calls to tone down the Washington partisan rhetoric. Obama, who had campaigned on bringing the country together in 2008, renewed his challenge to lawmakers to "disagree without being disagreeable," and there were vows on both sides of the aisle to conduct the nation's business with greater civility.[21] The change in tone in Washington was nice while it lasted, but in a pattern we have seen repeated several times, it faded, with a half-life of about three weeks.

Recalling President Clinton's acrimonious but ultimately successful bipartisan negotiations that produced budget surpluses, welfare reform, and the State Children's Health Insurance Program (SCHIP) after the 1994 midterms, as well as the surprise Obama "lame-duck" breakthroughs at the end of 2010, I hoped divided government would again lead to serious bipartisan negotiations to finally tackle the rising long-term national debt. Maybe the Republicans, who had done nothing but obstruct Obama's entire agenda during his first two years, would see control of the House as an opportunity to show they could participate in governing the country, not just say no. If the two parties wanted to work seriously on curbing future debt increases, they had the Simpson-Bowles blueprint to start from. With the addition of Domenici-Rivlin and all those other plans, there was no shortage of policy ideas backed by solid staff work.

One obvious opportunity for President Obama to reach out to Congress and throw his weight behind a bipartisan debt plan would have been his State of the Union address in January 2011, and I put this hope on the editorial page of the *New York Times*.[22] I hoped he would make the dual objectives of accelerating economic recovery and controlling the future debt increases the centerpiece of a post-midterm agenda and challenge the new House Republicans to join him. I did not think he should endorse Simpson-Bowles, but I was hoping he would say something like this: "I am committed to working with Congress to speed the recovery and control the rise of the national debt. I appointed this distinguished commission, which worked hard for a year to produce a balanced plan. *(Waves the commission report.)* I do not agree with everything the commission proposed, but I challenge the new Congress to work with me to craft a bipartisan plan that will speed up recovery and curb the future growth of debt."

The president disappointed those of us who were expecting an embrace of Simpson-Bowles that night. Obama mentioned that he had appointed a bipartisan budget commission that had "made progress," but he did not endorse its recommendations. He did not challenge the new Congress to work with him on a plan either for faster job creation or for long-term deficit reduction. In the eyes of those of us who hoped for leadership from President Obama, this seemed like a huge opportunity missed.

With the added perspective of time and after hearing from many of the people involved in the negotiations (either directly or through their articles

---

*President Obama must use his State of the Union speech to make clear his commitment to two economic imperatives: accelerating job growth and controlling the federal deficit. He must persuade Americans that we do not have a choice between the two. We have to do both, and we have to get the timing right. That means pushing hard for faster job creation, but also warning about looming federal deficits and their threat to prosperity. It means promising to work actively with Congress to control the rising debt.*

—Alice M. Rivlin, "Create Jobs Not
Deficits," *New York Times*,
January 22, 2011

---

and memoirs), I now understand that Obama was acting strategically. He and his advisors were convinced that he needed to maintain distance from Simpson-Bowles. When Congress was unable to create a deficit reduction committee, Obama had to create it. Then congressional Republicans walked away from endorsing its recommendations. If Obama said too many positive words about the commission report, he would own the compromises on the spending side without banking any of the gains on the revenue side. Instead of representing an effort to define the center, Simpson-Bowles would become the president's position from which he would still be negotiating to get a deal that, from the Democrats' point of view, would be worse than Simpson-Bowles.

Rather than moving to the center, Obama used the State of the Union to lay out his position in the negotiations, set limits on what was nonnegotiable, and make the case for his investment agenda. Word was leaking out that the Republicans were contemplating using the 2012 budget process, and even the nation's debt limit, to force concessions on federal spending, so rather than setting the stage for a bipartisan grand bargain, the White House was preparing for the hyperpartisan showdown that was about to unfold.

## THE BUDGET PROCESS BREAKS DOWN

I was not alone in being surprised when Republicans started talking about using threats of a government shutdown, and even a refusal to raise the debt ceiling, to gain leverage in negotiations and force drastic cuts in domestic spending. Hadn't we seen this kind of constitutional hardball before, when Newt Gingrich tried the same tactic to gain leverage over Bill Clinton? Didn't that end badly for Republicans? Beyond the question of whether elected officials should threaten harm to people they represent, because certainly closing the government is bad for the economy and for the voters back home, and a federal government debt default would be even worse, there was the simple question of why Republicans would expect the tactic to succeed this time when it had failed a decade earlier.

The newly elected Tea Party Republicans, and the Young Guns they chose as their leaders, viewed this as inside-the-beltway thinking. They rejected the assumed wisdom of past Congresses on the belief that previous Republican leaders had talked about cutting spending only to see budgets and deficits grow ever larger. Any warning that using government shutdown or debt default threats risked causing an economic or political disaster simply conveyed the power of these tactics and how much the Washington establishment feared their use.

The Republican House leadership identified three points of vulnerability for Obama and the Democrats in 2011: (1) the need to fund the government by extending the fiscal year 2011 budget's continuing resolution (CR),[23] which was set to expire on March 4, 2011; (2) the need for congressional approval of the fiscal year 2012 budget appropriations by October 1, 2011; and (3) the need to raise the debt ceiling sometime in the late spring (or, possibly, postponed into the summer). If all of this sounds familiar, it should, because Newt Gingrich had walked down the same path to gain leverage in negotiations with the Clinton administration, as detailed in chapter 7.

The budget battles of 2011 started off chaotic and ugly and went downhill from there. The first battle was over the continuing resolution expiring in March of that year, but this was already the fourth CR for fiscal year 2011, and it would not be the last. Unable to pass appropriations bills at the start of fiscal year 2011, just before the 2010 elections, Congress passed a CR to get to December. At that deadline, stymied negotiators gave themselves another two weeks, passing a second CR that ended just before Christmas, 2010. This was when Obama was making compromises and reaching deals on many issues, but the budget talks were deadlocked, so Congress passed another CR, extending into the new year, 2011. I doubt there was a single news organization in America that was not regularly using the phrase "kicking the can down the road," because the analogy so aptly fit the repeated behavior. Several times, the media went through the drill of reporting what would happen if negotiators failed to reach agreement and parts of the government were shut down. Cable television networks repeatedly showed countdown clocks to mark the time remaining to reach a deal.

The two sides were far apart. Republicans wanted deep cuts in spending. Democrats basically wanted to maintain current spending levels. Many numbers in the tens of billions of dollars were batted back and forth over the months of negotiating, but the gap seemed to grow wider as Republicans were emboldened following their election successes. In mid-February, about two weeks before the expiration of the third CR, House Republicans passed their own version of another CR bill that cut $61 billion from current funding. It was a negotiating tactic rather than a serious effort to reach compromise, because it included so many elements that were clearly unacceptable to Democrats, including restrictions on women's health service delivery through Planned Parenthood and zero funding for Obamacare. Senate Minority Leader Harry Reid announced it would not pass the Senate and soon made good on that proclamation.[24]

White House Budget Director Jack Lew countered with an offer to cut $30 billion, which Republicans called a meaningful starting point for negotiations. But Congress could not close the deal before the deadline, so it passed another CR into April, with Democrats accepting $6 billion in cuts.[25] Hours before the April deadline, the Senate and House passed a fifth CR funding the government through the end of the fiscal year, with an initial estimated $38 billion in savings.[26]

Subsequent analysis of the bill they passed proved that estimate illusory. Some put the budgetary savings at just a couple hundred million dollars,[27] while others projected that the CR had actually increased fiscal year 2011 spending. Budget bills are complicated, especially when they are negotiated against tight deadlines. It is very hard to save tens of billions from a budget year that is more than half over, so most of the savings—and they were real savings—were going to be realized in fiscal year 2012 and beyond. The Republicans believed they had been snookered. They had fought the Washington system, and the Washington system won. Pressure from the Tea Party flank was mounting on Speaker Boehner to be a tougher negotiator in the coming fights over the fiscal year 2012 budget and the debt ceiling.

## THE BATTLE OF THE 2012 BUDGET

The fiscal year 2012 budget process started in February 2011 with President Obama's budget getting a cold reception from Republicans as negotiations raged over the fiscal year 2011 continuing resolution. Obama's budget was fairly straightforward, funding much of the government at current levels, but in an effort to offer substantial deficit reduction, which Jack Lew called "steps to live within our means," it proposed freezing many areas of domestic spending, with a handful of program eliminations.[28] At the same time, Obama's budget included a focused investment agenda designed to spur job creation. This meant additional funding for education, infrastructure, and innovation, and new investments in research and development, and in bio-medical research at the National Institutes of Health.

On April 5, Paul Ryan released his House Budget Committee's budget proposal under the title, "The Path to Prosperity: Restoring America's Promise."[29] Ryan's budget was a clear signal the Republican majority in the House was going for huge spending cuts—$4 trillion in deficit reduction after additional tax cuts, which meant slashing entitlements and everything else.[30] To make matters worse—well, worse for me at least—every time he defended the entitlement cuts, he explained his premium support proposals invoking my name.

## "RIVLIN-RYAN" AND THE CONTROVERSY OVER PREMIUM SUPPORT

Both Simpson-Bowles and Domenici-Rivlin put major emphasis on slowing the growth of Medicare and Medicaid because they were central to the long-term debt problem. The Domenici-Rivlin health proposals were bolder and considerably more specific than those in Simpson-Bowles. In our task force's proposal, we recommended shifting to a premium support approach for financing Medicare.[31]

The details matter, and it was in the details that I first found, and then lost, common ground with Paul Ryan over premium support. The most important detail was whether the premium support would be optional or mandatory. If it were optional, seniors could choose to stay in traditional Medicare. If it were mandatory, traditional Medicare would be replaced altogether with a premium support plan. (This issue would affect future retirees, as any proposal would exempt current Medicare beneficiaries and those soon to enroll.) It also matters how generous the proposal is, what services are required to be covered in the private plans, the amounts of the subsidies offered, and how quickly the subsidies grow over time.

Back in 2010, Paul Ryan had released a fiscal year 2011 budget that made drastic Medicare cuts, with a stingy version of mandatory premium support replacing traditional Medicare for everyone under the age of 55. I would never have supported this plan because it was not optional, it did not spell out minimum service requirements, the premium support levels were too low (which would leave many seniors uninsured or underinsured), and it had a growth rate set at the rate of inflation plus 0.5 percent, which would not keep up with the cost of inflation in medical services.[32]

Later that year, after a version of the Domenici-Rivlin plan included a generous, optional premium support proposal, Ryan sought me out to collaborate on a bipartisan premium support plan to share with the Simpson-Bowles Commission. Working with me, Ryan proved likeable, smart, and surprisingly flexible. Like Bill Clinton, he obviously enjoyed immersing himself in policy details. I was impressed with his eagerness to work across the aisle and willingness to move toward the centrist plan I had developed with Pete Domenici. Ryan agreed to most of the main features of the Domenici-Rivlin version, including Medicare exchanges, retention of the traditional Medicare option, and capping growth of the per capita federal contribution at the growth of GDP plus 1.0% percent.[33] Paul and I discussed our proposal in a commission meeting but did not convince Simpson and Bowles to put it in their December 2010 chairman's mark (draft).

By 2011, Ryan had reverted back to his stingy premium support plan in his fiscal year 2012 budget proposal. Again the premium support was mandatory, not optional, replacing traditional Medicare for everyone under age 55. The budget was vague about what services would be covered, which meant much of the claimed savings would come from insurers offering thin plans that would force more costs onto future retirees. The growth rate of subsidies returned to GDP plus 0.5 percent instead of the GDP plus 1.0 percent growth rate that Ryan and I had agreed to suggest for the Simpson-Bowles plan. This difference may seem small, but compounded over ten or twenty years, it becomes a huge funding gap. In fact, I was hearing from a lot of friends and colleagues that I respect—experts in health care financing like economists Henry J. Aaron and Robert Reischauer—that the GDP plus 1 percent in Domenici-Rivlin was not going to be generous enough to avoid an unacceptable level of cost shifting onto seniors.[34] I was open to making changes in the plan to make it more generous, not less.

At no time did I endorse either of Ryan's stingy and mandatory versions of premium support, and I told him so, but he repeatedly invoked my name whenever he was defending his fiscal year 2012 budget. I'm sure he chose his words carefully to not say I endorsed this specific plan, but repeating that I endorsed premium support, and that he and I had worked on a plan together, created a lot of problems for me. The same was true for Senator Ron

Wyden (D-OR), who had also crafted a bipartisan premium support plan with Ryan that was close to the Domenici-Rivlin version.

Ryan continued to advocate for premium support and invoke my name and Wyden's as coauthors of two of his various proposals. I was forced to repeat my disclaimer, "No, I never agreed to that," over and over. Senator Wyden was doing the same thing.[35] Indeed, Ryan's endorsement of premium support made it anathema to many Democrats, who felt it would lead to unacceptable hardships for vulnerable seniors. Democrats even produced a campaign video that depicted a lanky Ryan-like figure pushing a sweet-faced old lady in a wheelchair off a cliff. It was unfair to Ryan and to the concept of premium support, but it was effective political theater.

## OBAMA RESPONDS TO THE STEADY DECLINE IN US MANUFACTURING

With the overall US economy, as well as the global economy, in a slow but steady recovery from the steep decline of 2008 and 2009, it would have been easy to miss some of the important economic trends that had been building beneath the surface. Obama was from Illinois, so as he was developing his platform to run for the White House, before the Great Recession, he was emphasizing the decades-long decline in US manufacturing, particularly in the Great Lakes region of the Midwest.

Nationwide, total manufacturing employment peaked in 1979 with more than 19 million working in the sector.[36] By the end of 2009, that number had fallen to just below 12 million, a decline of 41 percent, with only the last 10 percentage points attributable to the Great Recession. Obama had made several commitments to strengthen the manufacturing sector during the 2008 presidential campaign, and he was able to keep his commitments and maintain his focus on this issue through the many contentious fiscal policy battles with the Republicans, even if the press was not paying much attention to the decline in manufacturing or Obama's successful efforts to reverse the trends.

America's success in manufacturing is closely tied to its success in innovation of new products and new manufacturing techniques. This in turn depends on our success in advancing basic science, research and development, energy production, and education, especially in science, technology, engineering, and mathematics (STEM) subjects, and worker training and retraining. Obama had committed to supporting these activities by funding Advanced Manufacturing Partnerships (AMPs), Regional Innovation Clusters (RICs), and a National Network for Manufacturing Innovation (NNMI) through grants administered by the Department of Commerce, with the participation of the Departments of Energy and Defense, the National Science Foundation, and the Small Business Administration.

The basic goal for each of these initiatives was to connect manufacturers with other manufacturers and with university researchers developing new products and manufacturing techniques, at the local, regional, and national levels. Many of the projects focused on advanced manufacturing, defined as those sectors most dependent on continuous research and development investment, and manufacturing to support national defense and homeland security needs.

Obama also built on worker training programs developed in the Clinton administration, relaunching Clinton's Workforce Investment Act (WIA) under the new name of the Workforce Innovation and Opportunity Act (WIOA) and adding a Manufacturing Jobs for America component that passed both chambers of Congress overwhelmingly with strong bipartisan support in 2014, spearheaded by Senator Chris Coons (D-DE). Directed by the Departments of Education and Labor, WIOA focused on community colleges through competitive grant programs to support schools that connect out-of-work Americans with jobs in regional economies, placing special emphasis on the skills most needed by local manufacturers.

## LURCHING FROM CRISIS TO CRISIS

In the spring of 2011, after a series of continuing resolutions averted a government shutdown just before each deadline was reached, the government was finally funded through the end of the fiscal year, but the two sides were still far apart on agreeing to a budget for fiscal year 2012, which was starting October 1, and there was a debt ceiling which needed raising or the United States would default on its debt obligations, causing a global economic catastrophe. The new era of civility following the Gabby Giffords shooting had faded into memory. The Republicans were using hardball tactics in a multifront assault. The public had been seeing countdown clocks and "Shutdown Showdown" headlines on their televisions for months.

President Obama responded to Paul Ryan's budget with a speech at George Washington University on April 13. His new plan cut deficits by $4 trillion over ten years—the same figure the Republican plan claimed but with different priorities. Obama's plan emphasized investments in job creation and productivity, income tax reform that broadened the tax base and shifted the burden to upper-income filers, and long-term entitlement reforms that were not very clearly specified.[37] In other words, he was adopting a great deal of Simpson-Bowles. Both Simpson and Bowles were present at the speech as Obama lauded their efforts and pledged to work with Congress. It was the speech I had hoped he would give in January, and it would have been a good basis for bipartisan cooperation, but for one unfortunate circumstance. Paul Ryan, as a member of the Simpson-Bowles Commission, had been invited to the event but was not expected to attend. He showed up, however, but no one alerted President Obama. The first half of the speech trashed the Republican budget, and Ryan had to sit through the attack, although his presence was not acknowledged.[38] It was not a great way to embark on a new round of bipartisan negotiations.

John Boehner responded with his own speech to the Economic Club of New York, outlining his position. Cuts in Medicare and Social Security were on the table, but tax increases were not discussable. Boehner said Republicans would only support increasing the debt ceiling if the parties could agree on larger budget cuts than the amount by which the ceiling would be raised. "Without significant spending cuts and reforms to reduce our debt, there will be no debt limit increase. And the cuts should be greater than the accompanying increase in debt authority the President is given. We should be talking about cuts of trillions, not just billions."[39]

## A SUMMER OF DISAPPOINTMENT, IMPASSE, AND POSTPONEMENT

The negotiations seemed to be running in two contradictory worlds for Obama and Congress. In one reality, the negotiations were hopeless. Republicans were refusing any new tax revenue and threatening economic catastrophe to gain leverage in their quest to balance the budget by cutting far more deeply into Medicare, Social Security, and other popular programs than the Democrats could ever accept. Democrats were offering too little in the way of cuts to entitlements for the Republicans to accept.

In the other reality, the negotiations were substantially more hopeful. Democrats and Republicans were negotiating to avoid catastrophe by finding an agreeable balance of spending cuts and new revenue to close the budget gap without slashing programs or harming beneficiaries. It was unclear which reality was closer to the truth or what the outcome would be. If an agreement could be reached, it would not have to follow the exact contours of Simpson-Bowles, but at least the commission's report showed the task of reaching bipartisan agreement was achievable.

While many people like me tried to stay optimistic that a grand bargain, or even small bargains, would be possible, the same pattern kept repeating, proving the pessimists correct. What Obama and Biden did not know, and I suspect John Boehner did not fully understand or accept, was Boehner did not have enough control over his Republican Caucus to deliver the votes to pass a bill that balanced spending cuts with new revenue. Years earlier, in a January 2009 secret meeting called by former speaker Newt Gingrich and GOP strategist Frank Luntz—a meeting that did not include Boehner—the Young Guns and several other Republican senators and representatives agreed to stand together for conservative principles. Following the Republican takeover of the House with new Tea Party members, the Young Guns and their supporters now had enough votes within the caucus to unite around their definition of conservative principles.[40] They seemed unconcerned by the fact that their core conservative demands were mutually incompatible, as I noted earlier. The demands to balance the budget without any increase in taxes, as well as the full repeal of Obamacare, would require cuts in Medicare and Medicaid that most Tea Party supporters would strongly oppose.[41] The Republicans kept insisting that their adversary was President Obama, but their real enemy was arithmetic.

Two of the top three House Republicans, Paul Ryan and Majority Leader Eric Cantor, were in on the agreement to use the budget crises to gain leverage and refuse all tax increases, but all three (Ryan, Cantor, and Boehner) feared being jettisoned by anti-tax zealots if they agreed to new revenue, either from tax increases or loophole elimination. Eventually these fears would be realized as all three would be out of Congress as Republicans pushed for a more confrontational posture.

In 2011, the same pattern repeated several times over. Democrats were negotiating for a deal that balanced spending reductions and revenue increases, and Republicans negotiated spending cuts but never agreed to any revenue increases. The talks broke down, and the best that negotiators could get was an agreement to avert catastrophe by postponing the deadline without resolving the larger issues.

In May 2011, Vice President Biden led an initiative to try to reach agreement on having the fiscal year 2012 budget raise the debt ceiling while substantially reducing the growth of future debt. Eric Cantor and Senator Jon Kyl (R-AZ), negotiating for the Republicans, were asking for cuts of $6 trillion to raise the debt ceiling.[42] The Democrats, Biden and Lew, working from Obama's proposal of $4 trillion in cuts and new revenues, indicated a willingness to get long-term savings from Medicare and Social Security, but only if Republicans were willing to negotiate revenue increases. The Republicans agreed to move forward on that basis if they could negotiate the spending cuts first. The Democrats wanted to follow Tip O'Neill and Ronald Reagan's 1983 formula[43] of long-term spending cuts equal to the amount of new revenue, getting most of the savings from technical changes to cost-of-living adjustments (COLAs) and continuing the upward creep in the retirement age. But ultimately, negotiations reached an impasse when they returned to the revenue side. By some reports, Republicans were willing to discuss revenue options as long as they could say there were no net tax increases, but on June 23, Eric Cantor ended the talks, saying Republicans would not support any debt reduction plan that involved increased revenues.[44]

In June, President Obama and Speaker Boehner also began direct talks—beginning on a golf course—about forging a grand bargain. They made specific offers and counteroffers, had staff working on drafts, and reportedly got very close to a handshake twice before their efforts fell apart amid mutual accusations about who was to blame for the breakdown. The negotiations were following along the lines of the deficit reduction committees' deliberations. Boehner was reportedly open to $800 billion in revenue increases if he could do it by broadening the tax base and not have to raise any tax rates. Obama was offering essentially the same concessions on entitlements that Biden and Lew had offered to Cantor, including raising the Medicare retirement age gradually to 67 and modifying the Social Security COLAs and the way other benefits (and tax brackets) were adjusted for inflation,[45] but when word of this reached a broader audience of lawmakers, both conservatives and progressives were angered by the concessions their own side was putting on the table. Cantor and a small group of Republican House members met with Boehner to warn him that he could lose the support of his caucus if he agreed to any tax increases, and they were not buying the distinction between tax rate increases and revenue increases from closing loopholes. The next day, Boehner called Obama to end the discussions.[46]

When the talks broke down, the Boehner team accused the president of "moving the goal posts" by demanding an additional $400 billion in revenue. Obama denied agreeing to the previous number. I suspect the real story was that neither leader had the votes to deliver a bipartisan deal. Boehner was afraid of losing his speakership if he made concessions to the Democrats on taxes. Obama did not have strong enough support from Democrats to move ahead with changes in entitlements.[47]

This frenetic activity was mostly motivated by the approaching debt ceiling deadline, which the right-wing Republicans vowed not to raise without major concessions from Democrats.[48] Either these Republicans did not understand the risk of throwing the financial system into turmoil if the world's largest creditor defaulted on its debt or they did not care. During the late spring and early summer of 2011, Obama's treasury secretary, Timothy Geithner, had been deploying the same tactics that Robert Rubin had used to delay breaching the debt ceiling in the 1990s. The extraordinary measures included things like borrowing from the civil service retirement fund to gain extra time, but Geithner was running out of room while Republicans were extracting concessions from Democrats.[49] Early in August, Standard and Poor's (S&P) downgraded the United States' credit rating. The Dow Jones average dropped 635 points the next day, a warning signal of market nervousness about clearly irresponsible fiscal tactics on Capitol Hill.[50]

A few days earlier, at the very end of July, with the nation teetering on the edge of default, the president and congressional leaders had finally reached a deal, the Budget Control Act (BCA) of 2011.[51] It was, in reality, similar to a debt ceiling version of a CR.[52] The BCA was a deal to extend the crisis deadline by more than a year while setting up a new process to reach agreement on what to do about the long-term deficit. The debt ceiling was raised in two stages and by enough to cover necessary government spending for a few months into 2013.

But unlike a continuing resolution, the BCA had a lot of strings attached that would have a significant impact on future spending levels.

To start with, the Democrats had to accept budget cuts in discretionary spending just to get the BCA agreement. The constitutional hardball tactic of threatening a government default had been successful in getting the Democrats to accept bad economic policy. The price for Democrats was deep cuts in discretionary spending (the parts of the budget that were already small by historical standards and not projected to grow faster than the overall economy).

But the heart of the BCA was the process it set up to continue the negotiations. The BCA created a new congressional supercommittee with twelve members (three from each party in each chamber) to try once more to reach a grand bargain on long-term debt reduction, including new revenues and entitlements, the parts of the budget where long-term debt was projected to grow faster than the economy could sustain. The BCA gave the supercommittee less than three months to reach a grand bargain on taxes and entitlements by Thanksgiving and then get an up-or-down vote (no amendments) just before Christmas.[53] The BCA made the penalty for failure unacceptable to both sides, or at least that was the intention. If the supercommittee failed to reach agreement by Christmas, the BCA imposed a sequester—automatic, across-the-board cuts in discretionary and nondiscretionary spending, including the parts of the budget both sides had been protecting: defense spending for Republicans, and Medicare for Democrats. The legislation even specified extra cuts to agriculture to make the sequester worse for both sides.

The sequester was a serious threat designed as a sword of Damocles hanging over the heads of the supercommittee members to force a compromise.[54] The sequester was supposed to be bad policy, and it was, as I testified to Congress on several occasions. The sequester made cuts in all the wrong categories of spending.[55] Instead of addressing the real long-term debt problem by making structural changes to fund Medicare sustainably (and close much more manageable Social Security shortfalls), it would attack the false problem of the short-term deficit in a period of economic recovery by making immediate and indiscriminate cuts in discretionary spending. If the sequester took effect, nearly 50 million Americans living at or below the poverty line and even larger numbers facing food insecurity[56] would all lose critical support, including an estimated 75,000 children who would be dropped from Head Start.[57] There was an equally compelling case for conservatives against cutting defense spending while American troops were overseas. I thought there was no way lawmakers would fail to reach agreement and would allow the automatic sequester cuts.

## WHERE COMMITTEES HAD FAILED, A SUPERCOMMITTEE ALSO FAILS

The supercommittee was cochaired by the House and Senate Budget Committee chairs, Paul Ryan and Senator Patty Murray (D-WA). Despite press skepticism and budget fatigue, the cochairs worked hard and for a while appeared to be making progress. But just before Thanksgiving, they had to admit they had failed.[58] The sequester would take effect! But the dealmakers who crafted the Budget Control Act of 2011 made one huge mistake; the sequester did not start until January 1, 2013, more than a year away, a lifetime in American politics and after the 2012 election. The sword of Damocles was actually just a note proclaiming death in eighteen months. If Congress does one thing well, it is postponing difficult issues. But the timing was worse than the crafters of the BCA even imagined.

The debt ceiling extension date can only be estimated, but it was at most a few months into 2013 and turned out to arrive in March. In addition to the start date of the sequester, January 1, 2013, was also when the Bush tax cuts were set to expire. There were other legislative odds and ends, like the Alternative Minimum Tax and the extension of the Medicare "doc fix," that also needed legislative attention by New Year's Day or there would be unintended and undesirable consequences. Ben Bernanke, the chair of the Federal Reserve, began warning about the dangers of these multiple deadlines by giving them the ominous name of the "fiscal cliff."[59] Meanwhile, everyone breathed a little easier and departed to enjoy the holidays.

## ONE MORE TIME INTO THE BREACH

At the start of 2012, the two sides now had the task of reaching a budget deal before the nation headed over the fiscal cliff. But 2012 was an election year, and the fiscal cliff seemed far in the future, so beyond a few speeches, little was done to resolve the budget impasse. Republicans nominated Mitt

Romney, the former governor of Massachusetts, for president, and he chose Paul Ryan to be his vice-presidential running mate. This meant another round of statements from me that I had never endorsed the premium support proposal in Ryan's fiscal year 2011 and fiscal year 2012 budget proposals, but Ryan was also distancing himself from some of his more extreme past positions, saying that, as Romney's running mate, he now endorsed all of Romney's positions.

I was amused when both Romney and Obama praised Simpson-Bowles in the October 3 presidential debate.[60] "The president should have grabbed that," Romney said of the plan that Ryan had voted against, holding it below the threshold needed to force an up-or-down congressional vote. Romney also made it clear that he "absolutely" opposed raising additional revenue to close the budget gap, a key element of the Simpson-Bowles formula. Obama had never fully embraced Simpson-Bowles, but in the debate, he said it had formed the basis for his $4 trillion deficit reduction plan, which we now know was truer of his negotiation position that contemplated entitlement reforms than what his public statements had until then indicated.

Like most presidential contests, the 2012 election was billed as one of the most consequential in history, but when the votes were counted, it seemed like nothing had changed. Obama was reelected to the White House, and Democrats gained two net seats to retain control of the Senate. Democrats gained eight net House seats, although Republicans retained the majority. Policymakers returned to Washington and to negotiations to avert the worst effects of the fiscal cliff, with nearly everyone back in the same chairs. However, there may have been a subtle change in the power dynamic below the surface.

## ANOTHER HOLIDAY RUINED BY BUDGET BATTLES

The fiscal cliff was only partially a product of the 2011 deals to postpone making a deal; there were other tax and spending provisions scheduled to expire at the end of 2012. The sequester would mean $65 billion in automatic cuts. The Bush tax cuts had been set to expire at the end of 2010 but were extended by two years in Obama's lame-duck deal, so they, too, were expiring at the end of 2012. Combined with a few other expiring business tax cuts, the effective tax increase would total $400 billion. Extended unemployment benefits were expiring, taking $26 billion from millions of unemployed work-ers, and there was a payroll tax cut Obama had negotiated in 2010 that was expiring, adding up to a $112 billion cut in national take-home pay.[61]

All these tax increases and spending cuts would have reduced the defi-cit, but more than $600 billion hitting all at once would have landed as a negative blow to the fragile economy. The two sides seemed to have gone back to their two separate realities as the same set of negotiators—Obama, Biden, Boehner, Pelosi, Reid, and McConnell—returned from Thanksgiving to try yet again to avert disaster before the New Year's Eve deadline. And there was also another debt ceiling fight that would come in the first few months of 2013.

The White House had a new strategy—to end-run the Tea Party. Instead of starting with John Boehner in the House, Joe Biden turned to the Senate. The plan was to negotiate with Senate Majority Leader Harry Reid and, just as importantly, with Minority Leader Mitch McConnell, representing the Republicans. If they could reach a deal that could pass the Senate with bi-partisan support, it would then go to the House with momentum behind it. Both Boehner and McConnell were conservative Republicans, but McCon-nell had more room to maneuver because he, rather than the Tea Party, was in control of his caucus. He could make a deal that included enough new revenues (at least, more than zero) that Democrats could also support.

It is not exactly clear why this plan worked, but certainly McConnell was ready to end years of partisan standoff. It may have been personal relation-ships; at that point, it is not unreasonable to believe that McConnell found his former Senate colleague Joe Biden more persuasive than Boehner and the more extreme Tea Party Republicans to his right. It may have been that McConnell, having reached a very similar historical point after the 1996 elec-tion, reached the same conclusion he had in 1997 (as relayed in chapter 7): that the strategy of maximal confrontation had been pushed as far as it could go, and that, yielding few policy gains and following an election where little had changed, a new and less confrontational strategy was warranted. As Yogi Berra said, "It was déjà vu all over again."

After weeks of negotiations right up to, and even a couple of hours past the New Year's Eve deadline, the Senate voted 89–8 to pass the American Taxpayer Relief Act (ATRA) of 2012, at 2:00 a.m. on January 1, 2013. While ATRA did not resolve every issue, it reduced, rather than eliminated, the across-the-board sequester cuts and pushed remaining cuts back from January to March. The act resolved the issue of the expiring Bush tax cuts just as President Obama had wanted in 2010; the tax cuts continued for most families, but top rates returned to the Clinton levels for individuals making over $400,000 per year or $450,000 for married couples. The act also raised taxes on investment profits and dividends, and inheritance taxes on estates over $5 million.[62]

The size of the bipartisan Senate majority put enormous pressure on John Boehner in the House, and a day later he made the courageous decision he had been avoiding for two years. Boehner broke the "Hastert Rule" and allowed ATRA to come to the House floor even though it did not have majority support among House Republicans.[63] The act passed despite the opposition of the Tea Party, representing a dramatic political development. About one-third of the Republican members joined nearly all the Democrats to pass ATRA 257–167. The original Young Guns were divided, with Paul Ryan voting with Speaker Boehner, and Eric Cantor and Kevin McCarthy voting against the compromise.[64] The era of House Republicans' uncompromising opposition to tax increases had ended, but by no means did this mean all the outstanding issues were resolved and the partisan battles were over.

## A MORE "DELIBERATIVE" NEGOTIATION STRATEGY

Action was still needed to raise the debt ceiling, and the bulk of the sequester cuts had only been postponed until March 1. The debt ceiling was reached, suspended temporarily, and extended a few times but continued to hang over budget negotiations as a threat to bring the US and global economies to a crashing halt. There was even a government shutdown that lasted over two weeks at the start of fiscal year 2013 (the first and only shutdown while Obama was president), but this was more of a policy fight than a budget fight.[65] House Republicans withheld funding for the government to force a change to the Affordable Care Act, removing the tax penalty for individuals that did not have insurance. This effort failed when public opinion blamed the Republicans more than the Democrats for the government shutdown;[66] Congress later removed the tax penalty, in 2017, sending the issue to the courts.[67]

Budget negotiations for fiscal year 2014 were led by the two former supercommittee chairs, Representative Paul Ryan and Senator Patty Murray, and I believe they did an extraordinary job of managing the chaos. To be certain, both sides remained far apart, and Murray and Ryan were not able to pacify the partisan warfare, but though the road was rocky, they managed to reach agreement on a budget that passed both chambers. Other than the seventeen days of government shutdown in October 2013, Murray and Ryan managed to keep the government funded and open, and they avoided a national debt default. Perhaps it is a low bar, but after several years of government dysfunction their fiscal year 2014 budget deal delivered minimally functional government and, to this observer, that was an achievement.

Jill Lawrence interviewed many negotiation participants for her analysis of the deal.[68] She asserts that Ryan and Murray (whether knowingly or not) followed the four keys to "deliberative negotiation" as outlined by Mark E. Warren and Jane Mansbridge for the American Political Science Association's Task Force on Negotiating Agreement in Politics.[69] In Lawrence's telling, the negotiations were successful because Murray and Ryan (1) conducted nonpartisan fact-finding, (2) came together for repeated interactions and never let disagreements break off talks, and (3) negotiated in private rather than in the press. In addition, (4) both sides found negotiation failure, leaving the sequester cuts in place, unacceptable.

On substance, the deal was essentially a bipartisan agreement to undo the most oppressive aspects of the sequester, without raising taxes or closing tax loopholes, and without touching Social Security or Medicare. Nearly all new revenue came from fees for government services like security fees for airline tickets and fees states pay for management of mineral leases on public lands. Murray and Ryan proposed $20 billion in savings from COLA adjustments to military and federal civilian employee retirement, but that was whittled down to $6 billion when the plan became public. Simpson-Bowles had proposed $132 billion in ten-year savings from this approach, so therein was another secret to the Ryan-Murray process. They were adding up small numbers to get a deal without ambitions to solve the larger problems.

The fiscal year 2014 spending plan passed both chambers of Congress in January 2014. The plan made a small reduction in the deficit, while partially restoring some of the funds cut by the sequester from the military and

*Meeting the big challenges facing our economy, such as reining in the projected increase in national debt, requires sharing the pain as well as the gain. Austerity is bad economic policy in a recession; so is adding massively to deficits at full employment and continuously growing the debt faster than the economy.*

—Alice M. Rivlin, "In Defense of Centrists," Brookings Institution, February 27, 2018

domestic budgets in equal measure. It made no effort to address long-term challenges to the debt caused by the soon-to-be-retiring baby boomers. Still, after another failed government shutdown, only the most partisan politicians maintained that this deal was worse than no deal.

Effectively, Murray and Ryan struck a two-year deal because the fiscal year 2014 budget was extended through fiscal year 2015. This avoided budget negotiations in the late summer and fall of the 2014 election year, which would turn out to be at least as much of a catastrophe for the Democrats as the 2010 midterms were. Republicans won nearly every battleground race, gaining nine Senate seats and making Mitch McConnell the majority leader. Republicans gained thirteen House seats, strengthening John Boehner's majority. However, Boehner lost power as leader of his caucus because the energized conservative members organized themselves into a "Freedom Caucus" to assert right-wing opposition to taxes, Obamacare, and immigration. (Earlier in 2014, Boehner's top deputy, House Majority Leader Eric Cantor, had lost a highly symbolic Republican primary race to Dave Bratt, an economics professor who claimed Cantor was not conservative enough to represent Virginia's Seventh Congressional District, which ran from the farm country and suburbs just west of Richmond to Culpepper and the Shenandoah Valley.)

## A Seismic Shift in Republican Conservatism

John Boehner would struggle to maintain his position of leadership through one more round of intensive negotiations, this time over the fiscal year 2016 budget. Boehner drove a hard bargain for conservative principles in talks with President Obama to eventually produce a compromise that could pass both chambers. But Boehner had been working on the assumption that if he and Obama could agree on a bill that could pass in the Republican Senate, Boehner could pass it through the House with mostly Democratic votes. The strategy was a repeat of the end-run that had sidelined the Tea Party at the end of 2012, and while it worked to get the budget passed, it was a clear signal that Boehner no longer had control of his caucus. He resigned the speakership and retired from Congress before the budget came to the House floor.

Paul Ryan replaced Boehner as Speaker and passed the fiscal year 2016 budget, which President Obama signed into law. Yet, Ryan found himself caught, as Boehner had been, between the militantly conservative right wing of his party and the moderates who might be willing to work with Democrats on bipartisan solutions. The former Tea Party, now the Freedom Caucus, was taking full control of the Republican Party.

But the Freedom Caucus Republicans would themselves be replaced as leaders of the Republican Party when, in 2016, New York billionaire and reality television star Donald Trump defeated the Republican establishment to win the GOP nomination. Trump then defeated the Democratic establishment, in the form of former First Lady, Senator, and Secretary of State Hillary Clinton, to win the White House. The Freedom Caucus had unofficially become "the party of Trump," and it was now in control of the House, the Senate, and the White House.

Although Paul Ryan, as one of the original Young Guns, had once defined the conservative movement in Congress, he was as uncomfortable leading the House Republicans in Trump's first two years as the Freedom Caucus was with having him as the Speaker. Because I had always seen Ryan as a potential champion for bipartisan cooperation to reduce the long-term deficit, I was disappointed when Ryan and Mitch McConnell forced through the Tax Cuts and Jobs Act (TCJA) of 2017 without any Democratic votes in either chamber. The TCJA cut taxes for individuals and corporations, adding $2.3 trillion to the debt. I thought this was terrible policy because, again, it was cutting taxes in a growth phase of the business cycle, robbing the country of fiscal space for countercyclical spending that would be needed if the economy turned downward again (as it always does). Ryan was in step with his party in making it clear that they had always cared more about cutting taxes than they cared about cutting deficits, but Donald Trump's brand of conservatism was defined by more than just tax cuts. So I was extremely disappointed when Paul Ryan was challenged by, and ultimately failed to stand up to, the racist and xenophobic views of Trump and his followers within the Republican Party, and when Ryan decided, just fifteen months into Trump's presidency, that he had had enough and it was time to abandon his congressional career.[70]

## CHAPTER 10

# HYPERPARTISANSHIP IN MODERN POLITICS

I decided to write this book because I am as frustrated, concerned, and even fearful about American politics and governance today as I have ever been before. In recent years, there has been far less constructive problem-solving communication between Republicans and Democrats in the White House and Congress, and far more anger, name-calling, and finger-pointing. America has always been divided on many fault lines, sometimes viciously divided, and many times it has seemed that our differences were greater than our political institutions' ability to bridge the difference; but with the exception of the Civil War, we have always been able to reach political agreement.

This book has offered several themes that likely contributed to the election of Donald Trump in the 2016 election, and political scientists have not (yet, if they ever will) sorted out the contributions of each of them. The first is the broadest theme of this book, that hyperpartisanship has hobbled Washington's ability to solve problems and deliver real progress for the American people, leading to a decline in trust of Washington, and many of the institutions of government and society. This includes the partisan standoffs during the Obama Administration that convulsed Washington from crisis to crisis, forestalling sensible policy to strengthen the economy, and likely slowing the economic recovery out of the Great Recession—and this brings us to the second major theme.

As discussed in chapter 2, I believe policymakers in Washington failed to appreciate the pain and economic frustration of the people trapped in low wage jobs in declining small towns in the deindustrializing American heartland. Democrats campaigned in 2016 to keep the Obama recovery going, but this was out of touch and unpersuasive in the parts of America that had not experienced an economic recovery and were falling behind the surging coastal cities in the transition to a globally connected knowledge economy.

The third theme in American politics, discussed throughout this book, is explicitly racial, or to put a finer point on it, racist. This chapter explores the political science research on the current state of American politics and finds support for the proposition that Trump won a substantial number of votes by taking "politically incorrect" positions against Mexican and Muslim immigrants, African Americans, LGBTQ individuals, and women. While many Republicans have followed Ronald Reagan's lead in taking inspiration from Barry Goldwater's 1964 presidential campaign, it cannot be missed that Trump's campaign made deliberate appeals to the faction in American politics that supported George Wallace in 1968. But even if criticism can be lodged at a political opponent, common ground can still be made, and deals can be reached to move public policy forward.

## BIPARTISANSHIP HAPPENS MORE THAN WE THINK BUT LESS THAN WE NEED

The earlier chapters in this book include many stories of presidents and Congresses finding common ground across party lines to make progress on serious issues that were dividing the nation. Democratic President Lyndon Johnson and then Senator Hubert Humphrey (D-MN) worked with Senate Minority Leader Everett Dirksen (R-IL) to break the Southern Democrats' filibuster and pass landmark civil rights legislation. Republican President Ronald Reagan and Speaker Tip O'Neill (D-MA) negotiated a deal to put Social Security on a strong financial footing for decades. President George H. W. Bush made deals with Democrats and President Bill Clinton made deals with Republicans to limit spending and raise revenue that helped keep large deficits under control, eventually producing four years of budget surpluses.

In recent years, the two political parties have pulled apart; there are now fewer moderates, fewer bipartisan bills introduced, and fewer bills signed into law. Congressional achievement during Donald Trump's presidency is a continuation of the dismal trajectory of Washington dysfunction that was bad in the Clinton years, declined further under George W. Bush, and hit new lows during the Barack Obama administration. And yet, even after his Democrats got "shellacked" in the 2010 midterm elections, Obama and then Vice President Joe Biden were able to negotiate a huge economic stimulus with Senator Mitch McConnell (R-KY) and the Republicans in the lame-duck session before the Tea Party Republicans took their seats in Congress. I learned from these episodes that bipartisanship can break out at any time, even when it seems most unlikely.

With Trump in the White House, many important national challenges have gone unaddressed even when bipartisan agreement seemed within reach. Trump talked about potential deals on infrastructure before taking office but offered no proposals. Once in office, Trump pulled America out of the international climate agreements (Paris Accords) for all nations to limit greenhouse gas emissions and worked to undermine environmental regulations and vehicle fuel efficiency standards. Trump twice endorsed, and then rejected, a bipartisan Senate immigration deal that would have traded enhanced border security for resolving the citizenship status of young undocumented immigrants (aka "Dreamers") under the Deferred Action for Childhood Arrivals (DACA) policy.[1] The longest US government shutdown in history—thirty-five days—started at the end of 2018 over funding for Trump's southern border wall.

The Tax Cuts and Jobs Act (TCJA), Trump's first major legislative accomplishment, was also his largest economic mistake. Passed on a strictly party-line vote, it increased economic inequality and the deficit, leaving less room for countercyclical fiscal policy when the next economic downturn arrives. (George W. Bush made the same mistake at the start of his first term.) In increasing the national debt for a short-term stimulus to an already-growing economy, the act did the opposite of addressing our nations' long-term unsustainable debt problem.

My larger point is that this level of gridlock on policy, the inability to act on even the most urgent challenges facing the country, and even standoffs and shutdowns have all been common features during the past several administrations (as detailed in chapters 6 through 9).

There were also many bipartisan successes struck while acrimony seemed to have reached new high levels—and this is also true in the Trump years. Trump actively thwarted bipartisan cooperation on several issues, but he also signed into law many bipartisan bills that were passed in the 115th Congress. Some were on high-profile issues, like the First Step Act that reformed the criminal justice system and released thousands of nonviolent federal prisoners.[2] Others were less publicized, including bills to protect public lands, create a cybersecurity agency, expand veterans' health benefits, reduce deaths during childbirth, and modernize water infrastructure.[3] Most were initiated in Congress, but they were passed and then signed by Trump, proving that bipartisan agreement happens quite often, even in times that seem especially bleak.

University of Maryland professor Frances Lee[4] and James Curry of the University of Utah have compiled research showing that bipartisanship is not only quite common, but also almost essential for passing legislation through Congress.[5] Lee and Curry have been tracking all laws enacted by Congress over four decades and find that nearly all bills that become laws do so with substantial bipartisan support. Presidents tend to get one big piece of legislation passed through partisan force on a mostly party-line vote at the start of each term, such as Obama's Affordable Care Act (ACA) and the big Bush and Trump tax cuts, but these are the exceptions, not the rule. Generally, Curry and Lee tell us, bills that pass do so with "support from a majority of the minority party in at least one chamber and with the endorsement of one or more of the minority party's top leaders."[6]

Lee and Curry find this has been quite stable over the decades. The graphs in figure 10-1, taken from their book, *The Limits of Party: Congress and Lawmaking in a Polarized Era*, show the percentage of the vote from the minority party in both chambers for House and Senate bills enacted from 1973 to 2018. Two lines are plotted for each chamber, one for all laws and the other for "landmark laws" as determined using the method developed by Yale University Professor David Mayhew.[7] The "all laws" lines include major legislation as well as smaller bills naming national holidays, creating new national parks, funding individual infrastructure projects, honoring historical figures, or strengthening penalties for specific crimes. The landmark laws lines include only the major legislation covered in the news.

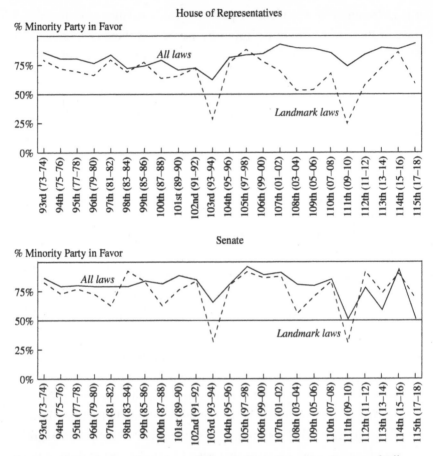

FIGURE 10-1.  Average Percentage of Minority Party Support on Passage of Bills, 1973–2018

*Source:* James M. Curry and Frances E. Lee, *The Limits of Party, Congress and Lawmaking in a Polarized Era* (University of Chicago Press, 2020).

The most notable points in the graphs are the two dips in each chamber for landmark laws in the 103rd and 111th Congresses, the first Clinton and Obama Congresses, both under Democratic control. Both presidents passed landmark legislation in their first two years with very little Republican support in either chamber. As detailed in chapters 6 and 8, passage of Clinton's deficit reduction package and Obama's economic stimulus bill required intensive negotiations to find compromises acceptable to progressive Democrats in the House and moderate Democrats in the Senate. The plotted points above the 50 percent line (often well above) in the other years tell us it is uncommon for the majority party to pass legislation over the objections of most members of the minority party, and these two Congresses were the exceptions. The data set starts with the 93rd Congress (1973–1974) and tells us that in over more than forty years, the character of how laws pass Congress has changed very little. For most Congresses, most legislation passes with majority support from the minority party. But other measures over this period show much more change.

## BIPARTISANSHIP IS NECESSARY BUT INCREASINGLY RARE

Curry and Lee tell us that laws still do pass through even these most recent Congresses, and most of the time it is through bipartisan cooperation that can be achieved even when government appears to be at crescendo levels of division and acrimony. But this is not happening enough of the time, especially on the most pressing issues like immigration, climate change, economic inequality, and unsustainable long-term national debt. We are not reaching bipartisan agreement even as these problems threaten to grow worse.

My Brookings colleague Sarah Binder[8] has data that supports my observations that recent Congresses have been more dysfunctional than those of decades past.[9] Instead of counting the number of bills that pass Congress, she counts the number of issues that get addressed or get tied up in gridlock. She reviews the editorial pages to identify the issues facing the nation during each congressional session and then assesses whether Congress has made progress on addressing each issue over the two-year period. She does not assess whether Congress came to the correct decision or passed legislation that will solve all of the problems, but just whether Congress passed legislation designed to do something about the issues raised on the editorial pages. She finds that a far higher percentage of issues are not getting addressed in recent Congresses than in those of the past. We are experiencing more gridlock and less problem-solving, which is what caused the frustration that drove me to write this book.

Figure 10-2 plots the level of deadlock for each Congress. The higher the point, the greater the percentage of problems are going unaddressed; the

Percent of salient legislative measures deadlocked

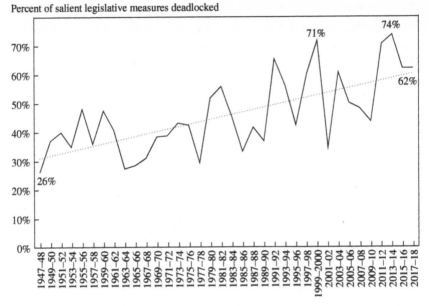

FIGURE 10-2.   Legislative Stalemate, 1947–2018: Percentage of Legislation
Deadlocked
*Source:* Sarah Binder, Center for Effective Public Management at Brookings.

lower the point, the more Congress has achieved. There has clearly been a
rising trend in the level of gridlock since 1947–1948, when President Harry
Truman gave the label "Do-Nothing Congress" to the 80th Congress despite
being able to reach agreement with it to pass legislation addressing 74 percent
of the nation's most pressing problems—allowing 26 percent to stall in legislative gridlock. The 115th Congress ended in January 2019 having reached
agreement with President Donald Trump to address just 38 percent of the
most salient issues. The 62 percent of issues stuck in legislative stalemate precisely matches the achievement of President Barack Obama and his final
114th Congress, but it was better than the 113th Congress (2013–2014), which
set record levels of dysfunction at 74 percent gridlock—or just 26 percent of
the nation's salient issues getting addressed—a reversal of the achievement
of the Do-Nothing Congress.[10]

Binder's "Legislative Stalemate" graph covers a longer time period than
the graphs from Curry and Lee showing the "Average Percentage of Minority Party Support." If we look at the period of overlap (starting in 1973, which

is toward the middle in Binder's graph), we see that over this period lasting more than 40 years, most laws that pass Congress do so with substantial minority support, but a far higher proportion of the nation's issues
are going unaddressed in later years than in the 1970s. This tells us we
will have to see more bipartisanship if we want to see more congressional
achievement.

Keith Krehbiel, professor at Stanford Graduate School of Business, has a
theory that yields insight on the key numbers that determine whether a bill's
passage is possible, discussed in his 1998 book, *Pivotal Politics: A Theory of
US Lawmaking.*[11] His "pivot points" include party control of the White House
and each congressional chamber, but he stresses the importance of the
threshold levels for breaking a filibuster in the Senate and overriding a presidential veto, as these levels determine whether most bills can get past the
choke points that too often are used to block legislation. The theory is consistent with Curry and Lee's finding that most legislation passes with bipartisan support. The theory also explains why so much attention is placed on
rule changes that alter the vote thresholds needed for passage, such as changes
in when bills are subject to a filibuster or when they can be fast-tracked or
qualified under the 1974 Congressional Budget Act's reconciliation provision: All of these details determine whether a bill can pass the Senate with
a simple 51-vote majority or will need a 60-vote supermajority.

In his 2011 book, *Partisan Balance: Why Political Parties Don't Kill the
U.S. Constitutional System*, David Mayhew looks at past instances when
Washington seemed divided and dysfunctional, and predicts that the increasing partisan dysfunction of Congress through the Bush, Clinton, Bush,
and Obama years will have a tendency toward self-correction.[12] I respect
the optimism in this view, but I am not counting on his hope that Congress
will solve its own problems. I believe those of us who want to see a less ad-
versarial, less contentious, more cooperative, and more effective Congress
must insist on a change in direction, and encourage any evidence that the
government is indeed self-correcting. We deserve a Congress and president
who can get things done to solve our enduring problems, and we must act
as a catalyst for correction or self-correction when Washington is falling
short of our expectations. My ideas for how both insiders and ordinary
citizens can work toward these goals are in chapter 11.

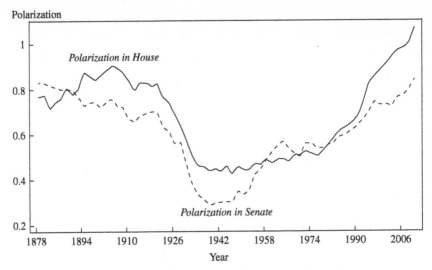

FIGURE 10-3.  Polarization in the House and the Senate, 1879–2011
The y-axis shows the average distance between positions across parties—that is, the difference in mean positions between the two parties in both the House and the Senate—using the DW-NOMINATE scores developed by Keith T. Poole and Howard Rosenthal.

*Source:* Jane Mansbridge and Cathie Jo Martin, eds., *Negotiating Agreement in Politics*, Report of the Task Force on Negotiating Agreement in Politics, American Political Science Association, December 2013, 20.

## POLITICAL SCIENTISTS FIND INCREASING POLARIZATION IN CONGRESS

There are several ways to measure polarization, but nearly every method confirms what we already understand: Congress has been growing increasingly polarized, a trend that covers more than six decades. Congress was unusually unified during World War II and into the 1950s but has been growing more polarized decade by decade up to the present Congress. Here we are defining "polarization" as the distance between the average Democrat and the average Republican lawmaker on the liberal-to-conservative scale. The graph in figure 10-3 captures the long-term trend of increasing polarization in both the Senate and the House. The lines bottom out in the 1940s, showing very low levels of polarization at the time when many conservative Democrats and many liberal Republicans in Congress became part of the shifting coalitions that Franklin D. Roosevelt formed to pass his New Deal agenda. The lines then rise through the decades as Democrats become increasingly more liberal, and Republicans to an even greater degree become increasingly more conservative.

This graph represents the work of many political scientists[13] and is just one of many that were collected in an excellent 2013 report from the American Political Science Association's (APSA's) Task Force on Negotiating Agreement in Politics.[14] Section 2 of the APSA report presents what is known and not known by political scientists about the "Causes and Consequences of Polarization."[15] It was written by Michael Barber of Brigham Young University and Nolan McCarty of Princeton University, and it convincingly claims to offer the consensus view of the profession because so many of the political scientists I have read on these topics, informing my understand for this chapter, and indeed this book, were members of the APSA working group that crafted section 2. They do not agree on everything, but nearly all agree that, however we measure it, Congress is more polarized today than it was one, two, or three decades ago, and this trend goes all the way back to the 1940s.

Another area of consensus among the political scientists in the APSA working group is that the shift in congressional polarization has not been symmetrical. The assertion that the Republicans moved to the right and the Democrats to the left in anywhere near equal measure simply does not fit the available data. The research finds that Republicans in Congress now are dramatically more ideologically conservative, while Democrats in Congress now are about as liberal as Democrats were during the Vietnam War. Democrats are more ideologically cohesive today than they were in the 1960s and 1970s, but that is because conservative Southern Democrats in Congress left the party and became, or were replaced by, conservative Southern Republicans.[16]

Political scientists build large data sets and use advanced statistical analyses to try to understand not only what is happening but also why it is happening. There are many data sets, but one in particular is used quite often to understand polarization in the American Congress. Every congressional roll-call vote ever recorded in Congress forms the basis for the data set called Voteview, which was used to generate the graph in figure 10-3, showing "Polarization in Congress and the Senate, 1879–2011," and figures 10-4 and 10-5. Political scientists Keith T. Poole and Howard Rosenthal were at

Number of Senators

93rd Congress, 1973–74

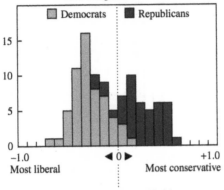

103rd Congress, 1993–94

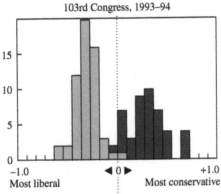

112th Congress, 2011–12

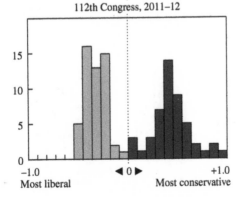

FIGURE 10-4.   Ideological Polarization in
the Senate, 1973–2012
Ideological scores of senators are based on
roll-call votes. Negative numbers represent
liberal views and positive numbers, conservative views.
*Sources:* Royce Carroll and others, Voteview.com;
PEW Research Center.

Number of Representatives

93rd Congress, 1973–74

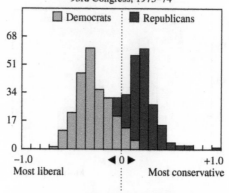

103rd Congress, 1993–94

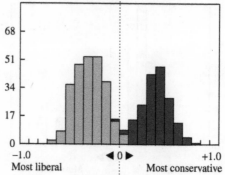

112th Congress, 2011–12

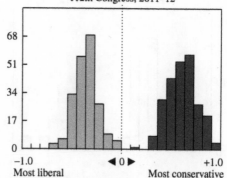

FIGURE 10-5. Ideological Polarization in
the House, 1973–2012
Ideological scores of senators are based on
roll-call votes. Negative numbers represent
liberal views and positive numbers, conservative views.
*Sources:* Royce Carroll and others, Voteview.com;
PEW Research Center.

Carnegie-Mellon University between 1989 and 1992 when they developed the "DW-NOMINATE" scores for estimating the position of lawmakers on a liberal/conservative political ideology scale based on the votes they each cast. The application can also tell us where the parties are in any given Congress by averaging the scores of party members on the same scale; the distance between those scores is shown on the graph in figure 10-3.

The graph in figure 10-4 shows "Ideological Polarization in the Senate," and the graph in figure 10-5 shows "Ideological Polarization in the House." Both show three different periods: 1973–1974, 1993–1994, and 2011–2012. The graphs were created by using the DW-NOMINATE scores to plot each lawmaker on the liberal/conservative scale and show the number of lawmakers of each party at each point. We can see that, in both chambers, there was a fair degree of overlap in the early 1970s, far less in the early 1990s, and almost none at all in 2011–2012.

The graphs also make it clear that the increase in distance is far more about Republicans moving to the right than Democrats moving to the left. They are a graphic depiction of asymmetric polarization. There are other data sets and other ways to evaluate these propositions, but generally the other data and methods do not contradict these findings.

This is just one way of analyzing what researchers call "elite polarization," where elites in this case are defined as senators and congressional representatives, although the category of elites is thought to also include their staffs and political parties, campaign workers, special interest groups, and anyone who gets paid to work on politics. There are other data sets that are used to understand "mass polarization," which refers to changes in the attitudes of voters as discussed later in the chapter, but for now our attention is on elites, specifically members of the House and the Senate.

Political scientists have teased a lot of insights out of the DW-NOMINATE data sets regarding the political behavior of members of Congress. Some of these assertions are the subject of vigorous debate, and some are less controversial and generally accepted as more robust findings. I could never convey all of the complexity of the political science research here, and remember, I am an economist, not a political scientist. But for much of the rest of this chapter, I relay some of the findings that I think are relatively uncontroversial and that shed light on some of the history and personal experience I discuss in this book.

## Lawmakers Sorting Themselves into Ideologically Distinct Parties

One of the major findings in political science is given the name "sorting," and there are lots of different but related types of sorting. Staying focused on the elite level, ideological sorting can be seen in how, while Congress at one time included large numbers of conservative Democrats and liberal Republicans, now nearly all Republicans are conservatives, with a small number who would call themselves moderates, and most Democrats would call themselves progressives, with a few who would call themselves moderates.

Political scientists agree that ideological sorting and the resulting polarization in Congress has been happening recently, but most see the trend going back in the data for many years and decades. The 1980 election of Ronald Reagan and the 1994 Republican congressional victory mark key shifts in the balance of power between the two parties, but many political scientists point to 1964 and the passage of the Civil Rights Act as a pivotal point defining our two political parties. President Lyndon Johnson was said to be aware at the time that Democrats may have just "lost the South for a generation." It was certainly true that Southern Democrats in the House and Senate who opposed the act, and their replacements, would continue to realign with the Republican Party. In my view, however, the story starts much earlier, as chronicled in chapter 3, because the interests of this key faction in preserving a system of racial inequality go back to the Constitutional Convention of 1787 and continue to drive political polarization today.

## Durable Fault Lines, and Evolving Factions and Parties

As discussed in chapters 3 and 4, we see how fault lines of race, religion, geography, and economics—along with differing views about the strength of the federal government *vis-à-vis* state governments, which divided the thirteen colonies when they met to write the Constitution—have proven remarkably durable and continue to divide us now. These fault lines have proven more consistent than the parties, which have formed and re-formed around different personalities, factions, and issues. One faction of lawmakers, in particular, has proven particularly pivotal: the representatives, mostly but not exclusively from Southern states, who supported slavery before the Civil War and then segregation and discrimination thereafter. This faction has changed its party alignment in different historical periods, often bringing enough votes in Congress to deliver a majority.

The Republicans Abraham Lincoln and Ulysses S. Grant defeated this faction in the Civil War, but Rutherford B. Hayes accommodated Southern Democratic segregationists in a deal that allowed him to win the disputed 1876 presidential election by reversing the Republican position on Reconstruction and allowing white rule in the Jim Crow South. Chapter 4 chronicles the slow migration of this faction from the Democratic Party at the start of the twentieth century to the Republican Party by the end of the century. Democratic Southern segregationists were an important element in Franklin Roosevelt's New Deal coalition, even though he passed some of his agenda with the support of Republicans to mitigate the influence of the Southern Democrats. This is reflected in figure 10-3, showing polarization in Congress and the Senate as very low scores for party conflict in the 1940s, when FDR formed coalitions with factions in both parties to pass the New Deal.

Southern Democrats asserted their independence by following North Carolina Senator Strom Thurmond's Dixiecrats in opposing Harry Truman in the 1948 election, and again as Thurmond supported Republican Barry Goldwater in 1964. That was the year President Johnson took up President John Kennedy's civil rights agenda by passing the Civil Rights Act, followed by the Voting Rights Act and the Fair Housing Act. Even though the votes of many Republicans were needed to pass this legislation, the Democrats were then firmly aligned with the issue of African American civil rights. From that point forward, the faction opposed to racial equality increasingly aligns with Republicans, first by supporting segregationist Democrat George Wallace in the 1968 presidential election and then by responding to Richard Nixon's Southern strategy in 1972.

Through the 1970s, more and more Southern state Senate seats would shift to Republicans, contributing to the Republicans Senate majority after the 1980 election that saw Ronald Reagan win the White House in a landslide. The House remained Democratic nominally but not functionally when conservative Southern Democratic House members calling themselves the Boll Weevils gave Ronald Reagan an effective governing majority to pass his budgets and tax cuts. This story would continue as Southern states and congressional districts, as well as many white, working-class districts in Northern industrial states, increasingly voted Republican, contributing to the 1994 Republican takeover of the House, the rise of the Tea Party faction, and eventually the surprise election victory for Donald Trump.

The shift in party identification from Democratic to Republican of the conservative senators and representatives from Southern states is just the most obvious example of what political scientists point to as the sorting of elected officials into more ideologically homogeneous political parties. Over the same period, the Democrats were electing more African American, Hispanic, and women House representatives, who tended to take more liberal positions. When Reagan came out clearly against the *Roe v. Wade* decision that gave women the right to have an abortion, evangelical Christian groups became a larger factor in Republican politics as women's groups insisted that all Democrats support a woman's right to choose. The right to own guns versus the need to limit gun violence became a wedge issue that divided urban Democrats from Democrats in less populated Western states, eventually contributing to a massive shift in favor of Republican representation. As noted in chapter 3, Democrats held eight out of the ten Senate seats from Iowa, North Dakota, South Dakota, Nebraska, and Montana in 1977, but just one of these ten seats in 2019.

The political scientists' theories of ideological sorting and the polarization of members of Congress fit my own experiences in trying to find common ground through the decades. In the 1970s, whether the topic was budget policy, health policy, military and foreign policy, immigration policy, or environmental policy, I could name as many Republicans who were willing to take moderate or even progressive positions as I could name Democrats taking fiscally conservative, strong defense, or pro-business positions. As these overlaps shrink and then disappear, it becomes increasingly difficult to find bargaining partners on the other side of the aisle.

By the time we get to the Obama administration, this trend had reached full fruition, and I experienced it personally in many ways. The ideologically diverse but unelected Domenici-Rivlin Task Force could get Democrats to consider reductions in the growth rate for Social Security and Medicare, and Republicans to consider increases in government revenue, especially if it could be done without raising tax rates. The same conversations could be had, under conditions of strict secrecy, with the members of the Simpson-Bowles Commission, but when it came time to vote, five of the six senators were willing to sign on, but only one of the six House members would endorse the deal, leaving it short of the supermajority needed to bring it to a vote on the House and Senate floors.

## PARTIES AT NEAR EQUAL STRENGTH EVOLVE INTO PARTISAN TEAMS

The increasing ideological elite polarization and sorting of lawmakers into distinct homogeneous parties does a lot to help me understand why efforts to reach a grand bargain were unsuccessful, but this is not enough to help me understand why Senate Republican Leader Mitch McConnell would say his goal was to see President Obama fail and become a one-term president, or why the grand bargain negotiations were happening against a backdrop of threats to default on the national debt, which almost surely would have caused a global economic catastrophe. To understand this, I need an additional theory, and I believe Frances Lee offers at least a partial explanation for these behavior changes in her persuasive 2016 book, *Insecure Majorities: Congress and the Perpetual Campaign*.[17]

Lee argues that when political parties see the potential for the next election to change control of one or both chambers in Congress, the parties behave differently than when one party seems to have a lock on the majority and the other is relegated to perpetual minority opposition status. Minority party members can only have a voice in crafting legislation if the majority allows them to participate, so they define their role constructively and work to help the majority to pass legislation that is less bad than if the majority shut the minority out of deliberations. This certainly is consistent with my experiences at the start of my career in Washington in the 1960s, as described in chapter 4. Committee chairs working closely together and having respectful, collegial relationships with members of opposite parties was common then, and often productive.

No one doubts that there was a huge change in Congress in 1980, when after decades of nearly unbroken Democratic control of both the House and Senate, Ronald Reagan's landslide victory flipped twelve Senate seats from

Democrat to Republican to win a Senate Republican majority for the first time since 1954. At the same time, the Democratic "Boll Weevils" delivered effective control of the House to the Republicans on budget issues.

From that point forward, House Republicans began to believe that full control of the House was possible, and they won a majority for the first time in 40 years in 1994. The House majority switched parties again in 2006, 2010, and 2018, and control of the Senate changed nearly as frequently. Party parity had arrived, and with it, a significant change in the behavior of both parties.

Lee asserts that parties viewing majority control as insecure are prone to prioritize aggressive, win-at-all-cost tactics over collegiality and compromise to solve the longer-term issues facing the nation. The aspect of the political process that resembles an ongoing contest causes the participants to view themselves as members of a team, and to rally around their team captains. The team that holds the White House becomes the "in party" (especially if it also controls one or both chambers on the Hill) wanting to pass legislation that will advance its chances of holding power or enhancing it in the next election. The "out party" adopts the goal of stopping the in party from achieving its goals while scoring points that can be used to throw the bums out in the next election.

The political battle between the in group and the out group can become a stronger motivation than even the ideological battle between liberals and conservatives, as I noticed in the political fight over Medicare premium support. Democrats and Republicans were taking positions that were the opposite of the policy positions they were taking in the fight over the Affordable Care Act. As I relay in chapter 9, neither side cared about the contradiction. Republicans just wanted to defeat Obama's signature legislative achievement and attack Democrats as big spenders, while Democrats just wanted to keep Obamacare and charge that the Republicans were ending Medicare as we know it.

Lee details dozens of specific changes in the behavior of both the majority and the minority in the Senate and the House that can be characterized according to several themes. A party that feels it faces a real prospect of losing power in the next election will concentrate tighter control over all activities in the leadership, as will a party that sees an opportunity to gain control of a chamber. This is especially the case when it comes to messaging, where efforts will be made to have every member speak from the same set of talking points, as in the Republicans' "Contract with America" or the Democrats' "For the People" agenda.

Hearings in committees and subcommittees are designed less to inform lawmakers about the details of policy tradeoffs than to make speeches or, better still, to make news, often at the expense of the other side. Lee draws particular attention to what she calls "messaging votes" on the House and Senate floors, which are votes taken not to resolve a legislative issue but to get members on record supporting or opposing a policy so it can then be used in campaign ads. There are dozens of examples that could be cited, but none is better than the dozens of votes taken to repeal the Affordable Care Act when Republicans controlled the House agenda but did not have enough power across Washington to actually repeal Obamacare nor an alternative health care policy with which to replace it.

Two of my favorite analyses of how the policy process has broken down, both with terrific titles, are Thomas Mann and Norman Ornstein's book *It's Even Worse Than It Looks*, which details the plunge of Congress into total dysfunction with the rise of the Tea Party,[18] and E. J. Dionne's *Why the Right Went Wrong*, which traces the Republican refusal to compromise dating back to Goldwater's losing 1964 campaign.[19]

Former Speaker of the House Newt Gingrich is a central figure in both books. The embodiment of Frances Lee's thesis in *Insecure Majorities*, Gingrich was first elected to Congress from Georgia in 1978, and in the GOP's 1980 capture of the White House and Senate, Gingrich saw a vision for Republicans to eventually win the House. He developed a combative style and recruited like-minded candidates with a message of small government and low taxes. But the message was also pointedly aggressive in attacking Democrats, individually and collectively, as corrupted by Washington power.

The plan worked when Republicans won the House in the 1994 midterm elections. Gingrich's style of politics, now proven successful, would be adopted by countless other Republicans. Gingrich consolidated power in the Speaker's office; handpicked members for the Rules Committee to give leadership complete control of bills reaching the House floor; eliminated several congressional committees and many subcommittees; and disregarded seniority to name committee chairs who understood the importance of a unified party message.[20]

The new House leadership continued to use the combative techniques that had brought them to power in negotiations with the Democrat in the White House. There had been a few short federal government shutdowns in previous administrations, but the Gingrich standoffs with Bill Clinton, detailed in chapter 7, were longer, more costly, and more acrimonious. They were paired with threats of a potential national debt default, which would have been far more damaging to the economy and America's standing in the world. However, Gingrich eventually had to end the 25-day second shutdown without achieving most of his goals and without public opinion on his side.

After overreaching with the shutdowns, Gingrich sought common ground with Clinton, and as discussed in chapter 7, there are reports the two discussed a grand bargain on entitlements before the Monica Lewinski scandal engulfed the White House and Gingrich resigned from the House after the poor Republican performance in the 1998 midterms. But nearly a decade later, Gingrich was again encouraging an uncompromising approach to politics when, from outside Congress, he advised the "Young Guns" on tactics and encouraged the rise of the Tea Party. As described in chapters 8 and 9, Barack Obama endured years of negotiations amid another round of government shutdowns and default threats, as Tea Party Republicans rejected compromise on taxes and pressured other Republicans and the leadership to show the same resolve.[21] Through the years, this tactic has frustrated Democrats and at the same time pushed many Democrats to insist that their party adopt positions rejecting compromise on many issues.

## FACTIONS WITHIN NETWORKED PARTIES

If Frances Lee worries about parties being too strong and in control, Seth Masket of the University of Denver has the perspective that parties are weakening and losing control, further adding to their insecurities. Masket describes the modern political party as a network of aligned individuals and groups without a hierarchical structure. Where parties once had a great deal of influence over policy platforms, candidates, money, and message, now they rely on others to perform those functions. Think tanks develop policy proposals. A network of political action committees (PACs) and large and small funders raise the money. Each party has allies in the media to provide an audience for the message. Masket points to the outsourcing and informality of the network as a major factor that has frustrated efforts to reform politics or to limit polarization. When reformers try to regulate campaign money or the message, they limit the parties or the candidates, but other elements of the network can compensate, raising money and delivering an unfettered message as an independent effort.

The same technologies and tactics that strengthened parties in the 1990s have evolved to serve factions within the parties that are now challenging the party establishment for control. Groups independent from the Democratic Party, such as Democracy for America[22] and MoveOn.org, have developed their own constituency, funding base, and policy platform designed to move Democrats to the left.

In chapter 9, I detail the rise of the Tea Party faction within the Republican Party, from an uncoordinated notion that soon took shape as a movement that quickly showed the limits of the power that the Republican Speaker of the House had to control the chamber. As the Tea Party has become absorbed by the party of Trump, many in the Republican establishment worry that they no longer have a home in the GOP.

The fact that there are semiautonomous factions within each major party should not be overinterpreted as suggesting symmetry. The many asymmetries noted in this chapter give the parties very different characteristics, goals, and tactics. The movement that flows from Goldwater to Reagan, to Gingrich, to the Tea Party, and to Trump has proven far more effective in moving the Republican Party to the right than the progressives have been in moving the Democrats away from the center to the left. The willingness of the Tea Party to see budget negotiations fail, and even the government fail, finds no parallel on the left, where progressive Democrats are as supportive of democratic institutions as are the moderate Democrats. All of this leads Norman Ornstein and Thomas Mann to label the Republican Party, now that it is under the control of its latest faction, as "an insurgent outlier—ideologically extreme, contemptuous of the inherited social and economic policy regime; scornful of compromise, unpersuaded by conventional understanding of facts, evidence, and science; and dismissive of the legitimacy of its political opposition." This insurgent faction has put enormous strains on policymaking especially when it comes to the budget process.

## A BUDGET PROCESS PUSHED TO (AND SOMETIMES BEYOND) THE BREAKING POINT

The budget process has been challenged, stressed, and at times almost broken down completely as the business of legislation becomes a secondary priority for lawmakers, losing out to the larger goal of sending a message to voters in the never-ending campaign for reelection. Here I want to define two ways budget work has been achieved in recent times—one of which I call the new normal, which is a dismal state of affairs, and the other I call the new abnormal, which is far worse. First, let's talk about the old normal, which is called regular order.

As discussed in chapters 4 and 5, the congressional budget process is defined by the Congressional Budget and Impoundment Control Act of 1974, which laid out a detailed timeline and rules for passing each year's annual budget through budget resolutions, and sometimes reconciliation bills, in Congress before the appropriations committees are given the task of writing twelve separate spending bills. However, this process stopped happening on schedule, and more recently, it does not happen at all.

The process is supposed to start in the cabinet departments and agencies, where policy analysts and budget analysts go through all the programs looking for inefficiencies, and opportunities to shift priorities. Their recommendations are passed to the White House Office of Management and Budget (OMB), which has a lot of budget analysts to make the tough decisions needed to prepare the president's budget proposal, which is supposed to be delivered to Congress in February.

The House and Senate Budget Committees, with the support of the Congressional Budget Office (CBO) and in consultation with twelve appropriations committees on each side of the Hill and the tax-writing committees, prepare the House and Senate budget resolutions. These resolutions are supposed to be passed by April 15. A budget reconciliation bill may be necessary if the House and Senate do not pass identical budget resolutions. These guide the appropriations committees in their work to prepare the twelve appropriations bills necessary to fund the government by the start of the new fiscal year on October 1.

Completion of the twelve separate spending bills has become a rarely attained goal. It is great when they can be passed in regular order, but more often than not, the bills that cannot get passed on time are rolled into a large omnibus spending bill. When this cannot get passed on time, Congress gives itself an extension of a few weeks or a few months in the form of a continuing resolution (CR) to fund the government at current levels. If Congress cannot even pass a CR, that's when we see a partial or total government shutdown.

What I call the new normal is what happens when the budget process does not get completely derailed by what I call the new abnormal: shutdown threats, budget standoffs, and up-to-the-deadline negotiations between the White House and congressional leadership. Even without the high drama, the budget process is facing additional stresses in the era of party parity and insecure majorities due to the dysfunction throughout the legislative process.

Budget resolutions are must-pass bills, and, by tradition, they usually reach the House floor under "open rules" that allow amendments. Budget bills offer the rare opportunity for members to propose amendments (often nongermane to the budget process) because leadership is now tightly controlling all other legislative activity. This is one of the reasons why Congress misses so many budget deadlines; work on the budget gets delayed by fights over things like funding abortion or flying the Confederate flag.[23] The result is a House budget process that is burdened with a lot of added politics and complexity, but the Senate side may be even worse.

The Congressional Budget Act of 1974 exempted budget resolutions and reconciliation bills from Senate filibusters. A budget resolution is a necessary first step in using the reconciliation process. Reconciliation bills are attractive opportunities to move legislation through the Senate with a 51-vote threshold rather than the 60 votes needed to break a filibuster. The Senate parliamentarian (a nonpartisan independent advisor) must agree that each element of a reconciliation bill qualifies as a budgetary matter according to the criteria set under the Byrd Rule (as discussed in chapter 5). Both the Affordable Care Act and the Republican effort to repeal the ACA (the one that failed when Arizona Republican Senator John McCain voted thumbs-down) were qualified under the Byrd Rule to reach the floor.

Senate budget bills can be amended, and this has caused an annual ritual called a vote-a-rama, where all 100 Senators stay on or near the Senate floor for a marathon session that can exceed 24 hours, where they vote up or down on as many as 100 amendments, sometimes more. This has become an opportunity for senators to raise ideas that have no other viable path to passage in the tightly controlled legislative atmosphere, and it often allows senators to force messaging votes that put every Senator on the record on controversial issues that are then raised in political ads.

All of these are just examples of the strains placed on the budget process by the increased politicization and tighter control of the legislative process that has evolved in response to party parity and increased polarization. But this is the new normal level of dysfunction. Chapter 9 describes how the budget process was taken to even greater heights of abnormality in the budget battles between the Obama White House and Tea Party-influenced Republicans. We can hope that the new normal era of omnibus bills, continuing resolutions, and vote-a-ramas does not often get replaced by a new abnormal of default threats leading to supercommittees and sequesters, but I have no reason for my optimism unless we change congressional rules and norms of behavior.[24]

We all pay a price for this lack of government function. The budget process is cumbersome, but when it functions, budget analysts and lawmakers have the opportunity to make decisions about spending and taxing priorities. Instead of lowering the deficit by changing policy—for example, by slowing the rapidly rising costs for providing medical care or eliminating unneeded special tax breaks—budgets passed as continuing resolutions at a deadline, and amid threats of default, just mean no real decisions are made.

From a policy point of view, the only thing worse than a long string of continuing resolutions is a budget sequester, which calls for across-the-board spending cuts from discretionary programs without regard to efficiency, quality, or necessity. Instead of a grand bargain that would adequately fund the social safety net, make the needed investments in future productivity, and put the national debt on a sustainable path, partisan hardball tactics gave us a sequester in the budget arena and no meaningful progress toward fixing a broken immigration system, reversing global warming, reducing economic inequality, raising people out of poverty, or providing economic security for the middle class. I believe the low level of congressional achievement in the years preceding the 2016 election helped set the stage for Donald Trump to defeat the Republican Party establishment in the 2016 primaries and the Democratic Party establishment in the general election.

## How Congress Works When It Does Not Work

From the point where party parity fully arrived in Washington following the 1994 election through to the present, both parties have become increasingly polarized; leadership in both parties has taken greater control over the legislative process, and over messaging, to prevail in the next election; and both parties have prioritized messaging over passing legislation, placing burdens on the legislative process that have pushed it to the breaking point on several occasions. And yet, as we know from the start of this chapter, legislation still passes, and most of the time it passes with bipartisan support. Many political scientists are studying the details of how lawmaking still happens, even in the current environment. Barbara Sinclair wrote a book about what she calls "unorthodox lawmaking."[25]

What we see is that on any issue large enough to become the subject of recurring segments on cable news, nothing gets passed unless it becomes the subject of intense high-level negotiations—either between the two parties or, on the rare occasion when one party tries to go it alone, between moderate members and either the Democrats' progressive wing or the Republicans' conservative wing, which history shows can be just as intense. Where once the compromises necessary to pass legislation could be worked out in committee, now everything becomes a negotiation between the White House and the leadership in Congress, both of which perceive themselves to be locked in a zero-sum game where the prize is victory for their team in the next election. Often, the incentives push lawmakers away from accommodation and compromise toward adoption of hardball tactics.

## Asymmetrical Constitutional Hardball: Staying within the Rules but Breaking the Norms

In chapter 11, I suggest several congressional rule changes that could help Congress function better in this age of intense polarization. Congressional rules are important, but it is equally important to understand how the leadership of the House and Senate has been using the rules. In this view, I join many political scientists, including Molly Reynolds, Sarah Binder,

Thomas Mann, and Norman Ornstein, who focus attention on congressional norms and the many ways in which Congress has broken with its past precedents.

We are firmly in an era of party parity and insecure majorities as described by Frances Lee, where both sides believe majority control of one or both chambers could switch in each next election, and both sides are insecure, aggressive, and behaving like teams to the point where seeing the other side lose becomes a more important goal of politics than seeing the American people win. It is the only explanation I can think of for the practice of political hostage-taking—threatening to do something that would cause harm to the public to gain leverage in achieving political goals. This is exactly what it means to threaten to breach the nation's debt ceiling, allowing the government to default on its debts and almost certainly causing a national and global economic catastrophe.

Legal scholars define "constitutional hardball" as tactics that push the constitutional envelope, straining unwritten norms of governance or disrupting established constitutional understandings. Constitutional hardball is played within the rules, but in ways that stretch the norms. Threatening to do something that would cause economic harm to the American people unless cuts are made in federal programs is certainly straining unwritten norms of governance. And constitutional hardball is being practiced asymmetrically;[26] Republicans have been using these tactics with increasing levels of aggressiveness as Democrats search for a response to the political hostage-taking that reaches a resolution without rewarding the tactics.[27]

Binder explains how the filibuster has evolved over two centuries from a rarely used and, indeed, accidental change in Senate procedures (as I note in chapter 4) to become routinely invoked by the minority party to raise the vote threshold for passing laws in the Senate from a simple majority to the 60 votes needed to end debate.[28] Reynolds has studied how budget reconciliation bills have become the exception to the filibuster rule, periodically (and under defined circumstances) allowing the majority party to sideline the objections of the minority party and pass legislation with a 51-vote simple majority.[29]

In their 2006 book, *The Broken Branch: How Congress Is Failing America and How to Get It Back on Track*,[30] Mann and Ornstein emphasize separation of powers, explaining that Congress is failing to act as an independent check on the power of the president. When the president and the majority of one or both chambers of Congress are from the same party, the majority acts like its mandate is simply to support the president's agenda. When a chamber majority is of the opposite party of the president, its members act as if they have a mandate to adamantly oppose the president's agenda. This relatively recent choice by congressional leaders to define their role in support or opposition to the president in no way reflects the independence that the framers of the Constitution envisioned.

The rules of Congress and the roles of the congressional leadership do not demand that leaders use constitutional hardball tactics to gain political leverage; these are choices that leaders make. Senate Minority Leader Mitch McConnell decided to use the filibuster on nearly all legislation, as well as on nominations to cabinet positions and for judges to the federal courts, as a method to thwart the Obama administration and retain court vacancies until Republicans could fill them in another Congress.[31] As reviewed in chapter 9, Obama was seeking compromise with Republicans for eight years, but McConnell in the Senate and the House Tea Party Republicans refused to compromise for most of those years. But on a few occasions, such as the lame-duck session after the 2010 election, there were breakthroughs that delivered real progress. The rules can be used to block negotiations, but when leaders on both sides want to negotiate, the rules do not stand in the way.

## USING ANTI-GOVERNMENT RHETORIC TO GAIN ASYMMETRICAL BARGAINING LEVERAGE

My own experience supports the political scientists' finding that the increasing polarization has been asymmetrical: Republicans have moved further to the right on the ideological scale than Democrats have moved to the left. I also would have to agree that the use of constitutional hardball tactics has been asymmetrical: Republicans have been more aggressive at most points in the escalation. But I would add an additional asymmetry in budget bargaining positions that began to arrive when Ronald Reagan declared in his first inaugural address—echoing statements he had made during his campaigns for president in 1980 and 1976, and even far earlier, in his 1964 speeches for Barry Goldwater's presidential campaign—that "government is not the solution to our problem, government is the problem."

As Republicans became increasingly the anti-government party, and now they are almost exclusively the anti-government party, all negotiations became asymmetrical. Republicans gain leverage from the Democrats' belief that government delivers real benefits to the American people. Democrats want negotiations to succeed so that the government can succeed, and the American people will succeed. Republicans, at least rhetorically, do not believe in government, so they are more willing to see negotiations fail.

I define "leverage" in any negotiation as directly related to either party's willingness to see the negotiations fail. When I am buying a used car, I only have leverage to get a better deal to the degree that the car salesperson believes I am willing to walk away from the lot. Sarah Binder and Frances Lee reach essentially the same understanding of leverage, writing in section 3 of the APSA Task Force report, "The greater (lower) is the cost to the minority of saying no, the greater (lower) is the majority's bargaining leverage."[32]

There are many used cars in town. By signaling my willingness to walk away, I (the minority) let the salesperson (the majority) know she or he has low leverage because the cost to me of saying no is low. Binder and Lee do not explain how the minority gains leverage over the majority. The logic of political hostage-taking, as in threatening a government shutdown or default, is that it raises the cost for the majority party of failing to reach a deal. When members of one party, the Republican Party, espouse anti-government rhetoric, they convince themselves that their supporters would welcome a government shutdown. They gain leverage (at least temporarily) from the view that saying no to a deal is low cost to them, but high cost for the majority that believes a well-functioning government is in the public interest.

In what I call the good old days, such as when President Ronald Reagan and House Speaker Tip O'Neill negotiated to extend the solvency of Social Security, Republicans and Democrats had strong differences of opinion over policy, but both sides wanted to reach a deal that would benefit the American people. As anti-government rhetoric increasingly became the guiding ideology of Republicans across the negotiating table from Presidents Clinton and Obama, the Republicans were gaining leverage from their willingness to let negotiations fail and allow a government shutdown. They lost this leverage when the government did shut down, and Republicans learned that, contrary to their rhetoric, the public really does appreciate and depend on their government and what it does for them on a daily basis. It was an expensive lesson to learn, and we can hope it does not need to be learned many more times.

The government was again shut down at the end of 2018, extending for thirty-five days and into 2019, but this time the Senate voted unanimously to pass a continuing resolution that was expected to pass the House as well. Donald Trump was on his own (although he was supported by some public conservative groups and news media) when he announced he would not sign the CR unless it included funding for the wall he promised to build on the US southern border. Eventually he backed off and ended the shutdown without gaining any concessions from Congress, having learned the lesson most in Congress already knew: the public does not want government shutdowns.

## INTEREST GROUPS TAKE UP THE CAUSE OF OPPOSING POLITICAL COMPROMISE

Before departing the topic of elite polarization in Congress, it is important to also examine the role of special interest groups, because while they take pains to claim that they speak for large numbers of voters and members of their organizations, interest groups are properly understood to be elites in the political process, and some have substantial influence. Special interest groups employ armies of staff to refine their message, lobby for their issue on Capitol Hill (including drafting legislation for lawmakers), and inform their members of their activities, but most of their attention is on building their membership base for the purposes of fundraising. An issue group is important if it has a large political action committee (PAC) so that it can donate to candidates, and a large bank account so that it can buy television and online advertising, and send more mail and email to build its membership and raise more funds.

Now, I want to be clear that I am not opposed to this activity. The right of citizens to assemble peaceably and to petition their government is guaranteed in the First Amendment to the Constitution. My problem is not with the existence of these groups—it is with a tactic that they have found especially effective in defining their positions on issues and mobilizing their constituents, and that may be having the effect of making Congress far less able to reach common-ground solutions to our national problems.

I do not have a problem with special interest groups, but I do see an issue with uncompromising special interest groups. Special interest groups become

*People can disagree on all sorts of things, but if they listen to each other and have respect for each other, they can work things out. And we've kind of lost that idea that you have to work things out and compromise and come to a conclusion. Because gridlock, which we have now in the budget, is the worst possible thing, especially with respect to a problem like the budget deficit, which gets worse if you do nothing. Gridlock is fatal for this problem. Because the course we're on now is hurtling toward disaster over time, and we have to do something. Nothing is not the answer.*

—Alice Rivlin, "Political Bridge
People," *On Being with Krista
Tippett*, October 25, 2012

problematic when they block political leaders from making the compromises necessary to pass legislation and solve problems.

The special interest group called Americans for Tax Reform, founded by Grover Norquist, may not have invented the tactic of defining an organization by the uncompromising positions that it holds and insists politicians endorse, but they used it to such great effect that they made political compromise on taxes nearly impossible for decades. As detailed in chapter 5, the group was formed to pressure Republican candidates into signing a pledge not to vote to raise income taxes. President George H. W. Bush echoed the pledge with his "read my lips, no new taxes" promise to the 1998 Republican Convention, which he regretted when a rising deficit threatened financial market stability and the national economy. Bush broke his pledge and joined Democrats in passing a compromise budget that raised some taxes and cut some spending; it also included the Budget Enforcement Act of 1990, which set caps on discretionary spending and added a pay-as-you-go (PAYGO) requirement that new legislation not add to the deficit. The move may have cost Bush reelection, but the compromise deal kept the deficit low enough to set the Clinton administration up for success in achieving four balanced budgets in a row (as detailed in chapter 7).

In my opinion, political compromise is necessary for a democracy to function, but that is not the lesson others seemed to have learned from this episode. Still following the lead of Americans for Tax Reform, nearly all other Republicans blamed Bush's loss on the reversal of the "no tax pledge," and they bound themselves more tightly to the absolutist position. This was a

driving force behind the budget battles of the Clinton and Obama administrations, leading to the standoffs and shutdowns.

The fact that many progressive interest groups on the Democratic side
have responded with similar tactics is evidence that they judge the aggressive posture as effective. Democrats are split between those who endorse an
equal and opposite reaction, and those who would set a higher standard. First
Lady Michelle Obama's dictum, "When they go low, we go high," was initially celebrated during the 2016 campaign, but after Trump's victory in the
presidential election, the sentiment became controversial.

The word "primary" has become a verb with an explicitly threatening
meaning. Interest groups on both the right and left now routinely threaten
"to primary" senators and members of Congress for the alleged transgres-
sion of compromising with the other party. This means Republican-leaning
interest groups recruit and fund Republican challengers to try to defeat Republican incumbents who are viewed as too moderate or who dare to compromise with Democrats. Of course, Democratic-leaning interest groups
have also been threatening to primary Democratic lawmakers, because the
tactic seems to be successful.

It is not clear that partisan primary campaigns lead to greater polarization in Congress. The record of political incumbents facing more extreme
partisans in primary elections is quite mixed despite the legendary status of
some of the more extreme partisans who have won in this fashion. More
often than not, the challenger loses the primary or she or he loses in the general election. One could suppose that it is the threat of the potential primary challenge that keeps elected officials in line, but the APSA report reviewed the available research and found little statistically reliable evidence
to support the assertions that primary elections have a consistent effect on
congressional polarization.[33]

## INCREASING POLARIZATION IN THE ELECTORATE

Over the same years that congressional polarization has increased, pollsters
and political scientists have also noted a similar shift in the views of voters. It is
not clear which is cause and which is effect. It may not be possible to determine
whether voters are becoming more polarized because their leaders in Congress
are or the other way around, but the data clearly show that supporters of the

two political parties are pulling further apart. It should also be noted, however, that there are still large numbers of American voters who remain in the center, even if their numbers are fewer today than one or two decades in the past.

The nonpartisan Pew Research Center has been conducting American voter surveys for decades and has cataloged the shift from political parties whose issue positions once overlapped to parties that are far more distinct. The three graphs in figure 10-6 show polarization among voters, and it looks a lot like the Pew-generated graphs in figures 10-4 and 10-5 showing polarization in the House and Senate (although they cover different periods). The figure 10-6 graphs were based on asking the same ten questions about issues and values on surveys conducted over twenty-three years.[34] The voters who gave the liberal or conservative answers to all ten questions were labeled "consistent partisans," and they made up just 21 percent of all voters in the 2014 survey, roughly evenly split between consistent conservatives (9 percent) and consistent liberals (12 percent).[35]

The same survey found these two polar opposites made up the majority (69 percent) of the politically active and engaged public, the group that drives political discussions among friends and family, on social media, and through active participation in politics. While it is undeniably true that America has been growing increasingly polarized, consistent partisans are responsible for us feeling more polarized than we really are.[37] These most consistent partisans are the most engaged voters, but they do not represent the views of most Americans, who hold mixed views on issues and values.

In 2018, Steven Hawkins, Daniel Yudkin, and Tim Dixon of More in Common, an international group that conducts research to support liberal democracies, fielded a survey that found most Americans dramatically overestimate how much we are divided on issues. The results are powerful, showing Democrats estimate that far larger numbers of Republicans hold the most conservative positions on a range of issues—for example, guessing that 49 percent of Republicans believe racism no longer exists, when in fact a 21 percent minority of Republicans hold this view. The reverse is also true, with the average estimate among Republicans for the proportion of Democrats who agree that "most police are bad people" is 52 percent, when the actual number is just 15 percent of Democrats hold this view.[38] Strongly partisan elites are ubiquitous on political media, and they convince their opponents that they are speaking for larger numbers than they in fact are.

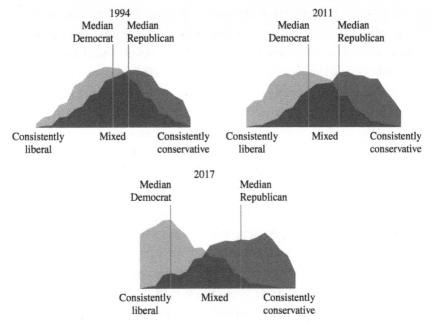

FIGURE 10-6.   Pew Research Center Surveys Show a Polarizing Electorate
*Source:* Pew Research Center surveys conducted in 1994, 2011, and 2017.

## VOTER POLARIZATION AND (ISSUE, IDEOLOGICAL, GEOGRAPHIC, SOCIAL, AND IDENTITY) SORTING

As when analyzing elites, the political scientists define two closely related but distinct concepts, polarization and sorting, when they look at the mass electorate. Polarization refers to the position of each voter on the ideological scale from strongly liberal through moderate to strongly conservative. If voters move from more moderate views to more extreme views, whether more conservative or more liberal, then political scientists say the electorate has grown more polarized (and there is evidence that it has over the last several decades).

There are several types of voter sorting. Political scientists say voter ideological sorting has occurred if conservative Democrats and liberal Republicans become less common (and this is happening, too). Democrats are now more likely to be progressives or moderates, and Republicans are more likely to be conservatives or moderates.

Social identity sorting is the alignment of people into more homogeneous groups on dimensions that define one's personal identity, such as race, religion, educational attainment, and geography, and this has been happening too. And to a greater degree than ever before, these personal identity characteristics have been aligning with political affiliation.

Issue sorting has occurred if voters hold positions across a wide range of issues that are more consistent with the views of others in their same party (and this is increasingly true). Where once pro-life or pro-gun Democrats or pro-choice or environmentalist Republicans were common, now the issue stances of the parties are sorted to the degree that those voters who do not align with the same party on all issues may feel peer pressure to either change their positions on the issues or change their party identification.

Voters may feel these pressures due to geographic sorting, ideological sorting, or social identity sorting. Republicans are now more likely to live near other Republicans with whom they share many personal identity characteristics on such dimensions as race, religion, age, marital status, and educational attainment. Their social circle is likely to include a high proportion of other Republicans who share their personal identity characteristics and views on leading issues. Of course, Democrats are also increasingly likely to live near and socialize with other Democrats who share their political views on the issues and most of their personal characteristics.

There is little debate that voters are becoming increasingly sorted on all these dimensions. The fact that these changes have been taking place over decades, going back at least to the middle of the 1970s, and that the same period saw increased polarization and sorting among political elites fuels deep and rich conversations among political scientists. They bring theories and hypotheses, data, and statistical analyses to conferences, research papers, and books that attempt to understand which of the changes preceded other changes, and the patterns of influence among the various factors.

## STUDYING SHIFTS IN PARTY SUPPORT

Political scientists like Alan Abramowitz of Emory University, Shanto Iyengar of Stanford University, and Lilliana Mason of the Johns Hopkins University and the University of Maryland base most of their research on the American National Election Survey (ANES), a series of surveys dating back to 1948 conducted by a consortium of academic researchers centered at the University of Michigan. Abramowitz's influential 2011 book, *The Dis-*

*appearing Center, Engaged Citizens, Polarization & American Democracy,*[39] details how polarization in Washington reflects the polarization of the public, especially among politically engaged voters and activists. Among less active and less informed voters, partisanship is weaker, and many voters hold moderate views and share some of the values of both parties. Many of the people in this group may be less engaged because they have been alienated, "turned off" by the hyperpartisanship of some activists. One of my hopes in writing this book is to encourage these voters to reengage and find more moderate leaders that are worthy of their attention and support.

Abramowitz's research draws attention to the long-term trends of racial, cultural, and ideological realignments that have roots in the 1960s and benefitted Republicans in 1980, 1994, and 2016.[40] The research confirms what we know about white, noncollege educated voters, especially males, migrating from the Democratic Party to cast votes for Republicans, joining conservative Christians to fuel the "Reagan Revolution." By the time Newt Gingrich and the Republicans won the House in 1994, the "Reagan Democrats" were fully aligned with the Republican Party, and they were motivated by partisan outrage to identify with the Tea Party Republicans in a backlash following the election of the first African American president, Barack Obama, in 2008.

Of course, Democrats were also winning elections throughout this period of major party parity, and they were doing so by activating the "Rising American Electorate" of women, younger voters, people of color and immigrant descent, and LGBTQ voters. We currently find the two parties at nearly equal strength, but to a greater degree than at any time since World War II, they are sorted into one party that is mostly white, less well educated, Christian, and nonurban, and another party that is well educated, diverse, and highly concentrated in the major cities, especially on the coasts.

The high concentration of Democratic voters in urban centers often adds to their frustration and sense that the system is unjust because Democrats frequently win a majority in the nationwide popular vote but come up short in the Senate or the Electoral College for reasons that go back to the founding of our nation. For Republicans, the concentration of Democrats in cities, with the attendant cultural power and wealth, also fuels grievance. But these negative emotions are just part of the story of anger, outrage, and contempt both parties experience when they reflect on the other party.

Lilliana Mason finds that voters' political affiliations are increasingly aligned with their personal identity characteristics, and this increases their partisan identity and their feelings of anger and antipathy toward the other party. Her research also finds that voters are more likely to hold strongly negative attitudes toward members of the other party when they also differ on identity dimensions of religion, urban versus rural residency, and college versus non-college educational attainment, as has increasingly become the case. More and more, voters consider their party identification to be their dominant identity and are unable to imagine ever voting for a candidate from the other party. These strong partisan bonds can lead to diminished political accountability, as Mason explained in an interview with Andy Fitch of the *Los Angeles Review of Books*:

> The problem comes when you begin to identify with your party so strongly that you cannot imagine ever voting for the other party. Democracy requires accountability. If an elected official does something that we don't like, that doesn't serve our interest, then we should have the option and the impetus to vote against this person next time. But really strong partisanship allows bad behavior to continue in government and allows representatives to ignore or even work against our interests with virtually no consequence.[41]

This is the mass voter-level equivalent to Ornstein and Mann's elite-level observation that Congress has grown more reticent to hold presidents of their own party responsible for misdeeds or bad policies.

## THE RISE OF NEGATIVE PARTISANSHIP

Over the roughly four-decade-long period that researchers have been noting increasing political polarization in the ANES data, they have also seen an increase in the proportion of voters that align with neither party, preferring to describe themselves as independents. This apparent contradiction gets an easy explanation from the same polls when we realize the increase in polarization is not driven by greater support for either the Democrats or the Republicans, but rather by greater antipathy to both political parties. The rise in the proportion of independents is easily explained by the dramatic increase in the pro-

Mean Therm Rating

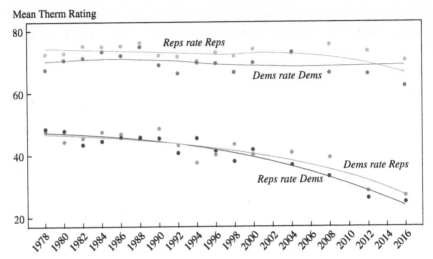

FIGURE 10-7.   Increase in Negative Partisan Affect, 1978–2016
Party identifiers rating their own party and the opposing party on a 0–100 "feelings thermometer" scale.
*Source:* Analysis of ANES data by Shanto Iyengar and Masha Krupenkin, "The Strengthening of Partisan Affect," *Political Psychology* 39:01 (February 13, 2018), 201–218, https://doi.org/10.1111/pops.12487.

portion of voters holding a negative view of both parties. Over the same period, partisans have been cultivating increasingly negative views of the other party. The time-series chart from a paper by Shanto Iyengar and Masha Krupenkin captures what has really been going on over a period of decades.[42]

The ANES polls ask voters to rate their feelings on a scale from zero (very unfavorable) to 100 (very favorable). The points are plotted to represent the rating for each party by members of the two parties, but the story is easier to follow by looking at the four lines that smooth out the trends. The two lines at the top of the chart show that Democrats' ratings for the Democratic Party have been very stable, hovering around 70 degrees on the "feelings thermometer," while Republicans' ratings for the Republican Party have been nearly as stable, dipping from just above 70 degrees to a bit below that level. What has really changed is the ratings Republicans give to Democrats, and Democrats give to Republicans; those ratings were just below 50 degrees in 1978 but have now fallen below levels that would indicate freezing on a Fahrenheit scale. The term "negative partisan affect" describes this increasing animosity partisans have for members of the other party. Negative partisan affect shows up in the extremely low job approval ratings Republicans gave

President Clinton and President Obama. After George W. Bush's inaugural honeymoon and a rise after the September 11, 2001, terrorist attacks, Democrats' job performance rating for Bush's presidency dropped to very low levels, but the gap between partisan ratings for Donald Trump has been nothing short of a chasm.[43]

Working with Jennifer McCoy of Georgia State University, Abramowitz analyzed the ANES Pilot Study of the 2016 presidential primary electorate to understand how negative partisan affect works to bind partisans to their party's eventual nominees. The survey was taken in January 2016, before any votes were cast in what would turn out to be hard fought and divisive primary contests in both parties for Donald Trump and Hillary Clinton. At that time, supporters of Vermont Senator Bernie Sanders had tepid feelings thermometer ratings for Clinton, averaging just 55 degrees, and on the Republican side, feelings for Trump among Republican voters supporting the other candidates in the primary were even cooler, at 50 degrees.

For the following several months, Trump and Clinton battled to win their respective nominations, and then set about the task of uniting their party to support them in the general election. But the task for Trump of getting supporters of Jeb Bush, John Kasich, Ted Cruz, or Marco Rubio on his side was not too difficult because their supporters' rating for Hillary Clinton back in January averaged a subfreezing 13 degrees. Supporters of Bernie Sanders were as easily convinced to support Clinton because they rated Trump at just 14 degrees back in January. As the year unfolded, other polls would find that both Trump and Clinton had low ratings overall, but Republicans turned out to oppose Clinton, and Democrats turned out to oppose Trump. This is the power and, it must be said, the purpose of cultivating negative partisan affect. But as we look in more detail at the way Trump activated a faction of ethnonationalist voters to come out and support his campaign, it is important to keep in mind that this is in addition to the support he received from other Republicans who were simply motivated to vote against the Democrat. Moving forward, it may not be possible to separate the more traditional Republican voters from the ethnonationalist faction that now seems to be dominant in the GOP, but the emergence of leading voices against Trump within the Republican Party—or perhaps separating themselves from the party altogether—may offer the best hope of reversing the downward spiral described in this book.

# "Us versus Them" Is Becoming the Driving Force Among Voters

In yet another case of it-started-before-Trump-but-Trump-made-it-worse, researchers are finding that voters are now identifying with their political party, and especially their opposition to the other party, to a degree that is becoming stronger than other political considerations. The same policy proposal can get a widely different reaction from voters if it is labeled as an "Obama policy" or a "Trump policy." Just as Frances Lee describes with elite political leaders, the public is now behaving like partisan teams that serve the function of defining an in group, "us," and the dangerous and untrustworthy out group, "them." Many researchers have found evidence that these definitions of "us" and "them" are gaining an importance that is greater than support for any issue positions or consistent adherence to ideologies expressed as liberal or conservative.[44]

Donald Trump exploited this trend to win the Republican nomination in 2016. Most of Trump's Republican opponents expected to win by proclaiming themselves the most conservative candidate in the race. They, and a large number of authoritative conservative Republicans, denounced Trump as insufficiently conservative because he had been a Democrat in the past and because he held nonconservative issue positions such as opposing free trade and vowing to protect Social Security and Medicare from budget cuts. But Trump proved the most gifted at attacking liberal Democrats and blaming them for every outrage he told his followers they had endured.

Lilliana Mason has been drawing attention to the intersection of negative partisan affect and social identity sorting in understanding Trump's appeal. Trump did not create either of these conditions, but he exploited them with consistent attacks on the groups that make up the Democratic coalition, the out groups for his constituents. Mason tells us that voters' identity characteristics such as gender, race, and religion are more easily activated for negative affect or anger than issue positions or political ideology.[45] Trump motivates his base not by making policy proposals in the traditional sense or setting an ambitious agenda, but by choosing opponents who are different from his core supporters. His policy pronouncements, such as the ban on Muslims entering the country or "Build the wall," were designed to signal his opposition to the out groups.

From Trump's attacks on immigrants from Mexico, Latin America, Muslim countries, and African and Caribbean countries; to his opposition to Colin Kaepernick and Black Lives Matter; to his disparaging descriptions of African American mayors of cities he described as "rat-infested" and "crime-ridden"; to his vulgar attacks on women and LGBTQ leaders, Trump was written off as "politically incorrect" by pundits on the right and the left because his assaults crossed all previous boundaries of political decorum. But the attacks helped him build a new "us" in affinity to, not conservatism or the Republican Party, but to Trump, because they signaled that he hated "them" more than did any other Republican in the race.

Working with Julie Wronski and John V. Kane, Mason used two surveys—one conducted in 2011, well before the period of Trump's influence on American politics, and the second when the same respondents were recontacted in 2017. The researchers were able to accurately predict support for Trump in 2017 using only the 2011 feelings thermometer ratings for African Americans, Hispanics, whites, Christians, Muslims, and LGBTQ individuals.[46] Negative feelings toward the four out groups Trump criticized in his campaign (African Americans, Hispanics, Muslims, and LGBTQ) predicted positive feelings toward Trump six years later, and this statistical correlation was far stronger than the same association for predicting support for the Republican party.

It is important to say that not all noncollege educated white voters are motivated by ethnonationalist antipathy. No one should be asserting that all working-class white voters, nor all Republicans, are racists. Trump had the support of many traditional Republicans in his pocket due simply to their partisan antipathy toward Hillary Clinton and the Democrats, but he realized that there were many others, be they Republicans, Democrats, independents, or nonpolitical infrequent voters, who harbored negative feelings toward the out groups he was attacking: gay and transgender Americans, Muslims, non-white immigrants, and African Americans. Trump did not create the animosities he exploited as much as he focused the anger of his supporters to a degree that far exceeded the trend line for other Republicans. In 2011, there were voters who were noncollege educated, heterosexual, white Christians (and others not in this category who shared their antipathy to at least one of the out groups) who harbored resentment of the other groups that they viewed as rising in economic, cultural, or political influence.

Trump assumed leadership of this team by stoking their racial and cultural grievances in a way that Jeb Bush, Marco Rubio, John Kasich, and Ted Cruz never imagined possible or desirable. Hillary Clinton called it "deplorable" but underestimated its potency.

By doing so, Trump has created political necessities for himself to keep stoking the passions of his base in ways that challenge any vision of multiracial democracy. In the words of the researchers, "From all the available evidence, Trump's political incentives point him further down the road of identity-based conflict. The voters who support Trump today are the same people who hated the idea of racial, religious, and cultural diversity well before Trump appeared on a debate stage."

Abramowitz, Iyengar, Mason, and many other political scientists are describing an American politics where people are more united by who and what they are against than they are supportive of the politicians and policies of their own political party.[47] Big policy promises may draw applause, but what really gets the crowd excited (and the viewers, listeners, and clickers tuned in) is the assertion that the opposition represents a dangerous threat to all we hold dear, and the vow to never surrender in the fight to stop "their" radical agenda. The politics of resentment triggers a reaction on the other side that intensifies the conflict. Criticized Democrats feel a need to defend themselves and, especially, the constituents of their coalition; African Americans, Latin American immigrants, Asian Americans, Muslim Americans, LGBTQ, and women, who all have long and painful histories of discrimination, hate crimes, and violence. Left-leaning media outlets find their support increases in proportion to the vehemence of their criticism of Trump and their warnings of the threat posed by his extremism.

Both Abramowitz and Mason conclude their research with expressions of alarm at the implications of their findings. The existence of an ethnonationalist voting segment and the apparent effectiveness of the politics of resentment in activating the passions of this segment—in raising those passions to levels that are stronger than the voters' commitment to any political party, conservative ideology, or any coherent set of policies, and are certainly stronger than the segment's commitment to our democratic institutions—raises fears that our American democracy could be endangered.

I share the researchers' concerns. It is easy to see how the coupling of identity politics and intensifying negative partisan affect could spiral downward into a complete breakdown of our political institutions. The hope of Democrats that the election of Barack Obama would usher in a new era of post-racial, post-partisan democracy and public policy was viewed as a threat to "our way of life" by the mostly white, mostly Christian conservatives who found expression in the Tea Party. Trump then raised the level of antipathy toward racial and ethnic groups, and in doing so he activated a loyal following for himself among the faction of white voters who had always opposed racial integration and acceptance of equal status for non-whites and other minorities. The George Wallace faction has joined the Republican Party and, with Trump as president, appears to be dominating the party, although it is not clear whether the Republicans who do not define themselves as racists and who believe in democracy, the Constitution, and the rule of law will continue to support the party if it opposes these values.

With Trump's active opposition to government and democratic institutions including a free and independent judiciary, many Democratic elites are voicing the fear that Trump could lead his followers into anti-democratic authoritarianism. There are many independents and Republicans (and former Republicans) echoing these fears.[48] My Brookings colleague Bill Galston gave an important speech in 2017, putting the Trump presidency in the context of an international retreat of constitutional democratic liberalism, and he is not alone in seeing global patterns with alarming implications.[49]

In a show of bipartisanship, two think tanks—the right-leaning American Enterprise Institute (AEI) and the left-leaning Center for American Progress (CAP), both officially nonpartisan but understood to have close ties to different political parties—joined together to hold a series of meetings and write a joint report to understand the "Drivers of Authoritarian Populism in the United States." The report, authored by Dalibor Rohac of AEI and Liz Kennedy and Vikram Singh of CAP, outlines the danger that rising support for authoritarian populist movements in the United States and Europe poses to the institutions of democracy.[50]

Not unlike my own view, the researchers find the causes of the anti-democratic movements' appeal in economic frustrations and political polarization, paralysis, and tensions as an old cultural order of social and racial hierarchy is challenged by a new, more egalitarian multiculturalism demanding political and economic inclusion. Most importantly, the researchers offer a path forward in a call for both parties to reinvent themselves for "constructive partisanship combined with bipartisan cooperation on critical issues" to get government functioning better and delivering for the public.

Rohac, Kennedy, and Singh call for a new patriotism based on respect for all groups in our society, writing that "the ugly nationalism and white supremacy on display during and after the 2016 election can best be countered by rebuilding patriotic sentiments around America's time-tested democratic values and institutions. This must be built on an honest understanding of America's history and an embrace of the nation's founding principles of government of, by, and for the people, with equal, inalienable rights for all."

The fact that this call comes from institutions on the right and the left suggests the potential for a new patriotic American majority that draws support from Democrats, Republicans, and independents uniting around a defense of democracy for all citizens regardless of social status. Constructive partisanship and bipartisan cooperation do not require people to give up their political beliefs, policies, or objectives, but instead to agree to resolve those differences more consistently and efficiently within democratic institutions for the benefit of all Americans. We must subordinate our desires to defeat the other party, and the social and ideological groups contained within that party, to the urgent necessity of defeating political stalemate and gridlock while fostering a patriotism that values all Americans.

We need to change the rules and norms of political behavior in Congress, and throughout our country, to increase opportunities for real legislative accomplishment. And we must change the tone of our discourse away from rage and blame toward greater listening, understanding, compassion, and problem-solving. In the age of Trump, rhetoric on both sides is as angry as I can remember, but there may be some advantage in the short term for Republicans in lowering the temperature of communications to avoid turning off voters that are uncomfortable with the level of confrontation. Democrats have an even clearer opportunity to speak calmly and moderately to appeal to Republicans and independents who are uninterested in supporting the Trump version of the GOP. If Democrats can find common ground between their progressive and moderate wings (something that has proven to be a substantial challenge in the past), they may find support for constructive action among independents and Republicans as well. There are far more Americans that believe in democracy than would work to undermine it.

## CHAPTER 11

# How We Can Change the Rules and Change the Tone of American Politics

Uncompromising partisan polarization causing legislative gridlock has been an increasing problem in American politics for a long time. We rarely solve problems in America. Our habit is to wait until problems grow to a crisis. Chapter 10 makes the case that partisan polarization is reaching the point where it will soon arrive as a crisis. Both Congress and the voting public have increasingly been sorting into two separate worlds that are bonded by their opposition to the other team. Hostile partisan sorting on both levels, in Congress and among voters, is robbing us of our ability to be a great and harmonious nation. Reversing the long-term trends that have engulfed Washington and the public will allow us to address other problems that are also reaching crisis proportions, including unsustainable federal debt, inequality in all its forms (by income, wealth, race, gender, geography, and educational attainment), a broken immigration system, and global climate change.

Donald Trump and a network of allies in right-wing political organizations and media channels have activated a faction within the Republican Party that views the multiculturalism on the left as a threat to its way of life. His "us" applaud Trump for his willingness to use whatever means necessary to stop "them." This has now increased in intensity to a degree that many on the left and in the center, and even many current or former Republicans, now view it as a threat to democracy and American constitutional government. Rising negative partisan affect took us past dislike between the groups a decade ago. Now both sides see the other as a dangerous threat in ways that make nonconfrontational communications increasingly rare.

I understand why many people express pessimism that bipartisan cooperation on policy is possible, when both parties view the other not as their political opposition, but as a direct threat that must be defeated. Given that chapter 10 features graphs showing decades-long trends of increasing elite and mass polarization and declining congressional achievement, it is fair to expect that the current hyperpolarization means bipartisan cooperation will become even more difficult and Congress will get even less done. To the degree that we see an emerging threat to our democracy, we cannot accept this level of dysfunction as an inevitability.

Partisan negativity is posing a threat to our democratic institutions, adding to the urgency of the need to get our government functioning for all Americans. We have divided into two Americas that live in different areas and rarely interact; the two sides do not like each other, and both sides view the other as a serious threat to values worth defending. This may make it harder to find common-ground solutions in Congress, but those of us who care about defending our democracy must fight to make Congress more effective at solving real problems, setting the conditions for equitable economic growth, and delivering real benefits for the American people. The best way to defend democracy is to make democracy work better.

We need a new patriotism that is inclusive of anyone who cares about our democracy and wants to work to strengthen it. It is not necessary to understand how to engage those who place a higher value on loyalty to Trump than commitment to respectful discourse, the truth, and our institutions of democracy. There are far more Americans that want to strengthen our democratic system than want to see it fail. This new patriotism may never take hold among the people who are currently members of any group with the word "patriot" or "militia" in its name. But I believe most Democrats, many political independents, and even large numbers of Republicans who have grown alarmed by the excesses of Trumpism would eagerly work to reverse the decline in American politics and recommit to constructive partisan engagement.

At the end of most books about public policy and government, the author arrives at the question, "What can we do about this?" Usually, the answer takes the form of a five-point plan (or three- or ten-point plan) and a list of policies that Congress and the president should enact to solve the problem. I know this because I have written a lot of books that end that way. But in this case, it is Congress itself and its rules, procedures, and norms of behavior that are at the center of the problem, so Congress cannot be the only "we" involved. This chapter is for everyone, whether inside the government or outside it, who believes Americans deserve a government that works and can solve problems. The plan has too many points to number them all, but as I break the challenge down into many subparts, I also spotlight many of the bipartisan and nonpartisan organizations that are already engaged on the front lines of each issue, so you can pick the battles you are willing to join.

There are literally dozens of ways "we the people" can join like-minded others working to address one aspect or another of the problems facing our democracy. And this is what it will take to regain a government that works for the people. As we understand from looking at partisan dysfunction from many perspectives, the challenges have been developing for a long time, there is no single cause, and there will be no single solution. We will have to fight battles on many fronts. We can only reverse the trends that have led us into hyperpartisan warfare if large numbers of us raise our hands, raise our voices, and reach out to others who share our resolve and insist that the greatest nation in the world should have the best government in the world.

At the local level or at the national level, you can join groups dedicated to dialogue, to listening, and to understanding among individuals across the political spectrum. There are groups that exist to gather issue experts with diverse points of view to seek common-ground solutions to our problems. Other groups are directly involved in politics, working within Congress to encourage bipartisan cooperation, and identifying, training, and supporting candidates for office who hold moderate positions on issues or who hold conservative or liberal views yet express a desire to work across the partisan divide to make progress on our most vexing problems.

In one respect, democracy is working well in America. Frances Lee's thesis in *Insecure Majorities: Congress and the Perpetual Campaign*,[1] discussed at length in chapter 10, tells us that the American people have a lot of influence over our government. Perhaps too much, in some ways. When the two parties are at nearly equal strength and believe control of one or both chambers of Congress could change in the next election, as has been the case for more than two decades, both sides prioritize politics and winning the next election over governing and enacting good public policy for the long term. Interest groups have a great deal of influence over policy positions, and as we see later in this chapter, politicians pay a lot of attention to funders, even those giving relatively small amounts.

In one sense, I want to say this is terrific! The ability to influence our democracy is just what the writers of our Constitution had in mind when they guaranteed the right to petition the government in the First Amendment. But the research tells us the activists who influence our government the most tend to be those who hold uncompromising ideological positions that do not represent the views of most Americans. Passionate partisans and political activists often support organizations that take strong positions on individual issues and in some cases actively oppose any compromise on those positions, even to the point of recruiting and funding challengers in primaries and general elections to unseat politicians who compromise on issues.

There is no way to restrain this activity because it is not only protected by the Constitution, it is also the kind of citizen involvement in politics we all should celebrate. Rather than trying to diminish the energy of ideologically committed activists, those of us who would like to see more compromise, cooperation, and progress will have to match the activists' passion. I believe most Americans would like to see less partisanship and more achievement from our elected leaders, but the minority of ideologically polarized activists work hard to have more influence in the system. Let this be your invitation to become just as engaged.

Communicate with the leaders we have already elected and make your views clear. Reach out to members of Congress and other politicians; find out which ones are already working across the aisle, or say they want to, and encourage them, support them, and reward them. Write to your senators and member of Congress. Go to town halls and candidate forums and use the opportunity to express your enthusiasm for bipartisan negotiation. (Be prepared for some boos and catcalls from the most dedicated partisans in the room.) Join forces with other concerned citizens and work together. You want to find, participate in, and support organizations that work with members on bipartisan policies that seem constructive to you. This chapter will tell you how and give you many options to get involved.

## CHANGE THE RULES AND CHANGE THE TONE

We know from chapter 10 that the problems of partisan polarization leading to legislative gridlock have been growing worse. Reversing these trends will require many efforts by many people. We must do at least two things simultaneously:

- Change the rules.
- Change the tone.

We know the rules that govern the White House, and especially Congress, matter a great deal in determining what legislation can become law and how quickly. We have seen (in chapters 6 through 9) how the rules can be used to make bipartisan compromise difficult to the point of seeming impossible. But we have also seen that even when the two parties seem impossibly far apart, if the leaders want to reach a deal, the rules do not stand in the way of bipartisan compromise. So if it is not the rules that determine whether deals are reached, we need to understand what other factors determine whether problems get solved and progress is made. After looking at the rules, I will examine ways to change the tone of relations between the parties and reduce negative partisan affect in Washington and across the country.

## CHANGING CONGRESSIONAL RULES, NORMS, AND PROCEDURES

Before I evaluate several potential changes to the rules that govern the process, including filibuster and reconciliation in the Senate, and discharge petitions and the so-called Hastert Rule in the House, it is important to first understand that most of the rules and procedures that guide congressional action, or inaction, today were themselves enacted as "reforms" for the problems of Congress a decade or more in the past. The history of congressional reform is replete with examples of reforms arising to correct the unintended consequences of reforms passed earlier to correct the unintended consequences of prior reforms.

Committee chairs were viewed as too powerful in the 1960s, in part because they had battled against civil rights legislation, so Congress enacted reforms to make committees more open and reduce strict adherence to the seniority system of selecting chairs. It loosened the rules allowing members to introduce amendments on the floor, until this new ability was abused and the number of floor amendments caused the legislative process to grind to a halt in the 1970s. Since Newt Gingrich and the Republicans took power in 1994, the leadership of both parties has taken tighter control over crafting and moving legislation. But this power has been used to prevent legislative proposals that could pass with bipartisan support from ever getting a vote on the House or Senate floor.

John Lawrence served many members of the House of Representatives over a long career as a congressional staffer, including eight years as chief of staff (2005 to 2013) to Nancy Pelosi (D-CA) when she was the Democratic leader and then Speaker of the House. He summarized his views on congressional rules and process reform in thoughtful testimony before the House Select Committee on the Modernization of Congress,[2] a bipartisan committee set up by Pelosi in 2019 to evaluate potential changes in rules and procedures. Lawrence noted the elusiveness of the balance that must be reached in the trade-off between efficiency and broad participation. As the number of legislators with influence over the outcome increases, the time to passage also increases. Democratization of the processes of democracy is desirable, but it has a cost that must sometimes be paid with patience—on matters that are too important for endless patience. When the process moves too slowly, leaders take greater control, and calls begin anew for another round of reforms.

## RULE CHANGES: THE BAD, THE PROMISING, THE GOOD, AND THE OVERDUE

### The Bad: The Hastert Rule

The "Hastert Rule" was never a rule. It was a policy pronouncement of Dennis Hastert (R-IL) when he was Speaker of the House from 1999 to 2007, designed to control the House agenda and frustrate bipartisan cooperation. Hastert, and later Speaker John Boehner (R-OH), who invoked the "rule" many times, made it clear it was not really a rule by repeatedly making exceptions when doing so served their interests. The policy of these recent Republican Speakers was that they would not allow any proposed legislation to reach the floor unless it was supported by a "majority of the majority." In other words, only bills with majority Republican support could become law, and bills that failed this test would gather dust, even if they were supported by a bipartisan majority of members of Congress. The existence of the Hastert Rule highlights how much discretion the rules grant to the Speaker. Anyone who supports bipartisan cooperation should oppose any reintroduction of a Hastert Rule.

## The Promising: "Break the Gridlock" Rules

Democrats could have done the same thing as the Republicans and enforced their own "Pelosi Rule," but they made a different choice at the start of the 116th Congress in January 2019. After the Democrats won the House majority in the 2018 election, Nancy Pelosi supported a set of congressional reforms designed to "Break the Gridlock." She was responding to a clear request from the moderate Democrats who represented half the membership of the bipartisan Problem Solvers Caucus (a congressional group devised by the nonpartisan advocacy group No Labels, which is discussed in more detail below). Members join the caucus in pairs, to ensure equal numbers of Democrats and Republicans.

Each member of the Problem Solvers Caucus had pledged to push for rule changes designed to further bipartisan compromise before they knew which side would be in the majority, and when Democrats won in November, they understood their moment of leverage over Pelosi had arrived as she worked to secure support to regain the Speaker's gavel. With specific requests from the moderate Democrats worked out in advance, Pelosi reached out to liberal Representative James McGovern (D-MA), the incoming Rules Committee Chair and Congressional Progressive Caucus (CPC) member, to also champion the Break the Gridlock reform package, because it benefitted not just moderates but any faction of House members (including progressives) that wanted to build an alliance with other factions to move legislation to the floor. The Break the Gridlock reforms were adopted, and Pelosi was named

Speaker by a united Democratic Caucus.[3] (Those seeking to understand how Nancy Pelosi has maintained leadership of the fractious House Democratic Caucus need look no farther than this story.)

The Break the Gridlock rule changes created a new "Consensus Calendar" process mandating a floor vote for any bill with more than 290 cosponsors, even if it was opposed by the Speaker and a majority of the majority—thus reversing the Hastert Rule. Pelosi was meaningfully surrendering power, but it was also a major step forward for bipartisanship, acknowledging the constituency for cooperation, and making progress possible.[4]

## HOW YOU CAN GET INVOLVED

### Join No Labels

The Problem Solvers Caucus is only for members of Congress, so most people reading this cannot join, but it was a direct outgrowth of No Labels, a nonprofit organization that Nancy Jacobson founded in 2013 to goad Congress into replacing partisan hostility with cooperative work to address policy issues. The rule change at the start of the 116th Congress was a direct result of citizen engagement of No Labels advocating for the formation of the Problem Solvers Caucus. You can add your voice and demand more progress like this by joining No Labels.[5]

### The Good: Discharge Petitions

The Consensus Calendar process is like a discharge petition on steroids, and the rules for discharge petitions were also liberalized for the 116th Congress in the Break the Gridlock reforms. Discharge petitions, which have been part of House rules since the 1910 congressional reforms,[6] also allow legislation to reach the House floor over the opposition of the relevant committee chair or the Speaker. When a majority of House members support a bill that is stuck in committee, they can sign a petition to discharge the committee of its duties, moving the bill to a floor vote.

Successful discharge petitions are quite rare. A 2003 analysis by Richard Beth of the Congressional Research Service found that in the seventy-two years since 1931, over 500 discharge petitions were filed but only forty-seven reached the signature threshold. Fewer than half of those measures (nineteen) were passed by the House, and of those, just two were passed by the Senate and signed into law by the president.[7] However, the importance of the discharge petition process is greater than these numbers would indicate, because it serves as a basis for discussions about bipartisan legislation. Some elements of the stalled discharge petitions eventually became parts of other legislation. When two or more representatives find common ground across party lines, the discharge petition is just one of many pathways by which bills could become law, and anything that creates more possibilities for bipartisan success is a small step toward reversing the trends of increasing party polarization and legislative paralysis. Anyone who supports bipartisan cooperation should encourage greater participation on bipartisan discharge petitions.

## The Overdue: Filibuster Reform

We should eliminate the Senate filibuster because, as it is currently being used, it is a greater impediment to than enabler of bipartisan deliberation and progress. The filibuster allows senators to block legislation from getting to the floor by keeping debate open, even if no one is debating it, unless sixty senators vote to end debate. When routinely invoked, as it is now, the filibuster raises the threshold needed to pass legislation from a 51-vote majority to a 60-vote supermajority, and a lot of bills that pass the House die by Senate filibuster, blocked from getting a vote by a minority of senators.

Most of what I know about the filibuster comes from my Brookings colleague Sarah Binder, who wrote a book with Steven Smith called *Politics or Principle? Filibustering in the United States Senate.*[8] I have shared her insights in nearly every chapter in this book. In chapter 3, I related that the filibuster is not in the Constitution because James Madison, Alexander Hamilton, and the other writers opposed a supermajority requirement in the Senate because, as Madison wrote in *Federalist* No. 58, "the fundamental principle of free government would be reversed. It would be no longer the majority that would rule: the power would be transferred to the minority."

Not only was the filibuster not designed by the Founding Fathers to make the Senate more deliberative, but, as discussed in chapter 4, the filibuster was not designed by anyone. It arose totally by accident. When Vice President Aaron Burr requested simplification of the Senate rule book in 1806, the senators inadvertently eliminated the rule to "call the previous question."

In 1917, the Senate rules were changed to allow two-thirds of senators to end debate by invoking "cloture," assisting Woodrow Wilson's efforts to involve the US in the First World War. Filibusters were used sporadically over the next five decades, but through the end of the 1970s, there was no two-year span of Congress where as many as ten cloture motions were filed in the Senate.

There were twenty-four Senate cloture motions filed in the 92nd Congress (1971–1972), an average of one per month. This would rise to three per month through the end of the Bill Clinton presidency. Routine use of filibusters started in this millennium, as both sides pressed each other and the Senate rules to gain as much advantage as they could.[9] But when Senate Minority Leader Mitch McConnell (R-KY) and the Republicans filibustered 252 Democratic bills and nominations backed by Senate Majority Leader Harry Reid (D-NV) and President Barack Obama—an average of eleven filibusters per month—in the 113th Congress (2013–2014), it was undeniable that the parliamentary tactic was being abused. It was not the rule that had changed; it was the norms as to how the rule was being used. For more than a decade now, the filibuster has become, in practice, something that it was never intended to be, and that it has not been through most of American history: a de facto threshold of a 60-vote supermajority needed to pass legislation through the Senate.

The majority party writes the rules for the Senate (if they have enough votes to pass them), and majorities have created many pathways for passage of laws, nominations, and other Senate business that were exempt from potential filibusters over the years. Another Brookings colleague, Molly Reynolds, wrote a book examining the at least 161 times the Senate has created *Exceptions to the Rule* in the forty-five years from 1969 to 2014.[10] These include majority up-or-down votes on congressional budgets and reconciliation bills, and fast-track processes for some trade bills and military base closings. More recently, and quite contentiously, Senate Democrats were frustrated with McConnell's obstructions, so Reid eliminated the filibuster for presidential executive appointments and lower-level court nominations in 2013. When McConnell's Republicans regained the majority, they eliminated the filibuster for Supreme Court nominations in 2017.

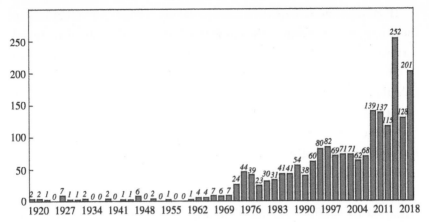

FIGURE 11-1.   Number of Senate Cloture Motions in Each 2-Year Session, 1917–2018
*Source:* US Senate, senate.gov/legislature/cloture/clotureCounts.htm.

On its face, it looks like the problem with the filibuster is that it encourages too much debate, but as it is being used today, the problem is that it forestalls debate. In the modern Senate of intense polarization, party parity, and insecure majorities (as described in chapter 10), there is very little real debate, if we understand debate to mean an exchange of arguments designed to persuade the other side or reach a common understanding. The positions of the parties are determined by leadership in consultation with the Senators on their side, and sometimes in negotiations with the leadership of the other side behind closed doors. Any Senate debate in public has been replaced by members of the two parties talking past each other, making speeches that deliver talking points for their own side. A modern filibuster is invoked with a phone call to the majority leader's office and does not imply any debate at all. The reality is that when the debate cannot be ended, the debate never starts.

Even if the filibuster was not part of the original design, there was a time when it could be argued that, in practice, the filibuster encouraged bipartisan cooperation. Laws could be modified to avoid engendering enough opposition to sustain a filibuster from the other party. But when the filibuster is nearly universally employed to raise the threshold for every bill to a 60-vote supermajority, the net effect is to diminish bipartisan cooperation. As it is used today, the filibuster is a weapon of hyperpartisan warfare not a tool to end it. Recent years have brought ever more frequent filibusters but no peace in the partisan battles.

There are some actions Democrats could take the next time they control
the Senate, such as limiting the number of filibusters that can be mounted,
further restricting the types of motions or measures that can be filibustered,
or returning to the practice of "talking filibusters"—requiring senators to
hold the floor and talk, as they did before the 1970s. These partial reforms
might be an improvement, especially as part of bipartisan negotiations that
help reduce partisan polarization and increase cooperation on legislation.
But we should not kid ourselves; the next step toward weakening the filibuster will either be the last stop or next to the last stop before elimination. The
filibuster benefits the minority, and the majority makes the rules. Both parties weakened the filibuster the last time they took control of the Senate, and
both must assume the other party will end it the next time they take power.

## REFORM THE CONGRESSIONAL BUDGET PROCESS

In 2015, Pete Domenici, G. William Hoagland, and I (with the full resources
of the Bipartisan Policy Center, or BPC) wrote a "Proposal for Improving
the Congressional Budget Process" with ten recommendations for reform,
arranged into three broad themes.[11] While I stand by all of these recommendations, let me highlight those changes that most directly address the issues
raised in this book—bipartisan cooperation, or its opposite, partisan standoff, as has been so commonly seen on budget matters in recent history—by
presenting five recommendations to reform the budget process.

### Include Everything

Instead of negotiating over a small fraction of the nation's balance sheet—
the part called "discretionary spending," which has not been growing faster
than the overall economy—we must include all the taxing and spending the
government does. There is no other way to get the unsustainable long-term
government deficit and debt problem under control. The idea of including
Social Security, Medicare, and Medicaid—which are collectively called "nondiscretionary" spending or "entitlements," and which threaten to grow far
faster than the economy—in the budget process will scare some Democrats,
but not as much as including the revenue side of the balance sheet—taxes

and so-called tax expenditures—will scare Republicans, as we learned from the Simpson-Bowles Commission (discussed in chapters 8 and 9).

Tax expenditures, which are written into the tax laws, are defined as all the specific deductions, credits, exclusions, and other allowable reductions to the income of individuals and corporations. The common word for tax expenditures is "loopholes," and they add up to a huge amount of potential revenue. The two categories taken together, nondiscretionary spending and tax revenues, dwarf the discretionary spending fraction of the budget that Congress has been fighting over.

The largest parts of federal spending cannot be left on autopilot as they are now. "Out of sight, out of mind" cannot be allowed to continue to yield deficits that are out of control. Even though Democrats are uncomfortable including nondiscretionary spending in the budget process and Republicans are uncomfortable including taxes and tax expenditures, we should include all government revenue and expenditures in long-term budgeting. We have no choice if we hope to get unsustainable long-term deficits under control.

We have had shutdowns over discretionary spending, the one part of the budget that is not growing faster than the economy, while the deficit is exploding because total revenue and total spending (including the slow-growing discretionary and the fast-growing and accelerating nondiscretionary) are completely out of balance. This cannot continue indefinitely.

The treatment for the nondiscretionary spending and tax policy categories does not have to be the same treatment as that for discretionary spending, but both categories should come under intense periodic examination, with caps and targets subject to regular review. The first three recommendations of the "Proposal for Improving the Congressional Budget Process" provide more details of how Domenici, Hoagland, BPC scholars, and I thought this could work.

But if Congress cannot reach agreement on the fraction of the government's balance sheet that is the discretionary budget without missed deadlines, continuing resolutions (CRs), and occasional government shutdowns, how will it manage the whole of the problem? The answer is the need to cut the workload in half by giving Washington twice as much time to get the job done.

## Replace Annual Budgeting with Two-Year Budget Cycles

Congress has been losing the race to meet annual budget deadlines most of the time—especially in election years. The CR has become the escape hatch that gets used most often, rather than using the front door for passing the budget on schedule. The best way to get Congress to meet the deadlines is to make them more realistic by changing the law to put the budget process on a two-year cycle. The president would propose a budget in odd numbered years, and Congress would keep to the current schedule to pass the budget before October 1 of that year. Even numbered years would be for authorizations, for long-term budget planning for tax policy and nondiscretionary spending, and, of course, for elections. This would allow Congress more time to prioritize its work and devote attention to program oversight and reauthorizations. Supplemental and emergency appropriations could still occur whenever needed at any point on the calendar.

## Make Continuing Resolutions Automatic

This recommendation and the next are offered to eliminate the deadlines that have become opportunities for partisan budget hostage-taking. Perhaps it should go without saying, but one American political party should not be able to threaten harm to the American people to get the other political party to agree to legislative changes. By making CRs automatic when the budget expires, neither party could threaten a government shutdown to get its way. The government would simply continue spending at the previous budget year's levels until a new budget is passed. Continuing resolutions are not as desirable a way to fund government as a well-crafted budget, but they are better than a government shutdown.

## Make Raising the Debt Limit Automatic

Similarly, once Congress and the president agree on a budget including revenue and spending levels, it should be as a matter of law understood that they have agreed to authorize the level of national debt implied by those choices. There is no meaningful purpose to a separate debt limit, which for most of our history has been raised as routine business, but in our worst partisan episodes has been exploited as a threat to gain leverage in budget negotiations. This is another case where the law did not change but there was a change in the norms of behavior in Congress as to how the law would be used; now the law needs to change to reflect that reality. The threat to default on the national debt is a hazard that should not be left lying in plain sight to be used for political leverage over the other party.

Any economist can tell you the cost of actually following through on the threat to not raise the debt ceiling would have been devastating to the national and global economy. The world runs on reliable forms of debt, and US Treasury bonds are considered the most reliable of all. If the US government were to default, there would be an immediate loss of value for nearly every asset on the planet as markets tumble around the world. The full faith and credit of the US government is worth that much to the global economy. Had lawmakers made good on their threats to block the debt ceiling increase, the world's richest people and the world's lowest-paid workers would all face widespread misery. There is no reason anyone would want to do this, and Congress should pass new laws so no one can threaten to do it.

Some might ask whether Congress would ever get its work done on a budget if we removed deadlines with consequences like a government shutdown or a default on the debt. But the consequences should fall on Congress, not on the American public (which is not to blame when a budget deadline is missed). For this reason, I have no problem with "no-budget-no-pay" provisions that hit members of Congress in the wallet when they do not get their work done. Domenici, Hoagland, and I included a no-budget-no-recess provision (although we did not call it that) in the BPC proposal we wrote.

## HOW YOU CAN GET INVOLVED

### Support the Bipartisan Policy Center and the Committee for a Responsible Federal Budget

In 2007, four prominent retiring Senate leaders, Bob Dole (R-KS), Howard Baker (R-TN), Tom Daschle (D-SD), and George Mitchell (D-ME), got together to start the Bipartisan Policy Center, with Jason Grumet as its president. Each of these Senate leaders and Grumet had been deeply worried about the extreme partisanship that was splitting the Hill. So, they founded a think tank to provide a safe space for members to explore difficult policy issues, listen to others' points of view, analyze alternatives, find common ground, and then work to facilitate implementation of bipartisan proposals.

I have been deeply involved with BPC for many years. It provided support for the Debt Reduction Task Force that I cochaired with Pete Domenici in 2010–2011. Domenici's former staff director of the Senate Budget Committee, William Hoagland, is a BPC senior vice president, and he worked with Domenici and me on our "Proposal for Improving the Congressional Budget Process." Beyond budget policy and process, BPC provides a forum for the development of bipartisan policy proposals on areas as diverse as energy, elections, education, health policy, and infrastructure.[12]

The Committee for a Responsible Federal Budget (CRFB) is another bipartisan policy organization with which I have been deeply involved for many years, and I have served on its board of directors. If you believe, as I do, that coming to agreement on bipartisan solutions is the only way the nation will get control of its unsustainable debt and deficit, this is an organization you should join. Former Representatives Robert Giaimo (D-CT) and Henry Bellmon (R-OK) founded the think tank in 1981. Maya MacGuineas has run CRFB as its president since 2003, and there is no better advocate for the case that the long-term debt problem must be addressed sooner rather than later.

Most people involved with the CRFB are federal budget experts and veterans of the Congressional Budget Office (CBO), the House and Senate Budget Committees, the Office of Management and Budget (OMB), and other fiscal agencies. The staff produces original research and analyses of fiscal issues and budgetary proposals. The CRFB's Fiscal Institute hosts policy projects like the Fix the Debt campaign; the FixUS program, which aims to understand growing polarization; and the Better Budget Process Initiative, whose objective is to develop concrete reforms that will improve the functioning of the budgetary process.

Erskine Bowles and former Senator Alan Simpson (R-WY), the cochairs of the National Commission on Fiscal Responsibility and Reform (Simpson-Bowles Commission), founded the Fix the Debt campaign. It brings together business leaders, former members of Congress, and fiscal experts around the goal of educating the public on America's fiscal problems to gather support for significant fiscal reforms. Fix the Debt's efforts are not to support any particular fiscal plan, but to encourage policymakers to work together on a bipartisan, comprehensive solution that will satisfy a set of fundamental guiding principles, including tax reform and changes to government spending.[13]

## Bring Back Earmarks

In chapter 2, I make the case for a major investment in the nation's infrastructure, stressing the importance of priorities driven by local needs and economic development strategies. Congress used to have a process that allowed individual members to deliver the funding needed for projects that would be most appreciated by constituents in their home districts—building a dam here, widening a highway there, or building an airport to unlock an underserved area—but Congress eliminated it. This process involved so-called earmarks—specific line items in the budget requested by an individual representative or senator—which became a symbol for what is wrong with Washington spending. However, earmarks have never added up to more than a tiny fraction of federal spending, they distribute power away from Washington out to states and local congressional districts, and they are essential to getting things done on Capitol Hill.

Since Congress banned earmarks in 2011, all legislation has become more difficult to pass, but especially infrastructure bills, which were once some

---

*Rising anger at government may have been fueled more by the growth of regulation (environmental, safety, employment) than spending, but it merged into widespread antagonism to "big government" and suspicion of bureaucrats and politicians. Railing against government spending became standard campaign rhetoric even on the left and led to surprising, often counterproductive political moves like getting rid of earmarks.*

—Alice M. Rivlin, "Thoughts About Monetary and Fiscal Policy in a Post-Inflation World," Brookings Institution, March 10, 2015

---

of the easiest major bills to get through Congress. It is not hard to see why. If you do not allow earmarks, then all of the authority to define priorities rests in the executive branch that administers the legislation. The Department of Transportation decides which highway projects to fund or delegates the decision to the states by a formula. Earmarks give Congress a say in which projects get funded, and as long as there are effective ethics rules to prohibit self-dealing, individual representatives and senators have every incentive to promote projects that their constituents view as best to support local economic development strategies.

The best argument for earmarks is their role in moving lawmakers to agreement on legislation. Rather than claiming credit for a whole package with vague benefits spread across the land, with earmarks a large number of lawmakers are able to stand by a specific construction site as proof they can deliver needed local priority projects. And when a bill is five votes short of passage, party leaders, committee chairs, and the bill's sponsors have extra incentives to offer lawmakers, in the form of earmarks that can help drag the bill across the finish line. When earmarks are banned, the chances increase that a bill stays a few votes short of passage, and Congress remains deadlocked on the issue.

## OTHER THINGS WE CAN DO TO REDUCE POLARIZATION AND PARTISANSHIP

### Improve the Economy to Deliver Sustainable and Broadly Shared Prosperity

In addition to my suggestions above to change the rules and procedures that govern Congress and the congressional budgeting process, I believe that any legislation to improve the economy and meaningfully address inequality in all its forms (gender, race, geography, educational attainment) will help reduce the destructive partisan polarization in the country and in Congress. The same political scientists discussed in chapter 10 have research that shows a link between increasing economic inequality among voters and higher levels of political polarization in the Senate, House, and state legislatures.[14] The high and increasing economic inequality we have seen over the past few decades is an important cause of the polarization that is leading to gridlock in Congress. This means we are facing the threat of a dangerous feedback loop. Inequality may be making it harder for political leaders to enact legislation designed to lessen inequality.

In chapter 2, I lay out my proposals for an economic policy that could break the feedback loop by garnering broad bipartisan support because the policy addresses the two kinds of inequality that have been driving our political divisions: income and wealth inequality and geographic inequality—or as I term them, vertical inequality and horizontal inequality. For too long, we have been underinvesting in our economic prosperity, letting our roads crumble, our bridges decay, and our public school buildings grow old. We have been patching water, sewer, and electrical systems, and even railroads and railway stations, canals and seaports, and airports and air traffic control systems that were built in another era—a time when there was broad support for government investment in the basic economic infrastructure that supports a prosperous economy.

This infrastructure neglect is a relatively recent symptom of our political dysfunction. When I started my career in 1960s Washington, infrastructure bills were nonpartisan, nonpolitical, and uncontroversial. America needed a thriving economy to win two World Wars and the Cold War, build a thriving middle-class, and become the world leader in technological innovation. I believe we can regain the national unity and sense of purpose to renew our investments in innovation, education, infrastructure, and healthy communities, especially if we take pains to ensure that the benefits of economic growth are broadly shared. After decades where America has been divided by economic inequality and unequal economic growth between regions, we can rebuild bipartisan support for investing in the American economy. The key is to make sure the benefits of growth flow to the people and places that have been left behind as the wealthiest people, mostly living in the largest cities, mostly on the coasts, have surged ahead.

My proposal (detailed in chapter 2) has several key features. The investments are designed to help all the people and places that have been left behind in the transition to a globally connected digital economy, including the pockets of poverty in the blue urban areas and in red small town and rural stretches of America. My proposal is comprehensive and strategic, addressing all the needs of a community in transition to a more productive and modern economy: education and job skills training; support for innovation and new products and techniques in manufacturing and agriculture; broadly defined infrastructure, including modernized data and energy grids, and support for childcare and transportation workforces; and healthy communities with a focus on public health and wellness, safe streets, welcoming common areas and Main Streets, and a functioning, responsive local government.

Finally, and importantly, these investments must be locally rather than federally controlled. Regional economic development councils should be supported, strengthened, and partnered with in the determination of local economic development strategies. While Washington has been trapped in partisan standoffs, nonpartisan local and regional stakeholder groups all across America have been forming to address critical issues.[15] These groups offer the best hope to move rapidly to a new era of civil discourse and community progress.

## Change Election Rules

There are a lot of proposals to reform election laws in America, either to make elections less partisan, more fair, and more inclusive, or because one side or the other believes reform would give that side an advantage. This last objective is, of course, never presented that way. There is always an argument made for the merits of any proposed change. In recent years, Republicans have spoken a great deal about election fraud, although they have produced little evidence that election fraud occurs in America with any significant frequency. President Trump formed a select Advisory Commission on Election Integrity cochaired by Vice President Mike Pence and Kansas Secretary of State Kris Kobach, an outspoken proponent of the claim that voter fraud is widespread, but the commission disbanded after months of investigations without producing any evidence of substantial voter fraud.[16]

Democrats have their own list of wrongs they want to see righted and far more evidence in the historical record. Efforts to stop minorities from voting were a matter of law in the Jim Crow era, until they were outlawed by the 1965 Voting Rights Act. But in 2013, in the *Shelby County* v. *Holder* decision, the Supreme Court overturned a key provision of the act—the requirement that states with a history of discriminatory voting laws must submit proposed changes in voting laws to the US Department of Justice to certify that the laws do not make it difficult for African Americans or other minorities to vote. After the *Shelby* v. *Holder* decision, Democrats started warning about new voter identification requirements, restrictions on early voting times and places, and other threats of voter suppression laws—that is, laws designed to make participation harder for certain groups of voters.[17]

Both parties should commit to election reform at the federal and state level to solve the very real problems with American elections. The legitimacy of both political parties, and no less than the whole of our democracy, rests on free and fair elections based on the simple standard of one person, one vote, which is known to every fourth grader. Our nation will truly be in crisis if the public trust in the legitimacy of our elections continues to decline. We must strengthen and renew our election infrastructure and institutions. To the greatest degree possible, we must get the politicians out of the role of writing the rules for the elections in which they compete and give this power to nonpartisan professional election administrators or nonpartisan citizen commissions.

## Tighter Regulation of Money in Politics

There has been a long tradition of efforts by Congress, often spurred on by major scandals, to regulate political campaign financing. These attempts have consistently run into two problems: (1) increasingly clever political operatives finding ways for money to flow around the restrictions, and (2) resistance in the Supreme Court. The first election reform bill, the Federal Corrupt Practices Act (aka the Publicity Act), became law in 1910 and passed without any Democratic votes in the Senate, but the law was largely invalidated by the Supreme Court in 1921. Within a couple of years, the Teapot Dome scandal revealed kickbacks for oil leases in the Warren G. Harding administration, forcing Congress to write some new anti-corruption laws.

For the next 100 years, Congress would continue to make periodic efforts to regulate money in politics. Congress banned solicitations of campaign contributions from military personnel, federal employees, and public utilities, and placed limits on spending in general election and primary campaigns. But each time, a skeptical Supreme Court invalidated or narrowed the laws. The narrowing of the laws created opportunities for creative accounting. When Congress placed limits on the actions of corporations and labor unions, political action committees (PACs) were invented to do the same functions because they were neither corporations nor unions. As the rules changed, different categories of organizations were created and given names based on the subparagraph of the Internal Revenue Service code that qualified them as outside the latest restrictions.

The Federal Election Campaign Act of 1971 required disclosure of contributions to candidates for federal office, political parties, and PACs. It passed the Democratic-controlled Senate and House by lopsided bipartisan margins and was signed by Republican President Richard Nixon in 1972—the same year the Watergate scandal began. Watergate is best remembered for the break-in at Democratic headquarters, but as it unraveled in 1973 and culminated in Nixon's resignation in 1974, the reporting and investigations unearthed many slush funds, hush-money payments, and other problems with money corrupting politics. The major reform that followed was the Federal Election Campaign Act Amendments of 1974, which created the Federal Election Commission (FEC). However, between the Supreme Court invalidating parts of the new law and the interpretations of it by the FEC, the effect was the definition of "hard money," where donations are capped and limited in their use, and "soft money" funds, which could not be used to solicit votes for candidates but could be received in any amount and could be used for "party building activities." This turned out to be a distinction with little difference in practice for a system that lasted for many election cycles.

This pattern repeated in recent years with the Bipartisan Campaign Reform Act (BCRA, aka McCain-Feingold) finally becoming law in 2002 but then getting mostly overruled by the Supreme Court. John McCain (R-AZ) will be remembered as one of the Senate's most ardent advocates of bipartisanship, and he partnered with Russ Feingold (D-WI) in 1995 to try to patch the holes in campaign finance laws. McCain and Feingold worked the problem for seven years and were eventually successful in getting the Senate to adopt the House version of their bill, introduced by Representatives Chris Shays (R-CT) and Marty Meehan (D-MA). But the court challenges started soon after President George H. W. Bush signed the bill into law. Most elements survived the first challenge by then Senate Minority Whip Mitch McConnell (R-KY). As the Supreme Court challenges continued, the law was narrowed and then, in 2009, most of the BCRA limitations on corporations and unions were invalidated as unconstitutional. The Supreme Court decided that corporations have the same First Amendment free speech rights as individual citizens do, and that spending for political messages is speech that cannot be limited, in its 2010 ruling in *Citizens United* v. *the Federal Election Commission*.[18]

After the *Citizens United* ruling, there essentially are no effective limits on special interests and corporations spending money to influence American elections and policy debates. Some rules still stand, such as the BCRA requirement called "Stand by Your Ad," which requires the candidate to say, "I approve this message." But anyone with a lot of money can place an ad that does not explicitly solicit votes for a named candidate, using a legal entity that can spend unlimited sums of what is called "dark money," because donor disclosures are not required. We no longer know, although there are estimates, how much money is being spent by wealthy individuals, American or international corporations, or even foreign governments to influence American elections.[19]

## HOW YOU CAN GET INVOLVED

### Join Common Cause, Democracy 21, or OpenSecrets

Common Cause, one of the oldest and most effective nonpartisan organizations working to improve the functioning and accountability of American democracy, has a program to promote effective regulation of money in politics.[20] Common Cause was founded by John Gardner, a Republican who I got to know when I was a holdover from the Johnson administration and Gardner came in to be Nixon's secretary of Health, Education, and Welfare. For more than two decades, Common Cause was also the home of Fred Wertheimer who developed its campaign finance program and helped pass the Federal Election Campaign Act and its amendments.

Democracy 21 is where you will find Fred Wertheimer today, still fighting to make elections better and control the influence of money in politics. Democracy 21 has many good government programs, but it is best known for crafting legislation including the DISCLOSE Act to limit dark money in politics and the "For the People Act," known as H.R. 1, the first piece of legislation introduced in the 116th Congress in January 2019.

OpenSecrets has developed a specialty in taking all the data that is disclosed through federal election reports and making them understandable to the public so people can know what individuals, labor unions, corporations, and special interest groups are spending, and who they are supporting, through the channels for money that must be reported.[21]

## Restore and Strengthen the Voting Rights Act

Congress should reaffirm and strengthen the Voting Rights Act as soon as possible. The Supreme Court explicitly invited Congress to do this in the *Shelby County* decision. The laws restricting voter participation are based on claims of voter fraud that have no evidence, but the history of racially motivated restrictions on participation by African Americans and other minorities is a stain on American democracy. Both parties should be able to unite to defend the principles of one-person, one-vote democracy and reassert the federal role in ensuring states do not engage in practices that have the effect of suppressing voter participation by any group.

## Fix Gerrymandering with Technology and Nonpartisan Redistricting Commissions

The political scientists I discuss in chapter 10 are not convinced that gerrymandering is a cause of congressional polarization, but I believe we should fix this problem because it would be easy to solve and doing so would add credibility to our elections system. The term "gerrymandering" comes from the whimsical description of congressional districts drawn by Massachusetts Governor Elbridge Gerry in 1812, where some of the districts were said to resemble a salamander.

Mickey Edwards is a Republican who represented Oklahoma's Fifth Congressional District from 1977 to 1993. He wrote a terrific book in 2012 called *The Parties versus the People: How to Turn Republicans and Democrats into Americans,* in which he proposed a number of solutions to congressional polarization, including an impassioned call for reform of the congressional redistricting process.[22] In most states, congressional districts are drawn by governors and state legislatures every ten years after each decennial census. This often means the process is controlled by the political partisans in control of the state government. When government is divided—for example, if state law requires involving a governor and a majority legislature that happen to be from different parties—redistricting decisions become bipartisan. In some states, either by state law or due to a court order, redistricting is done by an academic expert, an independent bipartisan committee, or a nonpartisan commission.

There is a big difference between a partisan process for drawing districts and a bipartisan process, but the best option is to move every state to an independent, nonpartisan individual or commission. Obviously, when one party draws the districts, there is a strong temptation to do so in a way that gives that party an advantage, and few would argue this is uncommon. The interactions of race, geography, and politics adds complexity. There are laws that prohibit "racial gerrymandering" that is district maps that have the effect of weakening racial minority votes, either by breaking minority neighborhoods into multiple districts or by concentrating the votes of minorities heavily in one district, allowing surrounding districts to be nearly all white. Yet, redistricting plans frequently face court challenges (often brought by the NAACP or another of the groups listed below) alleging both types of racially discriminatory redistricting.

Even when the process includes two parties, the results are likely to advantage incumbents over challengers. We need to get our whole system of running elections, especially the drawing of congressional districts, out of the hands of politicians. The best option is to have districts drawn by people who are not politicians. When politicians draw district lines, the most fundamental principle of democracy is turned on its head: Instead of voters choosing which politicians they want to lead them, it is the politicians choosing which voters they will campaign to represent.

My perspective on this is informed by my knowledge of statistical modeling. Computer models have come a long way since the econometric models we used in the early days at the CBO. Academic researchers and partisan political consulting firms now have extraordinarily accurate models to predict the effects of even small changes in the lines defining districts. The models can produce any number of maps that maximize the number of likely Republican seats or Democratic seats, or that minimize the number of incumbent losses. The models can also be set to draw district lines that produce the minimum advantage for either party or for incumbents, and to respect minority rights. It would not be hard for any governor to find five nonpartisan citizens with local knowledge to select the most sensible map from a half-dozen maps that the computer models defined as unbiased options. Our democracy has too many difficult problems to solve to get stuck on problems that could be so easily resolved if only we had political the will to do so.

## Continue Experimentation with Alternative Election Formats

There may be opportunities to make our elections more democratically representative through the use of alternative voting formats including blanket primaries and ranked-choice voting.[23] Low voter turnout in congressional primaries allows the most committed party activists to have an outsized influence in choosing the candidates for the general election.[24] Then when moderate and independent voters show up for the general election, they may not have the option to vote for a candidate who shares their values and policy positions. The simplest way to address this problem is to increase moderate and independent voter turnout in primaries. This is another case where those of us who would like to see more cooperation and achievement from government must match the passion, commitment, and energy of the smaller number of voters who are driven by their uncompromising ideology. This means I am asking you to get more involved, learn who the candidates are, and vote in every election for every office, from president of the United States to county or city council, and I am asking you to encourage your family and friends to do the same.

So-called open primaries may make it easier for independents and moderates to have their voices heard. In a closed primary, only voters registered as Republican can vote in the Republican primary, and likewise for Democrats. Some states have open primaries in which people who are not registered to a specific party can choose to vote for either the Democratic or Republican ticket. In some states, one party may have an open primary and the other a closed primary. This can make a difference in presidential primaries, where more moderate candidates will often put more resources into states where their party is holding an open primary, hoping to attract independent voters to come to the polls. The distinction between open and closed primaries may make less of a difference in down-ballot races that attract less attention and fewer votes, but nonetheless it is a step toward bipartisan co-operation whenever a state or local jurisdiction or party chooses to open their primaries.

Nonpartisan "blanket primaries" are an experiment that some states and jurisdictions have been trying to encourage participation and decrease partisanship. Also called "jungle primaries" and "top-two primaries," blanket primaries have been used in Louisiana politics since 1975 and have spread to other Southern states, California, and Washington. In a blanket primary, all candidates from all parties are listed on the same primary ballot and the top two vote getters advance to a general election runoff unless one candidate wins an outright majority of the primary vote. Proponents of increasing the number of states using this system or of employing it nationwide suggest it would be a moderating force because candidates need to appeal to the whole electorate, but the evidence is mixed that the blanket primary has had much of an effect in the states that use it.[25]

The logic behind blanket primaries is simple: bring the whole electorate into the selection of general election candidates, let voters express their preference among all of the candidates, and then have a runoff election for the most popular ones, where the winner must get a majority of votes. Problems arise when many candidates of one party run and split the vote of their base but only two candidates of the less popular party run; in this case, the general election may feature only candidates from the less popular party. The experience in California has shown this to be a serious concern.

In 2012, in the first California congressional primaries where the new top-two system was used, four Democrats and two Republicans ran for the seat in the Thirty-first Congressional District. Democrats combined to win more votes than Republicans, but the two Republican candidates advanced to the general election because the Democratic votes were split fairly evenly among the four candidates. Thus, a majority Democratic district was forced to elect a Republican representative, and some called for an end to the experiment.[26]

By 2018, many people feared the California primary elections were becoming too unpredictable and expensive, with twenty-seven candidates for governor and thirty-two candidates for US senator. Democrats were also concerned that a close national contest to retake the House could falter in four specific California districts where there were many Democratic candidates seeking the office, raising the possibility of a repeat of 2012 if no Democrat qualified for the general election. The danger was avoided by concentrating resources and votes, and at least one Democrat qualified in each of the districts.

While blanket primaries have added significant strategic concerns to California primaries, they have not yet proven they reduce polarization. My Brookings colleague Elaine Kamarck is an expert on primary elections and how they contribute to political polarization. She analyzed the 2014 congressional elections run by top-two runoff rules in California and Washington for evidence that blanket primaries result in more moderate candidates reaching office, but she did not find much support for the hypothesis.[27] Most districts ended up with a runoff between a Democrat and a Republican that was generally won by the incumbent. This means no change in the level of polarization in Congress from those districts. A small number of districts held a runoff between two Republicans or two Democrats, and an even smaller number advanced a minor party candidate to the runoff, although none were elected to Congress. Taken as a whole, there was little evidence to suggest that the voting system sent representatives to Washington who would be less polarizing. In most cases, it was the same person as the previous election.

We are going to need a lot more data points from a lot more blanket primaries to evaluate this proposition because the power of incumbency is so great. Currently, with more than 90 percent of incumbents generally winning, there are few races where nonpartisan primaries could deliver different, less partisan, results. Even if more states choose to experiment with alternative voting systems, there are few contested elections in each cycle that add data to the analysis of whether the alternative produces a different outcome. Of course, there are more ways to evaluate a change in election procedures than whether it leads to more moderate candidates getting elected to office. Blanket primaries could be an improvement if they allow greater participation of candidates and more choices for voters, if the number is not overwhelming, but the problem of strategic voting bedevils blanket primaries.

Voters face difficult decisions whenever there are three or more candidates for an office and their first-choice candidate seems unlikely to win. They may end up "wasting their vote" and helping to elect their least favorite candidate. This happens in standard primary and general election formats, and as we have just seen, problems of "strategic voting" can be even worse in blanket primaries. Ranked-choice voting (RCV) solves this problem by letting voters express more information about their preferences on the ballot.

Ranked-choice voting solves problems of strategic voting and "wasted votes" in a way that is appreciated by major party candidates and alternative candidates alike. Also called instant-runoff voting (IRV), RCV lets voters express their first choice as well as their second, third, and fourth choice (or as many choices as there are candidates in the race). When the votes are tallied, if no candidate has a majority, the candidate with the fewest votes is dropped and the second-choice votes of that candidate's supporters are counted and added to the totals for the remaining candidates. If still no candidate has a majority, another candidate is dropped and that candidate's votes are reallocated. The process is repeated until one candidate has a majority.

Ranked-choice voting was popular in many cities during the Progressive Era at the start of the twentieth century, with experiments in Cincinnati, Cleveland, Boulder, Sacramento, and New York City, and RCV has been making a comeback in recent years. Portland, Maine, has been using ranked-choice voting since 2011, and the full state of Maine started using RCV in elections for state and federal offices in 2018. Many municipalities across the country have also been experimenting with RCV, and several states are moving toward joining Maine by 2022 or 2024.

The biggest issue with RCV is that it sounds complicated and is perhaps more complicated to explain than it is in practice. Still, RCV has appeal for supporters of both moderate candidates and more niche candidates. More moderate candidates do better to the degree that they are able to amass second- and third-choice votes of candidates that have less overall support. But smaller political parties also like RCV because they can reach out for more supporters without hearing the concern that they will act as "spoilers" in the race between more popular candidates. Voters can cast a first-choice vote for the Libertarian Party or Green Party candidate and then a second-choice vote for their preference between the Republican or Democratic nominee. Getting those first-choice votes may not help the smaller parties win this time, but they can build on them to become a greater force in the future. Because voters are giving more information about their preferences, RCV can deliver results that more closely match voters' real preferences

States, cities, and towns should continue to experiment with alternate forms of elections as long as the motivations are pure—for example, to improve the voting experience, increase voter participation, or make the results better conform to the voters' preferences—and not to gain a partisan advantage or to discourage participation. Open primaries are a good idea, but there is only weak evidence that they would produce distinctly more moderate candidates. Blanket primaries can give bizarre results. Ranked-choice voting is promising, and proponents make the case that it allows more diverse candidates to enter the field, decreases the amount of negative campaigning, and increases civil discourse between candidates and their supporters, but those who suggest that a nationwide switch to nonpartisan primaries would cause a meaningful drop in congressional polarization are overstating their case.[28]

## HOW YOU CAN GET INVOLVED

### Join the NAACP, Fair Fight, The League of Women Voters, US Vote, UnidosUS, or the Brennan Center for Justice

We must make voter registration and voting accessible to every eligible American, and ensure every ballot is counted regardless of voter's race, ethnicity, language, age, or disability. This means increasing voter registration, expanding voter access, and working to end voter suppression. There are many nonpartisan groups that have taken on these challenges, and you can support their work. The oldest is the National Association for the Advancement of Colored People (NAACP), and perhaps the newest is Stacey Abrams's organization Fair Fight. The League of Women Voters was founded in 1920 to fight for ratification of the 19th amendment has been making elections better for nearly a century. The US Vote Foundation (US Vote) is a nonpartisan, nonprofit organization dedicated to improving voter access by providing each voter with individualized information on election dates and polling places, and offering vote by mail forms for every state and overseas.

There are many organizations with programs to protect voting rights and expand voter registration for communities that are historically underrepresented in the American electorate, like UnidosUS (formerly the National

Council of La Raza), the American-Arab Anti-Discrimination Committee (ADC), Asian and Pacific Islander American Vote (APIAVote), and the Native American Rights Fund (NARF).

I would also mention the Brennan Center for Justice, which has a strong program defending and expanding voting rights in honor of Supreme Court Justice William J. Brennan. I am sure there are many other great groups working for better election rules at the national and local levels that I am leaving off this list, but I encourage you to find them if you would like to help.[29]

## Ways We Can Change the Tone, in Washington and in Every Community

I have just listed dozens of ways we could change the rules governing the Senate and House—rules defining the federal budget process, rules regulating money in politics, rules governing elections, and rules designating local control of investments in our towns and cities across America. I have also provided contact information (mostly in the endnotes) for many nonprofit and nonpartisan organizations that are working to address these issues. But if I have learned one thing from my career in public policy, it is that changing the rules will not be enough to deliver a government that spends more time solving real problems and less time fighting for partisan advantage.

We have seen throughout this book that when leaders do not want to reach agreement, they can bend or stretch the rules to make compromise all but impossible; but when both sides are looking to reach bipartisan accommodation, the rules are rarely a hinderance. Chapter 10 examines

*The problem is that we have forgotten that our Constitution, which politicians and Supreme Court justices laud to the heavens, requires that politicians work together across party and ideological lines to get anything done at all. Recapturing the lost art of political compromise is essential to realizing our economic potential.*

—Alice M. Rivlin, "It's Not the Economy, Stupid—It's Failed Politics," SIEPR Prize Lecture, April 14, 2016 many potential causes of political polarization and congressional dysfunction, and perhaps the one thing that has changed the most over the last several decades in the data collected by political scientists is what they call negative partisan affect. Now more than ever before, Republicans hold negative views of Democrats, and Democrats hold negative views of Republicans. And yet, most of the laws that do pass the Senate and House do so with bipartisan support, so the two sides are able to find a way to work together for the good of the country despite the negative feelings.

Those of us who would like to see this happen more frequently and on the issues of greatest long-term consequence—including the national debt, climate change, immigration, infrastructure, public health, mental health, and addictions treatment, and investments in a faster-growing and more equitable economy—know that changing congressional rules and election laws will not be enough unless we also take meaningful steps to reverse the nation's decline into partisan animosity. We need to replace the blaming and name-calling with listening and civil discourse. Fortunately, we find that we are not alone in this goal. The rest of this chapter is dedicated to the many talented individuals and groups who are working to change the tone of public discourse and the culture inside Congress and in local communities across the land in ways that could lead to more compromise, cooperation, and progress in solving the most pressing problems we face as a nation. I will start with projects to improve interactions among lawmakers in Washington and then expand my focus to include efforts to create dialogue and understanding among people in communities across the country.

Efforts to forge a peace in the hyperpartisan warfare and social identity warfare in Congress have taken several forms. Allow me to distinguish three related but distinct levels for these activities: (1) informal relationship building, (2) civil discourse, and (3) national service.

## ENCOURAGE INFORMAL RELATIONSHIPS AMONG MEMBERS AND STAFFS IN CONGRESS

There are many proposals designed to increase the amount of informal time congressional members have to form relationships with members across the aisle. One suggestion is to eliminate the aisle altogether by mixing members' desks on the House and Senate floors and in committee rooms. This one change alone will not save the Republic from hyperpartisan dysfunction, but among many other changes, it could help get things moving in a more positive direction. The Maine State Legislature has tried this, and it seems to be working to improve cross party relationships.

Other ideas include holding bipartisan orientation for new members at the start of each Congress and encouraging bipartisan "buddy" selections. The House and Senate members could each go on retreats for members, staff, and families, as was done with House members in the 105th through 107th Congresses (1997–2003). Boating, golf, entertainment, and good food and drink help people relax a bit and forge new relationships. Some congressional members might worry about the optics of taking time off to have fun at taxpayers' expense but given the current state of partisan polarization and congressional dysfunction, any reasonable expense of this type would be a fantastic value for taxpayers. The nation's most successful businesses invest millions annually in these kinds of team-building activities.

There are also many bipartisan and nonpartisan organizations that have established programs to provide informal opportunities for socializing, discussion, dialogue, and problem-solving. Activities range from hosting policy-oriented retreats to holding seminars, sponsoring bipartisan fact-finding trips, and hosting breakfast meetings or pizza and beer parties.

## HOW YOU CAN GET INVOLVED

### Participate with the Aspen Institute, Lugar Center, Faith & Politics Institute, or Millennial Action Project

The Aspen Institute was founded in 1949 with a retreat in Aspen, Colorado, for philosophers, scholars, and business leaders to celebrate the German philosopher Johann Goethe. Under the leadership of Walter Isaacson, and more recently Dan Porterfield, it has maintained a level of excellence that makes it feel like an exclusive club. Memberships are expensive, however, a lot of the best ideas, seminars, and cultural events are shared for free on the Aspen Institute website, and if you join the institute's mailing list, you will see many opportunities to attend free seminars in person or streaming online.

The Institute's Congressional Program brings members of Congress together at weekly Capitol Hill breakfasts and offers bipartisan policy seminars for members in the institute's Washington, DC, headquarters, with expert analysis of problems and potential solutions. The Aspen Institute's Rodel Fellowships in Public Leadership, founded by former Oklahoma Republican Representative Mickey Edwards (mentioned earlier in this chapter), gather a diverse group of emerging political leaders for a two-year program of policy retreats and idea exchanges to help build bipartisan communications and deepen their commitment to the principles of American democracy.[30]

Former Senator Richard G. Lugar (R-IN) founded the Lugar Center on the principle that bipartisanship is not an ideology; rather, it is a commitment to doing the job of governing. Lugar believed strong conservatives and progressives do not have to give up their convictions as long as they keep doing the work of reaching agreement on new laws and spending bills. The key is keeping discourse civil, opening lines of communication, and continuing to work the problems until solutions are reached. The Lugar Center, working with Georgetown University, maintains a "Bipartisan Index" that ranks senators on their achievements in working across the aisle. The center also runs "Oversight Boot Camps" to strengthen the skills and resolve of congressional staffers to perform effective oversight of the executive branch. As a senator, Dick Lugar was particularly known for his support of bipartisanship in foreign policy and the Lugar Center continues this work with programs on global food security and arms control.[31]

Since 1998, the Faith & Politics Institute has led bipartisan congressional trips to Alabama to join Representative John Lewis in his remembrance of Bloody Sunday (March 7, 1965), when police attacked civil rights protesters as they attempted to march from Selma to Montgomery across the Edmund Pettus Bridge. More than 300 members of the US House and Senate and three presidents have participated in this nearly annual pilgrimage.[32]

The Millennial Action Project (MAP) was founded in 2013 by a small group of college students who met in 2011 after becoming Truman Scholars. They shared their concerns about partisan politics, especially after witnessing the 2011 debt ceiling dysfunction, and they decided to do something about changing the tone in Washington. In 2013, MAP started the Congressional Future Caucus, a bipartisan group of young members of Congress who meet formally to work on a broad range of issues and informally, such as on morning runs, looking for policies on which to work together. In addition, MAP organizes and supports similar caucuses in fifteen state legislatures. There is no cost or age requirement to join MAP's mailing list or support its work.[33]

## CIVIL DISCOURSE

Civil discourse is a more formalized way to strengthen relations among groups in conflict, and there have been efforts to bring this approach to the US Congress and state legislatures as well as communities across the country. I want to define what I mean by civil discourse, and here I rely heavily on Carolyn Lukensmeyer and Keith Allred of the National Institute for Civil Discourse (NICD) as well as Guy M. Burgess and Heidi Burgess of the Beyond Intractability Project. Both groups define "civil discourse" similarly and offer a list of guidelines for ensuring that discourse is civil.

Civil discourse is constructive engagement of individuals or groups across differences. Civil discourse is good in and of itself; it occurs whenever two or more people from different groups engage in discussions that value listening and understanding, mutual respect, and a search for agreement and common ground. Sometimes civil discourse can lead to agreement on a course of action, or in Congress it can lead to bipartisan legislative proposals, but this does not have to be a goal. It is enough just to get lines of communication open and to see the other side not as adversaries but as humans, replacing the lens of power and conflict with the lens of empathy and understanding.

It is important to say what civil discourse is not, as some people are suspicious of the concept because there have been times in history when protest movements—such as the suffragettes in the struggle for voting rights for women, Rosa Parks and the Student Nonviolent Coordinating Committee in the struggle for civil rights for African Americans, and protests against wars or for environmental sustainability—have been labeled as "uncivil" by those seeking to defend the status quo and quell the protest. Advocates of civil discourse would never use the concept to silence protest; precisely the opposite is true. Civil discourse is designed to foster constructive advocacy and allow expressions of discontent. But the greatest emphasis is simply on building relationships that include connections that are not limited to the points of conflict. The natural inclination to dehumanize opponents is replaced by an explicit and mutual effort to build human connections through respectful engagement.

## Congressional Civility Caucuses

Several bipartisan pairs of representatives have started civility caucuses in the House. In 2005, Representatives Shelley Moore Capito (R-WV) and Emanuel Cleaver II (D-MO) formed the Civility Caucus to hold "civility hours" on the House floor, where members come to respectfully debate national issues for the C-SPAN audience.

Representatives Charlie Crist (D-FL) and Mike Johnson (R-LA) established a bipartisan Honor and Civility Caucus in 2017 to promote a civility pledge written by Johnson and signed by 120 members. The two also sponsored a bill declaring National Civility Day on July 12 of each year.

Representatives Steve Stivers (R-OH) and Joyce Beatty (D-OH) founded the Congressional Civility and Respect Caucus in 2018. Membership is open to bipartisan pairs representing any state. The two founders from Ohio have set a model for others to follow of selecting a project that will show their constituents their ability to work together on a significant issue. Representatives Stivers and Beatty have presented a program in every high school in each of their districts promoting the importance of the democratic values of civility and respect and encouraging the students to find common-ground solutions to problems facing the schools and their community.

## The National Institute for Civil Discourse

We know that national tragedies like September 11, hurricanes, bombings, mass shootings, and presidential funerals often have the effect of bringing the country together for a temporary truce in the partisan warfare. Discussed in chapter 9, the January 2011 shooting of Representative Gabriel Giffords (D-AZ), causing her severe brain injury, wounding seventeen others, and killing six, was one of these national incidents that shocked the country and official Washington into a moment of silence. At the University of Arizona in Tucson, where the shooting took place, the effects of the tragedy were longer lived than in Washington. Giffords had been in discussions with the University of Arizona about forming an organization to address civility in politics just days before the shooting, and the National Institute for Civil Discourse (NICD) was launched within a few months. Giffords has served on the NICD board of directors, as have George H. W. Bush, Bill Clinton, and many leading political figures from both parties, including Thomas Daschle, former Senate Democratic majority leader, and Christine Todd Whitman, former Republican governor of New Jersey and head of the EPA. I have also served on the NICD board. Carolyn Lukensmeyer was selected as the founding executive director.

Lukensmeyer had been the founder and President of AmericaSpeaks since 1995, an organization that engaged diverse citizens and leaders in twenty-first century town hall meetings to ensure that citizens had a voice in the policies that most impact their lives. Under Lukensmeyer's leadership NICD established major program initiatives such as "Building Trust through Civil Discourse" which engages members of the public across the ideological spectrum; "Next Generation" which provides training for members of state legislatures in how to increase their capacity for bi-partisan problem-solving and policymaking; and "Divided We Fall" (which I think is a terrific title), a documentary demonstrating how Trump supporters and Trump detractors can discover that they have more in common than separates them.

Lukensmeyer stepped down in 2019 and was followed as executive director by Keith Allred who brought to NICD an already established initiative, CommonSense American, which fosters bipartisan policy problem-solving. Allred started CSA with a pilot project in Idaho, where he had run for governor in 2010. The idea was to pick a big issue and then bring together citizens and stakeholders representing diverse perspectives for a series of meetings to analyze the issue and seek common-ground solutions. Once two-thirds of the members agreed on a position, Allred would lobby for it in the state legislature. When Allred joined NICD, CommonSense American shifted its policy work to the United States Congress.

All of the NICD initiatives share a common mission to revive civility and enhance problem-solving across the partisan divide. The programs reach out to different populations to bridge divides and to engage decision makers at the community, state, and national levels.[34]

Through its programs, NICD has also been active in working with state legislators and state legislatures to build civil discourse and empathetic listening skills.[35] Legislators gather in national and regional working sessions to discuss their political views on a deeper level by sharing their personal experiences and values. Having made a connection with the NICD, its facilitators, and other participants, legislators have resources when their own states run into a bumpy patch. While NICD has been called into a long list of states to help build bridges between lawmakers when civility has been strained, the list of states that would benefit from the organization's attention is perhaps just as long. But NICD is not alone in working to create safe places for dialogue across political differences. There are many organizations that have formed to foster dialogue across party lines.

Following the 2016 election, independent bookstores across the country (including my neighborhood bookstore, Politics and Prose) started bipartisan book clubs where people come together to read and discuss contemporary books about politics and culture to increase understanding across political differences. The goal is to build relationships and increase tolerance, and the only rules are mutual respect, civil dialogue, no personal attacks, and no attempts at political conversion. The bipartisan book clubs are a project of the National Coalition Against Censorship in coordination with NICD and the American Booksellers Association.[36]

Better Angels[37] is a grassroots organization that aims to reduce political polarization by bringing liberals and conservatives together at the community level to understand each other beyond stereotypes, forming red/blue community alliances, teaching practical skills for communicating across political differences, and spreading the message of depolarization. Better Angels moderators arrange small workshops where seven conservatives and seven liberals come together to discuss and clarify disagreements, reduce stereotyped thinking, and build relationships across partisan lines.

Ask Big Questions hosts thoughtful discussions for small groups on college campuses to strengthen civic habits of listening, civility, and engaging diverse perspectives. The group was created by Hillel International to train student moderators and to offer conversation guides and other resources that can facilitate group discussions.[38]

Since 2015, the Bridge Alliance has been bringing together the fields of civic engagement, electoral reform, policymaking, and citizen empowerment. Bridge Alliance members don't all agree on solutions but do agree to be supportive and collaborate "when it makes sense." Their website

(BridgeAlliance.US) is a great place to connect with many organizations that are engaged in working together to strengthen our democracy.

The American Academy of Arts and Sciences (AAAS) has plans for strengthening American democracy in 2020 in a report that will be titled: "Our Common Purpose: Reinventing American Democracy for the 21st Century." AAAS was founded in 1790 by Benjamin Franklin, John Adams, and others of our country's founders to ensure that the new government would have knowledge and evidence to support their policymaking on difficult issues. The Commission has spent two years engaging people in communities across the country to explore ways to respond to the challenges facing our politics and civic life. You can follow the progress of the project at AmAcad.org.

One of the elements common to NICD, the bipartisan book clubs, and other experts in creating dialogue and moving groups from conflict to understanding and compromise is the importance of repeated and sustained contact. When people encounter one another at a town hall meeting or on the internet, we are often defined by the positions we take that others disagree with. But through repeated contact, we see each other as people and learn that, like us, others have children, coach soccer, and are worried about the health of their parents. Eventually we may learn that other people hold positions on some issues where we can actually agree (surprise!).

## NATIONAL SERVICE

Before the 2016 election, my Brookings colleague Isabel Sawhill started writing a book about *The Forgotten Americans*, which she defines as those without a college degree and earning less than $70,000 per year.[39] Her focus is on the economic policies needed to help the Americans who are falling behind, and she offers an economic plan that is not unlike the plan I offer in chapter 2. (It is not surprising that our plans are similar, because we talk often.)

Sawhill places emphasis on a proposal for national service with an American exchange program. I want to add my support for this proposal, but I am putting it here rather than in chapter 2 because I think this proposal would do a lot to heal the divisions in the nation. The idea of universal national service is bipartisan. John Bridgeland, who was domestic policy director in the George W. Bush White House, is a major proponent, as are (retired) General Stanley McChrystal and many others.

Under Sawhill's plan, every high school graduate would be expected to give a year of national service (military or civilian) in return for some help paying for college. She emphasizes the element of graduates working in communities that are unlike their own and bringing together teams of young people from diverse backgrounds to address local needs all across the United States. The contact theory from psychology[40] tells us these elements would be potent and effective in helping to lower the barriers of distrust, stereotypes, and misunderstandings across the many divisions in our country. In addition to the model offered by military service, the suggestion of civilian service projects builds on the successful and bipartisan models of the Peace Corps, Volunteers in Service to America (VISTA), and AmeriCorps, expanding them to reach as many high school graduates as could be convinced each year to participate in the voluntary program of national service.

## There Is So Much Worth Defending

Nearing the end of the book, I want to lay my cards on the table: I am hoping to recruit you into an army to defend American democracy. I am not trying to get you to be against anything. I want you to be for a lot of things. I want you to be for common sense. I want you to support an America that acts like a mature democracy. I want you to work for solutions to our long-term problems rather than sweeping them under the rug and leaving them to another generation, hoping they will get easier to solve. They will not; problems tend to get worse when left unattended. I believe most of America's most intractable challenges can be effectively addressed right now through policies that are supported by majorities of Americans and could be supported by majorities of lawmakers if the hyperpartisan battles did not stand in the way. Whether you have read every word of this book or you skipped to this chapter about things we can do, you have already taken the first step. The next steps are to support candidates and organizations that are dedicated to progress toward compromise positions on the issues where compromise is possible and, in many cases, has already been hammered out.

I want you to support comprehensive immigration reform and dramatic action to reverse global warming while developing new technologies and jobs in renewable energy.[41] We need to come to agreement on needed investments in innovation, education, infrastructure, and healthy communities to build an economy that will sustainably deliver broadly shared prosperity. I want you to support the people and policies that will help put the nation's finances and national debt on a sustainable path, by raising the revenue necessary to fund the government Americans demand by closing the loopholes and other expenditures in the tax system.

But more than anything else, I want you to recommit to patriotism and to the truth. I put these two values together quite deliberately. There may be nothing so dangerous in our world than patriotism that is divorced from the truth. I started chapter 3 by noting there are two views of American history, and both are true. One version views America as the greatest democracy in the world because the Founding Fathers wrote a Declaration of Independence, a Constitution, and a Bill of Rights that properly balanced federal, state, and individual rights and liberties. The other version remembers the darker truths of American history, the violence, subjugation, discrimination, and exploitation that helped some Americans achieve great wealth and power but maintained many others in a subordinate status. Extremes of economic and political inequality continue to divide America to this day.

Of course, it is wrong to deny the darker truths about America's past and present, but at the same time we should not let this truth blind us from celebrating American greatness. Many of America's greatest leaders in the struggle for equality—Frederick Douglass, Harriet Tubman, William Jennings Bryan, Susan B. Anthony, Thurgood Marshall, and Martin Luther King Jr.—all found ways to express their love of this country as they set about to improve it. America must always remember that we are a great nation with a constitutional democracy that still holds the promise of being an example of freedom and self-governance to the world.

With all of America's flaws and warts, Americans must recommit to the patriotic hard work of maintaining the great democratic republic bequeathed to us by the writers of the Constitution and the Bill of Rights. There is a reason why every public servant in the United States of America takes an oath to support and defend the Constitution: It is the glue that holds the nation together and defines our system of laws. The Constitution defines a system for lawmaking that requires a search for common ground and compromise to reach a majority agreement. The process can be corrupted unless all parties are committed to seeking rather than obscuring the truth.

As we recommit to patriotic efforts to see America, the American government, and the American people succeed, we must also recommit to seeking truth. It is normal for different sides in a negotiation to disagree about facts. This is, after all, the reason the CBO was created. Successful negotiations are aided by a common understanding of the consequences of different courses of action or, if that is elusive, then by agreement on a disinterested authority to provide best estimates of the objective reality. Short of outright lying, one of the most destructive actions we can take to subvert effective policymaking is to undermine the independent authorities designed to determine the truth, such as the intelligence agencies, inspectors general, and the large number of commissions, administrations, agencies, and offices that seek the truth in specific issue areas.

I understand that America has enemies, both foreign and domestic, that would be delighted to see America fail. There are some who would seek to replace the truth, in any area that is unpleasant, inconvenient, or unhelpful to their political aims, with untruth that serves their interests. But it is my sincere hope, and my strong belief and the source of my optimism, that the vast majority of Americans want to defend our constitutional system, seek truth and justice, and see America succeed.

# WHAT WOULD ALICE RIVLIN SAY NOW?

## Sheri Rivlin and Allan Rivlin

As we were working to complete this book, democracy was threatened as never before and certainly more threatened than it was at the time of Alice Rivlin's death. In her long career, Alice was a witness to a great deal of political and economic history, and we hope we have helped her tell those stories well in the chapters of this book. But history did not stop when Alice passed away in May 2019. The more than three years we have been working to complete this book have been some of the most eventful in the history of American politics and economics, with a pandemic, a disputed election, and an attempted coup d'état and Russian tanks and missiles invading Ukraine, putting the global order at risk. Because we have been so close to Alice's thinking and writings throughout this remarkable period, we believe we know how she would have responded to the many new challenges and questions of the moment.

## IS BIPARTISANSHIP STILL POSSIBLE IN THE AGE OF DONALD TRUMP, JANUARY 6, AND ALTERNATIVE FACTS?

Alice wrote this book to make the case that bipartisanship is always possible—that it happens all the time and often happens when it appears least likely. The best example is the huge, lame-duck, "just don't call it a stimulus" deal President Barack Obama and Vice President Joe Biden struck with Mitch McConnell (R-KY), John Boehner (R-OH), and the Republicans just after the disastrous (for Democrats) 2010 election that swept in the Republican Young Guns and Tea Party (which is all discussed in chapter 9). But as an advocate for bipartisan cooperation, Alice was always responding to the view that her position was now out of date because the other side was so radical now, so divorced from reality, as to make compromise impossible. So, allow us to continue the work of this book and Alice's work by noting the many bipartisan achievements (and frustrations) through the Trump years, beyond the January 6, 2021 insurrection, and into President Joe Biden's first year in office, to make the case that bipartisanship is still happening all the time—even when pundits proclaim it impossible and those who seek it are called naïve.

Perhaps the most instructive example of how Alice would hope to see bipartisan policymaking work best happened after her death, with the passage of the United States-Mexico-Canada Agreement (USMCA) on trade in January 2020. Alice would have credited the "Break the Gridlock" rule changes, negotiated in 2019 between the Problem Solvers Caucus and Nancy Pelosi (and progressive Representative James McGovern) as described in chapter 11, as being integral to the successful outcome. The rule changes created a "Consensus Calendar" process allowing a vote on any bill with more than 290 cosponsors even if the Speaker or a majority of Democrats didn't support it.

The trade agreement that President Trump negotiated—USMCA, the replacement for the North American Free Trade Agreement (NAFTA)—was gaining momentum in the House, with substantial support among Republicans and moderate Democrats, but Speaker Pelosi opened up the negotiations to include progressive House Democrats who wanted stronger labor provisions and environmental protections. Pelosi's actions had the effect of making Richard Trumka, then president of the American Federation of Labor and Congress of Industrial Organizations (AFL-CIO), a party to the discussions. Substantial changes were made, and USMCA passed by an overwhelmingly bipartisan 385–41 vote in the House in December 2019 and a vote of 89–10 in the Senate in January 2020.

In addition to the USMCA and the "First Step Act" reforms of the criminal justice system, the final years of the Trump presidency saw remarkably high levels of bipartisan cooperation on legislation, both in frequency and budgetary cost, in response to the coronavirus pandemic, which arrived at the start of 2020 (which was also an election year) and the final weeks of

Donald Trump's first impeachment trial. The preface of this book discusses several of the bipartisan COVID-19 response, relief, and recovery bills that were passed through July of 2020, as well as the nearly six-month partisan standoff from midsummer through the election and almost to the end-of-year deadline to fund the government. The Consolidated Appropriations Act passed the Senate by unanimous consent on December 21, 2020. After some amendments, it passed the House on the same day with a strong 359 to 53 bipartisan majority, and then the Senate accepted the House changes by a vote of 92 to 6. At $2.3 trillion, the resulting bipartisan bill that President Trump signed on December 27 was the largest spending bill in US history, eclipsing the $2.2 trillion bipartisan Coronavirus Aid, Relief, and Economic Security (CARES) Act that was passed in March 2020. No one can argue that bipartisan compromise proved impossible in the Trump years.

## DO DEFICITS STILL MATTER—EVEN IN A PANDEMIC?

Alice makes it clear in several places in this book that short-term deficit spending can be desirable during an economic downturn, but she would also say long-term deficit projections always matter because the retiring baby boom generation is a very real and very predictable challenge to the nation's future debt levels and economic capacity. Alice would also point out that a pandemic is a very unusual economic downturn.

In a typical recession, a drop-off in demand for goods and services can be reversed by economic stimulus, which can take many forms but often means deficit spending. But it makes no sense to stimulate an economy that is shutting down due to reduced human interactions that could spread disease. However, in both a typical recession and the coronavirus-induced recession, people have needs that must be met for food, housing, and education, so spending by federal, state, and local governments for basic social services should increase. Additionally, businesses and state and local governments need help to continue providing essential services while protecting essential workers. Alice would also have been an advocate for stimulus in the form of investments in productive capacity and human capital that would help the economy grow after the pandemic lockdown.

While Alice would have praised the bipartisanship exhibited in passing the many COVID response bills, and the many trillions of dollars committed to the emergency measures, we think she would have expressed some discomfort with the legislative dynamic that brought forth the spending bills. President Trump was never conservative on economic matters, prioritizing tax cuts over keeping the deficit manageable, but in 2020 he had only one priority—his own reelection. He believed there were two things that could save him: getting the economy reopened after the shutdown and sending out large checks with his name on them. Few, if any, Republicans would stand up to him at this point, so with Democrats turning reliably and correctly to their liberal economic experts in a crisis, there was no one representing the conservative point of view in negotiations over extraordinarily large spending bills. Where there were disputes between Republicans and Democrats over whether to get help to businesses or to workers, or whether to send checks to the unemployed, the poor, the middle class, or the wealthy, the answer was usually "all of the above." The tacit agreement between the parties was "We will let you borrow money to help the people you care about if you let us borrow money to help the people we care about."

We think Alice would have joined some of the economists she mentions in this book (like Christina and David Romer, who have analyzed the pandemic response) in the critique that some of the spending categories were far less central to, and efficient in, the mission of helping all Americans get through the pandemic and keeping the economy from collapsing. Alice was never a supporter of sending large government checks to the economically comfortable. It is important to understand that the mission was changing as the world was learning to respond to the pandemic. The initial strategy of shutting down the economy, and of compensating workers for staying home and business owners for closing, changed to a strategy of encouraging businesses to reopen and employees to return to work safely. Neither strategy was fully successful.

A nearly certain economic collapse was averted, a lot of good initiatives were funded, and many individuals and small businesses were extended a lifeline in a very troubling time. On the other hand, the COVID response bills added up to a huge amount of money and added to projections of America's long-term national debt, which is now on a path to double from a once-unthinkable 100 percent of GDP at the start of the pandemic to over 200 percent of GDP by 2050. The nation entered the pandemic crisis with far less fiscal space than it might have had if it were running smaller deficits in the preceding years, perhaps simply by forgoing the Tax Cuts and Jobs Act of 2017, but the amount of fiscal space available to policymakers at any given time has always been the subject of substantial debate.

## How Would Alice's Economics Have Evolved for a COVID and Post-COVID Economy?

In the political/economic debates of Alice's youth, the liberal side, generally buttressing its arguments with Keynesian economic theory, believed government's role was to use the revenue raised through progressive taxation to spend on government priorities like military defense, education, infrastructure, and other investments in future economic growth, and to help the poor, the infirmed, and the elderly cover their basic needs. The conservative side, often buttressed by the monetarist economic theory of Milton Friedman, pointed to the dangers of deficits and inflation to argue for a more limited fiscal policy, relying instead on expanding or constraining the money supply to target full employment and stable prices. Like many mainstream economists of her generation, Alice found merit in both schools of thought, and she worked to fashion a synthesis of the two that emphasized fiscal conservatism to keep long-term deficits under control in economic good times; strong automatic stabilizers (like unemployment insurance and food stamps) to surge in economic bad times and provide countercyclical spending even if they produce short-term deficits; and a Federal Reserve that is independent and insulated from political pressure to manage the money supply. The Democrats nominated, elected, and reelected two fiscally conservative presidents in Bill Clinton and Barack Obama, both of whom found value in Alice's economic perspective.

There are a lot of economic terms in the preceding paragraph, but they are all defined and explained in the pages of this book. The way the debate over economic theory has been ascribed to the left, center, or right over the decades is a gross oversimplification, but the depiction broadly describes the world into which two other economic theories, supply-side economics and Modern Monetary Theory (MMT), have competed for the attention of politicians and policymakers. Alice engaged supply-side economics throughout her career and throughout the pages of this book. Although MMT entered the political discussion more recently and after Alice's death, we are quite confident we know how she would have responded to MMT based largely on observing her response to supply-side economics.

Modern Monetary Theory rose to prominence in June 2020 when Professor Stephanie Kelton of Stonybrook University and the New School for Social Research published a book called *The Deficit Myth: Modern Monetary Theory and the Birth of the People's Economy*. This was a full year after Alice's death. While the theory predates publication of the book, and has more adherents than just Kelton, we have asked others (and, especially, Alice's husband, Sidney Winter, who is also a well-published economic theorist and who knew her thinking on most things economic or political) and are not aware that she ever formed or expressed an opinion on MMT.

The basic assertion of the theory is that government debt is not a problem to be limited but is instead a vast source of national wealth that could be used to fund national priorities like providing health care, ending poverty, and promoting higher education. The belief that the US government is "broke" or could ever run out of money is, in the view of MMT, a relic of the era when government repaid debt in gold bullion and has no relevance in a world where the government can "print" money with a few strokes on a computer keyboard. Governments that are able to borrow money in their own currency can never run out of money because they can always make more. By 2020, MMT was being championed by progressives like Senator Bernie Sanders (I-VT), who was using Kelton as an advisor to his presidential campaign, to provide an economic justification for funding Sanders's "Medicare for All" health care plan and other progressive initiatives, and then many others became interested in MMT as the pandemic relief bills were growing so large.

Modern Monetary Theory is a direct challenge to those economists who, like Alice Rivlin, spent their career warning about the danger posed by the long-term deficit and by rising national debt, and who insist that it is necessary to "pay for" government spending priorities. Supporters of MMT would say Alice was wrong to praise the pay-as-you-go (PAYGO) and spending cap congressional rules that were part of the budget reforms passed by George H. W. Bush, which Alice credits as instrumental to achieving four balanced budgets in a row when Bill Clinton was president. Adherents of MMT believe that PAYGO and budget caps were bad policy because its rules imposed arbitrary limits, misguidedly requiring that new federal spending and tax cuts be "paid for," which meant many good policies were not undertaken, and that all of this was for a false goal of balancing the federal budget (four times in a row).

Many prominent economists have criticized MMT as a crackpot theory—the left's version of the supply-side economics often invoked by conservatives to allow them to cut taxes without worrying about the implications for the deficit. We do not think Alice would have joined them in dismissing MMT, because as president of the American Economic Association in 1986, a nonpartisan position, she resisted those in the profession who wanted to dismiss supply-side economics. Rather than dismissing MMT, we believe Alice would have engaged it and found it provocative. She would have argued against those who wanted to oversimplify MMT. In her view, an economic theory must be developed and modeled. Databases must be found or created and used to test MMT's predictive ability in peer-reviewed journal articles. She believed economics is at its best when it is an evolving academic pursuit of greater truths.

But Alice would have cautioned politicians, or anyone, against adopting an economic theory, merely because it helps us justify what we want to do, whether it is supply-siders who want to cut taxes without worrying about the effects on the deficit or MMT proponents who want to spend money without worrying about the effects on the deficit. Theories should be evaluated based on the validity of their hypotheses, not based on their implications. Alice would not have accepted that the gross experiences of 2020–2021 could either prove or disprove MMT (although careful analysis of data collected in this period could add to the debate).

Early in the pandemic recession, when (as discussed above) there was a political consensus to dramatically increase government spending and run larger deficits—far larger than the country had run at any time since World War II—there were many casual conversations in the press speculating that all politicians were acting as if they had adopted the MMT philosophy and, when the sky did not collapse on the economy, some saw MMT vindicated. Then, as the economy gained momentum in 2021 and inflation and interest rates started rising, some people saw that as a repudiation of MMT. Alice would have asked for far more rigor before accepting either of these positions.

The details of this debate are more instructive than the surface simplifications. Sadly, Alice is not around to engage these details.

Alice would not have rejected MMT out of hand, but she would continue to believe that long-term deficits do matter. Unsustainable levels of government borrowing leave America with too little fiscal space when we need to respond to a crisis, and this is even more constraining when inflation and interest rates are rising. She would advocate for strengthening automatic stabilizers and for making smart, locally driven investments in human capital, physical infrastructure, technological advancement, and other measures that will enhance America's productive capacity and broadly shared prosperity. Further, she would continue to highlight the predictable decline in revenue and dramatic increase in spending that are starting to hit America as the baby boom generation retires. Alice would continue to support raising enough revenue by increasing tax rates on the wealthy, strengthening tax collections and enforcement of tax laws, and closing tax loopholes to pay for current and future spending needs, as well as calling for elected leaders to muster the political will to deal with the long-term deficit and debt problem before it becomes a crisis.

After its long absence, the return of wage and price inflation as an important concern is a major change to the United States and global economic landscapes. From the start of the 2008–2009 economic collapse and continuing for twelve more years, the Federal Reserve saw too little inflation (or worse, the possibility of deflation) as a greater threat to the economy than too much inflation. During this period, fiscal and monetary policy could push in one direction to stimulate the economy for greater growth and job creation. This historically unusual period ended when inflation heated up midway through 2021. Once again, Americans have returned to the more historically normal circumstance where fiscal and monetary policy must push in two opposing directions to balance the goals of full employment and price stability.

Inflation adds to the long-term deficit and debt risk because it forces a change in monetary policy toward higher interest rates to cool a potentially overheating economy at the same time as it adds to the cost of servicing the debt. The budgetary line item for interest paid on the national debt goes up when government adds to the debt by running a deficit, but it also increases when interest rates rise, as they are doing now. Alice would have seen the return of inflation as a very worrisome development because it arrived during the coronavirus pandemic. Alice lived through the "stagflation" of the 1970s, when supply-chain shocks in oil and food caused a long period in which the American economy experienced slow growth and high inflation at the same time. She would hope that fiscal and monetary policymakers can find the right balance to avoid a return to the stagflation trap.

## Biden Takes Office Facing a Choice Between Partisan and Bipartisan Paths

Joe Biden took over the White House amid a global pandemic, an economic crisis, and a political crisis, with an ambitious agenda that, in addition to significant action to address the pandemic, included all the economic policies Alice describes in chapter 2, a determination to strengthen American democracy against the assault directed by his predecessor, calls to protect voting rights and civil rights, and promises to meaningfully address the threats of climate change and a broken immigration system. On each of these fronts, he faced a choice whether to pursue bipartisan cooperation, try to pass legislation with only the Democrats who make up the razor-thin margins in both chambers, or follow a dual track combining bipartisan and partisan action.

President Biden's Democratic allies in the House and Senate were divided between a minority of members advocating bipartisanship to change the partisan tone in Washington and most of the party pushing to pass a bold progressive agenda (despite unified Republican opposition) to deliver real results for American families heading into the 2022 election. Alice would have supported nearly every element of the progressive agenda, but she would have placed a higher priority on changing the partisan patterns in Washington, for all the reasons stated in this book and especially due to the threat to democracy that she viewed as, at least partially, a consequence of hyperpartisan warfare.

Alice would have prodded Republicans and Democrats to be flexible, productive, and respectful in negotiations, and she would have extended the same advice to the two factions of Democrats in their negotiations and their standoffs over policy and procedures, which ended up dominating the news throughout Biden's first year in office. Americans had witnessed the protracted intraparty battles between progressive House Democrats and moderate Senate Democrats at the start of the Clinton and Obama presidencies, and the harm those conflicts caused for Democrats at the ballot box in both presidents' first midterm elections. The start of the Biden administration seemed like a third turn of a familiar wheel of frustration.

Joe Biden spoke frequently about the importance of bipartisan cooperation throughout the 2020 campaign. On October 6, 2020, he went to the Gettysburg battlefield in Pennsylvania, the site of the bloodiest battle in America's Civil War, and said this:

> Instead of treating each other's party as the opposition, we treat them as the enemy. This must end. We need to revive the spirit of bipartisanship in this country. A spirit of being able to work with one another. When I say that, and I've been saying it for two years now, I'm accused of being naive. I'm told, "Maybe that's the way things used to work, Joe, but they can't work that way anymore." Well, I'm here to tell you they can, and they must if we're going to get anything done.

Bipartisanship proved difficult in the early days of his presidency, following the January 6, 2021, Capitol insurrection and the refusal of Donald Trump to admit he lost the 2020 election. Republicans, led by Senate Minority Leader Mitch McConnell and House Minority Leader Kevin McCarthy (R-CA), having just supported the bipartisan Consolidated Appropriations Act in December, resisted another large spending bill to respond to the coronavirus pandemic. A group of ten Republican senators responded to the $1.9 trillion Democratic proposal with a $600 billion counteroffer. This was viewed as too great a gap to close through negotiation, so the Democrats passed the $1.9 trillion American Rescue Plan Act through reconciliation in the Senate and through their narrow House majority without a single Republican vote.

The negotiations over Biden's next big initiative started off in a similar place but then got a lot more complicated. The original idea was to pass a multitrillion-dollar bill to comprehensively address the nation's infrastructure needs defined as broadly as in chapter 2 of this book. This consisted of much more than just proposals to fix roads and bridges, to also include education and job training, universal access to broadband communications and safe drinking water, and a significant expansion to the nation's social safety net designed to reduce or eliminate poverty, especially among children and the working poor.

Republicans were only willing to support a far narrower definition of infrastructure, so the White House and Democratic leaders split the effort into two parts: an infrastructure bill that would be passed through bipartisan negotiations, and a social policy bill that would be passed through reconciliation without any Republican votes. The social spending bill was given the name "Build Back Better" (BBB) to make it clear that its elements were central to the economic plan that Joe Biden's campaign promised to deliver. The Democrats wanted to pass both bills before the August recess, with progressives tying the two bills together to maintain leverage over the Senate moderates.

The same dual-track approach was used for bills to defend democracy and protect voting rights. The House passed the For the People Act to counter new election laws emerging from several Republican-controlled states to make it difficult for African Americans and other racial minorities to vote, and to fix many of the election law problems Alice discusses in chapter 11. The House also passed the John Lewis Voting Rights Advancement Act to restore the full protections of the 1965 Voting Rights Act that had been weakened by the Supreme Court in 2013 and 2021. At the same time, Democratic Senator Joe Manchin of West Virginia and Alaska Republican Senator Lisa Murkowski were working to craft a voting rights bill that could get bipartisan support.

Alice would have been disappointed when the Republican Senate leadership and most Republicans voiced opposition to both of the Democratic voting rights and election reform bills that passed in the House in 2021, because Republicans had been instrumental in the bipartisan passage of the Voting Rights Act in 1965 and had overwhelmingly voted to reauthorize it in 2006. The only hope for passage of the new bills rested in suspending or eliminating the Senate filibuster rule. Alice calls for the elimination of the Senate filibuster in chapter 11, but two moderate Democratic senators, Joe Manchin and Arizona's Kyrsten Sinema, announced early on that although they supported the bills, both opposed changing the filibuster rule to pass the bills.

## Biden Gets a Bipartisan Infrastructure Deal as Partisan Legislation Stalls

On August 10, 2021, Senate Majority leader Chuck Schumer (D-NY) brought an infrastructure bill to the floor for a vote. The Infrastructure Investment and Jobs Act passed the Senate by a bipartisan vote of 69 to 30. The Senate had already passed the United States Innovation and Competition Act (USICA) on June 8 with a similar bipartisan vote of 68 to 32. The Senate was getting things done through bipartisan votes to help the economy and the American people. The infrastructure bill invested $1.2 trillion to create jobs across the country in building roads, repairing bridges, expanding access to broadband internet, modernizing the electrical grid, ensuring safe drinking water, and dozens of other priority projects.

The USICA bill was specifically targeted to improving US competitiveness in silicon chip manufacturing, with an estimated $110 billion to $250 billion investment in new manufacturing capacity, research and development, and job skills training to help workers qualify for the new high-paying jobs. The goal was to repatriate computer chip manufacturing from Asia to the US, especially in the midwestern industrial belt, and alleviate the chip shortage that was disrupting supply chains and exacerbating global inflation. However, neither USICA nor the bipartisan infrastructure bill was immediately taken up in the House.

Rather than celebrating the Senate's bipartisan accomplishments and getting the bills quickly to the president's desk for signing, House progressives criticized the infrastructure bill's investments as relatively unimportant compared with the far larger investments of the human capital, place-based social programs, and climate change mitigating Build Back Better bill they viewed as necessary to completing Biden's economic vision and addressing economic inequality. Progressives held up passage of the infrastructure bill for three months, insisting on linkage between the two bills to pressure the same two reluctant moderate senators, Manchin and Sinema, to accept a far larger social spending plan than they believed was prudent, especially as inflation was becoming a major concern to their constituents. This time the issue was not whether Manchin and Sinema would vote to weaken or eliminate the filibuster, because the BBB bill would pass using reconciliation, but their two votes were required to pass the bill with fifty Democrats in the Senate (plus the vice president's tie-breaking vote) over total Republican opposition.

The House progressive Democrats eventually dropped the requirement of linkage between the two bills, and most voted for the infrastructure bill. President Biden signed the Infrastructure Investment and Jobs Act into law on November 15, 2021, vindicating his faith in bipartisanship and making good on his campaign promise to heal America's broken politics by working across party lines to solve problems for the American people. But few Democrats were in a mood to celebrate bipartisanship. Just before Christmas 2021, Manchin broke off negotiations over the BBB bill, disappointing progressive Democrats while the White House vowed to keep fighting to pass the most important elements of the legislation.

As Biden's first year in office ended, the White House wanted to brag about Biden's legislative successes, including the American Rescue Plan, which had passed without any Republican votes, and the bipartisan Infrastructure Investment and Jobs Act. The press, however, was much more interested in covering the BBB bill that did not pass and the tensions, sometimes breaking into open hostility, between the progressive and moderate factions of the Democratic Party. The conflict was put on full display in January 2022 when Biden and the Democratic leadership tried to pass election reform legislation, knowing that they needed but did not have the votes of Senators Sinema and Manchin to change the filibuster rule. President Biden traveled to Atlanta, Georgia, to give a speech that many people heard as charging anyone opposed to changing the filibuster rule, which was fifty Republican senators and two Democratic senators, with being on the side of Bull Conner, a well-known Birmingham, Alabama, politician who used brutal tactics to oppose the civil rights movement in the 1960s. Biden also compared the senators to other historical racists and the speech was seen as a low point in his efforts to change the tone and improve Congress's ability to function.

A few days later, Manchin and Sinema voted with all fifty Republican senators against changing the filibuster rule to allow a vote on the Democrats' package of election reforms, and the measures failed. Democrats said they were putting all senators on record as supporting or opposing voting rights protections, and the Arizona Democratic Party voted to censure

Sinema. Alice would have been disappointed with everyone involved, because the Voting Rights Act is necessary legislation that gives voters tools to fight a long history of racist voter suppression, as detailed in several chapters of this book. She would have been displeased that Republicans reversed their past support for the legislation, especially now, when it is so clearly needed. She would have been frustrated with Manchin and Sinema for holding onto the filibuster in a manner that provided fresh evidence that the filibuster has become a tool for gridlock rather than deliberation and achievement. And she would have been disappointed in the other Democrats for failing to hear, respect, and work to reverse the positions of two of their colleagues. In her view, it is not the lawmakers' job to properly assign blame; it is their job to work with enough of their colleagues to get the deal done and pass legislation. Progressive Democrats reached the end of the year clearly convinced that the lack of success on Build Back Better and voting rights could be blamed on the two moderate senators. Alice would say the progressives and moderates were equally to blame because they failed to reach all available agreements to make progress on both partisan and bipartisan fronts.

## THE CAUSE OF PERPETUAL FRUSTRATION AND STALEMATE

Alice would have seen the disappointments of Biden's first year as highly predictable. Frances Lee and James Curry's research (discussed in chapter 10) describes how hard it is to pass legislation following either the bipartisan or partisan track. When bipartisanship proves difficult or seems unattainable, lawmakers try the partisan track, only to learn it has its own set of difficulties. Democrats learned this in the first years of the Clinton and Obama administrations through protracted battles between progressive Democrats and moderate Democrats over legislation. In 2021, when facing total Republican opposition on key issues, the Democrats had very few votes to spare in the House and none in the Senate, and again things got bogged down.

The repetition of this pattern across three Democratic administrations, spanning three decades, suggests that there is a structural cause for the pattern and in this case, it can be expressed in logic:

A majority of the majority $\neq$ a majority of the whole.

Here is a simple fact: Most Democrats today are progressive in their political views. Progressives are the beating heart of the Democratic coalition, turning out for every election and providing the energy and money to fuel election campaigns. Progressives have been inventive in creating public policy solutions to address poverty, racism, the environment, and many other issues that Alice strongly supported.

Here is another fact: From 1992 through the present, the progressive/liberal wing of the Democratic Party has never been close to a majority of American voters. Public opinion polls differ in their methods and over time, but most estimates of the proportion of all voters who would call themselves liberal Democrats or progressive Democrats range between roughly one-quarter to one-third of the total electorate. Rarely do estimates reach as high as 40 percent and never as high as 51 percent. Democrats have won a lot of elections (and even lost some) by winning a majority of the votes cast, and most Democrats are progressive, but Democrats win elections by combining the votes of progressive Democrats with those of more moderate (and even conservative) Democrats, independents, and even some Republicans.

The same is true in Congress, where, since 1992, progressive/liberal Democrats have never, by themselves, comprised a majority of members in either the House or the Senate. But three times, progressives/liberals have comprised the majority of the party in control of the Senate and the House of Representatives when there was also a Democrat in the White House. In each of these three times, progressives, as the majority of the majority, had high expectations that they could pass a progressive agenda, but they were frustrated by moderate Democrats, mostly in the Senate. Three Democratic presidents appeared weak and ineffective as their legislative agendas were stalled and compromised in protracted intraparty congressional negotiations, and Clinton and Obama saw Democrats' House and Senate majorities erased in disastrous first midterm elections.

It is important to understand that conservative Republicans have also never been a majority of American voters, and they have never held a majority of seats in the Senate or House, and the same can be said of Trump-supporting Republicans. The clearest evidence of this point came on July 27, 2017, when Senator John McCain of Arizona joined two other Republicans to vote thumbs-down on repealing the Affordable Care Act, as well as the small number of Republicans who have cast votes to impeach Trump or investigate January 6.

It is not possible for either side to reach a majority in contemporary American politics without finding common ground with moderates.

Alice uses chapter 4 to dispel the myth that this is a recent phenomenon, taking a close look at the legislative histories of Presidents Franklin Roosevelt and Lyndon Johnson. Large numbers of conservative, segregationist Southern Democrats opposed the most progressive elements of Roosevelt's and Johnson's achievements, which means both presidents passed many of their most celebrated laws by making compromises to earn bipartisan support. There was no time in the 1940s or the 1960s when liberal Democrats comprised the majority of voters or legislators in Congress, and most of the progressive legislation that made up the New Deal and the Great Society was passed by bipartisan coalitions.

The simple fact that progressive Democrats (and conservative Republicans) have sometimes been the majority of the majority but have never been the majority of the whole becomes a cause of perpetual frustration. When combined with the new politics of "no compromise" positions and hardball tactics that are now in fashion for Democrats as well as the Republicans who developed them, this simple misperception about who the majority represents becomes a recipe for protracted intraparty negotiations, but moderate senators have rarely buckled under the pressure tactics. Eventually, progressives (and conservatives) only get what the moderates are willing to agree to. It would be better for American democracy if everyone understood this going into negotiations and was therefore able to resolve them more quickly, and with less rancor and publicly expressed hostility.

## WHAT ABOUT THE "BIG LIE," THE COUP ATTEMPT, AND THE INSURRECTION ON JANUARY 6?

We know that, had she lived to see it, Alice would have been astonished, shocked, and saddened by the events of January 6, 2021. We know this because everyone was. We wish we could have called our mother on that day, just as many Americans had an instinct to do. Had we been able to talk to Alice on January 6, we expect that she would have expressed equal parts sadness and fear. She would have been worried for the safety of her family living in the city we share, for the vice president and congressional members who the mob was sent to threaten, for their staffs, and for the guards and police who were injured protecting them.

The events of that day, unfolding across our television screens (and in real life for those who were there) were unnerving to Americans across the political spectrum. Everyone was knocked off their center, from Sean Hannity and Laura Ingraham to Kevin McCarthy, Mitch McConnell, Ted Cruz, and Lindsey Graham, to Nancy Pelosi, Jamie Raskin, and Alexandria Ocasio Cortez. We know this from their public statements, speeches, tweets, and instant messages sent on that day and later uncovered by journalists and the House Select Committee to Investigate the January 6 Attack on the United States Capitol.

Within weeks or even days, many Republicans changed their position from revulsion back to support for Donald Trump. Artful talking points helped elected Republicans avoid the question of whether Joe Biden had legitimately won the 2020 election, while Republican candidates for offices from state legislator to the US Senate began courting Trump's endorsement in the upcoming 2022 midterm elections by openly embracing his false claims of 2020 election fraud. The Fox News Channel was initially a house divided over the question of whether Biden won the election, but decisions made by viewers to tune into more radical Trump-supporting media and by top executives turned the network toward a full embrace of Trump's false positions on the election, the insurrection, and, most consequentially, the anti-science position on face mask mandates and coronavirus vaccines. The defeated president was leading a movement denying he was defeated, and he had the support and trust of enough voters and Republican elites to gain effective control of the Republican networked party structure.

Once Alice recovered from the shock of January 6, we believe we know just how she would have responded, and we know the advice she would have offered to all those who see this moment as a time to stand for democracy, the truth, the rule of law, and the Constitution. It is written on every page of this book. The book started with her premonition that "the American Experiment is in danger of failing," to again quote the first line that she penned. Although she did not live to see the extent to which her fears would be justified, she was witness to many of Trump's words and actions that we now see as consistent with his increasingly revealed authoritarian impulses.

We know Alice was alarmed by Trump's endorsements of thuggery at his 2016 campaign rallies, where he began taunting the media and led the crowd in chants to lock up his political opponents. His efforts to delegitimize the 2016 election results as "rigged" mostly ended when he was declared the winner, but his assault on the institutions of democracy continued taking different forms that were relentless in their consistency. In addition to constant attacks on the free press as "the enemy of the people," these included rejections of the independence of the judicial branch, hostility toward congressional oversight over the executive branch, and continued efforts to undermine and politicize the professional diplomatic corps and career civil servants throughout the "deep state" in law enforcement, intelligence, and independent science-based regulatory commissions and agencies.

Chapters 10 and 11 include her thoughts on these breaches of the guardrails of democracy and the call to defend the institutions that are designed to be separate and insulated from interference from the chief executive. From her leadership positions and experience at the Congressional Budget Office and Federal Reserve, Alice had a strong appreciation for the importance of nonpartisan and unpoliticized expertise in economic analysis and forecasting, and she defended the necessity of truth-seeking expertise in science, public health and safety, military intelligence, and countless other critical areas. But it is unlikely that, in 2019, Alice could have anticipated the broad and deliberate Trump assault to undermine all the power centers that were designed to be independent from his control, to serve as a check on his power, or to release information to the public that challenged his narrative.

America is still learning the truth about the planning for January 6 and its connection to broader efforts to change the outcome of the 2020 presidential election after the votes were cast. The dogged efforts of the House Investigative Committee and its subpoena power, combined with the efforts of law enforcement agencies and investigative journalists, are revealing a criminal conspiracy to use violence, intimidation, and fraud to reverse the election results and return Donald Trump to power. With the release of the committee's full report, citizens are likely to gain confirmation that the violence at the US Capitol on the day Joe Biden would be certified as the 2020 winner was planned, coordinated, and connected to a propaganda campaign to sow distrust of the election results and efforts to replace slates of electors with fraudulent slates of Trump supporters.

Alice was aware that many of her professional colleagues, like William Galston of Brookings, were illuminating Trump's connections to some of the darkest racist and authoritarian impulses in American and European politics and history, but neither she nor her colleagues could have imagined the number of Confederate and Nazi symbols on display on January 6, and the level of coordination with white supremacist paramilitary organizations. Galston and others, like Stanford University's Francis Fukuyama, describe America as backsliding toward failure and warn of danger when the world's leading democracy is internally divided and stops acting as a reliable supporter of liberal democracies, leaving a vacuum as Russia's President Vladimir Putin and China's President Xi Jinping seek to expand their own territorial control and advance authoritarianism globally. Trump and many of his key allies (including Mike Pompeo, his former Secretary of State, and Tucker Carlson, his message carrier at Fox News) initially backed Putin before he invaded Ukraine targeting civilians for death destruction and appalling war crimes.

For Alice, the most distressing aspect of January 6 would have been that it marked more of a beginning than an end of the direct assault on truth, reason, and American democracy. Alice was a rationalist who believed in truth, facts, logic, and persuasion to settle political differences. Trump's evidence free assertions of 2020 voter fraud, the "Big Lie" and his supporters blind acceptance of the false claim, marked the culmination of a walled garden of disinformation, propaganda, and conspiracy theories that reject all evidence and reason. Alice would have been dismayed and insisted that Trump's rejection of truth and reason is inseparable from his rejection of democracy. And Alice would have been alarmed that the falsehoods have become so much a part of mainstream political discourse with several Q-anon embracing politicians holding seats in Congress and dozens of others seeking office, and Trumps endorsement in 2022 races for offices up and down the ballot.

While there have been some heroic counterexamples, far too few Republican politicians are standing up to Trump's clearly stated ambition to return to power by any means necessary, while many other Republican politicians spread the "Big Lie" to win Trump's favor and endorsement in their elections. Trump has effective control over the Republican National Committee and official Republican Party committees in many states. One of the two great parties in American politics has been taken over by people who do not believe in democracy or the truth as the way to settle political differences.

With all this being said, would Alice still call for greater bipartisanship? The answer would be an emphatic yes! The greater the actual threat to American democracy, the more important it is to unite to defend it. The Democrats would be making a catastrophic error to try to defeat this assault on democracy by themselves. It will take a coalition of progressive Democrats, moderate Democrats, independents, moderate Republicans, and conservative Republicans who believe in democracy and the rule of law to move Congress to effectively oppose the Trump faction. It will require exposing the Trump base for what it is—a small minority of American voters—by winning the support of independents and those Republicans who are more loyal to their country than to their political party.

To be clear, no one is suggesting that the minds of those in Trump's loyal base can be changed or even reached through the wall of "Make America Great Again" propaganda. The Oath Keepers cannot be talked into true patriotism, defined as support for the Constitution and the rule of law. There are roughly a dozen Senate Republicans, and many more than that in the House, who have taken Trump's side against democracy in a way that makes attempts at persuasion fruitless. House Minority Leader Kevin McCarthy has met his moment of history and chosen the wrong side, but the same is far from clear for Senate Minority Leader Mitch McConnell.

That McConnell agreed to support the Infrastructure Investment and Jobs Act and USICA was a major indication that he rejects Trump's definition of loyalty and partisanship. The fact that he has expressed a willingness to discuss changing the Electoral Count Act—the 1887 law defining the procedures for certifying national elections that Trump's coup attempt sought to exploit—is an even clearer sign that McConnell could be willing to join a coalition to defend democracy. Realistically speaking, American democracy will not be saved without the active participation of Mitch McConnell and the Republican senators who will join in if he asks them. If defending democracy is truly the Democrats' highest priority, they must work to include McConnell on the side of those who would defend American democracy against those who would seek to undermine it.

There are a lot of conflicted Republicans in the electorate, and in Congress, who are just coming to understand what is now at stake. The list of potential Republican members for an imagined "Defend American Democracy Caucus" starts with the thirty Senate Republicans and thirteen House Republicans who voted for the infrastructure bill over Trump's opposition. There are twenty-eight Republican members of the House Problem Solvers Caucus who could be approached with the proposition that maintaining the United States of America as a functioning democracy and a beacon to the free world is a problem to be solved independently from other, more mundane issues. The question must be posed simply as one of whether Americans want to live in a constitutional democracy, with the rule of law and a free press, or lose it, perhaps forever?

Israel recently faced the question of how to save constitutional democracy from the corrupt and authoritarian impulses of its prime minister, Binyamin Netanyahu. The solution was to form a coalition of eight political parties that span the ideological spectrum, from the pro-settler Yamina Party on the right to the centrist Yesh Atid and even including the Islamist United Arab List, with the single point of agreement being that Netanyahu's slide toward authoritarianism and corruption made removing him from office the only way to preserve Israeli democracy. Deep divisions in Israeli society remain to be healed, but the country will address them as a democracy. America needs its own version of this solution to stand up to the authoritarian impulses of Trumpism and defeat it electorally.

In our democracy, reforming the Electoral Count Act is imperative to ensuring that free and fair elections continue. If Joe Biden, Mitch McConnell, Chuck Schumer, Nancy Pelosi, Bernie Sanders, Joe Manchin, and the House progressives cannot find common purpose in defending the Constitution, then the United States is in even deeper trouble than it now appears. Everyone has a veto, so nothing will pass unless everyone agrees. Rather than trying to pass any particular agenda item that faces opposition, the top priority must be to pass whatever Democrats and pro-Constitution Republicans can agree on. Only by uniting progressive and moderate Democrats with moderate and conservative Republicans can those who would defend American democracy hope to prevail against all threats to it, foreign and domestic.

In 2018, Alice set out to write a book whose main themes were changing the rules and changing the tone of politics in Congress, in the states, and throughout the country, not just to avert a constitutional disaster, but more simply to get things done to solve real problems so that the many people who have tuned out of politics would agree that American democracy is worth saving. Alice believed the big problems can be solved if Americans work together toward consensus solutions, and in many cases the framework for workable compromises has already been hammered out but never adopted. Alice would hope that Americans will someday look back on January 6, 2021, as the date we hit peak government dysfunction, and that there will be enough leaders in both parties (leaving aside those who are all in with Trump's delusions) who now see the limits of political hardball tactics and the politics of never compromise. Alice did not want to write a book for political scientists, economists, and public policy elites. She was calling on all Americans, inside government or outside, to get involved in our jobs, in our communities, and, by joining groups, in efforts to find common ground, get things done, and make inclusive democracy work.

# NOTES

CHAPTER 1

1. Clara Hendrickson, Mark Muro, and William A. Galston, "Countering the Geography of Discontent: Strategies for Left-Behind Places," Brookings Institution, November 2018, brookings.edu/research/countering-the-geography-of-discontent-strategies-for-left-behind-places/.

2. A filibuster is an attempt to "block or delay Senate action on a bill or other matter by debating it at length, by offering numerous procedural motions, or by any other delaying or obstructive actions." United States Senate, Glossary, www.senate.gov/about/glossary.htm#F.

3. The Hastert Rule, named after former Speaker Dennis Hastert (R-IL), is an informal guiding principle for Republican House leaders that dictates most of the majority party must support any measure before it comes to a vote.

4. Forrest Maltzman and Charles R. Shipan, "Change, Continuity, and the Evolution of the Law," *American Journal of Political Science* 52:2 (2008), 252–67, jstor.org/stable/25193812.

5. James M. Curry and Frances E. Lee, "Congress at Work," in *Can America Govern Itself?* edited by Frances E. Lee and Nolan McCarty (Cambridge University Press, 2019), 181–219, https://doi.org/10.1017/9781108667357.008.

6. Clio Andris and others, "The Rise of Partisanship and Super-Cooperators in the U.S. House of Representatives," *PLoS One* 10:4 (2015), https://doi.org/10.1371/journal.pone.0123507.

7. Sarah A. Binder, "Polarized We Govern?" Brookings Institution, May 27, 2014, brookings.edu/research/polarized-we-govern/.

CHAPTER 2

1. Inflation returned as a problem in 2021 but this is written from a 2019 perspective.

2. Dionissi Aliprantis and Daniel R. Carroll, "What Is Behind the Persistence of the Racial Wealth Gap?" Federal Reserve Bank of Cleveland, February 28, 2019, clevelandfed
.org/newsroom-and-events/publications/economic-commentary/2019-economic
-commentaries/ec-201903-what-is-behind-the-persistence-of-the-racial-wealth
-gap.aspx.

3. Carol Graham and Sergio Pinto, "Unequal Hopes and Lives in the USA: Optimism, Race, Place, and Premature Mortality," *Journal of Population Economics* 32 (2018), 665–733, brookings.edu/wp-content/uploads/2017/06/working-paper-104-web-v2
.pdf.

4. Martha Ross and Nicole E. Bateman, "Meet the Low-Wage Workforce," Brookings Institution, November 7, 2019, brookings.edu/research/meet-the-low-wage-workforce/.

5. Annie Lowrey, "Who Broke the Economy?" review of *The Captured Economy: How the Powerful Become Richer, Slow Down Growth, and Increase Inequality*, by Brink Lindsey and Steven M. Teles, *The Atlantic*, December 11, 2017, theatlantic.com
/business/archive/2017/12/captured-economy/547967/.

6. There are positive aspects of the SALT deduction, but even supporters admit capping the deduction has the effect of raising taxes on wealthy individuals living in the high-tax states where Democrats tend to be the majority. See Tracy Gordon, "The Price We Pay for Capping the SALT Deduction," Tax Policy Center, February 15, 2018, taxpolicycenter.org/taxvox/price-we-pay-capping-salt-deduction.

7. See, for example, Angela Hanks, Danyelle Solomon, and Christian E. Weller, "Systematic Inequality: How America's Structural Racism Helped Create the Black-White Wealth Gap," Center for American Progress, February 21, 2018, americanprogress
.org/issues/race/reports/2018/02/21/447051/systematic-inequality/.

8. Ryan Nunn and Megan Mumford, "The Incomplete Progress of Women in the Labor Market," Hamilton Project, October 2017, hamiltonproject.org/assets/files
/incomplete_progress_women_in_labor_force_NunnMumford.pdf.

9. Supreme Court Justice Ruth Bader Ginsburg was at Harvard Law School about the same time I was at Harvard getting my economics Ph.D., and I can attest to many experiences similar to those depicted in the movie *On the Basis of Sex*.

10. The Hamilton Project has done a terrific job of chronicling geographic inequality in papers like this one: Ryan Nunn, Jana Parsons, and Jay Shambaugh, "The Geography of Prosperity," Hamilton Project, September 2018, brookings.edu/wp-content
/uploads/2018/09/PBP_FramingChapter_compressed_20190425.pdf.

11. Ethan Kaplan, Jörg Spenkuch, and Rebecca Sullivan studied county-level and precinct-level election results for president and congress and found that voters are increasingly sorting themselves into Democratic and Republican enclaves. See Ethan Kaplan, Jörg Spenkuch, and Rebecca Sullivan, "Measuring Geographic Polarization: Theory and Long-Run Evidence," January 2019, https://www.semantic
scholar.org/paper/Measuring-Geographic-Polarization%3A-Theory-and-Kaplan
/f7d46811792294547c17370b99f38977755798d4.

12. Bill Bishop, *The Big Sort: Why the Clustering of Like-Minded America is Tearing Us Apart* (Boston: Mariner Books, 2009).

13. See Mark E. Schweitzer, "What's Gone Wrong (and Right) in the Industrial Heartland?" Federal Reserve Bank of Cleveland, September 22, 2017, clevelandfed.org/en/newsroom-and-events/publications/economic-commentary/2017-economic-commentaries/ec-201714-whats-gone-wrong-and-right-in-the-industrial-heartland.aspx.

14. See Andre M. Perry, Jonathan Rothwell, and David Harshbarger, "The Devaluation of Assets in Black Neighborhoods: The Case of Residential Property," Brookings Institution, November 27, 2018. Perry, Rothwell, and Harshbarger's data analysis revealed that the true cost of housing discrimination is $48,000 per average home in majority Black neighborhoods compared with similar homes in neighborhoods that are nearly exclusively white.

15. Bradley Hardy, Trevon Logan, and John Parman have studied historical and current racially discriminatory policies and their implications for persistent gaps between races in income, wealth, and education. See Bradley L. Hardy, Trevon D. Logan, and John Parman, "The Historical Role of Race and Policy for Regional Inequality," Hamilton Project, September 28, 2018, hamiltonproject.org/papers/the_historical_role_of_race_and_policy_for_regional_inequality.

16. Hart Research Associates/Public Opinion Strategies, "August 2019 Social Trends Monitor," Study #19305, NBC News/Wall Street Journal Survey, documentcloud.org/documents/6336787-19305-NBCWSJ-August-Social-Trends-Poll.html.

17. Kim Parker, Rich Morin, and Juliana Menasce Horowitz, "Looking to the Future, Public Sees an America in Decline on Many Fronts," Pew Research Center, March 21, 2019, pewsocialtrends.org/2019/03/21/public-sees-an-america-in-decline-on-many-fronts/.

18. One of Alice Rivlin's earliest papers was this 1962 assessment of state and local capacity to raise revenue and fund local needs, serving as an analyst with Selma Mushkin as senior analyst. Selma J. Mushkin and Alice M. Rivlin, "Measures of State and Local Fiscal Capacity and Tax Effort," Congressional Advisory Commission on Intergovernmental Relations, M-16, October 1962, https://library.unt.edu/gpo/acir/Reports/information/M-16.pdf.

19. Alan Berube, "Policy to Help People and Help Places is Not a Zero-Sum Game," Brookings Institution, August 7, 2019, brookings.edu/research/policy-to-help-people-and-help-places-is-not-a-zero-sum-game/.

20. Thomas Piketty and Emmanuel Saez, "Income Inequality in The United States, 1913–1998," The Quarterly Journal of Economics, Vol. CXVIII Issue 1, February 2003. https://eml.berkeley.edu/~saez/pikettyqje.pdf.

21. Evan Smith, "TribLive: A Conversation with John Boehner," *Texas Tribune*, May 12, 2014, texastribune.org/2014/05/12/triblive-a-conversation-with-john-boehner/.

22. Paul Ryan, "Expanding Opportunity in America," remarks as prepared for delivery at the American Enterprise Institute, July 24, 2014, aei.org/research-products/speech/expanding-opportunity-in-america/.

23. Transcript of Teacher Town Hall, Federal Reserve Board of Governors, February 6, 2019, federalreserve.gov/mediacenter/files/teacher-town-hall-transcript-20190206.pdf.

24. Joseph Stiglitz and others, "Rewriting the Rules of the American Economy," Roosevelt Institute, May 12, 2015, https://rooseveltinstitute.org/publications/rewriting-the-rules-of-the-american-economy/.

25. The reader is reminded that this was based on 2019 projections. The actual deficit for the 2020 fiscal year was greater than $3 trillion.

26. See Adam Loony, "Will Opportunity Zones Help Distressed Residents or Be a Tax Cut for Gentrification?" Brookings Institution, February 26, 2018, brookings.edu/blog/up-front/2018/02/26/will-opportunity-zones-help-distressed-residents-or-be-a-tax-cut-for-gentrification/.

27. Clara Hendrickson, "Why Democrats Don't Have a Plan to Save 'Left-Behind' America," *Politico*, October 23, 2019, politico.com/magazine/story/2019/10/23/democrats-regional-inequality-plan-229869.

28. Robert J. Barro and Xavier Sala-i-Martin, "Convergence," *Journal of Political Economy* 100:2 (1992), 223–51, https://dash.harvard.edu/handle/1/3451299.

29. Benjamin Austin, Edward Glaeser, and Lawrence H. Summers, "Saving the Heartland: Place-Based Policies in 21st Century America," Brookings Institution, March 8, 2018, brookings.edu/bpea-articles/saving-the-heartland-place-based-policies-in-21st-century-america/.

30. Graham and Pinto, "Unequal Hopes and Lives in the U.S."

31. Thomas L. Friedman, "Where American Politics Can Still Work: From the Bottom Up," opinion, *New York Times*, July 3, 2018, nytimes.com/2018/07/03/opinion/community-revitalization-lancaster.html.

32. Thomas L. Friedman, *Thank You For Being Late: An Optimist's Guide to Thriving in the Age of Accelerations* (New York: Farrar, Straus, and Giroux, 2016).

33. Alan Berube and others, "Building Shared Prosperity in America's Cities," Brookings Institution, June 19, 2018, brookings.edu/research/building-shared-prosperity-in-americas-cities/.

34. James Fallows and Deborah Fallows, *Our Towns: A 100,000 Mile Journey into the Heart of America* (New York: Pantheon, 2018).

35. Mushkin and Rivlin, "State and Local Fiscal Capacity."

36. Because most public school funding depends on local taxes, schools in affluent districts have nearly three times as many resources as schools in low-income districts. This report details the data and the impact on students and teachers: Cory Turner and others, "Why America's Schools Have a Money Problem," NPR, April 18, 2016, npr.org/2016/04/18/474256366/why-americas-schools-have-a-money-problem.

37. Michael Jacobs and Mariana Mazzucato, *Rethinking Capitalism: Economics and Policy for Sustainable and Inclusive Growth* (Hoboken, NJ: Wiley-Blackwell, 2016).

38. See Richard R. Nelson and Sidney G. Winter, *An Evolutionary Theory of Economic Change* (Cambridge, MA: Belknap Press, 1985).

39. Sidney G. Winter and others, *Innovation and the Evolution of Industries: History-Friendly Models* (Cambridge University Press, 2016).

40. Jacobs and Mazzucato, *Rethinking Capitalism*.

41.  Alice M. Rivlin, *Reviving the American Dream* (Brookings Institution Press, 1992).

42.  Justin McCarthy, "Americans Still More Trusting of Local Than State Government," Gallup, October 8, 2018, https://news.gallup.com/poll/243563/americans-trusting -local-state-government.aspx.

43.  Jerome Powell, "Semiannual Monetary Policy Report to the Congress," Testimony before the U.S. Senate Committee on Banking, Housing, and Urban Affairs, February 26, 2019, federalreserve.gov/newsevents/testimony/powell20190226a.htm.

44.  Kansas Legislature, S Sub HB 2117, kslegislature.org/li_2012/b2011_12/measures /hb2117/.

45.  "Data: Breaking Down the Where and Why of K-12 Spending," *Education Week*, September 2019, edweek.org/ew/section/multimedia/the-where-and-why-of-k-12 -spending.html.

46.  Alexander Bolton, Juliegrace Burke, and Scott Wong, "Trump's Pursuit of Infrastructure Deal Hits GOP Roadblock," *The Hill*, May 3, 2019, https://thehill.com /policy/transportation/441909-trumps-infrastructure-plan-hits-gop-roadblock.

47.  "2017 Infrastructure Report Card" (n.d.), infrastructurereportcard.org.

48.  Business Roundtable, "Infrastructure" (n.d.), businessroundtable.org/policy-pers pectives/infrastructure.

49.  National Association of Manufacturers, "NAM Renews Call for Significant Infrastructure Investment," Press Release, April 29, 2019, nam.org/nam-renews-call-for -significant-infrastructure-investment-2314/.

## CHAPTER 3

1.  James Madison, *Federalist* No. 10 (1787).

2.  Alexander Hamilton, *Federalist* No. 9 (1787).

3.  James Madison, *Federalist* No. 58 (1788), https://founders.archives.gov/documents /Hamilton/01-04-02-0207.

4.  Alexander Hamilton, *Federalist* No. 22 (1787), https://founders.archives.gov /documents/Hamilton/01-04-02-0179.

5.  James Madison, *Federalist* No. 10 (1787).

6.  John Stuart Mill, "On Liberty" (1859).

7.  Center for Legislative Archives, "17th Amendment to the U.S. Constitution: Direct Election of U.S. Senators," National Archives (n.d.), archives.gov/legislative/features /17th-amendment.

8.  The population comparisons here are based on the first census, taken in 1790, which may have missed more than a few people, and the comparisons differ depending on who gets counted, which is discussed next.

9.  "State Population Totals and Components of Change: 2010-2019," US Census Bureau, census.gov/data/tables/time-series/demo/popest/2010s-state-total.html.

10.  For more information, see Ankita Rao, Erum Salam, and Juweek Adolphe, "Which US States Make It Hardest to Vote?" *The Guardian*, January 21, 2020, theguardian .com/us-news/ng-interactive/2019/nov/07/which-us-states-hardest-vote-supression -election.

11. Phillip A. Wallach, "Prospects for Partisan Realignment: Lessons from the Demise of the Whigs," Brookings Institution, March 6, 2017, brookings.edu/research /prospects-for-partisan-realignment-lessons-from-the-demise-of-the-whigs/.

12. "The Caning of Senator Charles Sumner," US Senate, May 22, 1856, senate.gov /artandhistory/history/minute/The_Caning_of_Senator_Charles_Sumner.htm.

13. "Landmark Legislation: The Fourteenth Amendment," US Senate (n.d.), senate.gov /artandhistory/history/common/generic/14thAmendment.htm; United States Senate, "Landmark Legislation: The Fifteenth Amendment" (n.d.), senate.gov/artand history/history/common/generic/15thAmendment.htm.

14. Mark L. Bradley, *The Army and Reconstruction, 1865-1877*, US Army Center of Military History (2015), https://history.army.mil/html/books/075/75-18/cmhPub_75 -18.pdf.

15. J. E. Hansan, "Jim Crow Laws and Racial Segregation," Social Welfare History Project, Virginia Commonwealth University (2011), https://socialwelfare.library.vcu .edu/eras/civil-war-reconstruction/jim-crow-laws-andracial-segregation/.

16. "Brown v. Board at Fifty: 'With an Even Hand,'" Library of Congress (n.d.), loc.gov /exhibits/brown/brown-segregation.html.

17. Lisa D. Cook, "Violence and Economic Activity: Evidence from African American Patents, 1870 to 1940," Michigan State University, October 2013, https://lisadcook .net/wp-content/uploads/2014/02/pats_paper17_1013_final_web.pdf.

18. "The Great Migration, 1910 to 1970," US Census Bureau Library, September 13, 2012, census.gov/dataviz/visualizations/020/.

19. Gary B. Nash and others, *The American People: Creating a Nation and a Society*, 5th ed. (New York: Addison Wesley Longman, 2000).

20. Drew E. VandeCreek, "Race and Ethnicity in Gilded-Age Illinois," Northern Illinois University Digital Library (n.d.), https://digital.lib.niu.edu/illinois/gildedage /race; Katie Bacon, "The Dark Side of the Gilded Age," *The Atlantic*, June 2007, theatlantic.com/magazine/archive/2007/06/the-dark-side-of-the-gilded-age /306012/.

21. Frances E. Lee, "Patronage, Logrolls, and 'Polarization': Congressional Parties of the Gilded Age, 1876–1896," *Studies in American Political Development* 30:2 (October 2016), 116–127.

22. Arthur Schlesinger Jr., "The Crisis of the American Party System," in *Political Parties and the Modern State*, edited by Richard L. McCormick (Rutgers University Press, 1984).

## CHAPTER 4

1. Theodore Roosevelt, *The Outlook*, Mem. Ed. XIV, 220, Nat. Ed XII, 237 (November 18, 1914).

2. Char Miller, "Play, Work, and Politics: The Remarkable Partnership of Theodore Roosevelt and Giffors Pinchot," in *Theodore Roosevelt, Naturalist in the Arena*, edited by Char Miller and Clay S. Jackson (University of Nebraska Press, 2020), 115.

3.  Thomas G. Dyer, "Theodore Roosevelt and the Idea of Race" (LSU Press, 1992).

4.  "Cloture Rule, March 8, 1917," US Senate (n.d.), senate.gov/about/powers-procedures /filibusters-cloture/senate-adopts-cloture-rule.htm.

5.  Sarah A. Binder and Steven S. Smith, *Politics or Principle? Filibustering in the United States Senate* (Brookings Institution Press, 1996), brookings.edu/book/politics-or -principle/.

6.  Sarah A. Binder, "The History of the Filibuster," Testimony before the US Senate Committee on Rules and Administration, April 22, 2010, brookings.edu/testimonies /the-history-of-the-filibuster/.

7.  Price Fishback and Valentina Kachanovskaya, "The Politics of the New Deal," Hoover Institution, July 19, 2016, hoover.org/research/politics-new-deal.

8.  William E. Leuchtenburg, "Franklin D. Roosevelt: The American Franchise," UVA Miller Center (n.d.), https://millercenter.org/president/fdroosevelt/the-american -franchise.

9.  David B. Woolner, "How Trump and Congress Failed the First 100 Days Test," Roosevelt Institute Blog, April 28, 2017, https://rooseveltinstitute.org/2017/04/28 /how-trump-and-congress-failed-the-first-100-days-test/.

10. "Public Works Administration (PWA), 1933-1943," Living New Deal (n.d.), https:// livingnewdeal.org/glossary/public-works-administration-pwa-1933-1943/.

11. "George Norris, July 11, 1861," US Senate (n.d.), senate.gov/artandhistory/history /minute/George_Norris.htm.

12. "Social Security History: 1935 Congressional Debates on Social Security," Social Security Administration (n.d.), ssa.gov/history/tally.html.

13. "The GI Bill: 20th Century America's Greatest Legislation," American Legion (n.d.), https://centennial.legion.org/gi-bill.

14. Kimberly Quick, "The Myth of the 'Natural' Neighborhood," Century Foundation, March 23, 2016, https://tcf.org/content/commentary/11312/.

15. Kilolo Kijakazi, Karen Smith, and Charmaine Runes, "African American Economic Security and the Role of Social Security," Urban Institute, July 2019, urban.org/sites /default/files/publication/100697/african_american_economic_security_and_the _role_of_social_security.pdf.

16. Otis Rolley, "The New Deal Made America's Racial Inequality Worse. We Can't Make the Same Mistake with Covid-19 Economic Crisis." Rockefeller Foundation, June 11, 2020, rockefellerfoundation.org/blog/the-new-deal-made-americas-racial-inequality -worse-we-cant-make-the-same-mistake-with-covid-19-economic-crisis/.

17. Leuchtenburg, "Franklin D. Roosevelt: The American Franchise."

18. Kari Frederickson, *The Dixiecrat Revolt and the End of the Solid South, 1932-1968* (University of North Carolina Press, March 2001).

19. Alonzo L. Hamby, "Harry S. Truman: Impact and Legacy," UVA Miller Center (n.d.), https://millercenter.org/president/truman/impact-and-legacy.

20. "President Truman and Civil Rights," White House Historical Association (n.d.), whitehousehistory.org/president-truman-and-civil-rights.

21. Rudolph G. Penner, "How Eisenhower and Congressional Democrats Balanced a Budget," Tax Policy Center, December 17, 2012, www.taxpolicycenter.org/taxvox /how-eisenhower-and-congressional-democrats-balanced-budget.

22. US Department of Commerce, "Current Population Reports: Consumer Income," US Census Bureau, October 1955, www2.census.gov/library/publications/1955 /demographics/p60-19.pdf.

23. "The Struggle for Civil Rights," UVA Miller Center (n.d.), https://millercenter.org /the-presidency/educational-resources/age-of-eisenhower/struggle-civil-rights.

24. Michael A. Boozer, Alan B. Kreuger, and Shari Wolkin, "Race and School Quality Since *Brown v. Board of Education*," in *Brookings Papers on Economic Activity: Microeconomics, 1992*, edited by Clifford Winston (Brookings Institution Press, 1992), brookings.edu/wp-content/uploads/1992/01/1992_bpeamicro_boozer.pdf.

25. "The Modern Civil Rights Movement and the Kennedy Administration," John F. Kennedy Presidential Library and Museum (n.d.), jfklibrary.org/learn/about-jfk/jfk -in-history/civil-rights-movement.

26. Ibid.

27. "The Senate and Civil Rights: Cloture and Final Passage of the Civil Rights Act of 1964," US Senate (n.d.), senate.gov/artandhistory/history/civil_rights/cloture_final passage.htm.

28. "About Filibusters and Cloture," US Senate (n.d.), senate.gov/artandhistory/history /common/briefing/Filibuster_Cloture.htm.

29. See "The Civil Rights Act of 1964: A Long Struggle for Freedom," Library of Congress (n.d.), loc.gov/exhibits/civil-rights-act/civil-rights-act-of-1964.html; "Civil Rights Filibuster Ended, June 10, 1964," US Senate (n.d.), senate.gov/about/powers -procedures/filibusters-cloture/civil-rights-filibuster-ended.htm.

30. Ibram X. Kendi, "The Civil Rights Act Was a Victory against Racism. But Racists Also Won," *Washington Post*, July 2, 2017, washingtonpost.com/news/made-by -history/wp/2017/07/02/the-civil-rights-act-was-a-victory-against-racism-but -racists-also-won/.

31. Lyndon B. Johnson, "January 8, 1964: State of the Union," UVA Miller Center (n.d.), https://millercenter.org/the-presidency/presidential-speeches/january-8-1964 -state-union.

32. Lyndon B. Johnson, "Remarks in Athens at Ohio University," delivered May 7, 1964, American Presidency Project, UC Santa Barbara, presidency.ucsb.edu/documents /remarks-athens-ohio-university.

33. Lyndon B. Johnson, "The Great Society," delivered May 22, 1964, American Rhetoric.com, http://hwcdn.libsyn.com/p/0/d/a/0dad185b8ba10c4f/Lyndon_Baines _Johnson_-_The_Great_Society.pdf?c_id=16351496&cs_id=16351496&destination _id=483011&expiration=1583279592&hwt=34e4807f986660cef811abf1fc702e53.

34. See Wilbur J. Cohen, "Reflections on the Enactment of Medicare and Medicaid," *Healthcare Finance Review*, December 1985 (Supplement), 3–11, ncbi.nlm.nih.gov /pmc/articles/PMC4195078/; Julian E. Zelizer, "How Medicare Was Made," *New Yorker*, February 15, 2015, newyorker.com/news/news-desk/medicare-made.

35. The vote of the final passage of the Social Security Amendments of 1965 was 307 to 116, with Republicans voting 70 to 68. The act passed the Senate 70 to 24, with 13 Republicans in favor and 17 opposed. "Vote Tallies for Passage of Medicare in 1965," Social Security Administration (n.d.), ssa.gov/history/tally65.html.

36. Alice M. Rivlin, "Republicans' Wrong Approach to Tackling Medicaid," RealClear Health, July 24, 2017, realclearhealth.com/articles/2017/07/24/republicans_are_tackling_medicaid_wrong_110682.html.

37. Barry Goldwater and Brent Bozell Jr., *The Conscience of a Conservative* (Lawrence, KS: Neeland Media, 1960).

38. Andrew E. Busch, "The Goldwater Myth," *Wall Street Journal,* January 11, 2006, wsj.com/articles/SB122531053433481295.

39. Kevin D. Williamson, "Desegregation, Before *Brown*," *National Review,* April 29, 2013, nationalreview.com/2013/04/desegregation-brown-kevin-d-williamson/.

40. "Thurmond to Bolt Democrats Today," *New York Times*, September 16, 1964, www.nytimes.com/1964/09/16/archives/thurmond-to-bolt-democrats-today-south-carolinian-will-join-gop-and.html.

41. The "Daisy" commercial officially aired only once. It can be seen here: youtube.com/watch?v=2cwqHB6QeUw.

42. Larry J. Sabato, "How Goldwater Changed Campaigns Forever," *Politico*, October 27, 2014, politico.com/magazine/story/2014/10/barry-goldwater-lasting-legacy-112210.

43. The LBJ 1964 Presidential campaign ad "Confessions of a Republican" did not air in the South, but it can be seen here: youtube.com/watch?v=LiG0AE8zdTU.

44. Kimberly Amadeo, "US Real GDP Growth Rate by Year Compared to Inflation and Unemployment," *The Balance*, January 30, 2020, thebalance.com/u-s-gdp-growth-3306008.

45. E. J. Dionne Jr., *Why the Right Went Wrong: Conservatism—From Goldwater to Trump and Beyond* (New York: Simon & Schuster, 2016).

46. Ken Hughes, "Richard Nixon: Domestic Affairs," UVA Miller Center (n.d.), https://millercenter.org/president/nixon/domestic-affairs.

47. Tim McMahon, "Historical Inflation Rate," InflationData.com, https://inflationdata.com/Inflation/Inflation_Rate/HistoricalInflation.aspx#table.

48. Jeffrey H. Birnbaum, "Ford Eventually Tamed Stagflation," Chron.com, December 29, 2006, www.chron.com/business/article/Ford-eventually-tamed-stagflation-1878125.php.

## CHAPTER 5

1. I advocated streamlining the committee structure on the Hill in testimony in 1973, including combining the appropriations and authorizing functions into a single set of "program committees." My conviction that such reforms would help Congress function more effectively was strengthened by my CBO experience and subsequent observation of the cumbersome congressional committee structure.

2. Democrats had demonized Barry Goldwater so much during the 1964 campaign—painting him not only as a hardhearted meanie who wanted to take away seniors'

Social Security, but also as a dangerous Cold War hawk likely to start a nuclear war—that I was surprised by the pleasant, gentlemanly senator I met when I started CBO about ten years later. When I left CBO in 1983, I received a lovely handwritten note from Senator Goldwater complimenting me on the fairness with which I had managed CBO.

3. Robert Shogan noted the change in Dole. See Robert Shogan, "Dole Joins Supply-Siders as Last Great GOP Convert," *Los Angeles Times*, September 6, 1995, latimes .com/archives/la-xpm-1995-09-06-mn-42698-story.html.

4. In his acceptance speech for the Republican nomination, Dole said, "Taxes for a family of four making $35,000 a year would be reduced by more than half—56 percent to be exact. And that's a big, big reduction. It means you will have a president who will help small businesses, the businesses that create most new jobs, by reducing the capital gains tax rate by 50 percent. Cut it in half." See "Text of Robert Dole's Speech to the Republican National Convention, August 15, 1996," CNN, cnn .com/ALLPOLITICS/1996/conventions/san.diego/transcripts/0815/dole.fdch.shtml.

5. They had a better case to make that Speaker of the House Newt Gingrich was hostile to Medicare. John MacDonald, "Gingrich Has Difficulty Escaping Medicare Comments," *Hartford Courant*, November 11, 1995, courant.com/news/connecticut /hc-xpm-1995-11-11-9511110142-story.html.

6. I expressed my admiration for Senator Dole in a June 1993 op-ed chiding him to change his position on the budget. He responded two days later with his own op-ed defending his position. The respectful though principled exchange of views illustrates the point I am making here, even if, chronologically, it is more pertinent to the next chapter. See Alice M. Rivlin, "Where is the Old Bob Dole?" *New York Times*, June 23, 1993, nytimes.com/1993/06/23/opinion/where-is-the-old-bob-dole.html; Bob Dole, "I'm the Same Old Bob Dole," *New York Times*, June 25, 1993, nytimes .com/1993/06/25/opinion/i-m-the-same-old-bob-dole.html.

7. Tribune News Services, "O'Neill Says Cheney Told Him, 'Deficits Don't Matter,'" *Chicago Tribune*, January 12, 2004, chicagotribune.com/news/ct-xpm-2004-01-12 -0401120168-story.html.

8. Based on an analysis of the CBO's 2019 Long-Term Budget Outlook. See Alan Auerbach, William Gale, and Aaron Krupkin, "If Not Now, When? New Estimates of the Federal Budget Outlook," Brookings Institution, February 11, 2019, brookings .edu/research/if-not-now-when-new-estimates-of-the-federal-budget-outlook; Congressional Budget Office, "The 2019 Long-Term Budget Outlook," June 2019, cbo.gov/system/files/2019-06/55331-LTBO-2.pdf.

9. Data from White House Office of Management and Budget Historical Tables, white house.gov/omb/historical-tables/.

10. A Treasury bill is an obligation from the federal government to pay the owner the face value (usually $1,000) in the future. Treasury bills have a duration of one year or less. Treasury notes have durations of two to ten years and have a monthly payout in addition to the payout at maturity. Treasury bonds have a duration of thirty years.

11. You can get the data from the White House Office of Management and Budget Historical Tables and explore it in any spreadsheet program: whitehouse.gov/omb /historical-tables/.

12. These figures are all given in the dollars of the time, that is, they are not adjusted for inflation. Of course, the value of a dollar in 1900 was quite a bit greater than our dollar today.

13. Treasury Secretary Steve Mnuchin repeated the claim as late as 2018, even as evidence that it was false was already mounting. See Bob Bryan, "Treasury Secretary Steve Mnuchin Doubled Down on a Claim about the Tax Bill That Almost Every Independent Group Says Is Wrong," *Business Insider*, August 28, 2018, businessin sider.com/mnuchin-gop-trump-tax-law-pay-for-itself-deficit-rising-debt-2018-8.

14. William R. Gale and Aaron Krupkin, "Did the Tax Cuts and Jobs Act Pay for Itself in 2018?" *Tax Policy Center*, March 13, 2019, taxpolicycenter.org/taxvox/did-tax-cuts -and-jobs-act-pay-itself-2018.

15. Ronald Reagan, "Inaugural Address," January 20, 1981, Reagan Quotes and Speeches, Ronald Reagan Presidential Foundation and Institute, www.reaganfoundation.org /ronald-reagan/reagan-quotes-speeches/inaugural-address-2/.

16. The filibuster is the rule that allows senators to continue debate on legislation indefinitely until sixty-six (changed to sixty in 1975) senators vote to invoke "cloture" to end debate. This means by Senate rules, it now takes sixty senators to pass legislation. There are many exceptions including the reconciliation process that allows passage of budget bills with a simple 51-vote majority.

17. Martin Tolchin, "The Troubles of Tip O'Neill," *New York Times*, August 16, 1981, nytimes.com/1981/08/16/magazine/the-troubles-of-tip-o-neill.html%20.

18. Alice M. Rivlin, "Statement before the Committee on the Budget," US Senate, March 31, 1981, cbo.gov/sites/default/files/97th-congress-1981-1982/reports/81doc19.pdf.

19. Congressional Research Service, "The Budget Reconciliation Process: The Senate's 'Byrd Rule,'" November 22, 2016, everycrsreport.com/reports/RL30862.html.

20. Here is the language of the Americans for Tax Reform (ATR) Taxpayer Protection Pledge: "I, _____, pledge to the taxpayers of the _____ district of the state of _____ and to the American people that I will: One, oppose any and all efforts to increase the marginal income tax rates for individuals and/or businesses; and Two, to oppose any net reduction or elimination of deductions and credits, unless matched dollar for dollar by further reducing tax rates."

21. See the June 1992 coverage of the campaign in Jeffrey Schmalz, "Voters; Words on Bush's Lips in '88 Now Stick in Voters' Craw," *New York Times*, June 14, 1992, nytimes.com/1992/06/14/us/the-1992-capmaign-voters-words-on-bush-s-lips-in -88-now-stick-in-voters-craw.html.

22. Here is a link to Clinton's 1992 ad "Read My Lips": youtube.com/watch?v=B -U0wFoYAXk.

23. "Perot Campaign Commercial 1992," C-SPAN, October 16, 1992, c-span.org/video /?33206-1/perot-campaign-commercial-1992.

24. Frances E. Lee, *Insecure Majorities: Congress and the Perpetual Campaign* (University of Chicago Press, 2016), https://press.uchicago.edu/ucp/books/book/chicago/I/bo24732099.html.

25. Doug Criss, "This is the 30-Year-Old Willie Horton Ad Everybody Is Talking about Today," CNN Politics, November 1, 2018, cnn.com/2018/11/01/politics/willie-horton-ad-1988-explainer-trnd/index.html.

26. See the Jesse Helms "Hands" ad here: youtube.com/watch?v=KIyewCdXMzk.

## CHAPTER 6

1. A value-added tax (VAT) is a form of a consumption tax that is common in most of the countries in the world except the United States. It is like a sales tax in that you pay a VAT when you buy something (goods or services). In the US, we have some state and local sales taxes but no federal sales tax. For more on the VAT, see the Tax Policy Center Briefing Book, "How Could We Improve the Federal Tax System?" Tax Policy Center, May 2020, taxpolicycenter.org/briefing-book/what-vat.

2. GDP growth was negative for three quarters in the recession of 1991. It was actually picking up as 1992 wore on, registering a strong 4.38 percent by the time of the election, economists would eventually tell us, but the public was not feeling it. The unemployment rate was above 7 percent for the whole of 1992. Interest rates for a thirty-year mortgage were above 8 percent for most of the year. See "US Real GDP Growth by Quarter," US Bureau of Economic Analysis, www.multpl.com/us-real-gdp-growth-rate/table/by-quarter; "US Unemployment Rate by Month," US Bureau of Labor Statistics, www.multpl.com/unemployment/table/by-month; "National Monthly Average Mortgage Rates," Mortgage-X Mortgage Information Services, http://mortgage-x.com/general/national_monthly_average.asp?y=1992.

3. Bob Woodward, *The Agenda: Inside the Clinton White House* (New York: Simon & Schuster, 1994).

4. "Laura Tyson," Interview with PBS for *Commanding Heights: The Battle for the World Economy,* July 23, 2001, pbs.org/wgbh/commandingheights/shared/minitext/int_lauratyson.html.

5. Christian Weller took a deep look at the 1990s, highlighting the importance of IT investment in the period. See Christian E. Weller, "Learning Lessons From the 1990s: Long-Term Growth Prospects for the U.S.," Economic Policy Institute, April 10, 2002, epi.org/publication/webfeatures_viewpoints_l-t_growth_lessons/.

6. For some perspective, a typical thirty-year mortgage could be found for 4.25 percent in 2019 compared with 7.31 percent in 1993. Comparable mortgage rates were over 16 percent in Reagan's first year of 1981, as Federal Reserve Chair Volker used rates to slow the economy to reduce inflation, and they were still above 10 percent as the decade ended. See Denny Ceizyk, "Historical Mortgage Rates: Averages and Trends from the 1970s to 2020," ValuePenguin by Lending Tree, October 13, 2021, valuepenguin.com/mortgages/historical-mortgage-rates#hist.

7. White House Office of Management and Budget Historical Tables, "Table 7.1—Federal Debt at the End of Year: 1940–2025," whitehouse.gov/omb/historical-tables/.

8. White House Office of Management and Budget Historical Tables, "Table 8.3—Percentage Distribution of Outlays by Budget Enforcement Act Category: 1962–2026" and "Table 8.4—Outlays by Budget Enforcement Act Category as Percentages of GDP: 1962–2026," whitehouse.gov/omb/historical-tables/.

9. The thirty-year Treasury bond rate had closed at 7.30 percent on Friday, January 22, 1993. It dipped to as low as 7.19 percent on Monday and closed at 7.22 percent, an unusually large drop that Bentsen attributed to his statements that Clinton favored deficit reduction. US Department of the Treasury, "Treasury Daily Yield Curve Rates," treasury.gov/resource-center/data-chart-center/interest-rates/Pages/Text View.aspx?data=yieldYear&year=1993.

10. Robert Burgess, "The Daily Prophet: Carville Was Right about the Bond Market," *Bloomberg Businessweek*, January 29, 2018, bloomberg.com/news/articles/2018-01 -29/the-daily-prophet-carville-was-right-about-the-bond-market-jd0q9r1w.

11. The PAYGO rules require lawmakers that want to propose a tax cut or a benefit increase to an entitlement program like Medicare or Social Security to also propose an equal and opposite (as scored by CBO) package of offsets (revenue increases or spending cuts) so the deficit would not increase over the next five or ten years.

12. "Clinton Signs Bill Ending Wool, Mohair Subsidies," AP News, November 1, 1993, https://apnews.com/473d1ccab33d8a59d4a8e47c16210f65.

13. We say a tax code is "progressive" if it taxes higher income, or wealthier taxpayers, at a higher rate. We say a tax code is "regressive" if it taxes higher income, or wealthier taxpayers, at a lower rate. On balance, the US tax code is progressive—except for provisions that allow wealthy taxpayers to avoid certain taxes, legally or illegally. For this reason, proposals for a "flat tax," where every taxpayer pays the same rate, are tricky schemes to lower taxes for the wealthy. I suspect that the flat tax would be less popular with middle-income taxpayers if more people understood this.

14. The balanced budget amendment is a terrible idea for many reasons. Requiring that the government spending not exceed government receipts is like outlawing cloudy days, because neither spending nor receipts are under anyone's control. A balanced budget requirement would block deficit spending during an economic downturn, when it is really needed. The Great Depression may never have ended if there was a balanced budget amendment in place.

15. Some of this hostility focused on me personally. For example, "White House sources" spread rumors that I was about to be fired. *Newsweek* ran a story, under the headline "Dead Man Walking," that quoted an anonymous source saying, "No one pays any attention to her anymore; she will be gone by the end of the year." These stories were painful and caused me considerable anxiety, although I had no reason to think the rumors were true.

16. Elizabeth Shogren, "Midnight Basketball Is a Winner on the Street: Crime: Players, Coaches, Police Officers Say the Prevention Programs Have Proved Their Worth.

But Some Lawmakers Aren't Convinced," *Los Angeles Times*, August 19, 1994, latimes.com/archives/la-xpm-1994-08-19-mn-28886-story.html.

17. Adam Clymer, "G.O.P Senators Prevail, Sinking Clinton's Economic Stimulus Bill," *New York Times*, April 22, 1993, nytimes.com/1993/04/22/us/gop-senators-prevail -sinking-clinton-s-economic-stimulus-bill.html.

18. "Power of Progressive Economics: The Clinton Years," Center for American Progress, October 28, 2011, americanprogress.org/issues/economy/reports/2011/10/28 /10405/power-of-progressive-economics-the-clinton-years/; "The Clinton Presidency: Historic Economic Growth," Clinton White House Archives (n.d.), https:// clintonwhitehouse5.archives.gov/WH/Accomplishments/eightyears-03.html.

19. Margorie Margolies gained a lot of respect in some circles for her vote and is currently a fellow at the University of Pennsylvania Fels Institute of Government. She may have lost a congressional seat, but she gained a daughter-in-law. Her son, Marc Mezvinsky, is married to Chelsea Clinton.

20. The deficit reduction plan was, of course, only one of many reasons for the midterm losses. Others would include the demise of health care reform, the assault weapons ban in the Crime Bill, NAFTA, and the congressional bank check-cashing scandal.

21. Republicans gained fifty-four congressional seats in the 1994 midterm elections to control the House for the first time since 1954 and eight Senate seats to control the Senate.

22. Bipartisan Commission on Entitlement and Tax Reform, "Final Report to the President," December 1994, ssa.gov/history/reports/KerreyDanforth/KerreyDanforth .htm.

23. For an example of how the newly leaked memo was described at the time, see Ann Devroy, "Memo Outlines Fiscal Options for President," *Washington Post*, October 23, 1994, washingtonpost.com/archive/politics/1994/10/23/memo-outlines-fiscal -options-for-president/02ab867d-2976-4ed2-b169-9e9527f557c2/.

24. For a balanced discussion of the Rivlin memo, see Peter Passel, "Economic Scene; A Deficit Plan Becomes the Administration's Latest Scandal," *New York Times*, October 27, 1994, nytimes.com/1994/10/27/business/economic-scene-a-deficit-plan -becomes-the-administration-s-latest-scandal.html.

CHAPTER 7

1. Thomas E. Mann, and Norman J. Ornstein, *It's Even Worse Than It Looks: How the American Constitutional System Collided with the New Politics of Extremism* (New York: Basic Books, 2012), 33.

2. Heather Krause, of the Government Accountability Office (GAO), studied the costs of continuing resolutions and government shutdowns. See Heather Krause, "Budget Issues: Continuing Resolutions and Other Budget Uncertainties Present Management Challenges," testimony before the Subcommittee on Spending Oversight and Emergency Management, Committee on Homeland Security and Government Affairs, US Senate, February 6, 2018, gao.gov/assets/690/689914.pdf.

3. The government reopened officially on Monday January 8, 1996, but Washington was closed that day due to a blizzard that blanketed the East Coast from Richmond, Virginia, to Boston, Massachusetts.

4. Based on the FCC website, radio spectrum auctions 1 through 17 netted $23,755,678,714 between fiscal year 1994 and fiscal year 1998. See Federal Communications Commission, "Auction 1: Nationwide Narrowband (PCS)" auction summaries (n.d.), fcc.gov/auction/1.

5. The other contract items were raising the amount of money retirees could earn before their Social Security income would be reduced and creating new avenues for small businesses to challenge government regulations in court.

6. Jerry Gray, "Debt and Line-Item Veto Bills Approved," *New York Times*, March 29, 1996, nytimes.com/1996/03/29/us/debt-and-line-item-veto-bills-approved.html.

7. Public Law 104-130-Apr 9, 1996.

8. Wolf Blitzer, "Clinton Disappointed by Line-Item Ruling; Welcomes McDougal's Release," CNN, June 26, 1998, cnn.com/ALLPOLITICS/1998/06/26/clinton .comments/index.html.

9. Richard Kogan, "Constitutional Balanced Budget Amendment Poses Serious Risks," Center on Budget and Policy Priorities, March 16, 2018, cbpp.org/research/federal -budget/constitutional-balanced-budget-amendment-poses-serious-risks.

10. David Rosenbaum, "Clinton Toughens Stand on Changing Constitution," *New York Times*, January 29, 1997, nytimes.com/1997/01/29/us/clinton-toughens-stand-on -changing-constitution.html.

11. "The Constitution: Amendments 11-27," National Archives, archives.gov/founding -docs/amendments-11-27.

12. Newt Gingrich had given Democrats a powerful quote to use against him when he predicted in 1995 that Medicare would "wither on the vine" due to the changes he had enacted. The Democratic National Committee (DNC) paired this with Bob Doles's vote in the House against Medicare when it was first passed in 1965 for a series of ads attacking the two Republican leaders. See Edwin Chen, "Gingrich: Today's Medicare Will 'Wither,'" *Los Angeles Times*, October 26, 1995, latimes.com /archives/la-xpm-1995-10-26-mn-61267-story.html; "Dole Voices Pride in '65 Anti-Medicare Vote," *Washington Post*, October 26, 1995, washingtonpost.com/archive /politics/1995/10/26/dole-voices-pride-in-65-anti-medicare-vote/a6c33c1b-fdec -4eb1-8fcf-578008dc0782/.

13. Todd S. Purdum, "Clinton Promises to Create a 'Coalition of the Center,'" *New York Times*, December 12, 1996, nytimes.com/1996/12/12/us/clinton-promises-to-create -a-coalition-of-the-center.html.

14. "Clinton Budget: Alive on Arrival. GOP Receptive: Both Parties Seek Agreement on Balanced Budget by 2002," *Baltimore Sun*, February 7, 1997, baltimoresun.com /news/bs-xpm-1997-02-07-1997038078-story.html.

15. James Bennet, "Clinton Presents '98 Budget, and a Goal," *New York Times*, February 7, 1997, nytimes.com/1997/02/07/us/clinton-presents-98-budget-and-a-goal.html.

16. "Clinton Budget: Alive on Arrival."

17. Richard W. Stevenson, "Republicans Offer to Forgo Drafting Their Own Budget," *New York Times*, February 5, 1997, nytimes.com/1997/02/05/us/republicans-offer -to-forgo-drafting-their-own-budget.html.

18. An Ipsos/NPR poll found strong support for abolishing inheritance taxes (65 percent), but an even larger (75 percent) majority wanted to abolish the "death tax." See "United States Tax Policy: Ipsos Poll Conducted on Behalf of National Public Radio," press release, April 13, 2017, https://assets.documentcloud.org/documents /3671669/NPR-Ipsos-Tax-Poll.pdf.

19. "Medicaid and Child Health Provisions of the Bipartisan Budget Agreement," Center on Budget and Policy Priorities, May 28, 1997, cbpp.org/archives/mcaidbud.htm.

20. Louise Norris, "What Was the Medicare 'Doc Fix' Legislation?" MedicareResources .org, May 1, 2020, medicareresources.org/faqs/what-is-the-medicare-doc-fix-legis lation/.

21. "Obama Signs 'Doc Fix' Bill, Changing Medicare Payments to Doctors," CBS News, April 16, 2015, cbsnews.com/news/obama-signs-doc-fix-bill-changing-medicare -payments-to-doctors/.

22. OMB projected a deficit of $120.6 for fiscal year 1998 on page 303 of the President's budget. See US Bureau of the Budget and US Office of Management and Budget, *Budget of the United States Government, Fiscal Year 1998*, February 1, 1997, https:// fraser.stlouisfed.org/files/docs/publications/usbudget/BUDGET-1998-BUD.pdf ?utm_source=direct_download.

23. Congressional Budget Office. "Table 2-1. CBO Deficit Projections (by Fiscal Year)," *The Economic and Budget Outlook: Fiscal Years 1998–2007* (January 1997), 18, cbo .gov/sites/default/files/cbofiles/attachments/Eb01-97.pdf.

24. Richard W. Stevenson, "$70 Billion Surplus as U.S. Closes Books on 1998 Fiscal Year," *New York Times*, October 29, 1998, nytimes.com/1998/10/29/us/70-billion -surplus-as-us-closes-books-on-1998-fiscal-year.html.

25. White House Historical Tables "Table 1.3—Summary of Receipts, Outlays, and Surpluses or Deficits (-) in Current Dollars, Constant (FY 2012) Dollars, and as Percentages of GDP: 1940–2025," whitehouse.gov/omb/budget/historical-tables/.

26. "US Real GDP Growth Rate Per Year," US Bureau of Economic Analysis, multpl .com/us-real-gdp-growth-rate/table/by-quarter.

27. Tony Long, "March 10, 2000: Pop Goes the Nasdaq!" *Wired*, August 10, 2010, wired .com/2010/03/0310nasdaq-bust/.

28. Emmanuel Saez and Gabriel Zucman, "Wealth Inequality in the United States Since 1913: Evidence from Capitalized Income Tax Data," *Quarterly Journal of Economics* 131:2 (May 2016), https://eml.berkeley.edu/~saez/SaezZucman2016QJE.pdf.

29. Economic Policy Institute, *The State of Working America 1998-99* (Cornell University Press, 1999), epi.org/publication/books_swa98/.

30. Benjamin Austin, Edward Gleaser, and Lawrence H. Summers, "Saving the Heartland: Place-Based Policies in 21st Century America," Brookings Institution,

March 8, 2018, brookings.edu/bpea-articles/saving-the-heartland-place-based -policies-in-21st-century-america/.

31. Henry J. Aaron, "Clinton's Got a Wise Plan for Surplus," Brooking Op-Ed, February 2, 1999, brookings.edu/opinions/clintons-got-a-wise-plan-for-surplus/.

32. Workforce Investment Partnership Act of 1998, H.R. 1385, 105th Congress (introduced May 5, 1998), congress.gov/bill/105th-congress/house-bill/1385/all-actions ?overview=closed&q={%22roll-call-vote%22:%22all%22}&KWICView=false.

33. George W. Bush was the forty-third president. His father, George H. W. Bush, had been the forty-first president.

34. Employment and Training Administration, "Workforce Innovation and Opportunity Act," US Department of Labor (n.d.), dol.gov/agencies/eta/wioa.

35. Steven M. Gillon, *The Pact: Bill Clinton, Newt Gingrich, and the Rivalry that Defined a Nation* (Oxford University Press, 2008); "The Pact Between Bill Clinton and Newt Gingrich," *U.S. News & World Report*, May 29, 2008, usnews.com/news/articles /2008/05/29/the-pact-between-bill-clinton-and-newt-gingrich.

36. Richard W. Stevenson, "The 2000 Campaign: The Budget Issue; Bush and Gore Revise Plans to Match a Growing Surplus," *New York Times*, June 13, 2000, nytimes .com/2000/06/13/us/2000-campaign-budget-issue-bush-gore-revise-plans-match -growing-surplus.html.

37. "The Clinton Presidency: Historic Economic Growth," Clinton White House Archives (n.d.), https://clintonwhitehouse5.archives.gov/WH/Accomplishments/eight years-03.html.

38. "US Real GDP Growth Rate Per Year."

39. "Table II-1, Receipts, Outlays, and Surplus," *Budget of the United States Government, Fiscal Year 2000*, February 1, 1999, 15, https://fraser.stlouisfed.org/files /docs/publications/usbudget/BUDGET-2000-BUD.pdf?utm_source=direct _download.

40. Congressional Budget Office, "Summary Table 1. The Budget Outlook Under Current Policies," *The Budget and Economic Outlook: Fiscal Years 2001–2010*, January 2000, XIV, https://www.cbo.gov/publication/12069.

41. The S&P 500 stock index went from 433.37 on January 20, 1993, as Clinton took office, to 1,342.54 on January 19, 2001, just before he left office. See "Standard and Poor's 500 Stock Index," Securities and Exchange Commission Archives (n.d.), sec .gov/Archives/edgar/data/357298/000035729801500016/sp500.html.

42. Alan Greenspan, "The Challenge of Central Banking in a Democratic Society," remarks given at the Annual Dinner and Francis Boyer Lecture of the American Enterprise Institute for Public Policy Research, December 5, 1996, federalreserve .gov/boarddocs/speeches/1996/19961205.htm.

43. Harry J. Holzer and Margy Waller, "The Workforce Reinvestment Act: Reauthorization to Address the 'Skills Gap,'" Brookings Institution Center on Urban and Metropolitan Policy, December 2003, brookings.edu/wp-content/uploads/2016/06 /20031218_Waller.pdf#:~:text=The%20Brookings%20Institution%20I.%20Intro

duction%20T%20he%20Workforce,needs%20to%20be%20extended%20or%20re
authorized%20by%20Congress.

44. Edward Alden and Laura Taylor-Kale, "The Work Ahead: Machines, Skills, and U.S. Leadership in the Twenty-First Century," *Council on Foreign Relations*, April 2018, cfr.org/report/the-work-ahead/.

45. Paul N. Van de Water, "Medicare is Not 'Bankrupt,'" Center on Budget and Policy Priorities, May 1, 2019, cbpp.org/research/health/medicare-is-not-bankrupt.

46. The filibuster is the rule that allows senators to continue debate on legislation indefinitely until sixty-six (changed to sixty in 1975) senators vote to invoke "cloture" to end debate. This means by Senate rules, it now takes sixty senators to pass legislation. There are many exceptions including the reconciliation process that allows passage of budget bills with a simple 51-vote majority.

47. "Summary of the Byrd Rule," U.S. House of Representatives Committee on Rules, Majority Office (n.d.), https://archives-democrats-rules.house.gov/archives/byrd_rule.htm.

48. Brian S. Wesbury, "The Post-9/11 Economy," *Wall Street Journal*, September 11, 2006, wsj.com/articles/SB11579348365065901.

49. White House Historical Tables, "Table 1.1." Summary of Receipts, Outlays, and Surpluses or Deficits (-): 1789–2025 whitehouse.gov/omb/budget/historical-tables/.

50. Congressional Budget Office, "Changes in CBO's Baseline Projections Since January 2001," June 7, 2012, cbo.gov/sites/default/files/112th-congress-2011-2012/reports/06-07-changessince2001baseline.pdf.

51. Adam Nagourney, "The 2002 Elections: The Overview; G.O.P. Retakes Control of the Senate in a Show of Presidential Influence; Pataki, Jeb Bush and Lautenberg Win," *New York Times*, November 6, 2002, nytimes.com/2002/11/06/us/2002-elections-overview-gop-retakes-control-senate-show-presidential-influence.html.

52. "O'Neill Says Cheney Told Him, 'Deficits Don't Matter,'" *Chicago Tribune*, January 12, 2004, chicagotribune.com/news/ct-xpm-2004-01-12-0401120168-story.html.

53. Final passage in the House was 220 to 215, with most Republicans in support and most Democrats opposed, but there was a substantial amount of crossover voting in both directions. See Clerk of the US House of Representatives, "Final Vote Results for Roll Call 669," November 22, 2003, http://clerk.house.gov/evs/2003/roll669.xml. A similar pattern held in the Senate, but support was stronger there and the bill passed 61 to 39. See US Senate, "Roll Call Vote 108th Congress—1st Session," Legislation & Records, senate.gov/legislative/LIS/roll_call_lists/roll_call_vote_cfm.cfm?congress=108&session=1&vote=00458.

54. "Military Base Closures: Estimates of Costs and Savings," Congressional Research Service, June 2001, everycrsreport.com/reports/RL30440.html.

55. Office of Rep. Jim Cooper, "Cooper and Wolf Weigh in on President's Debt Commission," press release, April, 20, 2010, https://cooper.house.gov/media-center/press-releases/cooper-and-wolf-weigh-in-on-presidents-debt-commission.

56. SAFE Commission Act, H.R. 5552, 109th Congress (June 7, 2006), congress.gov/109 /bills/hr5552/BILLS-109hr5552ih.xml.

57. This means the effort to craft legislation had support from both Republicans and Democrats in the House and the Senate. That is a good starting place for any serious proposal, but it is quite far from a guarantee of success.

58. Bipartisan Task Force for Responsible Fiscal Action Act of 2007, S.2063, 110th Congress (2007).

59. Emily Horton took a close look at the two Bush tax cuts and how much they added to the federal deficit (quite a lot) and economic growth (not much). See Emily Horton, "The Legacy of the 2001 and 2003 'Bush' Tax Cuts," Center on Budget and Policy Priorities, October 23, 2017, cbpp.org/research/federal-tax/the-legacy-of-the -2001-and-2003-bush-tax-cuts.

60. *Business Insider* produced a great chart showing estimates of how much each of many factors contributed to the transition from surplus to deficits. See Lucas Kawa, "CHART: How the Clinton Surpluses Turned into More Than $6 Trillion Worth of Deficits," *Business Insider*, January 8, 2013, businessinsider.com/how-clinton -surplus-became-a-6t-deficit-2013-1.

61. Gallup, "Trust in Government," polls from 1972 to 2021 (n.d.), https://news.gallup .com/poll/5392/trust-government.aspx.

62. Dan Roberts, "Wall Street Deregulation Pushed by Clinton Advisers, Documents Reveal," *The Guardian*, April 19, 2014, theguardian.com/world/2014/apr/19/wall -street-deregulation-clinton-advisers-obama.

63. Gillian B. White and Bourree Lam, "Could Reviving a Defunct Banking Rule Prevent a Future Crisis?" *The Atlantic*, August 23, 2016, theatlantic.com/business /archive/2016/08/glass-steagall/496856/.

64. Mark Landler and Sheryl Gay Stolberg, "Bush Can Share the Blame for Financial Crisis," *New York Times*, September 20, 2008, nytimes.com/2008/09/20/business /worldbusiness/20iht-prexy.4.16321064.html.

65. Eamon Javers, "Rubin: 'We All Bear Responsibility,'" *Politico*, April 8, 2010, politico.com/story/2010/04/rubin-we-all-bear-responsibility-035547.

66. US Department of the Treasury, "About FSOC" (n.d.), https://home.treasury.gov /policy-issues/financial-markets-financial-institutions-and-fiscal-service/fsoc /about-fsoc.

67. Bloomberg News, "Bush, Obama Response to Financial Crisis Likely Averted Depression, Economists Say," *Denver Post*, July 30, 2010, denverpost.com/2010/07/30 /bush-obama-response-to-financial-crisis-likely-averted-depression-economists -say/.

## CHAPTER 8

1. Clinton and the Republicans did sign a deal that extended the solvency of Medicare to 2026, but as detailed in chapter 7, the deal relied on a lower payment schedule for doctors and hospitals that never went into effect and had to be bailed out from general revenues in a series of annual "doc fix" bills.

2. The *Washington Post* produced a series of charts about the economic damage caused by the Great Recession. See Kate Rabinowitz and Youjin Shin, "The Great Recession's Great Hangover," *Washington Post*, September 7, 2018, washingtonpost.com /graphics/2018/business/great-recession-10-years-out/.

3. BuzzFeed collected personal stories from millennials about Great Recession hardships ten years after, and Brookings did a deep dive on the statistics. See Venessa Wong, "Here's How Millennials' Lives Were Changed by Recession 10 Years Ago," BuzzFeed, September 5, 2018, buzzfeednews.com/article/venessawong/millennials -lives-changed-by-recession-2008-2018; Michael Greenstone and Adam Looney, "Unemployment and Earnings Losses: A Look at Long-Term Impacts of the Great Recession on American Workers," Brookings Institution, November 4, 2011, brook ings.edu/blog/jobs/2011/11/04/unemployment-and-earnings-losses-a-look-at -long-term-impacts-of-the-great-recession-on-american-workers/.

4. Mark Thoma, "The Importance of Automatic Stabilizers to the Economy," CBS News, January 25, 2010, cbsnews.com/news/the-importance-of-automatic-stabilizers -to-the-economy/.

5. Heather Boushey and others, "Recession Ready: Fiscal Policies to Stabilize the American Economy," Hamilton Project, May 16, 2019, hamiltonproject.org/papers /recession_ready_fiscal_policies_to_stabilize_the_american_economy.

6. *Growth & Opportunity Project*, Republican National Committee 2012, http://online .wsj.com/public/resources/documents/RNCreport03182013.pdf.

7. John Hudson, "Could a Memo by Christina Romer Have Saved the Economy?" *The Atlantic*, February 22, 2012, theatlantic.com/business/archive/2012/02/could-memo -christina-romer-have-saved-economy/331392/.

8. Economists define "fiscal space" as the budgetary room that allows a government to provide resources for public purposes without undermining fiscal sustainability. See Christina Romer and David Romer, "Fiscal Space and the Aftermath of Financial Crises: How It Matters and Why," Brookings Institution, March 2019, brookings.edu/wp-content/uploads/2019/03/Fiscal-Space-and-the-Aftermath-of -Financial-Crises.pdf.

9. This was an estimate, and the value of the total package was reported as many different amounts in various news accounts and official scorings. Andrew Taylor, "Senate Passes its $838 Billion Stimulus Bill," SFGATE, February 10, 2012, sfgate .com/news/article/Senate-passes-its-838-billion-stimulus-bill-3251637.php.

10. American Recovery and Reinvestment Act of 2009, H.R. 1, 111th Congress, House vote #46 (January 28, 2009), govtrack.us/congress/votes/111-2009/h46, and House Vote #70 (February 13, 2009), govtrack.us/congress/votes/111-2009/h70.

11. Jim Myers, "U.S. Senate Passes $838 Billion Economic Package," *The Oklahoman*, February 10, 2009, https://oklahoman.com/article/3344755/us-senate-passes-838 -billion-economic-package.

12. David Rogers, "Senate Passes $787 Billion Stimulus Bill," *Politico*, February 13, 2009), politico.com/story/2009/02/senate-passes-787-billion-stimulus-bill -018837.

13. The $700 billion rescue plan that included TARP passed the House by a 228–205 vote, including ninety-one Republicans in support, and the Senate by a 74–25 vote, with thirty-two Republicans. See Joshua Green, "TARP, the Forbidden Bipartisan Success," *The Atlantic*, September 29, 2010, theatlantic.com/politics/archive/2010/09/tarp-the-forbidden-bipartisan-success/63803/.

14. Richard Wolf, "Obama's $825B Stimulus Plan Includes Spending, Tax Cuts," *USA Today*, January 15, 2009, https://abcnews.go.com/Business/story?id=6660263&page=1.

15. A CBO analysis of the 2009 Recovery Act found the effects on output and employment were smaller than the administration had hoped for. See "Estimated Impact of the American Recovery and Reinvestment Act on Employment and Economic Output in 2014," Congressional Budget Office, February 2015, cbo.gov/sites/default/files/114th-congress-2015-2016/reports/49958-ARRA.pdf.

16. Paul Krugman, "How Did We Know the Stimulus Was Too Small?" *New York Times*, July 28, 2010, https://krugman.blogs.nytimes.com/2010/07/28/how-did-we-know-the-stimulus-was-too-small/.

17. Mark Zandi and his team of econometric modelers at Moody's Analytics produced estimates of the multiplier effect of the many potential stimulus options under consideration in 2011. The findings show the importance of getting money into the hands of people who need it most because they will spend it right away, so permanently extending unemployment insurance (1.55), increasing food stamp payments (1.71), and child tax credits (1.38) give a high economic boost. Tax cuts that go to the wealthy, like corporate tax rate cuts (0.32) and accelerated depreciation of business assets (0.29), offer a much lower economic "bang for the buck." The full table of options can be found in Zandi's testimony before the Congressional Joint Economic Committee. See Mark Zandi, "Bolstering the Economy: Helping American Families by Reauthorizing the Payroll Tax Cut and UI Benefits," written testimony before the Congressional Joint Economic Committee, February 7, 2012, economy.com/mark-zandi/documents/2012-02-07-JEC-Payroll-Tax.pdf.

18. "CNN Poll: 3 of 4 Americans Say Much of Stimulus Money Wasted," CNN, January 25, 2010, cnn.com/2010/POLITICS/01/25/poll.stimulus.money/index.html.

19. An environmentalist proposal to "cap and trade" carbon credits led the list of Obama priorities that could not be passed in either of the two budgets. For details, see William Galston, "Will Obama's Agenda Pass Congress's Budget Resolution?" Brookings Institution, March 26, 2009, brookings.edu/opinions/will-obamas-agenda-pass-congresss-budget-resolution/.

20. Jesse Lee, "President Obama Signs Continuing Resolution," Obama White House Archives, March 6, 2009, https://obamawhitehouse.archives.gov/blog/2009/03/06/president-obama-signs-continuing-resolution.

21. Carl Hulse, "Budgets Approved, with No G.O.P. Votes," *New York Times*, April 2, 2009, nytimes.com/2009/04/03/us/politics/03budget.html.

22. "Helping Responsible Homeowners," Obama White House Archives (n.d.), https://obamawhitehouse.archives.gov/economy/middle-class/helping-responsible-homeowners.

23. The Constitution requires the president to report on the "state of the union" once a year. It does not have to be a speech, but this has become the tradition. But in the first year of a new president's term, the speech is simply called an address to Congress because the president is not expected to know the state of the union yet. Here is the text of Obama's first address to Congress: "President Obama's Address to Congress," transcript, *New York Times,* February 24, 2009, nytimes.com/2009/02/24 /us/politics/24obama-text.html.

24. "Obama's Remarks on the Economy," transcript, *New York Times,* April 14, 2009, nytimes.com/2009/04/14/us/politics/14obama-text.html.

25. "Opening Remarks at Fiscal Responsibility Summit," transcript, *New York Times,* February 23, 2009, nytimes.com/2009/02/23/us/politics/23text-summit.html%20 %20

26. Jonathan Weisman, "Obama Aims to Address Worries About Widening Deficit," *Wall Street Journal,* February 24, 2009, wsj.com/articles/SB123539969756547797.

27. Economists Alan Blinder and Mark Zandi did a terrific analysis of the Recovery Act and other policies that they argue were effective in reversing the decline of the Great Recession. See Alan S. Blinder and Mark Zandi, "How the Great Recession Was Brought to an End," Princeton University, July 27, 2010, princeton.edu/~blinder /End-of-Great-Recession.pdf.

28. The National Bureau of Economic Research (NBER) declares the official beginning and ending dates for recessions based on the rate of GDP growth or contraction, but the public may still be feeling the economic effects for months or even years after a recession officially ends. See "Business Cycle Dating," National Bureau of Economic Research, nber.org/research/business-cycle-dating.

29. Federal Reserve Economic Data, "Federal Surplus or Deficit [-] as Percent of Gross Domestic Product," Federal Reserve Bank of St. Louis (continuously updated), https://fred.stlouisfed.org/series/FYFSGDA188S#0.

30. The debt held by the public as a percentage of GDP was a stubborn legacy of the recession and it has not turned back, climbing above 60 percent in 2010, 70 percent in 2012, with projections that have it passing 100 percent within a few years from now. Federal Reserve Economic Data, "Federal Debt Held by the Public as Percent of Gross Domestic Product," Federal Reserve Bank of St. Louis (continuously updated), https://fred.stlouisfed.org/series/FYGFGDQ188S.

31. "Obama's Health Care Speech to Congress," text, *New York Times,* September 9, 2009, nytimes.com/2009/09/10/us/politics/10obama.text.html.

32. "House Minority Leader John Boehner: Where Are the Jobs, Mr. President?" *Washington Examiner,* June 22, 2009, washingtonexaminer.com/house-minority-leader -john-boehner-where-are-the-jobs-mr-president.

33. Andrea Fuller, "Boehner Says Not So Fast on Bipartisanship," *New York Times,* July 23, 2009, https://thecaucus.blogs.nytimes.com/2009/07/23/boehner-says-not-so -fast-on-bipartisanship/?searchResultPosition=34.

34. Sheryl Gay Stolberg and Jeff Zeleny summarized the state of bipartisanship in Washington. See Sheryl Gay Stolberg and Jeff Zeleny, "Obama Keeps Up Health Care

Push, Citing Uninsured," *New York Times*, September 10, 2009, nytimes.com/2009 /09/11/us/politics/11obama.html?searchResultPosition=1.

35.  "Pelosi Unveils House Health Care Bill," CBS News, October 29, 2009, cbsnews.com /news/pelosi-unveils-house-health-care-bill/.

36.  "The Five Democrats Who Voted Against the Public Option," *Huffpost*, November 29, 2009, huffpost.com/entry/the-five-democrats-who-vo_n_303700.

37.  Glenn Thrush and Carrie Budoff Brown, "Obama's Health Care Conversion," *Politico*, September 23, 2013, politico.com/story/2013/09/obama-health-care-conversion -obamacare-097185.

38.  Molly Ball, "How Nancy Pelosi Saved the Affordable Care Act," *Time*, May 6, 2020, https://time.com/5832330/nancy-pelosi-obamacare/.

39.  The filibuster and reconciliation process are discussed in greater detail in chapter 7.

40.  Sheryl Gay Stolberg and Robert Pear, "Obama Signs Health Care Overhaul Bill, with a Flourish," *New York Times*, March 23, 2010, nytimes.com/2010/03/24/health /policy/24health.html.

41.  The Kaiser Family Foundation tracked attitudes toward the ACA throughout this period. "KFF Health Tracking Poll: The Public's Views on the ACA," Kaiser Family Foundation (continuously updated), kff.org/interactive/kff-health-tracking-poll-the -publics-views-on-the-aca/#?response=Favorable—Unfavorable&aRange=all.

42.  "HealthCare.gov: CMS Management of the Federal Marketplace, A Case Study," US Department of Health and Human Services, Office of Inspector General, OEI-06-14-00350 (February 2016), https://oig.hhs.gov/oei/reports/oei-06-14-00350.pdf.

43.  Elaine S. Povich and Eric Pianin, "Support Grows for Tackling the Nation's Debt," *The Fiscal Times*, December 31, 2009, washingtonpost.com/wp-dyn/content/article /2009/12/30/AR2009123002576.html.

44.  Fred Hiatt, "Where Is McConnell's Sense of Leadership?" opinion, *Washington Post*, February 1, 2010, washingtonpost.com/wp-dyn/content/article/2010/01/31/AR20 10013101837.html.

45.  J. Taylor Rushing, "Senate Rejects Deficit Reduction Commission," *The Hill*, January 26, 2010, https://thehill.com/homenews/senate/78069-senate-rejects-fiscal-deficit -reduction-commission.

46.  Council of Economic Advisers, "Chapter 5: Addressing the Long-Run Fiscal Challenge," in *Economic Report of the President (2010)*, Executive Office of the President, https://obamawhitehouse.archives.gov/sites/default/files/microsites/economic -report-president-chapter-5r2.pdf.

47.  Office of the Press Secretary, "President Obama Establishes Bipartisan National Commission on Fiscal Responsibility and Reform," White House, February 18, 2010, https://obamawhitehouse.archives.gov/the-press-office/president-obama-establishes -bipartisan-national-commission-fiscal-responsibility-an.

48.  Grover Norquist, "Beware: The Taxman Cometh," *National Conservative Weekly*, May 17, 2010.

49.  Jonathan Weisman, "Republicans Blast Debt-Cutting Panel; GOP Leaders Say Legislation Is Needed to Ensure Up-or-Down Vote on Commission Recommenda-

tions," *Wall Street Journal*, January 21, 2010, wsj.com/articles/SB100014240527487
0340570457501555091596 0106.

50. The commission members were Alan Simpson (R), Dave Cote (R), Ann Fudge (R), Erskine Bowles (D), Andy Stern (D), Alice Rivlin (D), Bruce Reed (D), Paul Ryan (R), Jeb Hensarling (R), Dave Camp (R), John Spratt (D), Xavier Becerra (D), Jan Schakowsky (D), Judd Gregg (R), Tom Coburn (R), Mike Crapo (R), Richard Durbin (D), Max Baucus (D), and Kent Conrad (D).

51. Beyond the cochairs, myself, and former senator Pete Domenici of New Mexico, here are the members of the Domenici-Rivlin Task Force (listing only a few of the many current and former positions each had held): Robert L. Bixby, executive director of the Concord Coalition; James Blanchard, former governor of Michigan; Sheila Burke, former chief of staff to Senate Majority Leader Bob Dole; Dr. Leonard E. Burman, former director of the Urban Institute-Brookings Tax Policy Center, and former CBO senior analyst; Robert N. Campbell III, vice chair and public sector leader at Deloitte LLP; Henry Cisneros, former secretary of Housing and Urban Development, and mayor of San Antonio, Texas; Carlos M. Gutierrez, former secretary of Commerce; G. William Hoagland, former staff director, Senate Budget Committee; Frank Keating, former governor of Oklahoma; Karen Kerrigan, founder of Women Entrepreneurs Inc.; Maya MacGuineas, president, Committee for a Responsible Federal Budget; Donald Marron, former acting director of CBO; Edward McElroy Jr., former president, American Federation of Teachers; Joe Minarik, former associate director of economic policy for OMB, and former chief economist, House Budget Committee; Marc H. Morial, president and CEO, National Urban League; William D. Novelli, former CEO of the American Association of Retired Persons (AARP); and Anthony A. (Tony) Williams, former mayor of the District of Columbia and president of the National League of Cities.

52. David Leonhardt, "One Way to Trim Deficit: Cultivate Growth," *New York Times*, November 16, 2010, nytimes.com/2010/11/17/business/economy/17leonhardt.html.

53. I participated in a conference at Brookings that was dedicated to understanding the plusses and minuses of various premium support proposals. You can find the resulting paper here: Henry J. Aaron and others, "Premium Support: A Primer," Brookings Institution, December 16, 2011, brookings.edu/research/premium-support -a-primer/.

54. That Medicare Advantage was first proposed by a Democratic president and then extended by a Republican president suggests bipartisan roots; however, while the Medicare Modernization Act of 2003 passed the Senate with solid bipartisan support, the House Democrats resisted, and the final vote was close, controversial, and contentious.

55. The Democratic Congressional Campaign Committee produced a very amusing ad in 2011, showing seniors mowing lawns and even working as a stripper to earn money "because Republicans voted to end Medicare," referring to a vote on Representative Paul Ryan's premium support proposal. See Angie Drobnic Holan, "Democrats Say Republicans Voted to End Medicare and Charge Seniors $12,000," PolitiFact,

April 20, 2011, politifact.com/factchecks/2011/apr/20/democratic-congressional
-campaign-committee/democrats-say-republicans-voted-end-medicare-and-c/.

56. Alice M. Rivlin, "The Domenici-Rivlin Tax Reform Proposal," presented at the Annual Meetings of the American Economic Association, Chicago, Illinois, January 7, 2012, https://tinyurl.com/y523f3ko.

57. Pete Domenici and Alice M. Rivlin, "Restoring America's Future: The Domenici-Rivlin Debt Reduction Task Force Report," Bipartisan Policy Center, November 17, 2010, https://bipartisanpolicy.org/report/restoring-americas-future/.

58. The net effect of this rule was to establish a threshold that at least two of the six Republican elected officials needed to support the commission's proposal to reach support of fourteen of the eighteen members—assuming it had the support of the two chairs, all of the public members, and all of the Democratic elected officials. This was also true if the above party labels were reversed, but in the end, neither the requisite number of Republican nor Democratic votes was achieved as five of the six House members, one Senator, and one of the citizen members, voted against the proposal.

## CHAPTER 9

1. William Branigin, "Obama Reflects on 'Shellacking' in Midterm Elections," *Washington Post*, November 3, 2010, washingtonpost.com/wp-dyn/content/article/2010/11/03/AR2010110303997.html.

2. Brady Dennis, Alec MacGillis, and Lori Montgomery, "Origins of the Debt Showdown," *Washington Post*, August 3, 2011, washingtonpost.com/business/economy/origins-of-the-debt-showdown/2011/08/03/gIQA9uqIzI_story.html.

3. Sarah Childress, "Meet the GOP's 'Young Guns,'" *Frontline*, PBS, February 12, 2013, pbs.org/wgbh/frontline/article/meet-the-gops-young-guns/.

4. Abdon M. Pallasch, "'Best 5 Minutes of My Life'; His '09 CNBC Rant against Mortgage Bailouts for 'Losers' Ignited the Tea Party Movement," *Chicago Sun-Times*, September 19, 2010.

5. Erin O'Donnell, "Tea Party Passions," *Harvard Magazine*, January 2012, harvard-magazine.com/2012/01/tea-party-passions.

6. Samuel Best, "Why Democrats Lost the House to Republicans," CBS News, November 3, 2010, https://www.cbsnews.com/news/why-democrats-lost-the-house-to-republicans/.

7. David Corn, "The Deal That Worked," in *Showdown, The Inside Story of How Obama Fought Back Against Boehner, Cantor and the Tea Party* (New York: William Morrow, 2012), 65.

8. Garance Franke-Ruta, "The Most Productive Lame Duck Since WWII—and Maybe Ever," *The Atlantic*, December 22, 2010, theatlantic.com/politics/archive/2010/12/the-most-productive-lame-duck-since-wwii-and-maybe-ever/68442/.

9. Liberal Democrats are correctly quite wary of any cuts to the payroll tax, because the roughly 6.2 percent tax paid by both employers and employees (12.4 percent overall in 2010) is the principal funding stream for both Social Security and Medi-

care. The bipartisan lame-duck deal was partial and temporary, cutting just the employer share of the tax from 6.2 percent to 4.2 percent and just for the 2011 tax year. The cut was later extended through the end of 2012, but it was not made permanent, which would have been the liberals' great fear.

10. Brian Montopoli, "Obama Signs Bill to Extend Bush Tax Cuts," CBS News, December 17, 2010, cbsnews.com/news/obama-signs-bill-to-extend-bush-tax-cuts/.

11. The EITC is a tax rebate that helps millions of families, many headed by women, with low-paying jobs ("the working poor") stay out of poverty by sending them money in the form of a refund at tax time. See Natalie Holmes and Alan Berube, "The Earned Income Tax Credit and Community Economic Stability," Brookings Institution, November 20, 2015, brookings.edu/articles/the-earned-income-tax-credit-and-community-economic-stability/.

12. Chris Isidore, "Stimulus Price Tag: $2.8 Trillion," CNN Money, December 20, 2010, https://money.cnn.com/2010/12/20/news/economy/total_stimulus_cost/index.html.

13. The DREAM Act would have made citizens of millions of US residents who were brought into the country as children and had since lived typical American lives. Obama was never able to pass this legislation and eventually turned the DREAM Act into an executive order, which does not have the same power of law.

14. *PBS News Hour*, "Obama Marks 'Season of Progress,' But New Political Landscape Looms," December 22, 2010, pbs.org/newshour/show/obama-marks-season-of-progress-but-new-political-landscape-looms.

15. Kori Schulman, "President Obama on the Middle Class Tax Cuts and Unemployment Insurance Agreement: 'A Good Deal for the American People,'" Obama White House, Archives, December 7, 2010, https://obamawhitehouse.archives.gov/blog/2010/12/07/president-obama-middle-class-tax-cuts-and-unemployment-insurance-agreement-a-good-de.

16. Andrew Austin and Mindy R. Levit, "Trends in Discretionary Spending," Congressional Research Service, February 22, 2010, https://www.everycrsreport.com/files/20100222_RL34424_9da7e47c028124aabcaea01f053f9af89323a991.pdf.

17. Although Medicaid is principally known as the program that provides health benefits to the poor, it also pays for a large fraction of the cost of long-term care for the elderly, and for this reason it, too, was projected to grow dramatically as the population grows older.

18. The "Tax Reform" section of the Simpson-Bowles plan starts on page 28. See National Commission on Fiscal Responsibility and Reform, *The Moment of Truth*, White House, December 2010, ssa.gov/history/reports/ObamaFiscal/TheMoment ofTruth12_1_2010.pdf.

19. Office of US Representative Jan Schakowsky, "Schakowsky Offers Alternative to Simpson-Bowles Deficit Reduction Plan," press release, November 16, 2010, https://schakowsky.house.gov/media/press-releases/schakowsky-offers-alternative-simpson-bowles-deficit-reduction-plan.

20. Here are a few of the analyses: Henry J. Aaron and others, "Around the Halls: Analyzing the Plans to Solve the Budget Crisis," Brookings Institution, November 19,

2010, brookings.edu/blog/up-front/2010/11/19/around-the-halls-analyzing-the-plans-to-solve-the-budget-crisis/; Derek Thompson, "The Best Plan Yet? A Summary of the New Bipartisan Deficit Reduction Scheme," *The Atlantic*, November 17, 2010, theatlantic.com/business/archive/2010/11/the-best-plan-yet-a-summary-of-the-new-bipartisan-deficit-reduction-scheme/66695/; Richard Kogan, "What Was Actually in Bowles-Simpson—And How Can We Compare It With Other Plans?" Center on Budget and Policy Priorities, October 2, 2012, cbpp.org/research/what-was-actually-in-bowles-simpson-and-how-can-we-compare-it-with-other-plans.

21. Giffords was severely injured, requiring days of intensive care and years of rehabilitation to regain basic abilities to walk and speak. The dead included one of her staffers, a district court judge, and a 9-year-old girl. See Carl Hulse and Kate Zernike, "Bloodshed Puts New Focus on Vitriol in Politics," *New York Times*, January 8, 2011, nytimes.com/2011/01/09/us/politics/09capital.html.

22. Alice M. Rivlin, "Create Jobs Not Deficits," *New York Times*, January 22, 2011, nytimes.com/2011/01/23/opinion/23rivlin.html.

23. Continuing resolutions are budget bills to fund the government for a specified period and are passed to avoid or postpone a government funding lapse that could force the government to shut down some of its operations. Typically, a CR keeps most of the government funded at the same level as the expiring funding, although changes in levels can be negotiated. A CR can be as short as a few days or as long as several months, or it can last through the end of the fiscal year, when legislators hope another budget will have been passed to continue funding the government.

24. Paul Kane, "House Approves Dramatic Cuts in Federal Spending in 235–189 Vote," *Washington Post*, February 23, 2011, washingtonpost.com/politics/house-approves-dramatic-cuts-in-federal-spending/2011/02/18/AByHEsH_story.html.

25. Office of Federal Relations, "Congress Averts Shutdown Again, Passes Three-Week Continuing Resolution," Harvard University, March 17, 2011, https://ofr.harvard.edu/news/congress-averts-shutdown-again-passes-three-week-continuing-resolution.

26. Carl Hulse, "Budget Deal to Cut $38 Billion Averts Shutdown," *New York Times*, April 8, 2011, nytimes.com/2011/04/09/us/politics/09fiscal.html.

27. Associated Press, "CBO: Budget Deal Cuts This Fiscal Year's Deficit by Just $352 Million, Not $38 Billion Touted," April 13, 2011, https://web.archive.org/web/20110419191207/http://www.washingtonpost.com/business/cbo-budget-deal-cuts-this-fiscal-years-deficit-by-just-353-million-not-38-billion-touted/2011/04/13/AFFJnkWD_story.html.

28. Jack Lew, "The 2012 Budget," *Obama White House Archives*, February 14, 2011, https://obamawhitehouse.archives.gov/blog/2011/02/14/2012-budget.

29. Paul Ryan, "The Path to Prosperity: Restoring America's Promise," House Budget Committee, April 5, 2011.

30. Naftali Bendavid, "GOP Aim: Cut $4 Trillion," *Wall Street Journal*, April 4, 2011.

31. Premium support was also discussed in detail in chapter 7.

32. See Roadmap for America's Future Act of 2010, H.R. 4529, 111th Congress, 2nd Session (introduced on January 27, 2010), congress.gov/bill/111th-congress/house

-bill/4529. For a critical analysis of the proposals, see Paul N. Van De Water, "The Ryan Budget's Radical Priorities," Center on Budget and Policy Priorities, July 7, 2010, cbpp.org/research/the-ryan-budgets-radical-priorities.

33. In 2012, the Kaiser Family Foundation did a detailed comparison of many of the premium support proposals available at that time. It is worth noting the specific versions of the plans, as many of them are updates from the proposals discussed in this section. The November 2010 Rivlin-Ryan proposal is included in the comparison's appendix. See "Comparison of Medicare Premium Support Proposals," Kaiser Family Foundation, July 26, 2012, kff.org/wp-content/uploads/2013/01/8284 .pdf.

34. Paul N. Van De Water, "Converting Medicare to Premium Support Would Likely Lead to Two-Tier Health Care System," Center on Budget and Policy Priorities, September 26, 2011, cbpp.org/sites/default/files/atoms/files/9-26-11health.pdf.

35. Sam Baker, "Sen. Wyden Distances Himself from Medicare Plan He Crafted with Ryan," *The Hill*, August 13, 2012, https://thehill.com/policy/healthcare/243387 -wyden-downplays-medicare-plan-he-crafted-with-ryan.

36. Data from the Bureau of Labor Statistics. See Katelynn Harris, "Forty Years of Falling Manufacturing Employment," Beyond the Numbers, US Bureau of Labor Statistics, November 2020.

37. "Obama's Speech on Reducing the Budget (Text)," *New York Times*, April 13, 2011, nytimes.com/2011/04/14/us/politics/14obama-text.html.

38. Jackie Calmes, "Obama's Deficit Dilemma," *New York Times*, February 27, 2012, nytimes.com/2012/02/27/us/politics/obamas-unacknowledged-debt-to-bowles -simpson-plan.html.

39. Jake Sherman, "Boehner: Cut 'Trillions' as Debt Limit Nears," *Politico*, May 9, 2011, politico.com/story/2011/05/boehner-cut-trillions-as-debt-limit-nears-054604.

40. Robert Draper, *Do Not Ask What Good We Do: Inside the U.S. House of Representatives* (New York: Free Press, 2012).

41. Elspeth Reeve, "70% of Tea Partiers Don't Want to Cut Medicare Either," *The Atlantic*, April 19, 2011, theatlantic.com/politics/archive/2011/04/70-tea-partiers-dont -want-cut-medicare-either/349787/.

42. Manu Raju, "Kyl Predicts $6 Trillion in Cuts," *Politico*, May 9, 2011, politico.com /story/2011/05/kyl-predicts-6-trillion-in-cuts-054606.

43. Discussed in detail in chapter 4.

44. Laura Meckler and Gerald F. Seib, "Promise, False Starts Paved Road to a Deal," *Wall Street Journal*, August 2, 2011, wsj.com/articles/SB10001424053111190429250 4576481812376152944.

45. Economists thought shifting to a chained index for the price adjustment was just a technical change that made the inflation adjustment more accurate and happened to save a little money. But progressives were outraged because the shift would affect current beneficiaries rather than being limited to just future ones, as progressives had been promised.

46. Meckler and Seib, "Promise, False Starts."

47. Matt Bai, "Obama vs. Boehner: Who Killed the Debt Deal," *New York Times Magazine*, March 28, 2012, nytimes.com/2012/04/01/magazine/obama-vs-boehner-who-killed-the-debt-deal.html.

48. "Debt Limit Follies," editorial, *New York Times*, January 31, 2011, nytimes.com/2011/02/01/opinion/01tue1.html.

49. See Carl Hulse, "House Passes Spending Bill, But Not Happily," *New York Times*, March 15, 2011, nytimes.com/2011/03/16/us/politics/16congress.html; Carl Hulse, "Budget Deal to Cut $38 Billion Averts Shutdown," *New York Times*, April 8, 2011, nytimes.com/2011/04/09/us/politics/09fiscal.html.

50. Charles Riley, "S&P Downgrades U.S. Credit Rating," CNN Money, August 6, 2011, https://money.cnn.com/2011/08/05/news/economy/downgrade_rumors/index.htm.

51. Budget Control Act of 2011, Public Law 112-25 (August 2, 2011), govinfo.gov/content/pkg/PLAW-112publ25/html/PLAW-112publ25.htm.

52. Carl Hulse and Helene Cooper, "Obama and Leaders Reach Debt Deal," *New York Times*, July 31, 2011, nytimes.com/2011/08/01/us/politics/01FISCAL.html.

53. Robert Pear and Catherine Rampell, "Lawmakers in Both Parties Fear That New Budget Panel Will Erode Authority," *New York Times*, August 1, 2011, nytimes.com/2011/08/02/us/politics/02panel.html.

54. Alice M. Rivlin, "Growing the Economy and Stabilizing the Debt," Testimony to the Joint Economic Committee, US Congress, March 14, 2013, jec.senate.gov/public/_cache/files/a54db16c-c1a1-43f7-986e-8cbd92b5d42a/alice-rivlin-testimony.pdf.

55. Bill Heniff Jr., Elizabeth Rybicki, and Shannon M. Mahan, *The Budget Control Act of 2011*, Congressional Research Service, August 19, 2011, https://sgp.fas.org/crs/misc/R41965.pdf.

56. Kristin Butcher and others, *Understanding Food Insecurity During the Great Recession*, Russell Sage Foundation, March 2014, https://cpb-us-e1.wpmucdn.com/sites/.dartmouth.edu/dist/0/1994/files/2019/05/RussellSage.pdf.

57. Melissa Boteach, "New Poverty Data Provide Key Insights into Fiscal Cliff Negotiations," Center for American Progress, November 14, 2012, americanprogress.org/issues/poverty/news/2012/11/14/44898/new-poverty-data-provide-key-insights-into-fiscal-cliff-negotiations/.

58. Jennifer Steinhauer, Helene Cooper, and Robert Pear, "Panel Fails to Reach Deal on Plan for Deficit Reduction," *New York Times*, November 21, 2011, nytimes.com/2011/11/22/us/politics/death-of-deficit-deal-opens-up-new-campaign-of-blame.html.

59. Andrew C. Revikin, "Kicking Cans, Budget Woes and Other Risks Down the Road," *New York Times*, November 21, 2011, https://dotearth.blogs.nytimes.com/2011/11/21/congress-fails-to-find-common-ground-on-budget/.

60. Kim Dixon, "Romney, Obama Both Like Simpson-Bowles Plan, To a Point," Reuters, October 4, 2012, https://in.reuters.com/article/us-usa-campaign-taxes/romney-obama-both-like-simpson-bowles-plan-to-a-point-idINBRE89103Y20121004.

61. Congress also had failed to pass a "doc fix" bill (discussed in chapter 6), so Medicare would take an $11 billion hit unless action was taken, and the threshold for the Alternative Minimum Tax had not been adjusted for inflation, meaning millions more people would pay the higher tax rate intended to ensure that millionaires could not get away with small tax bills—another tax increase from policy on autopilot. See Jackie Calmes, "Demystifying the Fiscal Impasse That Is Vexing Washington," *New York Times*, November 15, 2012, nytimes.com/2012/11/16/us /politics/the-fiscal-cliff-explained.html.

62. Matt Smith, "Obama Signs Bill Warding Off Fiscal Cliff," CNN, January 3, 2013, cnn .com/2013/01/02/politics/fiscal-cliff/index.html; William G. Gale, "The Fiscal Cliff Has Been Avoided, But at What Cost?" Brookings Institution, January 2, 2013, brook ings.edu/blog/up-front/2013/01/02/the-fiscal-cliff-has-been-avoided-but-at-what -cost/; Michael Greenstone and Adam Looney, "The Fiscal Cliff Deal and Our Long-Run Budget Challenge," Brookings Institution, January 4, 2013, brookings.edu/blog /jobs/2013/01/04/the-fiscal-cliff-deal-and-our-long-run-budget-challenge/.

63. The Hastert Rule was never an actual rule of the House. It was a principle named for Rep. Dennis Hastert (R-IL), who was Speaker of the House from 1999 to 2007. He often refused to bring bills to the floor unless they had support of "a majority of the majority," even though he also violated this "rule" twelve separate times. The Hastert Rule should be eliminated through congressional reforms because it has the effect of blocking bills that could pass with a bipartisan majority, as I argue in chapter 11.

64. American Taxpayer Relief Act of 2012, Public Law 112-240, 112th Congress (January 2, 2013), congress.gov/112/plaws/publ240/PLAW-112publ240.pdf.

65. The headline may say "Government Shuts Down in Budget Impasse," but Jonathan Weisman and Jeremy Peters accurately report that the negotiations broke down when House Republicans tried to use the must-pass spending bill to postpone the Obamacare individual mandate. See Jonathan Weisman and Jeremy W. Peters, "Government Shuts Down in Budget Impasse," *New York Times*, September 30, 2013, nytimes.com/2013/10/01/us/politics/congress-shutdown-debate.html.

66. It was 53 percent blaming Republicans to 29 percent blaming President Obama in an ABC News-*Washington Post* poll in October 2013. See Dan Balz and Scott Clement, "Poll: Major Damage to GOP after Shutdown, and Broad Dissatisfaction with Government," *Washington Post*, October 22, 2013, washingtonpost.com/politics /poll-major-damage-to-gop-after-shutdown-and-broad-dissatisfaction-with -government/2013/10/21/dae5c062-3a84-11e3-b7ba-503fb5822c3e_story.html.

67. Rabah Kamal and others, "How Repeal of the Individual Mandate and Expansion of Loosely Regulated Plans are Affecting 2019 Premiums," Kaiser Family Foundation, October 26, 2018, kff.org/health-costs/issue-brief/how-repeal-of-the-individual -mandate-and-expansion-of-loosely-regulated-plans-are-affecting-2019-premiums/.

68. Jill Lawrence, "Profiles in Negotiation: The Murray-Ryan Budget Deal," Center for Effective Public Management at Brookings, February 2015, brookings.edu/wp -content/uploads/2016/06/BrookingsMurrayRyanv421315.pdf.

69. Mark E. Warren and Jane Mansbridge, "Deliberative Negotiation," in *Negotiating Agreement in Politics*, edited by Jane Mansbridge and Cathie Jo Martin (Washington: American Political Science Association, 2013), apsanet.org/portals/54/Files/Task%20Force%20Reports/Chapter5Mansbridge.pdf.

70. Tara Golshan, "Paul Ryan Says Trump's Presidency Was Worth It for the Tax Cuts," *Vox*, April 11, 2018, vox.com/policy-and-politics/2018/4/11/17224206/paul-ryan-retire-press-conference-trump.

## CHAPTER 10

1. Tal Kopan and Daniella Diaz, "Graham, Durbin Introduce Bipartisan Immigration Bill Despite Setbacks," CNN Politics, January 17, 2018, cnn.com/2018/01/17/politics/dreamers-bill-immigration-graham-durbin-congress/index.html.

2. David Shortell, "Thousands of Prisoners Released as New Reform Effort Takes Effect," CNN Politics, July 19, 2019, cnn.com/2019/07/19/politics/first-step-act-prisoners-released-doj/index.html.

3. Drew Desilver, "A Productivity Scorecard for the 115th Congress: More Laws Than Before, But Not More Substance," Pew Research Center, January 25, 2019, pewresearch.org/fact-tank/2019/01/25/a-productivity-scorecard-for-115th-congress/.

4. Since 2019, Frances Lee has been a professor at the Woodrow Wilson School at Princeton University.

5. See James M. Curry and Frances Lee, "Congress Is Far More Bipartisan Than Headlines Suggest," *Washington Post*, December 20, 2016, washingtonpost.com/news/monkey-cage/wp/2016/12/20/congress-is-far-more-bipartisan-than-headlines-suggest/.

6. The authors provided a prepublication draft. James M. Curry and Frances E. Lee, *The Limits of Party, Congress and Lawmaking in a Polarized Era* (University of Chicago Press, 2020), https://press.uchicago.edu/ucp/books/book/chicago/L/bo51795068.html.

7. Nearly every book or research paper on partisanship and legislation in the US Congress makes numerous references to David Mayhew, the Sterling Professor of Political Science at Yale University, because he pioneered the development of many of the research methods and assertions other researchers are exploring.

8. Sarah Binder is a Brookings senior fellow and a professor of political science at George Washington University's Columbian College of Arts and Sciences.

9. Sarah Binder, "Polarized We Govern?" Brookings Institution, May 2014, brookings.edu/wp-content/uploads/2016/06/BrookingsCEPM_Polarized_figReplacedText RevTableRev.pdf.

10. Sarah A. Binder, *Stalemate: Causes and Consequences of Legislative Deadlock* (Brookings Institution Press, 2003), data updated through 2018, jstor.org/stable/10.7864/j.ctvb937r3.

11. Keith Krehbiel, *Pivotal Politics: A Theory of U.S. Lawmaking* (University of Chicago Press, 1998), https://press.uchicago.edu/ucp/books/book/chicago/P/bo3616471.html.

12. David R. Mayhew, *Partisan Balance: Why Political Parties Don't Kill the U.S. Constitutional System* (Princeton University Press, 2013), https://press.princeton.edu /books/paperback/9780691157986/partisan-balance.

13. This graph is based on the DW-NOMINATE developed by Keith T. Poole and Howard Rosenthal. See https://voteview.com/about.

14. Jane Mansbridge and Cathie Jo Martin, eds., *Negotiating Agreement in Politics*, Report of the Task Force on Negotiating Agreement in Politics, American Political Science Association, December 2013, apsanet.org/Portals/54/files/Task%20Force %20Reports/Negotiating%20Agreement%20in%20Politics.pdf?ver=2018-11-28 -122632-157.

15. Nolan McCarty, a Princeton University professor, wrote an excellent summary of section 2 of the Task Force Report for nonacademic readers. See Nolan McCarty, "What We Know and Don't Know about Our Polarized Politics," *Washington Post*, January 8, 2014, washingtonpost.com/news/monkey-cage/wp/2014/01/08/what-we -know-and-dont-know-about-our-polarized-politics/.

16. The assertions in this paragraph are again taken from section 2 of *Negotiating Agreement in Politics*. Similar patterns of polarization were also found in most state legislatures by Nolan McCarty and Boris Shor of the Harris School of Public Policy of the University of Chicago. Nolan McCarty and Boris Shor, "Partisan Polarization in the United States: Diagnoses and Avenues for Reform," *Social Science Research Network*, November 11, 2015, https://datascience.iq.harvard.edu/files/pegroup/files /mccartyshor2015.pdf.

17. Frances E. Lee, *Insecure Majorities: Congress and the Perpetual Campaign* (University of Chicago Press, 2016), https://press.uchicago.edu/ucp/books/book/chicago/I /bo24732099.html.

18. Thomas E. Mann and Norman J. Ornstein, *It's Even Worse than It Looks: How the American Constitutional System Collided With the New Politics of Extremism* (New York: Basic Books, 2012), https://www.civilpolitics.org/content/mann-ornstein-its -even-worse-it-looks/.

19. E. J. Dionne Jr., *Why the Right Went Wrong: Conservatism–From Goldwater to Trump and Beyond* (New York: Simon & Schuster, 2016), simonandschuster.com /books/Why-the-Right-Went-Wrong/E-J-Dionne/9781476763804/. The book was written when Trump was still a candidate for the White House, but we know what Dionne thinks about the Trump administration; he tells us a few times a week in his *Washington Post* column, and our offices are so close, I see him nearly every day.

20. Frances E. Lee, "How Party Polarization Affects Governance," *Annual Review of Political Science* 18 (May 2015), 261–282, annualreviews.org/doi/full/10.1146 /annurev-polisci-072012-113747.

21. As discussed in detail in chapter 9.

22. Democracy for America (DFA) grew out of the (Howard) Dean for America presidential campaign in 2004 and has continued independently even as Dean served as the National Democratic Committee chair and after. It now supports candidates like Elizabeth Warren (D-MA) and Bernie Sanders (I-VT).

23. Cristina Marcos and Rebecca Shabad, "House GOP Halts Spending Bills After Confederate Flag Fight," *The Hill*, July 10, 2015, https://thehill.com/blogs/floor-action/house/247512-house-gop-halts-spending-bills-after-confederate-flag-fight.

24. Molly Reynolds, "This Is Why the Congressional Budget Process Is Broken," *Washington Post*, October 26, 2017, washingtonpost.com/news/monkey-cage/wp/2017/10/27/this-is-why-the-congressional-budget-process-is-broken/.

25. Barbara Sinclair, *Unorthodox Lawmaking: New Legislative Processes in the U.S. Congress*, 4th ed. (Washington: CQ Press, 2011), https://us.sagepub.com/en-us/nam/unorthodox-lawmaking/book236939.

26. Joseph Fishkin and David E. Pozen, "Asymmetric Constitutional Hardball," *Columbia Law Review*, 118:3, https://columbialawreview.org/content/asymmetric-constitutional-hardball/.

27. This is the conclusion of E. J. Dionne, Norm Ornstein, and Thomas E. Mann, "How the GOP Prompted the Decay of Political Norms: The Republican Party Laid the Groundwork for Dysfunction Long before Donald Trump Was Elected President," *The Atlantic*, September 19, 2017, theatlantic.com/politics/archive/2017/09/gop-decay-of-political-norms/540165/.

28. Sarah. A. Binder, "The History of the Filibuster," Brookings Institution, April 22, 2010, brookings.edu/testimonies/the-history-of-the-filibuster/.

29. Molly E. Reynolds, *Exceptions to the Rule, The Politics of Filibuster Limitations in the U.S. Senate* (Brookings Institution Press, 2017), brookings.edu/book/exceptions-to-the-rule/.

30. Norman Ornstein and Thomas E. Mann, *The Broken Branch: How Congress Is Failing America and How to Get It Back on Track* (Oxford University Press, 2006).

31. It was then Senate Majority Leader Harry Reid's decision to exercise the "nuclear option" eliminating the 60-vote requirement to end a filibuster for presidential nominations (except for Supreme Court justices) in 2013. The majority leader writes the rules for the Senate (if she or he has the votes to pass them). McConnell was majority leader in 2017 when he eliminated the Senate filibuster for Supreme Court nominees.

32. Sarah Binder and Frances Lee, "Making Deals in Congress," in *Negotiating Agreement in Politics*, edited by Jane Mansbridge and Cathie Jo Martin (Washington: American Political Science Association, 2013), 70, apsanet.org/Portals/54/files/Task%20Force%20Reports/Negotiating%20Agreement%20in%20Politics.pdf?ver=2018-11-28-122632-157.

33. Mansbridge and Martin, *Negotiating Agreement in Politics*, 29.

34. "The Partisan Divide on Political Values Grows Even Wider," Pew Research Center, October 5, 2017, pewresearch.org/politics/2017/10/05/the-partisan-divide-on-political-values-grows-even-wider/. There actually were seven surveys, but only three are shown here.

35. "Political Polarization in the American Public, Section 1: Growing Ideological Consistency," Pew Research Center, June 12, 2014, pewresearch.org/politics/2014/06/12/section-1-growing-ideological-consistency/.

36. "Political Polarization in the American Public, Section 1."

37. "Political Polarization in the American Public, Section 1."

38. Daniel Yudkin, Steven Hawkins, and Tim Dixon, *The Perception Gap: How False Impressions are Pulling us Apart,* More in Common, June 2019, https://perceptiongap .us/media/zaslaroc/perception-gap-report-1-0-3.pdf.

39. Alan I. Abramowitz, *The Disappearing Center: Engaged Citizens, Polarization, and American Democracy* (Yale University Press, 2011), https://yalebooks.yale.edu/book /9780300168297/disappearing-center.

40. Alan I. Abramowitz and Kyle L. Saunders, "Ideological Realignment in the U.S. Senate Electorate," *Journal of Politics*, 60:3 (August 1998), jstor.org/stable/2647642; Alan Abramowitz and Jennifer McCoy, "United States: Racial Resentment, Negative Partisanship, and Polarization in Trump's America," *Annals of the American Academy of Political & Social Science* 681 (January 2019), 137–56, https://journals .sagepub.com/doi/pdf/10.1177/0002716218811309.

41. Andy Fitch, "As the Rhetoric Escalates: Talking to Lilliana Mason," interview with Lilliana Mason, *Los Angeles Review of Books*, January 25, 2019, https://blog.lareview ofbooks.org/interviews/rhetoric-escalates-talking-lilliana-mason/.

42. Shanto Iyengar and Masha Krupenkin, "The Strengthening of Partisan Affect," *Political Psychology* 39:01 (February 13, 2018), 201–18, https://doi.org/10.1111/pops .12487.

43. As Alan Abramowitz and Steven Webster noted, "After only one week in office, President Trump's approval rating in the Gallup tracking poll was 89% among Republicans but only 12% among Democrats." See Alan I. Abramowitz and Steven W. Webster, "Negative Partisanship: Why Americans Dislike Parties But Behave Like Rabid Partisans," *Political Psychology,* 39:01 (February 13, 2018), 119–35, https://doi .org/10.1111/pops.12479.

44. Donald R. Kinder and Nathan P. Kalmoe, *Neither Liberal Nor Conservative: Ideological Innocence in the American Public* (University of Chicago Press, 2017), https:// press.uchicago.edu/ucp/books/book/chicago/N/bo25841664.html.

45. Lilliana Mason, "Ideologues without Issues: The Polarizing Consequences of Ideological Identities," *Public Opinion Quarterly* 82:S1 (March 2018), 866–87, https:// academic.oup.com/poq/article/82/S1/866/4951269.

46. There was no association between negative feelings for Christians or whites and support for the Democratic Party. See Lilliana Mason, Julie Wronski, and John V. Kane, "Trump Support Is Not Normal Partisanship," *New America*, December 11, 2019, newamerica.org/political-reform/reports/political-parties-good-for/trump -support-is-not-normal-partisanship/.

47. Alan I. Abramowitz and Steven W. Webster, "The Rise of Negative Partisanship and the Nationalization of U.S. Elections in the 21st Century," *Electoral Studies* 41 (March 2016), 12–22, https://doi.org/10.1016/j.electstud.2015.11.001; Shanto Iyengar, Gaurav Sood, Yphtach Lelkes, "Affect, Not Ideology: A Social Identity Perspective on Polarization," *Public Opinion Quarterly* 76:03 (September 17, 2012), 405–31, https://doi.org/10.1093/poq/nfs038.

48. See for example Nahal Amouzadeh, "Former RNC Chair Steele: 'Insanity That Has Engulfed' Trump Administration Threatens GOP," WTOP News, October 10, 2017, https://wtop.com/government/2017/10/former-rnc-chair-steele-insanity-engulfed -administration-threatens-gop/; "Full Text: Jeff Flake on Trump Speech Transcript," *Politico*, January 17, 2018, politico.com/story/2018/01/17/full-text-jeff-flake-on -trump-speech-transcript-343246; and Matthew MacWilliams, "The One Weird Trait That Predicts Whether You're a Trump Supporter," *Politico Magazine*, January 17, 2016, politico.com/magazine/story/2016/01/donald-trump-2016-authoritarian -213533/.

49. Adapted from the fourteenth annual Seymour Martin Lipset Lecture on Democracy in the World, delivered on November 29, 2017, at the Canadian Embassy in Washington. William A. Galston, "The Populist Challenge to Liberal Democracy," Brookings Institution, April 17, 2018, brookings.edu/research/the-populist-challenge -to-liberal-democracy/.

50. Dalibor Rohac, Liz Kennedy, and Vikram Singh, "Drivers of Authoritarian Populism in the United States: A Primer," American Enterprise Institute and Center for American Progress, May 2018, aei.org/research-products/report/drivers-of-authoritarian-populism-in-the-united-states-a-primer/.

CHAPTER 11

1. Frances E. Lee, *Insecure Majorities: Congress and the Perpetual Campaign* (University of Chicago Press, 2016), https://press.uchicago.edu/ucp/books/book/chicago/I /bo24732099.html.

2. John A. Lawrence, "Congressional Reforms of the Past and Their Effects on Today's Congress," Testimony before the Select Committee on the Modernization of Congress, US House of Representatives, March 27, 2019, https://docs.house.gov/meetings /MH/MH00/20190327/109172/HHRG-116-MH00-Wstate-LawrenceJ-20190327 .pdf.

3. Editorial Board. "Opinion: The Democratic House Wants to Reform Democracy. It's Not a Panacea—But It's a Start," *Washington Post*, January 3, 2019, washing tonpost.com/opinions/the-democratic-house-wants-to-reform-democracy-its-not -a-panacea--but-its-a-start/2019/01/03/54a0cb54-0fa0-11e9-8938-5898adc28fa2 _story.html.

4. House Committee on Rules, "Restoring Congress for the People," January 2019, https://rules.house.gov/sites/democrats.rules.house.gov/files/documents/115 /Reports/Restoring%20Congress%20for%20the%20People.pdf.

5. No Labels is active on Facebook and many other social media channels, and can be found at this web address: nolabels.org/.

6. A version of a discharge petition was introduced in a package of reforms in the congressional "Revolt of 1910" (aka "Revolution of 1910") by progressives of both parties against Republican Speaker Joseph Cannon (who also chaired the Rules Committee). See Olivia B. Waxman, "The Old-School Trick That Finally Pushed the House to Move on Immigration," *Time*, June 13, 2018, https://time.com/5308755/discharge

-petitions-definition-purpose-history/; "The House's All Night Session to Break Speaker Joe Cannon's Power (March 17, 1910)," US House of Representatives, History, Art and Archives (n.d.), https://history.house.gov/Historical-Highlights /1901-1950/The-House-s-all-night-session-to-break-Speaker-Joe-Cannon-s -power/.

7. Richard S. Beth, "The Discharge Rule in the House: Recent Use in Historical Context," Congressional Research Service, April 17, 2003, https://web.archive.org/web /20060228233412/http://www.rules.house.gov/archives/97-856.pdf.

8. Sarah A. Binder and Steven S. Smith. *Politics or Principle? Filibustering in the United States Senate* (Brookings Institution Press, 1996), brookings.edu/book/politics-or -principle/.

9. In November 2013, Senate Majority Leader Harry Reid dropped the threshold for confirming presidential nominees from 60 votes to a simple majority of 51 votes. See Jeff Zeleny and Arlette Saenz, "Senate Goes 'Nuclear,' Changes Nominee Filibuster Rules," ABC News, November 21, 2013, https://abcnews.go.com/Politics /senate-nuclear-filibuster-rules/story?id=20964700.

10. Molly E. Reynolds, *Exceptions to the Rule: The Politics of Filibuster Limitations in the U.S. Senate* (Brookings Institution Press, 2017), brookings.edu/book/exceptions -to-the-rule/.

11. Alice M. Rivlin, Pete V. Domenici, and G. William Hoagland, "Proposal for Improving the Congressional Budget Process," Bipartisan Policy Center, July 2015, brookings.edu/wp-content/uploads/2016/06/Economy-proposal-for-improving -the-congressional-budget-process.pdf. To be precise, there were more than three themes and ten recommendations. Recommendation 9 had eight separate proposals for relatively smaller changes, and Recommendation 10 was to create a commission to evaluate at least 7 other ideas for accounting changes.

12. Here is the Bipartisan Policy Center's website: https://bipartisanpolicy.org/.

13. You can learn more about the Committee for a Responsible Federal Budget at crfb .org/ and about the CRFB initiatives Fix the Debt at https://fixthedebt.org/, FixUS at https://fixusnow.org/, and the Better Budget Process Initiative at crfb.org/project /better-budget-process-initiative.

14. Nolan M. McCarty, Keith T. Poole, and Howard Rosenthal, *Polarized America: The Dance of Ideology and Unequal Riches* (MIT Press, 2006), https://mitpress.mit.edu /books/polarized-america; James C. Garand, "Income Inequality, Party Polarization, and Roll-Call Voting in the US Senate," *Journal of Politics*, 72:04 (October 2010), 1109–28, researchgate.net/publication/231964084_Income_Inequality_Party_Pola rization_and_Roll-Call_Voting_in_the_US_Senate.

15. James Fallows, "How America is Putting Itself Back Together," *The Atlantic*, March 2016, theatlantic.com/magazine/archive/2016/03/how-america-is-putting -itself-back-together/426882/.

16. Joseph P. Williams, "Trump Panel Finds No Voter Fraud," *U.S. News and World Report*, January 10, 2018, usnews.com/news/national-news/articles/2018-01-10 /trump-commision-on-election-integrity-found-no-evidence-of-voter-fraud.

17. Adam Liptak, "Supreme Court Invalidates Key Part of Voting Rights Act," *New York Times*, June 25, 2013, nytimes.com/2013/06/26/us/supreme-court-ruling.html.

18. Adam Liptak, "Justices, 5–4, Reject Corporate Spending Limit," *New York Times*, January 21, 2010, nytimes.com/2010/01/22/us/politics/22scotus.html.

19. Bob Biersack, "8 Years Later: How Citizens United Changed Campaign Finance," Open Secrets, February 7, 2018, opensecrets.org/news/2018/02/how-citizens-united -changed-campaign-finance/.

20. Common Cause was founded in 1970, long before the invention of the internet, but that may be the best way to find the organization today, at commoncause.org.

21. The website for Democracy 21 is https://democracy21.org/. Open Secrets, a project of the Center for Responsive Politics, can be found at opensecrets.org/.

22. Mickey Edwards, *The Parties versus the People: How to Turn Republicans and Democrats into Americans* (Yale University Press, 2012).

23. William A. Galston and Elaine Kamarck, "Make U.S. Politics Safe for Moderates," Brookings Institution, February 23, 2011, brookings.edu/opinions/make-u-s-politics -safe-for-moderates/.

24. Elaine C. Kamarck, "Increasing Turnout in Congressional Primaries," Brookings Institution Center for Effective Public Management, July 2014, brookings.edu/wp -content/uploads/2016/06/KamarckIncreasing-Turnout-in-Congressional -Primaries72614.pdf.

25. Eric McGhee and Boris Shor, "Has the Top Two Primary Elected More Moderates?" *Journal on Perspectives on Politics*, 15:4 (September 2017), 1053–66, cambridge.org /core/journals/perspectives-on-politics/article/has-the-top-two-primary-elected -more-moderates/1F65856812342373F4A51B233E9BD593.

26. Harold Meyerson, "Op-Ed: California's Jungle Primary: Tried It. Dump It." *Los Angeles Times*, June 21, 2014, latimes.com/opinion/op-ed/la-oe-meyerson-california -jungle-primary-20140622-story.html.

27. Alexander R. Podkul and Elaine Kamarck, "The Primaries Project: Blanket Primaries Have Yet to Deliver," Brookings Institution, October 10, 2014, brookings.edu/blog /fixgov/2014/10/10/the-primaries-project-blanket-primaries-have-yet-to-deliver/.

28. David Karol, "Charles Schumer's Flawed Diagnosis of Polarization," *Washington Post*, July 23, 2014, washingtonpost.com/news/monkey-cage/wp/2014/07/23/charles -schumers-flawed-diagnosis-of-polarization/.

29. The NAACP website is naacp.org/. The League of Women Voters website is lwv.org/. Fair Fight is found at https://fairfight.com/. The website for US Vote is usvotefoundation.org/. UnidosUS is found at unidosus.org. The Voting Rights Project of the American-Arab Anti-Discrimination Committee is found at adc.org/voting-rights/. The Asian and Pacific Islander American Vote website is apiavote.org/. The Native American Rights Fund website is narf.org/. The Brennan Center for Justice can be found at brennancenter.org.

30. The web addresses for the Aspen Institute's Congressional Program and the Rodel Fellowships are aspeninstitute.org/programs/congressional-program/ and aspen institute.org/programs/rodel-fellowships-public-leadership/.

31. The Lugar Center can be found at thelugarcenter.org/ourwork-Effective-Bipartisan-Governance.html.

32. The Faith and Politics Institute web address is faithandpolitics.org/.

33. The website for the Millennial Action Project is millennialaction.org/.

34. You can learn about all these programs at the NICD website: https://nicd.arizona.edu/.

35. Sarah McCammon, "Can We Come Together? How Americans Are Trying To Talk Across The Divide," NPR, April 4, 2019, npr.org/2019/04/04/709924342/can-we-come-together-how-americans-are-trying-to-talk-across-the-divide.

36. See the National Coalition Against Censorship, Open Discussion Project, at https://bipartisanbookclub.org/about https://ncac.org/project/open-discussion-project.

37. Before the 2020 election cycle, Better Angels renamed itself Braver Angels and can now be found at https://braverangels.org/.

38. You can learn more about Ask Big Questions at askbigquestions.org/.

39. Isabel V. Sawhill, *The Forgotten Americans: An Economic Agenda for a Divided Nation* (Yale University Press, 2018). See also Brennan Hoban, "An Economic Agenda for the Forgotten Americans in a Divided Nation," Brookings Institution, October 15, 2018, brookings.edu/blog/brookings-now/2018/10/15/an-economic-agenda-for-the-forgotten-americans-in-a-divided-nation/.

40. Jim A. C. Everett, "Intergroup Contact Theory: Past, Present, and Future," *Inquisitive Mind*, 2:17 (2013), in-mind.org/article/intergroup-contact-theory-past-present-and-future.

41. Mark Muro and others, "Advancing Inclusion Through Clean Energy Jobs," Brookings Institution Metropolitan Policy Program, April 2019, brookings.edu/wp-content/uploads/2019/04/2019.04_metro_Clean-Energy-Jobs_Report_Muro-Tomer-Shivaran-Kane.pdf.

# INDEX

*Figures and tables are indicated by "f" and "t" following page numbers.*